Catholic Girlhood Narratives

CATHOLIC GIRLHOOD NARRATIVES *The Church and Self-Denial*

Elizabeth N. Evasdaughter

Northeastern University Press
Boston

Northeastern University Press

Excerpts from *I Tell You Now: Autobiographical Essays by Native American Writers,* edited by
Brian Swann and Arnold Krupat, by permission of the University of Nebraska Press. Copyright
© 1987 by the University of Nebraska Press.

Excerpt from "A Tin Butterfly" in *Memories of a Catholic Girlhood,* copyright 1951 and renewed
1979 by Mary McCarthy, reprinted by permission of Harcourt Brace & Company.

The illustrations on pages 36, 112, and 158, which form the triptych *Embroidering Earth's Mantle,*
by Remedios Varo, are © 1996 by Artists Rights Society (ARS)/VEGAP, Madrid.

Library of Congress Cataloging-in-Publication Data
Evasdaughter, Elizabeth N.
    Catholic girlhood narratives : the Church and self-denial /
Elizabeth N. Evasdaughter.
        p.   cm.
    Includes bibliographical references and index.
    ISBN 1-55553-269-1 (cloth : alk. paper)
        1. Autobiography—Women authors.   2. Biography as a literary form.
3. Catholic women—Biography—History and criticism.   4. Girls—
Biography—History and criticism.   5. Women in the Catholic Church.
6. Evasdaughter, Elizabeth N.   I. Title.
CT25.E96   1996
920.72′008′822—dc20   95-46088

Designed by Joyce C. Weston

Composed in Garamond by Coghill Composition Co., Richmond, Virginia. Printed and bound
by Thomson-Shore, Inc., Dexter, Michigan. The paper is Glatfelter Supple Opaque Recycled,
an acid-free stock.

MANUFACTURED IN THE UNITED STATES OF AMERICA
00   99   98   97   96   5   4   3   2   1

To Mary Louise Salstad,
incomparable interlocutor

contents

Preface   *ix*

Chronology of Autobiographers   *xiii*

Chronology of Autobiographies   *xiv*

Introduction   *3*

Part 1.

AUTOBIOGRAPHY AND THE CATHOLIC WOMAN   *19*

Part 2.

PUZZLING CHEERFULNESS AND
PUZZLING COMPLAINTS

Chapter 1. The Conundrum of a Too Pleasant Surface   *39*

Chapter 2. Unexpected Frustration and Grief   *73*

Part 3.

THEOLOGIES OF WOMEN

Chapter 3. The Message of Subordination   *115*

Chapter 4. The Message of Equivalence   *145*

Part 4.

SPIRITUAL COMBAT

Chapter 5. Catholic Girls in Defense of Their Spiritual
Well-Being   *161*

Chapter 6. Catholic Women Autobiographers Keep Up
the Good Fight   *192*

Notes   *229*

Works Cited   *249*

Index   *257*

preface

---

*I*N the mind of a Catholic, the catechism has left more traces than one might think, not only of the belief system, but also of the structural sequence:

> Q. *Who made us?*
> A. God made us.

At some point in a Catholic's life, when the role of one's parents becomes more clear, this answer may be doubted, but the need to raise questions and look for answers may never let up.

As I wrote *Impossible Autobiographers*, a study of girlhood narratives written in the twentieth century by Catholic women, I soon realized that I was raising questions and working up answers—interrogating the texts, as the French say. The women may have sat in catechism class as children, as I did when I entered the convent, memorizing question-and-answer pairs. The catechism has one quality I do not want to imitate, however. My questions of the texts were real questions, not lead-ins to answers I already had. I wanted my book to be natural and logical, rather than artificial and dogmatic; still, like the writers of the catechism, I aimed at respect for the tradition being discussed, however dissimilar it may be from the evolving tradition of autobiographies by Catholic women. Though I was often tempted to investigate related issues such as the celibacy of priests or the ordination of women, I have limited myself to features of the texts.

This study is itself autobiographical in that it follows the path I took in reading and thinking about the texts. As a literary scholar and a former Dominican nun, I thought my background might help me with this project. But the first set of autobiographies I read dismayed me with what seemed to be an ersatz sunniness; to explain the atmosphere of falseness to myself I looked up my old catechism and found there rules against criticism. Reflecting again on the cheery autobiographies I found that they contained reactions to censorship. Interested by their concealments and half-revelations I looked for more of the texts, checking various bibliographies and libraries. In this exhaustive sweep I found a good number of girlhood narratives that were frank about both negative and positive experiences. The negative side of these texts presented a constellation of difficulties and hardships that puzzled me, probably because they were unlike those of my Protestant girlhood. To be frank, I could not understand why parents, priests, nuns, and other Catholic teachers would impose the prohibitions and frustrations that were leveled at these girls. To solve this puzzle, I turned to more authoritative sources than the Baltimore catechism and its counterparts in France and Spain; I tracked down writings by "the Fathers of the Church" and Thomas Aquinas, a copy of the Catechism of Trent, and a Jesuit book on the popes who reigned during the girlhoods I was studying. These sources answered my questions by explaining that Catholic priests have a very definite concept of the Catholic Woman and have labored diligently to train Catholic girls to live according to it. When I realized that the official expectation of women was dehumanizing, I could no longer remain in accord with the clerical or official Catholic position and, in fact, became quite discouraged. I began to reread the texts, and this time I found responses to the femininity training of the Church, coming both from the remembered girls and the remembering writers. I saw that the young girls had resisted attacks on their human dignity, and as autobiographers they continued that opposition. Chapters 5 and 6 reveal their courage and resolve. Only at this point did I rediscover the theology that is more in harmony with Christ's attitude toward women and that, I believe, animated the refusal of these Catholics to accept the later and un-Christian teaching on women that has crept into their religion.

I appreciate the interest and critiques offered by my editors John

Weingartner and Maria Casali, by professors Mary Louise Salstad and Helga Braunbeck of North Carolina State University, Evelyn Torton Beck of the University of Maryland, Joan Hinde Stewart of North Carolina State University, and Elaine N. Orr of North Carolina State University, who read all or part of the manuscript and offered constructive comments.

I am indebted to members of the interlibrary loan and reference departments of the University of Wyoming and North Carolina State University for their helpfulness. I also want to thank the ministers of First Christian Church in Tulsa for explaining Protestantism to me as I grew up, and Dominican nuns and priests in Wisconsin and Illinois for explaining Catholicism to a convert eager to learn, not only from their sermons and theology classes, but also from their manner of living. This gratitude does not imply that my Christian mentors would agree with what I say. I learned whatever I know of literary analysis and interpretation from professors at the University of Tulsa, especially Lester Zimmerman, and at the University of Wisconsin, Madison, especially Helen C. White, and from years of reading and discussion, in and out of the classroom.

With the exception of Simone de Beauvoir's *Mémoires d'une jeune fille rangée*, all translations of autobiographical texts are mine.

Chronology of Autobiographers

1836–1936	Juliette Lambert Adam, France (*Le Roman de mon enfance et de ma jeunesse*)
1844–1923	Sarah Bernhardt, France (*Ma double vie: Mémoires de Sarah Bernhardt*)
1849–?	Sister Xavier Farrell, United States (*Happy Memories of a Sister of Charity*)
1855–1950	Agnes Repplier, United States (*In Our Convent Days*)
1861–?	Elizabeth Schoffen, United States (*The Demands of Rome*)
1865–?	Mary Hunt Benoist, United States (*Memories*)
1873–1954	Colette, France (*La maison de Claudine* and *Sido*)
1880–1945	Lucie Delarue-Mardrus, France (*Mes mémoires*)
1880–1966	Kathleen Norris, United States (*Noon: An Autobiographical Sketch*)
1883–1967	Marie Noël, France (*Petit-Jour: Souvenirs d'enfance*)
1887–1964	Sister M. Madaleva Wolff, United States (*My First Seventy Years*)
1888–1969	[Béatrix] Dussane, France (*Au jour et aux lumières. Vol. 1, Premiers pas dans le Temple*)
1888–1971	Elise Jouhandeau, France (*Joies et douleurs d'une belle excentrique. Vol. 1, Enfance et adolescence d'Elise*)
1890–1955	Mary Mellish, United States (*Sometimes I Reminisce: Autobiography*)
1892–?	Sister Consolata Carroll, United States (*Pray Love, Remember* and *I Hear in My Heart*)
1898–	Rosa Chacel, Spain (*Desde el amanecer: Autobiografía de mis primeros diez años*)
1904–1988	María Teresa León, Spain (*Memoria de la melancolía*)
1908?–1963	Remedios Varo, Spain (*Embroidering Earth's Mantle*)
1908–1986	Simone de Beauvoir, France (*Mémoires d'une jeune fille rangée*)
1912–1989	Mary McCarthy, United States (*Memories of a Catholic Girlhood*)
1914–?	Barbara Mullen, United States (*Life Is My Adventure*)
1926–	Ana María Matute, Spain (*El río*)
1927–	María Asquerino, Spain (*Memorias*)
1940–	Clara Janés, Spain (*Jardín y laberinto*)
1943–	Linda Marie [Pillay], United States (*I Must Not Rock*)
1943–	Mary Gilligan Wong, United States (*Nun: A Memoir*)
1948–	Wendy Rose, United States ("Neon Scars")
1951–	Peggy Joan Fontenot, United States (*I Almost Burned in Hell: A Confession*)
1952–	Sheelagh Conway, Ireland (*A Woman and Catholicism: My Break with the Roman Catholic Church*)
1953–	Mary Brave Bird (Crow Dog), United States (*Lakota Woman*)
1959–	Rigoberta Menchú, Guatemala (*Me llamo Rigoberta Menchú y así me nació la conciencia*)

Chronology of Autobiographies

1902	*Le Roman de mon enfance et de ma jeunesse* (Adam)
1905	*In Our Convent Days* (Repplier)
1907	*Ma double vie: Mémoires de Sarah Bernhardt*
1917	*The Demands of Rome* (Schoffen)
1922	*La maison de Claudine* (Colette)
1925	*Noon: An Autobiographical Sketch* (Norris)
1929–30	*Sido* (Colette)
1930	*Memories* (Benoist)
1937	*Life Is My Adventure* (Mullen)
1938	*Mes mémoires* (Delarue-Mardrus)
1941	*Happy Memories of a Sister of Charity* (Farrell)
1941	*Sometimes I Reminisce: Autobiography* (Mellish)
1947	*Pray Love, Remember* (Carroll)
1949	*I Hear in My Heart* (Carroll)
1951	*Petit-Jour: Souvenirs d'enfance* (Noël)
1952	*Joies et douleurs d'une belle excentrique.* Vol. 1, *Enfance et adolescence d'Elise* (Jouhandeau)
1955	*Au jour et aux lumières.* Vol. 1, *Premiers pas dans le Temple* (Dussane)
1957	*Memories of a Catholic Girlhood* (McCarthy)
1958	*Mémoires d'une jeune fille rangée* (Beauvoir)
1959	*My First Seventy Years* (Wolff)
1962	*Embroidering Earth's Mantle* (Varo)
1963	*El río* (Matute)
1970	*Memoria de la melancolía* (León)
1972	*Desde el amanecer: Autobiografía de mis primeros diez años* (Chacel)
1977	*I Must Not Rock* (Pillay)
1978	*I Almost Burned in Hell: A Confession* (Fontenot)
1983	*Me llamo Rigoberta Menchú y así me nació la conciencia*
1984	*Nun: A Memoir* (Wong)
1987	*Memorias* (Asquerino)
1987	"Neon Scars" (Rose)
1987	*A Woman and Catholicism: My Break with the Roman Catholic Church* (Conway)
1990	*Jardín y laberinto* (Janés)
1990	*Lakota Woman* (Brave Bird)

Catholic Girlhood Narratives

introduction

---

*I*N *Inessential Woman: Problems of Exclusion in Feminist Thought* (1988) Elizabeth V. Spelman proposes that feminist thinkers should explore differences within the movement.[1] Ethnic background, class, and racial experience affect our lives as women, and that should alter conclusions about what living as a woman means. As she points out, not only feminist political activity but also feminist theory would benefit from "examination of the significance of [the heterogeneity of women]."[2] The thesis of the present book is that if Catholic women autobiographers are studied as a part of this exploration by feminist thinkers, what will be found is a group of women who have suffered a repression of their human possibilities by their Church in the name of "the Catholic Woman" and who have repudiated this training both as girls and as autobiographers.

The category *women* may not have a single feature common to all its members, since even the power to bear children is far from universal among human females. Perhaps we women will eventually be described as belonging to one category because of scattered or familial resemblances to one another rather than because of any common traits. I base this reasoning on Wittgenstein's notion *"family resemblances,"* which is that the members of a group may not all have all the distinguishing properties of the group.[3] This idea corrects the impression many people have, that a class or subclass must be homogeneous. In that way he opens the door to a redefinition of *women* as a term referring, of course, to adult female humans, but now thought of as more diverse than before. One of the enriching subclasses that should be considered in this group, if and where it has been left out, is Catholic women.

Like Wittgenstein, Spelman is calling for a correction of the illogical habit of assuming that all members of a group are alike. In fact, having to work harder to survive physically, growing up in one religion rather than another, or obtaining a better education results in marked differences among people. I am presenting this study of Catholic women's autobiographies partly in the hope of communicating to readers of other backgrounds a more complete notion of "women" and a more accurate idea of Catholic women than they might have without considering these texts.

What seems to link girlhood narratives by twentieth-century Catholic women is their desire to discuss what it was like to grow up under the pressure of Catholic gender training. Gérard Genette has made the point that genre definitions always include a thematic element like social class, in addition to a modal element like narrative or theater.[4] Other themes as well as education in the Catholic Church characterize one or another of these works, but when they are considered as a group, the thematic presence of the Church with its gender beliefs shows as dominant. The ups and downs of the remembered relationship of these girls with an institution that was determined to form them into examples of Catholic Womanhood is more important to them than the history of their psyches, unless we conclude that institutional obstacles can be made a path toward the self.

Spelman calls our attention to differences in the way women have been subjugated: "The claim that all women are oppressed is fully compatible with, and needs to be explicated in terms of, the many varieties of oppression that different populations of women have been subject to."[5] The situation Catholic girls grow up in is a specific variety of oppression, for the ideal presented to them has been that of "the Catholic Woman," a term used frequently by clerical writers before the successes of second-wave feminism in the 1960s and 1970s and roughly definable as a kind of idealized domestic not given to female pleasures or intellectual pursuits and not willing to participate seriously in the working world. Because of the difference in cultural context, some of the positions these girls and women have worked out do not parallel those of other feminists. For example, the intense concern of some Catholic women to prove that they are rational is not caused by any comparison the women themselves have made with men, but by the teaching of their tradition that women were not created for intellectual functions.[6] Sexual pleasure can become quite a different issue, too, since for Catholic women asserting their right to sexual pleasure often has less to do with what other people think of as gender rules, such as the rule against adultery for women, and more to do with whether the sexuality of women is corrupt and wrong on all occasions. Again, since the pattern of home life is much more monarchical for Catholics than it is for some other religious or ethnic groups, the issue of independence and self-direction may be taken up in a different way by Catholic women than by women who live in other circumstances.

Wanting to cover as full a range of Catholic women as possible, I have located thirty-three twentieth-century girlhood narratives from six countries: one from Canada about a childhood in Ireland, sixteen from the United States, one from Guatemala, one from Mexico about a girlhood in Spain, five from Spain, and nine from France. The Mexican/Spanish narrative is a triptych painted by Remedios Varo on her memories of convent school and her escape through romantic love into a rugged world.[7] Three areas where I hoped to find more texts than I have are Bavaria, Great Britain, and Hispanic America. My inquiry and reading have not located any narratives by Catholic women there that begin before marriage or entrance into religious life, college, or career, but I think field research might be able to do so, especially in Bavaria. The material I have been able to collect will have to suffice, for no other book has been done on Catholic women's autobiographies, with the result that the importance they have given their religious gender formation has not been analyzed.

As I compared the texts, I was as faithful as I could be to Wittgenstein and Spelman by recognizing among the autobiographers a minority that shifts its membership according to the issue involved, for the subclass "Catholic women autobiographers of the twentieth century" is not homogeneous. However, in spite of variations among them, family resemblances in their convictions and behavior can be worked out, and the outcome of my book, though it was not the original purpose, has been a statement of their attitudes taken as a whole. In the beginning I did not know what they had written, what they thought, or what they had accomplished by their lives. After studying their autobiographical work for several years I have concluded that they chose not to belong to the class "Catholic Woman." Not only Catholic girls as remembered by autobiographers, but also Catholic autobiographers commenting on their memories, have fought for the right to become women carrying out their faith—I would say faith in a creator's love for them—in the form of spiritual self-direction, study, an authentic sexuality, and above all, creativity, without renouncing devotion to an intimate circle. Their efforts have thus been directed against clerical limitations on women and could be considered a matter of interest only within the Church, yet the results may alter mainstream concepts of "women." For one difference between these narratives and other girlhood narratives as described by autobiographical theory is that the latter deal with the psychological history of the self, the important personal relationships the writer recalls, or the development of a career, whereas the Catholic writers describe a struggle between themselves and an institution. What they have done shows what other women could do in similar circumstances. The difference, incidentally, means that feminist theorists may wish to include girlhood narratives by Catholic women of the twentieth century when they are distinguishing women's autobiographies from those of men.

In the case of Simone de Beauvoir (1908–1986), and in other lives as well, the Catholic factor in a person's history may explain some feature that has exasperated or confused critics unnecessarily. Certain writers, female as well as male, have complained of Beauvoir that she was intellectual and cold, that she allowed philosophical principles to come between her and life, or that she rejected her femininity, living like a man.[8] Suzanne Lilar, for example, imposes her definition of femininity so completely on Beauvoir as to say that *Le deuxième sexe* calls on all of us to renounce our femininity.[9] In my study, I hope the role of Beauvoir's Catholic background in her choices will become clear. Because of the way the Catholic defines *woman* as "feminine" and *masculine* as "human," a good or true Catholic Woman is discouraged from complete humanity in this life. If she feels a great desire to employ all her personal powers in this world, as Beauvoir did, she has to reclaim certain aspects of life that have been assigned by the Church to the masculine side of the equation. Onlookers who have accepted the Catholic distribution of activities (whether they learned it in the Catholic Church or elsewhere) and who assign self-direction, public life, sexual enjoyment, and intellectual development to men assume that activity in these districts of life will make a woman masculine. Critics from this type of background intensify their error by thinking of *feminine* as "virtuous" or "normal" for women. Autobiographies by Catholic women suggest that personal history, family relationships, spiritual ideals, or personal endowments sometimes prevent an individual woman from following a path socially labeled "feminine." This knowledge could change definitions of "femininity" also.

If the autobiographies of Catholic women were taken into account, ideas on the genre of autobiography in general would also change. For example, these autobiographies manifest a much different interest in childhood from that given by theorist Roy Pascal, in his book *Design and Truth in Autobiography* (1960). Pascal explains the genre with a deceptive clarity. Because he has not read autobiographies by Catholic or by any representative group of women, his ideas are often incorrect or incomplete. When Pascal discusses childhood as an element in autobiography, he is hampered by his belief that the goal of an autobiography is to explain a man's acknowledged achievement and perhaps his philosophy.[10] Probably owing to the influence of the Romantics and of Freud, Pascal believes one cannot grasp a personality without the story of its childhood; in his view childhood should be analyzed as the cause of much that happens later. Accounts by Catholic women, at least, do not for the most part focus on childhood as a preparation for a career, though Sarah Bernhardt includes foretastes of her later glory. To Pascal's credit, he calls on autobiographers not to insist too much on causality or on the continuity of childhood and maturity.[11] The reasons he gives are that one may play many roles, that many factors may be involved in the outcome of these, that indeterminacy is significant. Children, after all, do not realize which elements of their experience will have consequences. Most important to Pascal, realism is lost by presenting the dominant direction of the life as the only one it might have taken. Pascal's distinction is therefore between childhood as the one potential that was taken up and childhood as a bundle of potentials of which several might have been developed.

However, the diversity of our possibilities is not the only fascinating aspect of childhood narratives. The way a child's mind develops is among the most interesting and useful areas to study, as can be seen in an autobiography by one of Spain's finest philosophical novelists, Rosa Chacel's *Desde el amanecer: Autobiografía de mis primeros diez años* (Since dawn: Autobiography of my first ten years [1972]).[12] Children also explore violence and death. Their interest in such realities is of immense importance to those who deal with children, even though its study has been neglected. In this area the great innovator is Ana María Matute in *El río* (The river [1963]). Sociologists and others grant the necessity and health of breaking away from one's parents at a certain age; a superb study of how this can be done when parents resist is found in Beauvoir's *Mémoires d'une jeune fille rangée* (1958). A child must break away, not only from her parents but also from earlier selves, a human challenge poignantly described by Repplier in her amusing book *In Our Convent Days* (1905). Certain factors in the onset of anorexia—excessive parental supervision, physical abuse, and sexual suppression—are pinponted by Barbara Mullen in *Life Is My Adventure* (1937); these factors are not faced up to in later accounts of anorexia. None of these five topics of narrative are particularly Catholic or female; they are problems children have to resolve in order to reach adulthood. Yet these books with all their universal value and appeal were written precisely because the authors were Catholics. They were reflecting on their girlhood struggles against Catholic gender rules, respectively, those related to the development of the mind, mildness, reality orientation, independence, self-directed growth, and the will to exist.

By speaking of my desire to communicate with non-Catholic women about the lives of Catholic women and with genre theorists about work Catholic women writers have done in autobiography, I do not mean to exclude Catholic women readers. Catholics and ex-Catholics often enjoy reading about the youthful experiences of other Catholics, and more than one Catholic has mentioned to me that you can tell who in an audience was raised Catholic by what they laugh at. Autobiographies of women can give readers of any background the pleasure of comparing their past experiences and present reflections with those of the writers.

One group of Catholic readers will want me to describe in these pages the Church as they know it, or as it has changed for the better since the Second Vatican Council, or as it appears in the person of an exceptional priest or nun. But in the book I am writing the only Church that matters is the Church of the autobiographers, the one they remember from about 1850 until about 1960. Without the character of that Church, these complex and innovative autobiographies would not have been written. Moreover, though one could understandably wish it were not so, the gender training of the Church does still need correction to bring it into harmony with Christ's teaching and his behavior toward women.

It should go without saying that I do not consider my reading or interpretation of the texts the one and only possible version. For example, Mary McCarthy, after relating a tale about a theft and a beating, undercuts the accuracy of her memory. Liz Stanley, in her book *The Auto/biographical I* (1992), sees this doubt as McCarthy's recognition of the impossibility of finding one true version of anyone's life.[13] I have always read the same passages in the light of McCarthy's scrupulosity as a younger child,[14] and as a result I have taken them as another instance of worry about one's sinfulness—in this case, about whether she had written the truth. *Scrupulosity* is a technical term Catholics use for a disorder of conscience in which one goes over and over a sin extracting all possible guilt and discouragement from it, even when the action was clearly either quite minor or not a sin at all. This understanding of the problem was taught to me in a Dominican novitiate; I learned it again when one of my students in Chicago suffered from it and again when one of my friends told me about having suffered from it as a girl. I learned it the fourth time when I read the autobiography of Saint Thérèse of Lisieux, for she too went through an episode of scrupulosity. A person can justifiably read McCarthy's notes on various versions of the theft as a comment on the nonauthoritative authorial voice; read as a too frequent fault among Catholics, her comments lose their intellectual charm, while they gain in autobiographical power. I offer my Catholic-oriented reading of the whole group of narratives because I hope by limiting my discussion to a single aspect, the ecclesiastical, I can perhaps guarantee that the complexity of the narratives will not be underestimated.

Generic analysis has been helpful to me in calling attention, for example, to the difference between the remembered and the remembering voices in an autobiographical text. As a way of recognizing the remembering voice, I have found it useful to rely on an analysis Philippe Lejeune makes of autobiographers' attitudes toward their remembered selves. In his handbook on the genre, he identifies three such dispositions or stances: identification, amusement, and distance; he divides the last category into nostalgia and shame.[15] Having read Catholic women's autobiographies leads me to add a category to his list: self-effacement and a determination not to be effaced. Lejeune further distinguishes between cerebral and emotional identification with the earlier personality; he calls analysis of causes of the present personality cerebral, and analysis of results of the past in the present personality, emotional identification. Since the present-tense "I" is the voice controlling autobiographical texts, Lejeune's discussion is important for reading them.

Interpretation of the more literary texts of the set should also consider factors like narrative design, figuration, and symbolism, because these dimensions of a text, in addition to giving aesthetic pleasure, may carry or reinforce its primary meaning or contradict one of its explicit messages. Texts with literary features can be identified from internal evidence, of course, but external evidence also exists. Before undertaking an autobiographical project, Repplier, Colette, Delarue-Mardrus, Norris, Noël, Wolff, Chacel, León, Beauvoir, McCarthy, Matute, Janés, and Rose had published biographies, novels, poetry, articles, or works of philosophy. Colette, because of her charming, disciplined style and her realistic fictions about intimate experience, was elected to the

Belgian Royal Academy of French Language and Literature in 1935. The Académie Goncourt elected her first to membership in 1945 and then to the presidency in 1949; and she rose in the Légion d'Honneur to the rank of grand officer in 1953. Jacob Stockinger credits P. O. Walzer with being the first critic to treat Colette as one of the great artists of early modern French literature, "officially placing her in the company of Proust and Gide."[16] Noël, though she wrote only for the devout, won the Grand Prize for Poetry of the Académie française in 1962.

Repplier published many of her articles in the *Atlantic Monthly.* Wolff published seventy books, as well as articles in *American Mercury, Commonweal, New Republic, New York Times,* and *Saturday Review of Literature.*[17]

In Spain in this century, special merit in a writer is almost always indicated by large monetary prizes because the reading public is too small to provide an adequate income for a writer. Matute won the Café Gijón prize in 1952 for *Fiesta al noroeste,* the Planeta prize in 1954 for *Pequeño teatro.* In 1958 and 1959 she won the Premio de la Crítica and the Miguel de Cervantes national literary prize for *Los hijos muertos;* in 1960, she won the Nadal prize for *Primera memoria.* Chacel won the four-million-peseta Spanish literary prize in 1988, and in 1992 she was awarded the two-and-a-half-million-peseta Madrid prize for literature. In her turn, Janés won the Barcelona prize two times, once for her 1975 biography of Federico Mompou and once for her 1983 book of poems, *Vivir.* These women had experience and skill, but, even for them, autobiography presented special problems, as I will explain a little later.

Partly because of the skill of such writers, literary analysis—semantic, linguistic, and figurative—has been helpful to me, not only in discovering how the sections of a text work together, when they do, but also in recognizing the frequent ironies in the girlhood memories of Beauvoir, textual signs of censorship evasion in Matute and Colette, and so forth. At the University of Tulsa in the early 1950s, I learned that literary texts can be understood better if their cultural context is understood, and I have found the principle valid at times in relation to even the briefest phrases. When, for example, Beauvoir says that she knew her unbelief to be "plus ferme que le roc" (more firm than the rock), the irony may not appear to readers who do not know that Catholics extend the Apostle Peter's rocklike faith to the popes. One of Beauvoir's translators, James Kirkup, seems to have missed the wryness of her remark, for he changes "the rock" to "a rock," thus removing the originality and pertinence of her metaphor.[18]

In addition to literary analysis, numerous disciplines may be brought into play when one is reading autobiographies by Catholic women. Sociology describes such factors as institutional or sectarian pressures in general, which may make otherwise bizarre behavior understandable. Philosophy, psychology, and cultural history explain the range of definitions of the self implied by various autobiographies. Autobiographies in general have a double historical context; that is, they present recollections, but they also refer in various ways to the setting during the time of their composition. Modern pluralism has also had an effect on these life-stories, one not evident in the autobiographies of medieval mystics.

Particular scholars in other than literary fields offer theories I have found very helpful. I have already explained the value of Wittgenstein's notion of family resemblances. A respected definition of the term *institution,* coming from the Inter-University Research Program in Institution Building, is "an organization which incorporates, fosters, and protects normative relationships and action patterns and performs functions and services which are valued in the environment."[19] Catholic girlhood narratives show great interest in the way the Church "incorporates, fosters, and protects normative relationships and action patterns." The logic of definitions as studied by philosopher Richard Robinson invalidates the definitions of Woman that have been taught to Catholic girls, in general because they are persuasive but are presented as if they were descriptive. The illogic of such a procedure is probably one reason the girls disliked their femininity training. In order to analyze the resistance of the girls to this training, I turned to Sun-tzu's *Art of War,* a book apparently irrelevant to the classrooms and domestic interiors of most women's memories, but nonetheless a study of strategy that proved to be applicable and enlightening.[20]

More important than any other subject in understanding the texts is Catholic theology. Since these are personal narratives, I expected a great deal of reference to Catholic lifestyle and none to doctrine; I was surprised to find that in remembered encounters with adults, gender theology dominates other contextual factors. To explain differences among Catholics on gender theology, I turned to Rosemary Radford Ruether's concept of two theological traditions regarding women, one hostile, the other supportive. Since both these theologies had influence on the girls studied here, both are verified in my study from Catholic theologians, the hostile tradition in chapter 3, the supportive one, more briefly, in chapter 4.[21] In making this analysis of the ideological situation in which these girls were raised, I depended on my education in theology by Dominican priests teaching at Rosary College. And although ecclesiastical and theological issues are crucial in the texts, the texts are no more theological treatises than they are humanities essays. As it does for other narratives, literary analysis offers the best approach to their interpretation, but it should be an analysis informed by awareness of other disciplines.

When I first began reading the life-histories, I kept thinking of them as works of art, not so much in their style, for that varies widely, as in their response to genre. For that reason as well as because I had become interested in the relations of the girls with the Church, I did not exclude autobiographies written by nonliterary women. Like Liz Stanley, I find ordinary autobiographies as valuable and as worthy of study as those that are written with distinction, but not only for the light they throw on history and society.[22] Some poorly written accounts can bring out a feature of the genre, potential or actual, that may be overlooked in a very beautiful, much-worked narrative like Colette's. Two examples of this are Mary Mellish's erratic repression of her anger and Peggy Joan Fontenot's transparent inability to erase her earlier passion. Either process may appear in the autobiographies of literary women in more subtle forms.

Fontenot did not attend college; Mellish had little or no experience as a writer. However, the unusually well-educated and skillful Catholic woman, if she accepts the standard clerical definition of the Catholic Woman, would theoretically find autobiography an impossible task. This definition, which I will examine more fully in chapter 3, excludes from the lives of women erotic pleasure, egalitarian marriage, deviations from heterosexual monogamy, advanced education, engrossing careers, political activity, and independent decisions. These prohibitions, if obeyed, remove almost all paths to self-development and personal history from the landscape girls must set out on. Therefore, part I looks at past autobiographies and at definitions of autobiography to ascertain whether a "selfless" woman can write in this genre. I found that if a Catholic woman is also a would-be autobiographer, she could find assistance in certain characteristics of the genre, but only if she did not believe that she was selfless. Some male and some feminist theories would be serviceable as well, but the autobiographers in question do not seem to have had access to such writers.

Part II attempts to learn why some Catholic women's life-histories are saccharine or joyful, and others angry or wounded. Chapter 1 deals with those girlhood narratives that seem too sweet to be entirely honest, and therefore seem to disqualify themselves as thoughtful examples of the genre. As I read the first seven or eight Catholic girlhood narratives I had found, I was very much dismayed, not because of the poor style or lack of literary and psycholog-ical sophistication of some of the women, but because neither they nor their literary sisters seemed to analyze the significance of the remembered past in an earnest way. The autobiographies I found by Catholic women, ranging in quality from Mellish's repetitive and poorly proportioned *Sometimes I Remi-nisce* (1941), to Agnes Repplier's flawless *In Our Convent Days* (1905), seemed all to be reminiscences rather than autobiographies, offering light entertain-ment rather than any insight or any vital confrontation with the writers' mem-ories.

The frothiness puzzled and frustrated me because the Catholic women I had worked with and talked with, mostly nuns, mothers, and young girls, while not all alike, were much more in touch with social reality, much more disillusioned, and much more determined about their faith than these writers seemed to be. At the time, I had not yet read the autobiographies of Simone de Beauvoir or María Teresa León, nor seen the autobiographical triptych painted by Remedios Varo. These and other narratives that recognize harmful aspects of the way the girls were brought up come from writers better able to express their anger and their hurt, better trained in analysis, or more able to propose healthy climates for growing girls. I am glad that I found the more confident works only later, because I might otherwise have denied the superfi-ciality of so many autobiographies by Catholic women. Instead, I have come to view the disciplined openness of León, Beauvoir, McCarthy, and others as a deliberate resistance to that false pleasantness.

In comparison with women in other traditions, we Catholic women (and of course I do not speak of all of us) often give the impression of coasting or floating, of not being in gear, perhaps even of wearing smiles painted on plaster as if we were imitating poor statues of the Blessed Virgin Mary. I would not say of Catholic women that we feel we are living on a plane superior to every-day life, or that we are excessively inhibited, or that we are submissive to a peculiar degree. Nevertheless, studying the more cheerful of the narratives has led me to the conclusion that we—the group of women these authors repre-sent—may be attempting to pass ourselves off as mere pleasantries. No one need worry about us, our manner says, because we are already living in another world. Yet several of these texts contain realistic or negative passages, and four of them—those by Matute, Repplier, Colette, and Janés—present telling criti-cisms of the Church that are concealed in networks of lyrical imagery, symbol, and charming incident. At the end of chapter 1, a look at the catechisms that were taught during the childhood of these girls shows that the Church prohibited criticism, especially criticism of one's parents and teachers. This inhibition is what has interfered, in certain Catholic women autobiographers, with the duty of social criticism imposed by the genre.

Chapter 2 analyzes those of the narratives that overcome the no-criticism rule in an explicit manner. These works face up to the negative side of Catholic girlhood, acknowledging and publicly criticizing faults in Catholic femininity training. Their authors accept the challenge of personal history, wrestle with the angel of socialization, and are most definitely autobiographical. Chapter 2 raises the question why Catholic parents, priests, and teaching nuns had often opposed the girls' efforts to mature. In my mind the condition of maturity entails self-direction, but in the girlhood narratives, even the most rational self-direction was sometimes considered wrong by adult Catholics. To solve this difficulty I went to the libraries of Catholic colleges, where I learned again, as till then I had more or less forgotten, that official Catholic gender teachings define the Woman as lacking the rational or intellectual nature of Man and, therefore, as owing subordination to him.

Chapter 3 explains that the girls' priests, nuns, and parents began at some point to demand conformity to this theology of Woman, which Rosemary Radford Ruether calls "the theology of subordination," and which could equally well be called "the theology of subrationality." As Ruether explains it, this theology was a cluster of themes that had taken over early Christianity by about the middle of the second century and considered women "less capable of independent life in all respects" than men.[23] In chapter 3 I have identified elements of this instruction in their sources, namely "the Fathers of the Church," Thomas Aquinas, the Catechism of Trent, and theologians and popes of our time. Popes do not seem more important than other bishops to many of the American Catholics I talk to; nevertheless, when the pope is involved, an institution is involved, not just a parent or priest who may not be thinking as a Catholic at every hour of every day. Chapter 3 also verifies the influence of these beliefs in the way the local representatives of the Church worded the Womanhood program to the girls.

To acknowledge the experience of those girls who had a more pleasant and healthful experience of the Church, chapter 4 provides an analysis of what Ruether calls "an eschatological theory of equivalence," that is, an equivalence with men in this life based on what is coming after the apocalypse. As she describes the first views of Christianity, "Early Christianity originally . . . read itself . . . as overturning systems of social discrimination" and gave women equal access to spiritual gifts and public power in the Church. Ruether states that this "theology of inclusion" has persisted in the Church as a minority view from the second century to the present and has very strong support in Scripture, particularly in Genesis 1:27, the Gospels, Galatians 3:28, and Acts 2:17.[24] For this reason I will call it *the primary theology of women* as well as *the minority tradition*. Chapter 4 explains why most of the girls rejected the dominant view. They appear to have been taught in early childhood that they were as worthy as boys and had as much potential for a complete human life in this world; that is, they had been taught the primary theology of women. From this it follows that the girls' rebellion against the dominant theology, when it came, was in fact an obedience, for it was carried out in a spirit of loyalty to their first faith. As rational humans, they could not accept traditional gender teachings, namely, that women should not be equal to men in this world.

In the lives of the girls the theology of inclusion led them to expect equality, but the theology of subordination led certain Catholic adults to attack their expectation of equality. Part III traces strategies of resistance of the young and looks at the way they maintained an active opposition while writing these autobiographies. Against efforts to postpone their equality and rationality until after their death, most of the girls resorted to a variety of means of defense. As I studied their methods of resistance, I discovered that, considered as a group, the girls practiced a high degree of strategic intelligence or prudence. Yet prudence, though it is known as the queen of the virtues, is not ordinarily attributed to women, much less to girls. Chapter 5 proves, almost incidentally, that the theology of subordination fails to describe the nature of women, since the girls are here described as directing their spiritual progress in a rational and virtuous way.

Chapter 6, after establishing how readers can recognize the voice of the remembering self, investigates whether the autobiographers are still fighting the battle with Catholic femininity or have repented of their earlier rebellion. My conclusion is that almost all of them side with their earlier selves. This means that in their maturity most of them did not accept the dominant Catholic view and, if anything, rejected it more vigorously than ever. This chapter will contend that these women—all of them—argue against any element of Catholic Womanhood that in girlhood opposed their healthy and virtuous desires. In the area of adult opinion and persuasive discourse, the variety among the women comes from differences either in what they wanted or in the type of persecution they encountered, and not from disagreement on the spiritual value of women. Even the celibates among the autobiographers reject some of the Church's teachings on women, especially the notion that women are less rational than men. When considered together, the arguments the women present demolish the official definition of the Catholic Woman—which Rome has never dropped or revised. The autobiographers reject it because they find it wrongly limits the potential role and goodness of women.

The second part of chapter 6 argues that one of the ways in which the autobiographers kept up the Christian fight against the diminution of women was through writing with intelligence and imagination. In taking on a complex subject, one seldom if ever explored in autobiography—namely, the relation between the protagonist both recalled and recalling, and a partly nourishing, partly hostile institution—these artists have already shown themselves to be innovators. From the standpoint of genre study, classifying this group of auto-biographical works as serious and innovative indicates that present generic definitions should be expanded to account for them. The Catholic women writers have been creative on the level of text generation and textual problem solving, deploying devices ranging from metaphor to hypertext to be so. Their exploitation of creativity may be due to the little encouragement their Church gives creativity in Catholic women. Tacking against the winds of low expectations and antagonism, they have held their course, thus proving their skill and courage—in short, their full humanity as women. I argue that such numerous demonstrations of rational writing come from a mental program inculcated in women by the Church not to function in a rational way, together with an override feature that allowed for the defense of one's human dignity.

When I talk about this research with Protestant women they usually say that some of the flaws I have found in the Catholic system appear in Protestant life, too. Ruether makes the point that "the Reformation as a whole cannot be said to have had a liberating influence on women."[25] It may be that early Protestant churches retained some Catholic beliefs and customs without being aware that they were Catholic. Today, as Ruether says, liberal churches see the theology of equivalence or inclusion of women as much truer to the gospels and the earlier books of the New Testament than the theology of subordination is.[26] This more Christian theology has survived in the Catholic Church as well precisely because it is in harmony with Christ's teaching and behavior. However, many Christians, both Protestant and Catholic, still assume that God revealed the theology of subordination; otherwise, they wonder, why would their priests and ministers be teaching it?

My motive in writing is not to assign blame for the damage done by Catholic femininity training, but, by uncovering its character, I hope to help correct all efforts, conscious or unconscious, deliberate or systemic, to prevent human development. One way of looking at my study and at the autobiographies themselves would be as suggestions for revisions in systems of socialization, so that nothing in these systems will any longer tend to extinguish women or to encourage any form of death in the living. Catholic women autobiographers of this century, because they identify with life and not death, have rejected the idea of the Catholic Woman in favor of another, earlier belief, left for the most part implicit in their writing, that a loving God created them and the world and desires the fulfillment of both.

I often discuss in the light of the Catholic factor some incident or remark that may have other dimensions: racial, as with Native American autobiographers; socioeconomic or political, as with certain daughters of working-class families; psychological, as with Noël's submissiveness. In the case of Beauvoir I will be looking at the Catholic aspect of one problem she herself analyzed in terms of class. By limiting my remarks to the one dimension, I do not mean to overlook the importance of other dimensions. However, one book cannot cover all aspects of a subject.

The selection of girlhood narratives as the set I would study has basically come from my lifelong interest in learning. Girlhood as an experience involves awareness of one's direction toward womanhood, in that girls form some concept of what their lives as women will become, have become, or may become. Remedios Varo (1908?–1963), a Spanish-born Mexican painter, in her autobiographical triptych, *Embroidering Earth's Mantle* (1962), shows how in convent school she and the other girls were taught to create the kind of world men want. Such concepts of the future role of women greatly affect the choices and actions of girls. An incidental result of my limitation to girlhood is that the accounts discussed include a range of lengths and wholeness: a prose poem of 168 words, two pamphlets, girlhood sections of book-length autobiographies, a number of ordinary-sized books devoted entirely to girlhood, a triptych corresponding to a book with three chapters, and a two-volume written work of approximately 256,000 words. The variation in length, probably owing to temperament and publishing opportunities, accords with the diversity of attitude and approach of the texts, which were written in divergent circumstances.

Since the collection includes thirty-three narratives by thirty-one narrators, the study is not quantified. No one knows or can know how many other Catholic girls are represented by each of the women discussed here. If I obtained a large number of autobiographical accounts by oral interviews or questionnaires, they would not be spontaneous, and so would be affected to some degree by the outline I would offer and by my directions, explanations, or wishes. I hope that these thirty-three narratives show that Catholic women vary considerably and bring out what their most important common features are.

The subject on which I am writing arouses deep emotions and is extremely controversial. Some readers will think that my knowledge of the Catholic background of the texts, while it enhances the interpretations given here, means that I must inevitably harm the study by pious denials of unpleasant truths. Other readers will think that I welcome and exaggerate flaws in the Church, as if this book had arisen from personal animus. In reality, the book preceded and caused my disaffection from the dominant theology of Woman. Another problem for some readers will be that not all the texts can be found in every library, nor are they all available in English. As a result, I rely much more on example and quotation from the autobiographies than I would do with a neutral subject such as narrative epistemology. An abstraction like "Barbara Mullen, as is typical of battered children, defended her mother" does not convey the same information as the statement "Once during a raid on the speak-easy, when Mrs. Brady was pouring a pot of whiskey down the drain and a cop grabbed her mother's hands and twisted them, Barbara threw a bowl of hot pigs' feet at him."[27] With the less abstract version, readers come away with a truer concept of Catholic women.

part **I**

AUTOBIOGRAPHY AND THE CATHOLIC WOMAN

*A*LTHOUGH some definitions of autobiography have been worded in such a way as to exclude women, most female Catholic autobiographers have not been familiar with such theories. The main obstacle to their writing in this genre has been the Catholic definition of Woman, a definition rooted through all its transformations in the idea that "She is different from man as body is from soul."[1] A woman who had internalized such a belief could not write a history of the self and would not be wondering whether the self is unitary or multiple, static or dynamic. Since in fact, however, women are not more like the body than they are like the soul, some Catholic women have written autobiographies anyway, in defiance of their gender training. In what must have been a difficult struggle to overcome internalized remnants of this training, the genre itself might have been a great help. I am not claiming that this genre can be friendly or unfriendly, like a Romantic universe, or that it has many fixed characteristics, but I do argue that it makes a strong demand for a narrative about the history of a self. Attempting to write in the genre, then, could make self-recognition more likely.

Catholic teaching is not the only intellectual pressure that opposes the writing of autobiography by women, of course. Five properties or functions of men's autobiographies over the centuries emphasized by certain male commentators have tended to exclude women, as follows: (1) limitation of the narrative subject to achieving in the public sphere or to "fathering the future";[2] (2) a restriction to writers with assertive personalities and whose public significance is already established;[3] (3) emphasis on truth to the exclusion of other, "feminine" values like love, goodness, vitality, or imagination;[4] (4) transformation of the autobiographer's life into "a coherent story," otherwise described as an "extended, organized narrative," perhaps with a view to distinguishing it from journals and letters, perhaps with a glance at the writer's desire to prove to himself that he has a coherent personality and history, even an "entire destiny";[5] and (5) review of the life from a particular moment in time, a formal convention followed in most autobiographies as a convenience, as a way of enhancing the illusion of the unitary self, or as an expression of the author's role.[6] Many of these characteristics also mark biographies and novels the women might have read, but I think only the third, which focuses on the public persona, might have damaged the autobiographies under discussion. If these women found topics like dreams and personal relationships avoided in all autobiographies they read (as Jon Saari found in Graham Greene's autobiography, of which he complains, "There isn't a gram of Greene in this book"),[7] they could either attempt to write cerebral autobiographies as well or abandon autobiography altogether.

Even if all definitions of autobiography were favorable to women, and some have been, Catholic women would have a specific problem: the expectations their Church has for them mean that they should not or cannot write autobiography. In the history of Catholic life, a phenomenon similar in its effect to masculine definitions of autobiography has occurred. *Woman* or *Catholic Woman* has been defined by priests in ways that discourage Catholic women from developing selves or lives about which autobiography could be written.

As I will show in chapter 3, if a woman accepts the Church's definitions of the Catholic Woman, she will not be able to give a history of her erotic development for the reason that, although a good Catholic woman is expected to reproduce as often as God wishes, her sexual pleasure is considered somehow connected to the Fall of Man and, therefore, to be evil. She will not be able to include any experiences differentiating her from other women or any experiences related to her self-concept, since her duty is to acquire the traits of the Catholic Woman and no other important characteristics. In medieval and modern times, the most emphasized feature of the Catholic Woman's life has been her obligation to subordinate herself to some male: father, husband, priest, or, if worse comes to worst and she must work, employer. The constant duty of subordination means that self-direction, self-originated action, and rational decision are not allowed her. Moreover, she cannot engage in profound analysis, since that task belongs to men. Now the development of a personality or self without regular access to power, money, books, and sex is difficult to imagine and probably impossible. Since the Catholic Woman is expected to sacrifice all these unless and when a man with authority over her grants them to her, autobiography, which writes of the self and its life, is not only forbidden to her but also impossible. Since I am a baptized Catholic, the book you have before you is also impossible and probably does not exist.

Lest my description of the adverse effects of Catholic femininity training seem to come from an unfounded hostility or bias, or even from a too-limited experience of Catholic life (six years as a laywoman, fifteen as a nun), I will include some observations of the Catholic Church from *Women and Self-Esteem,* by Linda Tschirhart Sanford and Mary Ellen Donovan (1985). Sanford and Donovan present a fair and balanced picture, pointing out that "Protestantism, Catholicism and Judaism all have the potential to affect women's lives in myriad positive ways," and even that "many people throughout history have found in Judaism and Christianity important sources of strength, solace and moral integrity that have inspired them and enabled them to stand up against oppression and injustice," and so forth.[8] At the same time, "While Protestantism, Catholicism and Judaism can and often do affect women in myriad positive ways, these religions also can and often do cause women great pain, and they often do great damage to women's self-esteem."[9] Among the women damaged in the United States, these authors include immigrant and Native American women who have been influenced by these three religions.[10] Among the autobiographers I will study, Barbara Mullen was an immigrant, and Mary Brave Bird and Wendy Rose, as well as Rigoberta Menchú of Guatemala, are Native American women.

Sanford and Donovan explain how some of the features of these religions have harmed women's self-esteem; among attributes they find most damaging are the beliefs that men but not women were created in God's image, that God is a white man, "that woman, through Eve the temptress, brought evil into the world," and that women must and will suffer for this. Further, the prohibition against questioning authority—the demand that one must obey without raising doubts—has deprived women of an ability needed "in order to fully experience our potential and to fully respect ourselves."[11] In regard to this problem,

Sanford and Donovan say of Catholic women that they "often have equally great difficulties [as Jewish women] becoming their own authorities, learning to rely on their own powers of judgment to decide what is right for them, what is wrong. As Mary Gordon has put it, many women who are raised Catholic, are 'fighting a life's battle to stop being overawed by authority.'"[12] Yet the Catholic Church, like Protestant sects, teaches that the individual's conscience is the final recourse when an ethical decision must be made.

Sanford and Donovan close their chapter on religion and women's low self-esteem with words attributed to Jesus in the Gnostic *Gospels of St. Thomas*: "If you bring forth what is within you, what you bring forth will save you. If you do not bring forth what is within you, what you do not bring forth will destroy you."[13] Here modern psychotherapy joins Rosemary Radford Ruether, quoted in the introduction to this study, in preferring a theology of equivalence and inclusion to the dominant theology, which would silence women. The Gnostic text almost commands us to assert ourselves and develop life-histories—"Bring forth what is within you."

Catholic women who are fighting for their spiritual survival and who want to write autobiographies could find considerable sustenance among feminist theoreticians of the self or of the self as the subject matter of women's autobiographies. Karen Horney's *Self-Analysis* encourages women to discover their individual existence. "The elusive concept of 'self' . . . is perhaps best indicated by William James's concept of 'the real self' as distinguished from the material and social self. In simple terms it concerns what *I* really feel, what *I* really want, what *I* really believe, what *I* really decide. It is, or should be, the most alive center of psychic life."[14]

Psychologist Horney has nothing against bonding or collective life; nor does sociologist Liz Stanley have any desire to oppose personal history when she stresses interconnectedness with others or membership in overlapping groups.[15] Catholic women are taught to value both prayer and service to others, so that views of those like Horney and Stanley, while not identical with Catholic views, would not seem alien.

Literary scholar Elaine Showalter summarizes feminist theories on what is different in women's lives as distinguished from those of men. "Women's writing has its own unique character, whether because it draws on female body images, uses a 'woman's language,' expresses the female psyche, or . . . reflects women's complex cultural position."[16] All four types of language would help a woman autobiographer; the first would help Catholic autobiographers in particular overcome taboos against the female, and the fourth would give them support as they analyze their complicated institutional situation.

Domna Stanton puts forward an excellent interdisciplinary idea, that women's autobiographical writing has "a global and essential therapeutic purpose: to constitute the female subject." More specifically, "in a phallocentric system, which defines her as the object, the inessential other to the . . . male subject—that, *The Second Sex* has proved beyond a doubt—the *graphing* of the *auto* was an act of self-assertion that denied and reversed woman's status. It represented, as Didier had said of Sand's *My Life,* the conquest of identity through writing. Creating the subject, an autograph gave the female 'I' substance through the inscription of an interior and an anterior."[17]

While this fifth type of women's language, that of academic feminists, might have put off the embryonic Catholic female autobiographer, Stanton's message describes what the autobiographer had in mind to do, however inchoately at first. After translating the concept into terminology she could understand, she would no doubt have found it clarified her intention.

Hélène Cixous and Catherine Clément present (in order to oppose) a list of polarized masculine and feminine traits that is probably derived from French culture.

> Where is she?
> Activity/passivity,
> Sun/Moon,
> Culture/Nature,
> Day/Night,
> Father/Mother,
> Head/Heart,
> Intelligible/Palpable,
> Logos/Pathos.
> Form, convex, step, advance, semen, progress.
> Matter, concave, ground—where steps are taken, holding—and
>   dumping—grounds
> Man
>
> ———
>
> Woman. . . .[18]

Similar bipolar lists are implicit in cultural practices in all the countries included in this study, but reading an explicit list would help one who had not thought about such problems to understand some of her past conflicts. Difficulties with mothers who opposed a girl's adoption of one or another "masculine" trait, for example, come into some of the Catholic women's narratives; perhaps they would be recounted in more of them, if such lists had been accessible to their writers.

Biddy Martin applies the notion of multiple selves-in-process to the topic of lesbian identity. Sexual preference is not the only predilection women have, so that our identity comes not only from our erotic side, but also from other groups we belong to, ethnic, political, class, and, I would add, geographic, intellectual, aesthetic, among others.[19] When this multiplicity is insisted on for lesbian women, the complexity of other women may be brought out as well. The same would be true for autobiographers wanting a clear idea of their past.

From her study of women, literature, and psychiatry, Shari Benstock has concluded that "Autobiographical writing—whatever form it takes—questions the notion of selfhood rather than taking self for granted. The coordinates of self cannot be graphed or plotted. Like autobiography, which slips in and out of genre definitions, self is both culturally constituted *and* composed of all that culture would erase—rather like a fishnet, composed both of string and empty spaces between the fibers. Or a skein of tangled yarn that cannot successfully be untangled—where knots and frayed elements remain."[20] Here what might have caught the attention of a Catholic woman beginning an autobiography is the recovery of "all that culture would erase."

For the most part the autobiographers studied here did not have the opportunity to read feminist theorists of the genre and the self because of the date at which they were educated or wrote, but a determined Catholic woman could overcome internalized censorship against the project of writing autobiography by reading autobiographies herself and theorizing on her own. She could have found features of autobiographies that contrast with those listed above as exclusive, and some of those features could have helped free her from the Procrustean concept of Woman. Some such characteristics of the genre follow; these properties are found both in autobiographies, some written by women, and in the work of some male theoreticians.

(1) Autobiography is an art, even "a flourishing and sophisticated art," as Francis R. Hart puts it, "and literary critic and theorist alike pay it increasing attention."[21] William L. Howarth expands the point, "An autobiography is equally a work of art and life. . . . Artfully shaped, it doesn't reproduce its model but is far different. It is not factual, unimaginative, nonfictional, for it welcomes all the devices of skilled narration and observes few of the restrictions of other forms of historical literature—accuracy, impartiality, inclusiveness."[22]

The more literary of the Catholic women writers might have felt they could move their awareness into the literary dimension of the genre as a way to forget Catholic rules forbidding self-centeredness and intellectual operations in women.

(2) Autobiographies tell about the writer's life. Catholic women in particular have been taught that their inner life will change and improve over the years, and for this reason they may have more interest in this genre than some other people do. As for the temporal life Catholic women are not supposed to have, if a woman remembers a course she pursued or was led along, or if she engaged in a series of choices, meditations, actions, developments—or, in a more receptive mode, observations, responses, appreciations, or losses—she has led a life, however hidden, and will probably assume she can write it up. Women are often skilled at turning their experience into stories. As Carmen Martín Gaite puts it in her essay, "La búsqueda de interlocutor," "Stories are born as such in telling them to oneself, before the necessity presents itself, as it will, of telling them to one another."[23]

(3) Autobiographical works by Hildegarde of Bingen, Julian of Norwich, Margery Kempe, Teresa of Avila, Thérèse of Lisieux, and others, if read with an open mind, prove that for centuries we have had a tradition that not only opposes diminution of the dignity of women but also asserts a woman's duty to participate in society in a spiritually independent and responsible manner. This tradition has been influential as a weak force. Many readers might have been altered by it, but only a few women autobiographers have consciously mined it, to my knowledge. I do know that Sarah Bernhardt owned the *Life* (1565) of Teresa of Avila and that Beauvoir commented on it in *Le deuxième sexe*.[24] Lucie Delarue-Mardrus in her autobiographical pact compared her life-study to that of Thérèse of Lisieux, *Histoire d'une âme*, (History of a Soul, 1897).[25] Rosa Chacel wrote a part of her autobiography as a variation on motifs in Thérèse's autobiography: a child's ball as a symbol of one's spiritual style and the divine prisoner as an archetype for living an intense life in a very limited space.[26] In Wendy Rose's telegraphic autobiography one of the themes (the outsider) and one of the images (apricots) play a variation on McCarthy's *Memories of a Catholic Girlhood* (1957).[27] Thus a stream of social commentary and meditative writing has been flowing all along.

Similarly, Georg Misch writes that the subject of autobiography should be one's relations with the deeper self and with others, with one's work and with the public. The chief source of autobiography, he says, is meditation on self and the world.[28] The spiritual training of Catholic women would make them feel at home with this aspect of the genre. For example, Beauvoir wrote the most useful and applicable section of *Mémoires d'une jeune fille rangée* precisely to show how, when her personal environment deprived her of nourishment for the inner self, she searched Paris for what she needed. Though what she found nourishing was secular, not Catholic, her narrative is about spiritual development.

Defining the subject matter of autobiography as "a life," began in Isocrates's *Antidosis* (354–353 B.C.E.), which Misch calls the first literary autobiography.[29] Isocrates was accused in his eighties of a fault against citizenship, and he said that as a defense he would construct "a discourse which would be, as it were, a true image of my thought and of my own life."[30] Even though Isocrates built up this image by listing his contributions to public life and did not include his childhood, his philosophical development, or his erotic history, his concept of the *Antidosis* as "a true image of my thought and of my own life" does allow for understandings of human value other than his. Once the genre was established, it carried in itself the option of following whatever strands of one's history seem important to the writer.

(4) Like Isocrates, a great many modern autobiographers have wanted to persuade their readers of their merit. Of itself the genre offers "an opportunity for a sincere relation with someone else," so that "the 'I' is confirmed in the function of permanent subject by the presence of its correlative 'you,' giving clear motivation to the discourse."[31] Teresa of Avila wrote her *Life* to defend herself against the courts of the Inquisition;[32] any autobiographer may want to convince the "you" of her version of events. This possibility may appeal to women who have lived out their lives unheard; moreover, it gives rhetorical form to a mass of material that might be otherwise overwhelming.

(5) In addition to defense, other ways of relating to readers would be to work out "an original interpretation of experience"[33] or, one would think, to offer one's narrative as a model—negative, positive, or mixed—that could be a useful comparison to the reader's life. Philippe Lejeune proposes that the interesting thing in autobiography is not whether it is objectively true, but what view the writer takes of the life and how the life led to this view.[34] These cognitive gifts to readers, considered as a form of justice or charity, may especially attract intellectual and dedicated writers.

James Olney has called attention to the universality of an autobiography, which he argues is not undermined by its focus on one person. Just as "a dream . . . is like a complex metaphor for the process of self as it is at the given moment of dreaming," so the autobiography as a whole is a metaphor or symbol of an individual's experience. What we take from autobiography is a symbol, and "any autobiography, the image of a life, is such a symbol."[35] If a Catholic woman has found some other individual's history comparable to her own or symbolic of her own, she may realize that she, too, could write an autobiography that would be beneficial in the cognitive order. *Histoire d'une âme,* the best-seller among Catholic autobiographies, makes of this Carmelite's life-story a symbol others can remember as a positive or negative model, depending on their values. The idea of life-history as a symbol or the idea of giving an interpretation of experience could sustain a woman writing out of a desire for intellectual communication.

(6) An interpretation of experience that is worthwhile can be and often is developed by a person who is not widely known. People lacking all fame, passive people, or marginal people have written autobiographies. Examples include Julian of Norwich and Leonor López de Córdoba.[36] As Misch argues, the autobiographer may be the subject of suffering, if kept at the center of the story.[37]

(7) Autobiography is oriented toward the future,[38] just as the postmodern self is; the self in process must involve the future. The writer of an autobiography is working in the present and to some degree is aware of the present, but she begins her rummaging through the past, sometimes, if not always, because she realizes that the future is going to be different. Biddy Martin appreciates autobiography that illuminates "discontinuities between past and present and, as a consequence, opens up possibilities for a different future."[39] Autobiography is written as a way of choosing among multiple available future selves. To stand poised where many paths can be seen leading into the future does not require any particular gender, and a number of female autobiographers have already employed the future tense for closure.[40]

These reflections indicate the appropriateness for autobiography of a definition of the self drawn from philosopher David Wiggins, that *the self* is a process of recollection of the past, perception of the present, and intention for the future.[41] Wiggins's definition of the self is appropriate to an art like autobiography, in which time is the topic. The only revision women might suggest is a change from *perception* to *attention,* as being more descriptive of the way they usually relate to the present. A definition of the self as process is bound to be attractive to orthodox Catholic women, who believe they are constantly changing under the impact of meditation, the gifts of the Holy Spirit, the sacraments, prayer, and good works.

(8) Without the assistance of any theorist, a Catholic woman might have

noticed the special situation of death in this genre. Whereas in the novel any character can die before the novel's end (unless the principal narrator is considered a character), in autobiography the main character does not die before the last period. But that prohibition does not exclude death from the genre. To think of writing an autobiography calls one's death to mind; further, other occasions on which death has come to mind may be important in one's life-history. Death is central to the autobiographical challenge; that is, an autobiographer not only has to look for a different closure for the life-history, perhaps a less purely biological closure, but may or should also deal with the place of death in the beginning and middle of life-history. All this could attract a Catholic woman for personal reasons, and her religion would support her as she reflects on death. Women, who are expected to bear the brunt of everyone else's sickness and death as well as their own,[42] can turn the difficult triumph over sickness, bereavement, and the fear of death to literary advantage. Many Catholic women autobiographers (as yet I have not read other women autobiographers with this question in mind) introduce death into their personal stories sometime before the end. Chacel is able to recreate an experience in which she nearly died. Beauvoir expresses her close call with psychological death the more poignantly by narrating the death of a close friend, her alter ego. Noël describes her death as she imagines it will unfold. Janés meditates on her father's premature death in order to decipher its effect on her life. All four of these autobiographers derive significance and insight into their personal development from involving death in their narratives; Beauvoir and Noël also employ these deaths for closure, a way of playing off convention and "upsetting expectations."[43] Both of them expand the interchange with the genre by constructing the death-account as an epitome of the autobiographer's life, in the one case, by contrast, in the other, by resemblance. These examples, together with others in the autobiographies of Colette, Norris, Carroll, McCarthy, Wong, and Menchú incidentally demonstrate the originality, imaginative power, and analytic discrimination of which women are capable.

(9) Catholic women, because of their long training in the power of hope, may be attracted also by the comic dimension of the genre. As Stephen A. Shapiro has pointed out, because the main character cannot die, autobiography is a comic genre, reflecting "the individual's ability to rise above circumstances, if only through retrospective analysis."[44] Unfortunately, part of the comedy may be the inability to rise above circumstances; as the bandit chief in *Don Quixote* said, he couldn't finish his autobiography because he hadn't died yet.

As potential qualities of an autobiography, these nine characteristics could give the women a hand in overcoming whatever Catholic teachings interfered with desires to write about themselves, to interpret their own stories, to participate in public life, and to address an audience beyond their ordinary reach. As we have the autobiographical texts the women produced, we know they must have found a way to overcome such teachings. One approach they have taken is to narrate the history of their inability to form an attitude toward their sexuality or to change one already established, to develop serious intellectual or artistic interests, to complete important endeavors, to build up a self, to know what they felt or wanted, to act without consulting some male authority figure. McCarthy and Beauvoir include in their autobiographies their lack of erotic history as girls. Mellish and Schoffen write histories of their inability to acquire the education they wanted. Mullen writes the history of her efforts to live with her father, from whom she thought she could obtain a good moral example. Brave Bird writes the history of her inability to find social support within the Church. Carroll, though unintentionaly, writes a history of occasions when self-development should have occurred but did not. Such stories are tales of false starts, nonevents, inconclusive initiatives, projects interrupted and blocked. These narratives have dealt with the self by its absence, and have provided social analysis by revealing some results of Catholic femininity training.

In a second subgenre, the confession, one would think a good Catholic woman could function well. As the later self went on disapproving an earlier self, the internal voices of her confessor and catechist and parents would all speak appreciatively to her. The confession is not monopolized by Catholics, but among its most famous examples is the *Life* of Teresa of Avila, a work first prepared for a confessor. In this century, Peggy Joan Fontenot (1951–   ), though she might never have heard that Teresa had written a confession, wrote one herself and published it with a vanity press. *I Almost Burned in Hell: A Confession* (1978) seems to have come from a retreat Fontenot made. Perhaps she and others wrote general confessions at the retreat master's suggestion. Although her text is rhetorically a confession, in substance the narrative vindicates her goodness. As a woman she finds it impossible to lie about her past love and ends by establishing that she was not much at fault for the failure of her marriage.[45] Fontenot's continual reference to sin and escape from sin are unsurprising in a Catholic; what may be surprising is that the other Catholic women on the list do not share her interest in fall and redemption. When what fascinates an autobiographer is not sin, confession is difficult to write. Very few of these writers disapprove of their earlier selves or mention any belief that they were sinful. The exceptions are ironic, for Mary Mellish expresses regret at having adopted Catholic "bigotry and inhibitions," and Simone de Beauvoir expresses amusement at the conceit Catholic devotions had taught her.

A third possibility for a Catholic woman wanting to write an autobiography would be to look to energetic, well-known, accomplished women, like those studied by Lynn Z. Bloom, as models.[46] Imitation of the courageous heroines of non-Catholic autobiography seems to have determined Bernhardt's history of her girlhood, a history that emphasizes her courage and talent and classifies other characters according to whether they loved her or did not. In a sense, Beauvoir's girlhood account fits here, in that she makes a point of inner experiences that show her early existentialism and her desire for a life-companion like Sartre. However, famous models could easily paralyze a Catholic woman because of her internalized self-abnegation, self-denial, and self-contempt. Of course, if she were the type of Catholic who was not allowed to read non-Catholic books in the first place, like Thérèse of Lisieux, this alternative would not arise, and, if it did, it would seem disloyal to her Church.

Once that possibility comes to mind, at least three other options open to this hypothetical autobiographer. The fourth type of autobiography she might write evades the teaching that she must be selfless, yet this option is Catholic as well as constructive; by basing her narrative on other Catholic doctrines such as the unique value of every soul, spiritual progress, or hope (a virtue related to the orientation of the genre toward the future), she can fence off her attention from discouraging effects of the Church's teaching on Woman.

Stephen Crites, a theoretician of the function of autobiography, offers support for writing about oneself under the auspices of the theological virtue of hope. He synthesizes the passion of hope with the process of writing autobiography as personal therapy. Hope is a virtue of major importance in Catholic symbols, rituals, and ethics, with their themes of resurrection, of reform, of restitution, of rebirth. By thinking only in terms of hope, a Catholic woman may prevent herself from adverting to definitions of Woman that would work against her progress and against public actions like writing books.

Crites connects hope with autobiographical form by arguing that without hope, a writer cannot form a sufficiently coherent concept of her life-history to produce an autobiography. In his view, the function of "digging out, archaeologically, [the] past," as autobiographers do, is to give the writer greater understanding of the self so as to sketch a future. The future does not provide predictability, but acts as "the lure" for our efforts. A lack of hope means a writer does not "project [the self] hopefully into the future" or does not "appropriate [the] personal past by making a connected, coherent story of it," in this way forming an identity. The identity is Crites's solution to disintegration. Thus by imagining a future the identity is modified over time.[47]

Crites's terms *coherence* and *identity* may be different names for the Christian soul or for the self as the static, fixed, delusory self that postmodernists reject. However, in Catholic pastoral theology, the soul is expected to undergo continual spiritual change, so that for Catholics, hope would not lead to the formation of a stable self, but rather, as in Clara Janés's autobiography, *Jardín y laberinto*, to the choice of a single path into the immediate future.[48] The self may overcome disintegration in this way, or achieve a kind of unity, but it will be the unity of embarking on a single process, not the unity of an imaginary essence (such as "Woman's essential nature . . . self-surrender and entire devotedness").[49] Like Janés, I prefer a concept of the self that is neither random nor fixed, neither static nor scattered. I think a combination of process and choice is appropriate to animals like us, who, as philosopher James Baillie has pointed out, have only one brain apiece, and who, because of that brain, can move from the present into the future with a sense of continuity.[50]

Crites refers to the passion rather than the virtue of hope. "Considering . . . the birth of all things out of [the future's] play of possibility, we again encounter the passion of hope."[51] In this way he puts his argument on a secular basis, but this would not offend Catholics. Since hope as both virtue and passion has been deeply inculcated into Catholic minds through much repetition in all available forms, his psychology of hope offers one way in which Catholic women can evade the Church's language of opposition to selfhood—that is, to selfhood in the sense of individual autonomy—so as to give their attention while writing to the topic of their personal growth.

The autobiography of Catholic hope has been written in two modes by Catholic women of the twentieth century, that of human hope and that of feminine hope. In the autobiography of feminine hope, the remembered self is understood as a soul on a path to happiness; one's femaleness and independence of mind (but not one's intelligence), are sidestepped in favor of a life of service to the institutional Church. Only Noël and the three nuns, Farrell, Carroll, and Wolff, write this feminine autobiography, which could almost be called the true Catholic Woman's autobiography. However, it is a near miss because writing an autobiography is an intellectual and public action, and therefore this type of book clashes substantially with the official beliefs on femininity that the Church attempts to uphold. When the clergy permit women to use their intellects in the Church's service, they demolish their own theology of Woman.

In the autobiography of human hope, hope comes from one's having been created out of love, progressing through this world under the care of the Holy Spirit or Providence, and living toward future completion. Here the self is understood as a person developing toward a life of intelligent justice. This kind of autobiography has been written by Adam, Bernhardt, Schoffen, Colette, Norris, Dussane, Jouhandeau, Chacel, León, Beauvoir, Janés, Pillay, Conway, Brave Bird, and Menchú. A secondary form of human hope inspires those autobiographies that stay with protest; that is, some of these autobiographers persevere in working out their objection to injustices without moving on to the justice they hoped to practice. In this group I would place Repplier, Benoist, Jouhandeau, McCarthy, Mullen, Matute, Asquerino, Wong, and Rose. Their argument does not contradict a just future, but does not reach it or describe it; the subject does not come up.

The fifth type creates a new virtue that could be called intellectual exchange or polylogue, in which the woman writes to communicate with other humans. It is difficult to ascertain whether any work is absolutely original, in a world with so many books, but in my reading experience Repplier, Chacel, Matute, and Janés offer new interpretations of life. Autobiographies that form symbols others can compare to their own lives are those by Beauvoir, McCarthy, and Mullen. Writing as a way of conversing with those not present is a project that gains support from the moral virtues of prudence and justice, the theological virtues of faith and charity, and from certain gifts of the Holy Spirit, in particular the gifts of knowledge, understanding, and wisdom. Autobiographies of spiritual progress, hope, or intellectual communication practiced as a form of charity allow their writers to ignore any Catholic teachings that are repressive of women; these texts are selectively Catholic and marvelously vital.

The sixth type is the most direct of a Catholic woman's options, that of basing her narrative on activities forbidden by the gender system, thus reversing the system. Some Catholic women have been able to stand aside from their gender training to develop an authentic, that is, a changing self through ordinary experiences, through spiritually autonomous decisions, personal friendships, exploration of the world, contact with non-Catholics, sexual love, and participation in public life. Their autobiographies could be called autobiographies of defiance and recount the fully human life, lived or desired, written by Repplier, Colette, Delarue-Mardrus, Norris, Dussane, Jouhandeau, Chacel,

León, Beauvoir, McCarthy, Janés, Mullen, Matute, Pillay, Conway, Brave Bird, and Menchú. Of this list, those who provided a narrative rationale for engaging in all major forms of human activity are Chacel, McCarthy, Matute, Mullen, Pillay, Beauvoir, and Janés. In addition to the six types I have identified, others may exist or may be written in the future.

With the exception of the confession, none of the six kinds of autobiography could have been written without rejecting or evading Catholic definitions of Woman. Moreover, any narrative about the self proves that the writer has a history and an individuality. To publish such writing without the 'nihil obstat' of the Censor Librorum and 'imprimatur' of the archbishop or bishop, which the lives of saints sometimes bear, carries the opposition farther because it involves the writer in public life under no authority but her own. Consequently, the women discussed in this book are all rebels to a degree, even those who base their work on some positive tenet of their faith or who accept one or two elements of the clerical concept of Catholic womanhood. To dismiss part of their Catholic heritage or to turn one part of it against another, as they all do, is spiritual combat indeed.

Social struggle through the centuries may finally have improved the situation of Catholic women, so that clerical rules and definitions have less power to discourage them from living fully human lives. One development that suggests as much is the increase in the number of autobiographies by Catholic women during the twentieth century. For a Catholic woman, the twentieth century has been a propitious time for writing autobiography, primarily because more Catholic women now have access to secular universities and to books written by non-Catholics. The magnitude of this change is indicated in Beauvoir's autobiography by the fervor of her parents' reaction against it. Economic and political changes have allowed some less highly educated women partial escape from Catholic enclaves as a result of migration, work outside the home, or membership in international organizations—all giving opportunities to mingle with people who are not Catholics. During the twentieth century, the progress of technology, shifts in the economy, and other major social forces have led to changes in the life cycle of women, such that unqualified credence in the old Catholic system seems now impossible. Without these developments, not enough autobiographies would have been written by Catholic women to create a representative set.

Although topics related to their Catholic upbringing appear repeatedly in the autobiographies, the writers sometimes attach a special value to experiences, relationships, and reading not allowed in the Catholic enclosure. In

Beauvoir's *Mémoires d'une jeune fille rangée,* which extends into the author's college years, she treats contact with the outside world as necessary to her human development. Her ventures outside the Catholic cultural tower were in themselves, as I will explain in chapter 3, a defiance of Catholic femininity rules. In these autobiographies in general, almost all passages with emotional power, almost all passages offering praise for or protesting features of socialization, have to do with these rules. While Catholic women have various personal histories to tell, they share the memory of a struggle with their Church's definition of *the Catholic Woman.*

The issue of the self as continuous/discontinuous, the most important formal problem as yet discussed by feminists writing on the genre, does not seem important in the texts studied here. Some have accepted a definition of autobiography involving a present-tense narrator looking over the past in order to compose an illusion of continuity and a coherent self. Others have no particular interest in proving their personal continuity. The prose-poem cycles composed by Colette, Matute, and Janés narrate incidents that are discontinuous in time but gradually connected in their themes. Next on the discontinuity spectrum might come Agnes Repplier's *In Our Convent Days* (1905), a series of narratives each with a different topic or aspect of the self: for example, the classroom self, the self that hears sermons, the self that is allowed to play outdoors, the self that loves. She unites these topics by a common theme, the efforts of schoolgirls to evade monastic discipline.[52] Perhaps next would come McCarthy's *Memories of a Catholic Girlhood,* a series of narrative essays or episodes explaining various periods of her girlhood, periods that were unusually discontinuous in the cultural sense. McCarthy also links the separate elements of her narrative, but she does so by providing an introduction or autobiographical pact and by appending commentary to each essay. An interested reader has the option of linking the narratives in McCarthy's and Repplier's essay cycles by looking for a pattern of development that traverses the whole work. Neither of these works follows a regular or steadily chronological pattern. The other narratives seem to follow the usual method of narrative in mainstream novels of the time, that is, to write as if one were covering the whole period referred to and not omitting a great deal. Only Sister Consolata Carroll seems to make an attempt to describe her entire youth, for she takes two volumes to account for a relatively standard Catholic girlhood.[53]

Primarily in the context of chapter 6, which analyzes the reaction of the autobiographers to their remembered selves, I present a few theoretical assumptions more related to autobiographers in general than to Catholic women autobiographers in particular. "Autobiographers" and "remembered selves" are textual phenomena and may not correspond to real-world phenomena; they cannot exhaust the real-world phenomena to which they refer, though they have their own cognitive value and interest. With Jean Starobinski I see autobiography as "a narrative discourse in which 'I' is both subject and object,"[54] or a genre of two voices, the writer's "I" in the present tense and the main character's "I" in the past. Autobiographies seem to be dominated by the past "I," but they are all the time directed and controlled by the present "I," a factor that may account for much of the pleasure of writing in this genre. Pinning down this elusive present voice is the aim of chapter 6.

I write not only as if the autobiographers give truthful accounts of their memories, but also as if their memories are correct. I do this partly to avoid tangling my readers in a long, debilitating series of qualifications. In addition, I respect our memories, which, even though they fuse and shift over the years, still form databases more useful to our correlating, deciding brains than Aladdin's treasure would be. I assume that autobiographers are sifting through their treasure of recollections, searching for whatever will best meet present and future need, including the needs of the text they are producing. What they find will probably be more helpful than a repetition of the remembered experience. In other words, mental life is a reality in itself, not just for its reference to external events but for its own processes. In this way, narrative resembles it.

Autobiography may have a function in society. Rigoberta Menchú (1959–), winner of the Nobel Peace Prize in 1992, wrote in her autobiography, *Me llamo Rigoberta Menchú y así me nació la conciencia* (1983), how in her village on the tenth birthday a child has a conversation with all members of the family older than she. "My older sister, who was already big enough, about twenty-four I think, told me her experiences when she was young. Ten, twelve, thirteen, fifteen years. . . . And also my mama, my papa, my brothers told their experiences."[55] Their personal narratives let her know that she had become an adult and could count on receiving information and emotional support from others. They let her know, too, that they were not stagnant but were moving forward. She did not have to resemble them completely in order to benefit from their memories. Just so, the autobiographies of any cultural subcategory can be beneficial to readers without threatening their independence or their loyalties.

part 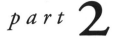 **2**

PUZZLING CHEERFULNESS
AND PUZZLING COMPLAINTS

chapter one

The Conundrum of the
Too Pleasant Surface

AUTOBIOGRAPHY requires that its practitioners undertake a serious analysis of their personal history. Read with
this assumption, the girlhood narratives of some Catholic women seem excessively sunny, avoiding obvious criticism of the Church and of Catholic authority figures. Such writers seem either dishonest or blind, but they might have
been blinded.

Supposing that the Church has a human dimension and therefore not only
a tendency to develop defects but also a capacity to change and reform itself,
then for Catholic writers of any gender to ignore either the flawed condition
of the Church or its improvability would be an embarrassment and a disap-
pointment. Moreover, if they are making a serious and persuasive study of
their life-history, readers may expect them to include an analysis of a relationship between the self and society and the overcoming of some difficulties.[1]
Many orthodox and loyal Catholic women who write autobiographies do not
include girlhood narratives, perhaps because they learned as girls the common
Catholic maxim, "If you can't say something good, don't say anything." Some
of those who include girlhood narratives seem intent on expressing a simplistic
delight with the Church and everyone in it. Unless these women have been

unusually lucky in their experiences and contacts in the Church, the breadth of their enthusiasm and the cheerfulness of their surface narrative present a conundrum.

Sister M. Xavier Farrell (1849–?), author of *Happy Memories of a Sister of Charity* (1941), expresses more love for the Catholic Church than any of the other autobiographers do.[2] She was ninety at the time she wrote, and a woman ninety years old who is perfectly happy seems a remarkable person. She dictated the girlhood section to another Sister who was working on a history of her community but who had agreed not to edit the dictation.

Farrell points out that she gave up nothing to join the convent, because when she entered, "boys" meant her brothers, her students, or her brothers' acquaintances. The nearest approximation to a suitor she had was an affected young man with a gold-headed cane whom she could not endure.[3] Joining the convent was therefore doing exactly what she wanted, she implies, and had nothing to do with sacrifice.

The Sisters of Mercy had been her teachers, and their ceremony of entrance was grander than that of the Sisters of Charity. Farrell is quite critical of the Mercies' reception ceremony for its lack of harmony with the Gospels. She wanted to become "a plain, common Sister of Charity"; as a result, when the priest at her own reception did not speak clearly enough for her to know whether she had become Sister Xavier or Sister Louis, she did not mind. She was too happy to care, because she felt as though she "had been transported to some wonderful country of beauty and peace."[4]

The reason she felt so happy was that she had become a citizen of her mother's country. Farrell's mother used to sing her children songs she had learned when she went to a school run by the Sisters of Charity in Pittsburgh. In other words, Farrell saw these Sisters as a way of rejoining her mother emotionally. The Charities were kind and courteous to Farrell,[5] and by entering their community she satisfied her deepest need—to find a permanent bond with other women like her mother.

Because her mother died young, and because Farrell did not attend a Catholic school, she might not have received the usual gender training, or if she did, she does not refer to it. Consequently, she has no important reason to be personally unhappy with the Church, and, on the level of her deeper needs, she has every reason to be grateful.

Sister Consolata Carroll (1892–?), a Sister of Mercy and home economics professor at Mount St. Mary's College in North Plainfield, New Jersey,[6] wrote an implausibly merry and garrulous autobiography, never, apparently, seeing through her resolute pleasantness. Her two-volume autobiography was an outcome of a creative writing class she took.[7] The first volume, *Pray Love, Remember* (1947), is a tribute to her parents, and the second, *I Hear in My Heart* (1949), is a tribute to religious vocation. Her memory for detail, particularly the detail of her mother's dressmaking (now a lost art), may make her first volume useful to historians. However, her verbosity, especially by comparison to Repplier, Colette, and Matute, is appalling. The flood of detail recorded here does offer one solution to the conundrum of the pleasant surface: Carroll uses her prolixity to put off facing what lies underneath as long as ever she can.

Carroll portrays herself in the third person as Viola Farrell, at first a girl brimming with enthusiasm for her parents and later a young woman grieving for her recently deceased mother but brimming with enthusiasm for convent life. While claiming that her parents were great blessings, she never explains why and incongruously portrays her mother as obsessed with trivia, her father as high-handed. As a girl she was especially preoccupied with her mother and tended to love female authority figures as such, perhaps as a result of Catholic gender training, perhaps because of her mother's personality or the way she treated Viola.

Carroll recalls herself as reaching a kind of ultimate in devotion to her mother. When she was still fairly young, she and her mother had once been nearly killed in a carriage accident, but to the daughter the important lesson of the accident was the value of the mother to the family. Viola's relief at her mother's survival dominates the account so thoroughly that we cannot learn from the narrative whether Viola felt any joy at being herself still alive.[8] Here Carroll's work as a Catholic home economics teacher and her self-abnegation as a nun may have affected her writing. In any case, this passage comes from a selfless writer, centering on her mother and thus writing reminiscence, not autobiography.

Viola's mother put an absolute value on beautifully detailed feminine attire, no doubt as a statement of her femininity and as a method of training Viola in femininity. When Viola once spilled iodine down the skirt of her white dress, her mother made her wear it back to school after lunch as a punishment. As Viola went along, the iodine split the skirt from hem to waist, and she crawled under the park shrubbery to hide. "She felt she was going to die. She couldn't go to school nor could she go home." She lay there, afraid of the worms and ants, afraid because her attendance record would be broken and afraid of the truant officer, and cried herself to sleep. She felt her mother must hate her. When she did go home, she was delirious.[9] The degree of despair Carroll communicates through this narrative contradicts her general tone of eulogy. Perhaps she refrained from censoring the episode because she did not see it as especially critical of her mother; perhaps she thought it would help her home economics students understand children better than their grandmothers had done.

What appears all too clearly is not the mother's severity but the inflated importance she attached to pretty dresses. Being seen in a pretty dress must have been the principal way the women of her class established how feminine they were. If some women in that social class also believed that femininity is essential to the moral goodness of a woman, then skilfully made clothes understandably took on an excessive importance. Certainly Viola Farrell learned that she had to have a pretty dress or lose her mother's support and protection. Paul Benson describes the social pressure that converts an equation between physical appearance and femininity into an undermining of self-respect. "Women whose looks never measure up very well or who never try hard to sculpt themselves . . . are lazy or selfish or ignorant or mentally or physically ill. Worse still, they might be mannish, not real women at all. Thus, many women are brought up to believe that constructing a feminine appearance is indispensable to their personal worth."[10] Carroll believed this, but because she believed her parents' disapproval of her was correct in the Catholic view, and because she belonged to a Church that emphasized subordination, she never seems to have realized what would result from the absence in herself and her text of any conviction of her personal value. Carroll's flaw seems to have been oversocialization, that is (applying a process described by Shively and Larsen), the strictness of her parents caused Viola Farrell to manifest excessive loyalty and to display primarily conformist behavior.[11]

By the end of her second volume, *I Hear in My Heart,* in accounting for her vocation, Carroll finally succeeds in spinning out the secret, she thinks, of her happiness. I think the secret she discovers is considerably more complex than she realizes. Her first volume inadvertently tells us that Viola's ego had been overwhelmed by the strong personalities of her parents or by an excess in her love for them. She must have been saturated with the homiletic of selflessness, sacrifice, and the love of one's mother. Yet in her second volume she writes that she finally managed to save herself from completely drowning by joining the convent. After her mother died, while Viola was still a student at Pratt Institute, she was not able to imagine any future for herself, a dangerous condition which, Crites explains in his analysis of hope, warns of psychological disintegration. To convey the gravity of her predicament, Carroll recalls a swimming accident when she almost died in a patch of quicksand. Sinking in the water but roused by a friend from her apathy, Viola suddenly put up a fight and saved herself.[12] In her despair after her mother's death, the offer of a job at a Catholic women's college came to her like her friend's cry from the shore of the swimming hole. Once she had taught among nuns, Viola wanted to be one of them.

By entering the convent, Viola found a way to turn self-abasement into self-will. The novice mistress made it clear that she doubted whether Viola should enter, and her father did not want her to do so.[13] In response to them, Viola gathered her energies together and persisted. Instead of submitting to the wishes of the authorities at hand, she struggled to win them over and succeeded. In that sense she established herself as a mature woman, grounded on her own choice of lifestyle. In this way she overcame her grief over her mother's death and her despair over her lack of a personal identity and plan of life.

Paradoxically, entering the convent saved her ego by allowing her to win her struggle with the angel of death. Though she limped from the field, she was victorious by her lights. The convent worked well for Viola Farrell in a number of ways. Life there would not arouse any conflict with her belief in self-erasure. By permitting her to become a home economics teacher, it gave her a most feminine role without her having to engage in sexual activity, a prospect that horrified her. Joining the convent maintained her adjustment by giving her a number of strong mother figures to strive to please, thus replacing her mother. Most important for autobiography, it sealed her self-respect. Carroll was able to think well of herself especially because as a good Catholic girl she loved female authority figures and developed a system for engaging their concern.[14] All this satisfaction explains the contented tone of her writing.

Despite Carroll's enthusiasm, she never makes the least effort to conceal any hurt or anger she remembers, and she seems delighted with her inferiority and her parents' flaws of character. She describes old hurts and contentions, but she does not analyze them in order to admit they could have been avoided or to face the faults of Catholic parenting and teaching, much less to urge reform. As a result, her joy does not carry conviction. It does not arise like the ebullience of fulfillment; her mood is more that of determination and denial.

The reason that Carroll did not censor her autobiography was that she did not realize that anyone might read it as a condemnation of the Church and its training of young girls. She describes openly how she was startled and dismayed when she saw pictures in a medical text explaining reproduction, how her mother was completely involved in domestic activity, how her father manipulated her out of driving a car and stopped her from dating a boy because he was Protestant.[15] She does not seem to know that non-Catholics or a group of Catholics educated in the social sciences, biology, and the humanities might disapprove of the Church because of these incidents. It never occurs to her that her parents were wrong to conceal the joys of sexuality from her or to break up a relationship of hers that might have led to a happy marriage, or that her mother should not have conditioned her to feel safe and virtuous only when cooking, sewing, or caring for the young, or that her father should have taught her to drive better, or that her general misery might have come from the thorough way in which her parents narrowed her horizons. She assumes throughout that her parents were correct. Just as Benson argues, if oppressive socialization aims at interiorization rather than coercion, those socialized will be less able to recognize worthy reasons for action.[16]

Carroll assumed that all her readers would see the beauty of a Church that could so provide for a lonely young girl. Carroll's gratitude and joy represent the strongest possible internal censorship, and her frankness about her struggles makes the strongest possible yet unintentional criticism of the Church.

Sister M. Madaleva Wolff, C.S.C. (1887–1964), served as president of Saint Mary's of Notre Dame from 1934 to 1961, and wrote poems and articles that were published by prestigious reviews and book publishers. In *My First Seventy Years* (1959), she does not offer her readers an intelligent analysis of her long and close relationship with the Church, except by scanty clues.[17] Possible explanations might include an introverted temperament, family rules of reserve common in her youth, or an inability to think narratively.[18] She might have been commanded by her superior to write the autobiography and felt the command was wrong or a violation of her style of virtue, which might have emphasized service to others and not self-development. Or she might have been angry for so long she didn't realize she was angry. Or perhaps her experience with the Church was too uniform to constitute a history. Or, finally, she might have felt an analysis would be ungrateful. The Church had demanded an unusual amount of work from her, and she had received unusual approval from the Church. Few nuns are sent to the University of California at Berkeley to study, promoted, and encouraged to write, much less to publish their writings. Perhaps it is not surprising that Wolff's autobiography finds almost no negative feature of Catholic life other than being given administrative responsibilities she did not want.

Her girlhood account devotes more space than most to playing with other children—in the yard, up in the trees, in her father's harness shop, or in the nearby lake. She mentions her mother in three incidents, in all of which mother and daughter were sharing something beautiful in nature or religion. Wolff describes her remembered fear when her mother almost died in child-birth. As a little girl, the future poet sat with her father in his big chair on Sunday afternoons in winter to read his scrapbook of poems clipped from periodicals.[19]

Wolff's childhood home in Cumberland, Wisconsin, was so far from a Catholic school that the children attended public school. However, because of the many nationalities in the neighborhood the parish priest had to know several languages, and the priest who prepared her class for first communion had been educated in Rome. Instead of drilling the children on the catechism, he dictated the theology of the Blessed Sacrament to them. She indicates her appreciation of his exceptional knowledge and the superior content of his in-struction. "Few children, I think, have ever been so honored in the quality of their instruction."[20] She might have entered the convent because she liked theology; she does not really give her reason.

In general, Wolff's experiences as she was growing up are reported in glowing terms; for example, she writes, "The lake is one of the deep loves of my life. . . . From the time I could balance myself precariously on skates I was the first girl on and the last girl off the ice in winter." And valuing her opportu-nities, "No children now, and few at any time, have had a harness shop for a playhouse. We had."[21]

Wolff has only two complaints to make of her girlhood, one that she was forced in public school, in however kindly a manner, to switch from her left to her right hand for writing, and the other that she was overworked as a young nun to the point of illness.[22] These complaints were made in support, I would guess, of educational reforms Wolff felt would have a good chance of success. Her book thereby furnishes a precedent, however scanty, for loyal criticism. Of her life at home and in her parish, she offers only praise. She speaks only superficially of her student days at St. Mary's; consequently, she does not thoroughly analyze her relations with the Church in girlhood. From reading her work and inquiring about her from people who have worked with her, I infer hesitantly that much of her personality, including its most poetic side, remained repressed. As a result of this truncation, a low-grade, permanent anger seems to have accompanied her brilliance and her devotion to all that merits devotion. The terseness of her autobiography seems almost bitter, a distillation of her inability to speak of herself or perhaps even to learn what she might want to write about her life.

Kathleen Norris (1880–1966), an enormously successful women's novelist, had such difficulty in criticizing her good Catholic parents that in her girlhood narrative, *Noon,* she sometimes slips into self-contradiction and incoherence.[23] Moreover, like Carroll, she is barely visible in her history until near the end. Less well-known now than Colette, in the twenties Kathleen Norris prospered. Her ninety-three novels left her at the end of her life with $1,234,613.[24] Her particular path to wealth was defined by Louise Maunsell Field in the review "Kathleen Norris Smiles Back at Life: 'Noon,' an Autobiographical Sketch [1925], Has a Happy Ending and No Disagreeable People." Field observes, "The narrative resembles in many ways a typical Kathleen Norris novel. We have the large and happy family, the gay acceptance of poverty, the optimism and the 'happy ending,' with the attainment of wealth, success and love. There is the same rosy glow cast over everything, the same simple, somewhat sentimental and unsophisticated point of view. . . . Her belief is, always more babies and you will be glad and virtuous."[25]

In quoting Field I am relying on a contemporary reader to support my first impression that Norris's autobiography is frivolous. Field does not exaggerate; in *Noon* Norris writes of her mother, "What she felt for her children was an actually consuming devotion and concern. She built about us a world of love. Sometimes she would get all five of us as close to her knees as possible, or into her arms, and amuse us with the histories of her childhood, in the floods and quicksands of a pioneer cattle ranch, or she would tell us of our irresistible charms in babyhood. She made us feel that of all wonderful achievements the acquiring of a family of small children was the most worth while."[26] This summary of her mother's storytelling is meant to appeal to the heart and to our denials of all evil. Yet Norris does not name her mother, as she did in her longer 1959 autobiography, *Family Gathering.*[27] (Her mother was Josephine Moroney, and her father was James Alden Thompson.) In *Noon,* when Norris eulogizes her father, turning him into a role rather than telling us his name, she writes with even greater enthusiasm than she expresses for her mother.[28] One can easily imagine how a novel full of such writing would cloy. However, both Field and I read *Noon* the first time without noticing all the features of Norris's topography. Or perhaps we were so caught up in her sunny passages as to be only briefly distracted by the tiny, dark, and violent storm tucked away in the middle of the book: "They were terrible years. They were years of hundreds of cares and responsibilities heavier than such youth should ever know."[29] This explicit and dramatic protest is startling by comparison with the earlier part of *Noon*. Norris refers here to a period after the perfect parents she describes had died and, quite unnecessarily, left their children unprovided for. She complains quite openly about that period, as a good Catholic would not do. A mind trained in Catholic beliefs would be thinking that Providence provides and that the time of death is in God's hand alone. Yet people can finish reading *Noon* without having noticed that Norris, however briefly, disagrees with Catholic teaching.

Readers may not register the negative passage in its full force, owing to its brevity. Another factor that somewhat softens it is its introduction by the obligatory loyal remarks about her parents and their idealism. Finally, she returns to a sunny tone before closing. She purges the ideal of evangelical poverty, which had harmed her and her brothers and sisters, by the experience of real poverty, and then, writing on, she counters their desperation with their cooperative efforts to earn money. She and her older siblings at first supported the younger ones, and then she teamed up with Charles Gilman Norris, whom she soon agreed to marry. Thus Norris reestablishes textually the lost happy family—twice, as if to make sure she could both recover it and keep it. Her second and third families, the orphans and the romantic couple, respectively, were based not only on love but also on a drive toward prosperity.[30] In other words, she is unable to exclude all storms from the landscape of her memory, but she makes sure she neither begins nor ends her narrative with one.

Yet near the end of *Noon,* Norris speaks of mortally dangerous weather four times. She mentions real snow falling in California; she imagines dying in an avalanche of rejected manuscripts in a snowy New York winter; she went ice skating on a "bitter winter night"; she thought, when Charles suggested going to New York, of failing and being evicted into "snow fluttering down about one's broken shoes." Her reason is to bring out love's triumph. Charles Norris came into her life at the ice-skating rink on that bitter winter night in 1908, and, later as they sat in the Vienna Bakery, she herself displaced the vision of failure with a real gesture and real speech, taking his hand across the table and agreeing to go to New York with him, where, she said, she would be able to "get twenty-five a week."[31] In this way Norris argues that the poverty her father visited on her was in time overcome. The danger and the humor that save her closing passage from excessive sentimentality probably stem from Norris's awareness that her readers remembered financial fear themselves and very probably knew how safe and prosperous she had become.

Field understandably does not give Norris credit for her realism, but Norris knew she couldn't have happy endings without storms in the middle. The title *Noon* is a denial of the darkness it contains, but in the text she never denies the existence of poverty and death, and, unlike her father, she rejects them as completely as she can. To this extent, Norris fulfills our expectation that an autobiographer will make a genuine effort to explain her life.

Her limping manner of criticizing her parents, however, she does not overcome. Perhaps Norris wanted to shield her parents from public disapproval: her mother for having had so many babies as to weaken her health, and her father for not having provided for the children adequately when he could have done so. To explain her personal drive toward wealth, she has no option but to object to their attitude. Reluctant to make this necessary criticism, she mentions her father's improvidence but attempts to minimize it. She discusses his Catholic belief in evangelical poverty before his death to explain why he had no estate to leave his children, but she places this negative fact about him toward the end of a eulogy of his virtues and enthusiasms. After telling us that her father had several times refused salary increases at the bank he managed, she notes his praise of poverty. In this passage she never mentions the words "Catholic," "Church," "belief," or "evangelical," and comes near to implying he had acquired the ideal of poverty from reading the Declaration of Independence. "He set poverty, service, and hard work before us in such glowing terms that we quite gloried in the thought of them. There was a goodness, and earnestness, a fundamental faith in the right, back of everything he said and that could not but influence children. Lincoln was his hero; Washington only a lesser light; and in America he believed with all his heart. He read us the Declaration of Independence and the Gettysburg Address, and talked to us of the glories of our own nation."[32] In *Family Gathering,* Norris acknowledges the influence of Catholicism on her parents, but for its benign aspect. "My mother was extremely religious; she and my father had married with old-fashioned seriousness, old-fashioned vows, and they never lost consciousness of them. We were raised in the Roman Catholic faith, urged to pray our way out of any tantrum, any revengeful fury, any panic."[33] The passage in *Noon* falsely linking ideal poverty to the Declaration of Independence is among those that create the puzzle I am working on. Nowhere in the text does Norris confront its origin in her hesitation to complain of the Church in writing, or, ultimately, in her father's Catholic education, nor does she ever work out the contradiction between the clear admiration she expresses at this point in the text with her later condemnation of his improvidence.

Norris achieves neither the whole truth nor paragraph unity in this passage, and had Lejeune in 1971 been classifying autobiographies written in the United States instead of those written in France, he would no doubt have thought this one scattered, if not flawed by its non sequiturs and its apparent ignorance of the Gospels. A Protestant reader in 1925 might have thought how so many Catholics insisted on their patriotism in the hope of reducing Protestant fear of their "allegiance to the Pope." As a Catholic reader with a literary education, I ask why a skillful writer like Norris distorts the very story she is attempting to tell and half conceals the social criticism her story implies.

Proof that Norris is leaving out a significant part of her narrative appears in an article in *California History,* in which the disparity between her private and public attitudes is made clear. "While she publicly advocated no form of birth control, she privately counseled young mothers to practice abstinence to avoid an unwanted pregnancy. No half-baked boy from Ireland with his collar turned around had the right to tell some woman that another baby was a blessing when she and her family were already emotionally and financially hard-pressed, she confided to her niece, Rosemary. Regrettably, Kathleen never revealed this sentiment to her reading audience."[34] Here the distinction between private and public criticism is strong. In Norris's comment to Rosemary, a connection between poverty and babies is made that is not directly made in *Noon,* and which would astound Field. A protective attitude toward the Church, as well as toward her parents, may in this way explain why Norris attempts to camouflage the anger in her text.

Norris sings a song of affection, interrupted by passages of anger; Mary Mellish (1890–1955) sings an angry aria, interrupted by passages intended to diminish any impression she may have given of being angry. Mellish was an operatic and concert singer of minor importance,[35] but Enrico Caruso had let her know she could have gone farther had she begun singing earlier. In the girlhood pages of *Sometimes I Reminisce: Autobiography* (1941), Mellish circles the topic, saying that her mother insisted on her attending normal school, and she never says in so many words that her mother felt singing on the stage was not appropriate for a good Catholic girl. Instead she insists, without much fear of contradiction, that her mother was a grand human being.[36] This erratic description of experience is puzzling.

Mellish must have sensed that the origin of the difficulty was the Church, for she complains at some length about nuns and priests. However, she does her best to soften or minimize her outbursts. In fact, her ways of avoiding sins of uncharitable speech sound like nuns' lessons. The resulting text, alternately erupting and tamping down, lacks formal beauty and at times even an ordinary degree of organization, omitting connections and investing more detail in some incidents than others without any evident reason. Her lack of training in composition is indicated also by her style, which is often indistinguishable from ordinary speech.

At first glance, Mellish's diction in her girlhood account expresses more happiness than anger, for example, "My grandfather, who was too lazy to work, would sit for hours at a time and sing Thomas Moore's Irish melodies. Grandfather had the asthma, but his choking and gasping for breath never bothered me. I would curl up at his feet and beg for one more song."[37] This heartless child did not herself choke and gasp for breath until the Sisters at her parochial school, St. John's Academy, got as far as astronomy. Mellish began to doubt the existence of a physical heaven when, visiting Dudley Observatory, she saw the rings of Saturn, Uranus, and Jupiter with its four moons. She was "strangely thrilled" but found it "very disconcerting because when I was study-ing astronomy I still had an idea that heaven was up there in the blue. Coming back, I lived with all these conflicting thoughts for days." Emotionally polar-ized, Mellish turned to a nun at school for enlightenment. "Sister, I am upset about a great many things. Sister, where is heaven?" Sister replied, "Child [Mellish was sixteen at the time], heaven could be on the tip of your little finger."[38] This kind of answer is somewhat standard in Catholic life, and be-cause of the way the asker experiences it, it could be called the nonanswer. Its typicality appears in a memory of Mary McCarthy's. "In *Our Sunday Visitor,* sold after church every Sunday, . . . there was a gripping Question-and-Answer column that advised you, if you were a doctor, which to save, the mother or the child, in a perilous childbirth—readers seemed to write in the same ques-tions week after week, maybe in the hope of getting a different answer."[39] In other words, the answers did not meet the questions, but in the astronomy incident, Mellish's immaturity of intellect was the cause. At sixteen she did not understand metaphorical language, and so she did not get the nun's point that heaven may not be a physical place. The text does not indicate whether Mellish is telling her readers an amusing story about stupidity, which we all share, or whether she wants to blame the Sisters for confusing her younger self. She seems to excuse them by adding, "to hear suddenly that maybe there were inhabitants on other planets was a bit confusing." "A bit" cannot be so very harmful. But then the language of the autobiographer shifts into a grimmer mode. "How often indeed we travel along strange roads, make detours, seem lost, suffer confusion, perhaps despair."[40] This diction allows the depth of her adolescent distress to emerge for a moment, even though she tries to generalize it by using a plural pronoun for herself and to soften it by implying that these things occur frequently and unavoidably. Why does Mellish say *we*? Is it egotistical and socially unacceptable to attribute spiritual suffering to herself? Or is it too hard to admit that her nuns bore a part of the blame?

Mellish as philosopher cannot seem to endure the mention of despair at all, for with only a comma, she continues, "and then suddenly we come upon an oasis of enlightenment and the way all seems so clear. I walked along many of those roads, but always there was . . ." As a reader accustomed to coherent texts, I felt sure I was about to hear of a nun who *did* have an answer, or of a religious experience that answered the problem of heaven. Instead, Mellish identifies her oasis as provided entirely by herself and her love for singing: "but always there was a great urge for self-expression with me and I kept an inner light burning before its shrine."[41] She could hardly be more open about the transfer of her faith from worship to music, and from religion to art, but she has not made us expect or understand the change. Her confusion must have been more than "a bit;" it was sufficient to destroy her childhood concept of a physical heaven without any more mature concept having replaced it. Although she attempts to conceal the causal connection to the loss of a child's literal faith, she indicates that the result was despair.

Perhaps one reason she tried to universalize loss and despair is that the catechism and most examinations of conscience listed doubt as a sin. The *Official Revised Baltimore Catechism Number One* (1944) in an exercise on the first commandment states, "Faith requires us to b[elieve] firmly what God has made known."[42] (This exercise calls for filling in blanks, which I have done.) Mellish must have felt that her textual efforts to contain her distress had failed, for she goes over the problem again in different terms (an instance of poor writing that most of the women would be ashamed of).

> At an age when I could recite the French and Latin poets and knew that the sun was ninety-three million miles from the earth, I was very naive.
>
> I thought that God the Father sat on a large throne, in His blue heaven in the sky. The Holy Ghost was on the left side and God's only Son, Jesus Christ sat on His right side. Then came the angels, archangels and saints in a huge stadium much like our present Hollywood Bowl. Behind this august assemblage there was seating room for all good Catholics who died in the faith. Far below that spot was Hell, where a red devil and his busy assistants kept piling on coal, I suppose oil burners are used now, so that the seething flames will never die out. All sinners were consigned to these flames never to return.

But there was a middle place called Purgatory for the in-betweens. If you were not good enough to enter immediately into the sight of God, you made a stop-over in Purgatory. I have recently heard a young priest describe its tortures as being equal to those of Hell, except there is a release from Purgatory and in time one can get to Heaven. . . . The priest's description of Purgatory was so vivid that one could easily get the impression that he had spent a week end there.[43]

This time Mellish's irony has two targets: Mellish herself, because her best concept of grandeur was the Hollywood Bowl, and the teaching Church, because the manner of an eyewitness should not be used to convince people of beliefs. The implication of experience destroys any need for faith. But her humor on this issue has not made Mellish feel entirely safe from her desire to criticize, for at this point she turns to the cerebral defense, inserting a parenthetical paragraph on a possible source of "the Purgatory idea" in the Hebrew Bible.[44] This display of biblical erudition is her last effort to stave off the real problem, which finally emerges. "On All Soul's Day, three days after my mother's death, I heard a young priest speak, from his fount of wisdom. He told us that one had to be almost a saint to immediately enter the Divine Presence. And that most of our loved ones were assuredly in Purgatory. My mother was no saint, she was just a grand human being. She never did burn in Purgatory but went on to a blessed and well deserved peace."[45] The phrase "fount of wisdom" is not ironic but sarcastic. In Mellish's statements about her mother I see white-hot anger, an absolute condemnation of this priest, his sermon, and his condescending beliefs. This time Mellish does not excuse the Church's attitude or minimize the Church's responsibility.

Mellish might have told people orally about her experiences of Catholic teaching on the Four Last Things—Death, the Judgment, Heaven, and Hell— and heard the usual excuses for the Church, for she credits the Church with its improvements, even though she does so in a ritual, disgusted manner. "I believe that in recent years, the Catholic Church dwells less on singing angels with harps, the agonies of Purgatory and the tortures of Hell fire." However, the young priest let her know, that among other things, the Church is still teaching the same doctrines; consequently, she refuses to accept any "change" in the Church as an excuse for its earlier ways. "But we got plenty of it in my youth and what with my bigotry, intolerance and inhibitions, I found myself a confused soul. I was years in cleaning off the stubborn barnacles."[46]

Even later, when through many zigs and zags she has reached some degree

of refusal to excuse the Church dishonestly, Mellish claims the bigotry, intolerance, and inhibitions as her own, almost as if she had arrived at school already
in this condition. As she does not know where she acquired her bigotry and
inhibitions, she takes the responsibility for them. But at fifty-one years of age,
she is able to admit that the harps and flames came from the Church.

In addition to rejecting the excuse that things have changed, Mellish rejects another traditional formula for denying evil of the Church, namely, to
say, as Norris and Repplier say, that the results have been good, that no harm
was done. Mellish regrets the trouble she had getting rid of her confusion and
"barnacles," a word that answers the metaphorical harps and flames with its
own spiritual significance, that of slowing down a ship that might otherwise
have made good headway.

Had Mellish written concisely or in an organized way, the text might not
have revealed so clearly how thin the crust of internalized censorship sometimes is, or how the heated emotions beneath have worn it away and in some
places broken through. This eruption of anger, paradoxically, may explain the
superficiality of Norris, Wolff, and certain other Catholic women autobiographers. Their superficiality may not be that of a scatterbrained, feminine
woman, but that of an angry woman who has been trained never to express
anger, at least not on certain subjects. Their internal censorship may have been
stronger, explaining the artificial blitheness of the texts they wrote. Yet in all
three the crust has weakened, so that occasionally bitter criticism bursts
through it. Perhaps censorship also explains why, when these eruptions throw
problems onto the surface of the text, none of the three women resolves the
problems, as one would expect an autobiographer to do.

Farrell is the only autobiographer in the first part of this chapter who does
not present social criticism. However, Carroll, Wolff, Norris, and Mellish criticize their socialization without intending to. Their objections are excessively
limited or are made almost against their wills. In contrast, Repplier, Matute,
Colette, and Janés have written lyrical, symbolical, flawless narratives, so lovely
that the works seem to be reminiscences—that is, recollections of others, lacking the self as a central character and thus not attaining autobiographical
status. Yet under the surface they do turn on the self and present considered
disagreements with the Catholic system.

The Spanish novelist Ana María Matute (1926–   ) has written in *El río*
(1963), a slender work usually taken to be an inconsequential, charming
reminiscence of childhood vacations in the mountains.[47] I propose that it be

read in the context of Matute's heroic struggle against General Francisco Franco's censors.

El río was published under a government that licensed no publications that were critical of the Church. Matute had reason to know that a straightforward autobiography that described, for example, her divorce, would not be published. Pope Leo XIII prohibited books that defended suicide or divorce in "Officiorum ac munerum."[48] Spanish censors had forbidden the publication of two of Matute's novels as first composed, *Pequeño teatro* (Little Theater), written in 1943, published in 1954, and *Las luciérnagas* (Fireflies), which had to be rewritten in order to obtain a license in 1955.[49] *El río*, however, was published in 1963 without incident; Matute concealed its message by literary indirection.

El río may be the most arcane of this group of Catholic women's autobiographies, yet it can be decoded simply by looking for camouflage. Matute relies on the pretended insignificance of nostalgia pieces written for a weekly called *Destino*;[50] fragmentation and scattering of her judgments; suppression of narrator and author comments;[51] suppression of anger and omissions of persons who had made her angry, especially the nuns;[52] symbols like the chalice as disguises for desire and love; and biblical tales that could satisfy traditional readers by reminding them of the theology of subordination, while throughout she incorporates attitudes from the theology of equivalence.

Because Matute presents this description of Spanish life as a series of local color sketches, which it is, I can imagine the censor tossing *El río* on his desk, dismissing it as trivial, disorganized, sometimes self-contradictory, and therefore, he would think, making no argument. A series of recollections about an inglorious village and a group of grubby little kids could not possibly have national importance. Such an attitude is represented in *El río* by the country boy Pinitos, who scatters and stamps on Ana María's souvenirs and calls them idiocies.[53]

Matute's array of disguises work so well that not only the censor but also her desired readers may not find the concealed attitudes. When camouflage succeeds, a secondary evasion becomes necessary: evasion of one's own indecipherability. Matute does this in two ways. First, through iteration, blood becomes a sign of suffering or unnecessary torment of harmless beings.[54] Second, she uses transformations of the usual clerical message about traditional texts, especially the positive valuation of sexuality in her Genesis tale and the negative valuation of persecution in her Crucifixion tale (in contrast to the clergy's usual emphasis of the value of Christ's suffering).[55] Phrases indicating Matute's sorrow at suffering imposed on the innocent and other phrases pointing to her approval of pleasure signal an affinity to readers with similar values. Camouflage alerts sympathetic readers to the presence of secret messages; affinity signals present them with the messages.

Matute argues by examples against beliefs that girls should stay inside and learn to be feminine, and especially against the belief that a Catholic style of femininity is natural to women. In instance after instance, by running the countryside with boys she learned more about her nature than she could have done inside, organizing doll tea parties. If our potential activities are described in terms of the three systems of the brain, as neurologist Paul MacLean proposes, they include pursuits related to ritual and survival (reptilian), food and territory, sex and defense (paleomammalian or limbic), and greater sensory information, reasoning, and altruism (neomammalian or neocortical).[56] This list parallels the types of adventures Ana María and her companions pursued during vacations. Away from her family's summer home and outside the femininity system, she was able to learn about layers of the self that adults commonly conceal, for example, our fascination with death, which she attributes to the question, "And if it were I?" By sneaking away from the house during siesta she was able to experience friendship, debate, and the dread of future suffering, all described in "The World Was an Orange"; she learned to see the world whole and good, as obedient girls in her social class could not. If she had stayed inside and never run with boys, how would she have known what she was missing or to what extent she wanted to participate? *El río* tells the story of how Matute, when she explored sex and violence, found sex to be joyful though dangerous, but found violence against the innocent repugnant and rejected it, together with idealistic language that excuses it. She attained this integration of the elements of personality at about the age of ten, her "age of reason."[57]

She tells us in *El río* that children allowed to explore the world can study the possibilities of human life. Matute's narrative argument is that children play and run about the world as a form of experimentation, to try themselves out. If authority prevents that, it prevents them from living complete lives as adults. She herself had the dedication and will even as a child to evade all customs and influences opposed to her complete development as an individual both animal and intelligent.

Learning to decipher *El río* helps one learn to read texts written under a censorship that is not official, but social or internalized. It raises the possibility that pleasant texts written in other countries may also only pretend to conform to Catholic views. The censors Catholic women face in France and the United States are not salaried government officials, but one's former schoolmates, as with Repplier, or readers and bookbuyers trained in Catholic beliefs opposed to frank criticism of the Church or to open description of the autobiographer's confidence and success. In France, such an audience would explain why Colette's objections to the Church are made indirectly, through her mother's voice; equally, it explains Dussane's false modesty and self-effacement, which climaxes in her displacement of self-praise onto another actor.[58]

Agnes Repplier (1855–1950), an American essayist, states explicitly that she values the discipline she and her friends received from the nuns at their boarding school, but her narrative describes the flaws of that discipline. She defends convent-school discipline in the introduction to what purports to be a sweet reminiscence. *In Our Convent Days* is Repplier's wittiest and warmest work. The convent school under examination is Eden Hall, named no doubt in a passion of hope and without conscious irony. Located in Philadelphia, the school was run by Religious of the Sacred Heart, who are called the Ladies of the Sacred Heart by McCarthy in her exceptional courtesy, but are usually spoken of by American Catholics as "the Madams." Repplier begins her recollections of life at Eden Hall by saying that she does not believe every instance of modernization of the convent has been for the better. She objects that "even the iron hand of discipline has been relaxed," and she wonders "if liberty, coupled with discretion, is worth having when one is eleven years old."[59] Readers expect the book that follows to extol a golden, lost paradise in which eleven-year-olds had much that was worth having. In these words, she has provided an *autobiographical pact,* to use Lejeune's term, but, as he cautions, readers should not always believe such contracts.[60]

Some scholars may not view *In Our Convent Days* as an autobiographical work because it covers only two years of Repplier's life. However, the two years comprise her total experience at Eden Hall, and she exhibits the wholeness of the narrative by touching on all aspects of her life there, including change and the passage of time. In dealing with a small convent school and acting entirely against the will of the nuns, Agnes had been able to confront guilt and pride, contempt and love, sacrifice and pleasure, death and rebirth. By studying Agnes's rapid evolution under pressure from the nuns and the other girls, Repplier was able to write a complete treatment of girlhood as Catholics lived it and were made to live it, rather than as their theory described it. Thus the scale of life can be small and the mood light, without omitting any important issues.

In Our Convent Days has an ebullience about it, probably because Repplier wrote it as a gift to her classmates for a reunion, perhaps their thirtieth. This first audience may also explain her cheerful attitude toward convent discipline. She attended the school for only two years because the Madams expelled her.[61] Even so, she seems to have emerged with the usual gratitude and amusement of graduates of such schools. She recalls with great love her favorite nun; her friends and their games, escapades, and fantasies; her yearnings after higher things and forbidden, worldly things; her loneliness for her mother. Even her anecdotes about those girls and nuns who were excessively pious or repressive are told in a way that would have brought laughter from other alumnae, as they do today from anyone familiar with convent life before its modernization after Vatican II.

An example of how Repplier played for that laughter is when she speaks of a nun (whom she calls Mme. Dane), who would not let the girls open their desks during study hours (there was a rule against it) and who was "constitutionally incapable of distinguishing between wilfull murder and crossing one's legs in class."[62] These insights show the sophistication of Repplier and her contemporaries in 1905, when they would have been about fifty years old. As children they perhaps sensed only that Mme. Dane was in error. Along with her impression that rules are valuable in themselves and not susceptible of variations went her belief that all girls and women should behave alike. "At night and morning prayers we were obliged to lay our folded hands in exactly the same position on the second rung of our chair backs. If we lifted them unconsciously to the top rung, Mme. Dane swooped down upon us like a falcon upon errant doves—which was dreadfully distracting to our devotions."[63] Neither the behavior at issue nor Mme. Dane's dogged enforcement of rules can function as a serious criticism of the Madams, or so one thinks on a first reading. Mme. Dane was more trivial than cruel, a kind of sheepdog to the saved children of saved Christians. These anecdotes are comic, after all, and Repplier does not seem to have wanted reform.[64] Her attitude appears rather indulgent, that nuns are like that, and we all understand.

It seems odd today that a writer in 1905 would defend the old convent-school discipline, which was a hopeless and almost crazy mixture of medieval and Victorian rules and customs. But Repplier's appreciation is as sincere as her critique. After all, the very use of an autobiographical pact must have come from the intellectual discipline given her at Eden Hall. Of the American women among these autobiographers only Repplier and McCarthy, members of the same social class and educated by the same French order, begin by indicating what and in what spirit they intend to write, as they had apparently been taught to do.[65] Repplier may be putting forward this advantage in subtle support of her case for convent discipline. In her autobiographical pact, the introduction, Repplier lists the topics she will discuss. By putting these in question form she shows her awareness that form ought to be appropriate, for questionnaires have a scholastic atmosphere about them. "Do [our successors to-day] live their lives as vehemently as we lived ours; do they hold the secrets of childhood inviolate in their hearts as we held them in ours; are they as untainted by the commonplace, as remote from the obvious, as we always were; and will they have as vivid a picture of their convent days to look back upon, as the one we look at now?"[66] A subtext of opposition to the convent and its values already tugs at the reader's attention. The phrasing of Repplier's list of narrative subjects raises questions as to how an iron hand could cause children to live with more vehemence than others, to keep secrets better, to lack familiarity with ordinary life, to be preternaturally alert. The book that follows is a series of illustrations of the way rules, surveillance, and punishment stimulate the mind—to evasion of the rules, true, but to activity and ingenuity all the same. Her narrative makes it clear that the group schedule suppressed the spontaneity and vitality of the girls most of the time, that they were afraid of unmerited punishments, that they were not allowed to educate themselves about everyday human experience.

Although she was expelled for the mischief she and her friends loved, she proposes that their friendship and even their misbehavior played a part in their maturation. Just as she left her doll behind, she and her friends dropped their crushes on the senior girls at the moment when an attractive new server appeared at Mass. When she takes the latter episode out of its chronological order and puts it first, besides playing for laughs from other alumnae, who were her first readers, she also emphasizes that a girl has a history, that like a wheel she moves forward when some aspect of her potential self touches the ground or comes into reality, and then passes backward and upward and out of present time, making way for the next. Her rearrangement of events argues that the nuns who expelled her had not understood and were attempting to stamp out behavior that in time would have led, paradoxically, to the behavior they wanted. *In Our Convent Days* conveys, along with its protestations of love, a criticism, which seems to me deadly, of traditional monastic discipline. A significant part of the impact of the text comes from the remembered sorrows of the children, a suffering the writer was unable to conceal or perhaps did not wish to conceal. She implies throughout that the pruning of innocent impulses while calling them sinful was a hurtful and unnecessary mistake, yet she appears to have felt confident that her audience of fellow alumnae would not respond to her humor by raising their voices against the nuns, or at least, not against their method of training girls. Perhaps she was calling on her peers—educated Catholic laywomen—to reform their lives, to apply the gift of discernment to demands made on them for sacrifices and suffering, to accept only those with some practical function.

Colette's two autobiographical works, *La maison de Claudine* (1922) and *Sido* (1929), are sufficiently creative in their form that Lejeune explicitly rejects them in his manual on French autobiographies, saying that Colette never wrote "a consecutive autobiography," but only "a stroll through scattered memories." In spite of his reaction, *La maison de Claudine* and *Sido* are truly autobiographical, for they "collect childhood memories on which the central figure confers coherence and even sanctity."[67]

Sidonie-Gabrielle Colette (1873–1954), stage personality and writer, wrote fictions about intimate experience. Her autobiographical work deserves the same respect as her fiction, both for her play with generic convention and for her insight into a girl's development. *La maison de Claudine* and *Sido* are literary studies of her formative years; for all their Parisian elegance and indirection, they have special interest for the study of Catholic training of girls. These works, particularly the first, have an inimitable allure, no more diminished by their sorrowful passages than was *In Our Convent Days*. The most apparent difference from Repplier's work is in the tone; Colette is lyrical rather than comic. Her deftness with language and imagery have given her prose such a shimmer as to make its topics sometimes almost disappear. Her thousands of women readers have not taken her as inconsequential, but her scintillating style apparently so dazzled Lejeune that he missed both the conscious artistry and the social implications of these two works, neglecting his responsibility to study formal innovations in the genre.

Perhaps the reason for his mistake is that earlier literary scholars had left autobiography to philosphers or historians. Lejeune does not realize that Colette is writing a literary work, a part of the artistic upheaval then in progress in Paris. Claire Dehon has made the case that Colette wrote in the spirit of Art Nouveau. Particularly interesting among the similarities Dehon notes is the sudden transformation of objects into living beings.[68] A fusion of Colette's literary attention to emotion with Art Nouveau's interest in vegetative forms appears in Colette's phrase about Sido, that she was "curved under storms."[69] Most relevant to Lejeune's comment, Dehon writes, "The desire to conceal artistry is not found in Art Nouveau, which, on the contrary, took pleasure in exhibiting skill. However, the decoration and the secondary detail do draw one's attention from the center of the work and therefore may hide its 'real' meaning."[70] Tendrils and curlings are characteristic of *La maison de Claudine,* and help explain, if they do not excuse, Lejeune's error. His lack of aesthetic awareness explains why he did not concede meaning or autobiographical status to either of her histories of girlhood. When I first read the set of autobiographies discussed in the present chapter, I also missed their import because of their manner.

Other artistic movements of the 1920s offered Colette riches to rummage through. She uses a surrealist interweaving of art, dream, and reality in *La maison* to explain her mother's attitude toward her growing up.[71] Again, the fragmentation of Colette's narrative or the omission of links between narrative units suggests that she might have been influenced by the Delaunays and the Cubists as much as by Art Nouveau. In *La maison de Claudine,* Colette creates a sparkling, many-faceted surface by breaking up both narrative and narrative themes into vignettes or prose poems, each with a title and closure. Having isolated and identified incidents that made her history what it was, she leaves the synthesis of these elements of her story to the reader. By allowing her readers to arrive at the implications of her narratives on their own, she frees herself to suggest with a few lines, in the manner of certain Oriental prints, as much or more experience than earlier writers could present with masses of unassimilable detail. In *La maison* Colette absorbs her autobiographical themes—independence, natural sexuality, and community—so completely into incident as to make them disappear as themes, at least during a first reading. This sleight of hand is unusual among Catholic women autobiographers, and could hardly be excelled by another autobiographer of any background or gender.

The religious factor in her distillation of themes remains to be examined. The elements of Catholic life on which these two texts turn are, for *La maison de Claudine,* the femininity program, and for *Sido,* the necessity of pleasing one's parents, an essential phase of the femininity program. Lejeune was not completely wrong to read Colette as feminine and her text as scattered, guilty of a charming inconsequence. This impression is part of a style she herself valued and labored to achieve, but it should be seen as the costume of the Catholic Woman worn by an authentic person. The enchanting texture, if Colette's readers fully absorb it, changes into a language of analysis and protest. For example, incidents dealing with conformity and independence reveal Colette's commitment to personal autonomy.[72] Another way in which Colette creates a surface with double implications is by locating her adult critique of the Church in her mother, for this mother can be read both as remarkably free and inner-directed, and as a model Colette came in time to resemble. The displacement allows the author to avoid interrupting the narrative continually with statements of her current attitude.

Colette's mother, Sidonie Landoy Colette (1835–1912), referred to in her daughter's writing as Sido, was an unusually devout Catholic in the France of her day, because she attended Mass every Sunday and visited the sick. She did her duty as a Catholic Mother by presenting the perfect example of a devoted wife, at least to her second husband, Colette's father; she had not greatly loved her first husband. Christiane Milner has noted that Colette always admired Sido's love for Captain Colette.[73] Sido met the Church's standards for a Catholic Mother, too, when she allowed Colette to join a catechism class. On the other hand, although Colette as a child had enjoyed the class, she disables the reader's inclination to respond to her delight by bringing in her mother's disapproval of the catechism itself.[74]

To understand the argument of Colette's autobiographies, then, a reader must view them as works of art in which elegance is achieved by indirection, but the central figure—not Sido, but Colette—can still be deciphered amid its graceful decoratons. The protests Colette makes in *Maison* and *Sido* are fundamental, which raises the question whether she deliberately threw dust in the eyes of certain of her readers, perhaps readers loyal to the Church and its femininity training or at least averse to their criticism in print.

Clara Janés (1940–), a member of a Barcelona publishing family and a disciplined writer, recently added a childhood narrative, *Jardín y laberinto* (Garden and Labyrinth, 1990) to the list of her works in various genres. *Jardín y laberinto* is distinguished for its beautiful style: "a night fifteen years ago on which an adolescent girl leaps out of the window of her room and climbs into a tree that by its form allows her to sit on one of its branches, like a cat, contemplating the silent, empty street and the stars that are seen above the uppermost line that on one side sharpens into St. Peter the Martyr and on the other reaches the Tibidabo."[75] Poetic moments like this tend to absorb more of the reader's attention than does the overall narrative flow. Thus *Jardín y laberinto,* though presented in two parts rather than Colette's fifty, has a fragmentary air like that of Colette's autobiographical works and Matute's *El río.* Janés does not link her memories of musical and other cultural experiences, parties on the terrace, customs, personalities, and journeys small and great as she narrates.

Janés sees the Catholic way of life as resulting in unhappy women. Born during Franco's regime but writing after his death, she grew up in a Catholic setting but, more important to her, among adults actively interested in publishing, music, literature, and theater. Above all, she writes of her father, who brought composers and other cultured people to the house, and who had a tremendous enthusiasm for publishing and was about to begin publishing foreign titles when he was killed in a road accident. Possibly as a result of her aesthetic childhood, Janés expresses her judgment of the Catholic Church most frequently by what I will call "textual secularization," that is, a transformation of something Catholic into something human, a reclassification. For example, when she joined a study-abroad group, she and a friend spent a long while seated, silent, in a chapel in the cathedral of Poitiers because of the life-size representation of the burial of Christ. The next sentence introduces their first lovers, Janés's a blond, blue-eyed Dutchman.[76] This sequence of a Catholic incident and its secularization is typical of *Jardín y laberinto*. Since she supplies no commentary, the reader is free to infer that Janés views Catholicism positively, as providing symbols of human episodes, but this process simultaneously points to its caterpillarlike characteristics. In other words, for her, Catholicism is what she transformed into mature human life and left behind. Though she was raised Catholic, Janés could not have remained a caterpillar nor could she return to the caterpillar state without dying as a butterfly.

She clarifies her belief that human life is more valuable than the religion in two ways: first, by always leaving any reference to a Catholic object or incident behind immediately in favor of a fuller description of related personal actions outside that context, as she did with her contemplation of the figure of the beautiful young male, and second, by contrasting her aunts. Her Aunt Angelina, bitter and ill, going from church to housework, could not laugh when the time came for fun. Janés says Angelina found relief from her sufferings only in "the masochistic resignation that Catholicism offers." The emptiness of her life was made all the more evident by Janés's Aunt Montserrat, who could laugh herself to death, and even in the nursing home would dress up to put on a love scene with another resident or recite a poem she had written or play the piano for people, thus increasing her enjoyment and that of others.[77] The implication is that the Church tends to keep women off paths that lead to a morally irreproachable happiness because these are not Catholic paths.

Toward the end of the work Janés expresses concern that her memories from her third and fourth year are vague and may lack anything that would lead one to tell them to a third person. This remark must be a transitional device or a concession to an imaginary critic, for she answers herself that the shards of memory may be important in that they "transmitted [to her] real knowledge of a distinct way of life, tied to practices and customs that were not dehumanizing and were in a certain way mysterious, since every gesture, in them, signified something more than its concrete realization, carried a symbolic load rooted in the earth, a profound meaning." Only at the end of the disjointed series of recollections does Janés transform it into a whole, by means of a discovery about her personal orientation. Her memories of her father's death and dismemberment in an automobile accident and her visit to the dusty cemetery where he was buried are tied forever in her mind to his joy in creating, whether three-dimensional scenes for Christmas or a translation of Francis Thompson, a British Catholic Revival poet. Janés's elegiac subject leads her to lyricism, and the lyricism leads her to her own commitment to her father's way of life. Howarth would say that her reminiscence becomes a poetic autobiography when it becomes an autobiography of discovery. The whole work unites when she decides to commit herself again, this time more consciously, "to follow ardently."[78] When she finishes traversing the labyrinth of memory, she does not deny that monstrous death lives there, but she finds the rose garden of human vitality, friendship, and culture at its heart.

Janés's conclusion about her girlhood is that it directed her ardor toward the infinite, not of another world, but of the artistic community of Barcelona. From her girlhood perch she could see the lights of Barcelona at night, and she felt this as a promise that she could in some way join her father in his work there, a work that went beyond the limitations of life in the house.[79] She has followed his pattern by not limiting her efforts in writing to any one genre. She has written poetry and fiction as well as analytic narrative. Her commitment is to a public career understood as involving a secular infinite. Secularization viewed as progress away from Catholicism is a very important part of the conclusions and narrative strategies of other autobiographers, especially Chacel, Delarue-Mardrus, and Beauvoir. Janés is courteous and wise; she, too, never states her opposition to Catholic femininity explicitly.

Of the writers discussed in this chapter, only Farrell seems to be as cheerful as she says. Norris and Mellish, Wolff and Carroll, while suffering from anger or some unadmitted deep distress, seem at first to be cheerful, but the reason may be that they feel their parents, the local priest, or their own nun at school should be beyond criticism. Colette, Repplier, Matute, and Janés give so much pleasure by the delicate beauty of their style that they almost hide the clear stream of criticism that runs underneath; the desire to hide may be as strong a force in their artistry as the desire to speak.

Probably the most reliable way to explain all this concealment, so dangerous to the generic responsibilities of an autobiographer, would be to look at the Church's written statements of its teaching for children in catechisms and prayer books. Not all the autobiographers studied here attended Catholic schools, but even if they did not, they had to learn the catechism in preparation for their first communion and first confession. Benoist, Delarue-Mardrus, and Sheelagh Conway criticize the way the catechism was taught or written, basically because it was incomprehensible to them. Apparently only Colette enjoyed it, but everyone was put through it in some form.

The *Official Revised Baltimore Catechism Number One* (1944), "number one" meaning "for grade school children," is a useful edition for this study in that all the women so far discussed except Janés must have completed their catechism class before that date, and in Spain in the 1940s, when she would have been preparing for her first communion, no modernization would as yet have occurred. (Although "things have changed" since Vatican II and a new catechism came out in 1992, the older edition is appropriate for the context.) In *Baltimore Number One,* the lesson on the fourth commandment of God, "Honor thy father and thy mother," asks, "What are we commanded by the fourth commandment?" The answer given is "By the fourth commandment we are commanded to respect and love our parents, to obey them in all that is not sinful, and to help them when they are in need." I have nothing against helping one's parents in need, but this obligation is not stated or implied in the fourth commandment. The catechism also asks, "What does the fourth commandment forbid?" and answers, "The fourth commandment forbids disrespect, unkindness, and disobedience to our parents and lawful superiors."[80] Again, disobedience to one's parents is not forbidden, nor is the equation of other lawful superiors with one's parents necessarily implied in the commandment itself. Yet this teaching seems benign enough at first reading, and some observers have credited it with the eventual Protestant acceptance of Catholics as workers and employees in the United States.

The catechisms of various countries teach the same basic concepts. The Paris catechism of 1863, which would have been studied by Colette and perhaps others of these autobiographers, told the children, "Par le quatrième commandement, Dieu nous ordonne d'aimer nos père et mère, de les respecter, de leur obéir, et de les assister dan leurs besoins" ("By the fourth commandment, God commands us to love our father and mother, to respect them, to obey them, and to assist them in their needs"). Even the motives for this love are given. Children were to love their parents and meet their needs out of gratitude for life and for having survived infancy; they were to respect and obey their parents "parce qu'ils tiennent auprès de nous la place de Dieu" ("because they occupy with us the place of God").[81] Until the 1960s brought some revision of Catholic teaching, a long series of catechisms, priests, and Sisters told Catholic children and adult converts that priests, nuns, and parents represented God's will to them. The idea was probably to guarantee that parents would be able to get their children to cooperate with the Church in establishing a virtuous society. But the identification of the parents' worthiness and commands with those of God has proved to be unwise in the case of battering, encroaching, or incestuous parents, as autobiographies by Mullen, Adam, and Pillay show. Even when parents were only dishonest, cold, exploitative, or tyrannical toward their children (like Jouhandeau's mother), or talked in the presence of children about avoidance and hatred of other groups of people (as did Schoffen's mother, McCarthy's paternal grandmother, and Beauvoir's father), the children would have been able to function better without worrying whether the behavior of these honored authority figures was God's will.

The Church has made a very grave error in assuming that all Catholic parents are able to correct morals and train their children in virtue or, if they are not so to begin with, can be persuaded to become morally good. If it happens that a girl's parents are basically good and give for the most part wise directives, their ability to care for their children physically or culturally can still suffer suddenly owing to the loss of one or both parents or financial incompetence or reverses, as happened with Mullen, Chacel, Norris, Bernhardt, Beauvoir, and McCarthy. This connection between death and diminution of family nurturance is suggested in *Becoming Mature* (1989) by Valerie Malhotra Bentz.[82] To think that when a good parent had departed, God had in some degree done so, too, could cause severe emotional problems for a child. In the best of cases, the equation of the parents with God puts an unduly heavy burden on small children. Unfortunately, the same concept of parental authority was taught in U.S. Catholic schools as well.

If the near-divinization of parents, nuns, and priests is taken lightly, as by Repplier and her friends, or if it is set aside in maturity, as by Colette, it does not seem harmful. But many Catholic children take these things too much to heart. Such a response explains both Mellish's feeling of betrayal by Sisters and priests, and Carroll's excessive devotion to her parents, particularly her mother, and later to nuns with authority over her. The inflation of parental authority may have caused or aggravated the puzzling emotional conflict about criticism of her parents in Norris's autobiography; frustration would be intensified by the importance given respect for the parents by equating their authority, rules, decrees, and judgments with God's absolute will. Later on, if children catechized in this way themselves became parents, teachers, or priests, they could think of themselves as having divine authority and therefore divine wisdom and soundness of judgment.

Similarity in these teachings in the catechisms of various countries may go back to the *Catechism of the Council of Trent for Parish Priests: Issued by Order of Pope Pius V* (1566), the source of them all. This proto-catechism was composed at the time of the "Protestant Rebellion" "to stem the tide of error that was sweeping over Christendom," and one of its dimensions was a desire to improve the impression that Protestants had of the Church.[83] In analyzing the fourth commandment, the Catechism of Trent expounds the terms *honor* and *longevity*. Less logically, the writers of this catechism derive authority in adult organizations, not from the whole people or from social necessity, but from family bonds. The extension from parents to others is made by listing types of men called "fathers": "the prelates of the Church, her pastors and priests," "those who govern the state," "those to whose care, fidelity, probity and wisdom others are committed, such as teachers, instructors, masters and guardians," and "finally, aged men, advanced in years." About thirty lines of print are devoted to this list, and it is followed by about four lines on "mothers," whose authority at that time was not yet extended to teaching nuns. Of the mother we are told only the reasons why we should honor her, namely, "the care and solicitude with which she bore us, and . . . the pain and labor with which she gave us birth and brought us up.[84]

The second significant revision the Catechism of Trent makes in the fourth commandment is in analyzing the "manner of honoring parents" to include "the spontaneous offering of sincere and dutiful love . . . To supplicate God in their behalf . . . Submission to their wishes and inclinations . . . The imitation of their good example; for, to seek to resemble closely anyone is the highest mark of esteem towards him . . . Not only ask, but follow their advice . . . Relieve their necessities, supplying them with necessary food and clothing." At the time of their parents' deaths, children are also to make sure they receive the sacraments and must attend their funerals.[85]

The list seems long, even when summarized. However, for this study of girlhood narratives, the items on the list are important, particularly in Trent's interpetation of the commandment to *honor* one's parents as a command to *obey* and *imitate* them, an interpretation I believe children in middle-class and lower-class Protestant sects in the United States, at least, are not taught. For them, the emphasis is on obedience to God and conscience. The Catholic interpretation may explain why Colette's second autobiographical work, *Sido,* acknowledges her imitation of her father, and why many Catholics are so hesitant to evaluate priests and, in some cases, even politicians. The extension of the fourth commandment to others in addition to one's parents, and the addition of obedience and imitation to the duty of honor, does much to explain the differences between Catholic and other women.

Since the situation of Catholic children in regard to the fourth commandment is unfamiliar to most readers in the United States, let me provide a little more acquaintance with it. In a catechism class, the teacher has to expand and apply the lessons, if for no other reason than that the class time must be filled. Accordingly, the classroom edition of the Baltimore catechism includes study exercises for each lesson, which offer some applications, including the following cases that the children are asked to judge.

1. Eddie always tries to do what the teacher asks. [Note the unexplained extension of respect for parents to teachers.]
2. Ben always finishes what he is doing before he does what his father has asked him to do.
3. Eleanor has the habit of pouting when she does not like what her mother asks her to do.
4. Carl always speaks with greatest respect to his father and mother . . .
6. Irene always tries to do the things that will please her mother . . .
10. Florence hates to go home immediately after school, but she goes home promptly and never complains. Her mother told her to do it.[86]

The language here, while it does not explicitly forbid disagreement or criticism of one's parents, nevertheless prohibits such behavior. Children are taught not to make even the silent protest of pouting; they are taught not only to obey, but to obey promptly and politely, and even try to please when they have not been asked to. In fact, the standard the children are asked to meet is that of heroic monastic obedience, namely, to think spontaneously of ways to please one's superiors. Also of interest in this list is the division of obedience, and, by implication, of modeling; that is, the boy is to obey the father, and the girl, the mother. Although this separation was common early in the twentieth century, Catholic teachers seem to have put more emphasis on the matter than other teachers did, and the effort to prevent girls from imitating their fathers becomes important in several of these autobiographies.

In catechism class, values and customs not originating with Christ may be taught side by side with those he practiced or approved. When Repplier's Mme. Dane confused uniform position of the hands during prayer with goodness and sanctity, and when Carroll's mother associated the gender customs of her day with moral principle, they had a model in the catechism.

In *Baltimore Number One,* the lesson on contrition for sins returns to the subject of obedience in its study exercises, asking the children to decide which actions in a list are "occasions of sin"; for example, "(4) obeying their mothers, . . . (7) going to movies that their teachers tell them not to attend, . . . (9) doing things that their fathers told them not to do, (10) obeying their teachers and pastors, (11) doing what their fathers say to do."[87] Numbers 7 and 9 are evidently meant to be actions that could lead a child into committing a sin. Children who took this on faith could have had no idea that their teachers and fathers might forbid them to do certain things that were not only morally safe, but even broadening and beneficial, such as seeing a movie praising Protestants, or one portraying women who resembled their fathers in some way. Although the catechism warns them not to obey sinful commands, somehow children are taken off guard if they are ordered to submit to incest, as Pillay's Catholic stepfather ordered her to do. The obedience training of these children was so time intensive, so closely associated with their awe of God, and approached in so many ways that they often found it difficult and painful to admit that a parent was requiring sinful behavior.

The Church's lessons on obedience were also taught through prayerbooks. The sample I will refer to was given for first communion in 1935 (at about the date of Matute's first communion) to a young Irish girl in Hibbing, Minnesota. I have talked with this woman several times, and know that she went on to bear twelve children that lived. She now has thirty-four grandchildren. Her husband owns a funeral home, thus devoting himself to the care of people at the time of the last rites and of bereavement. Her prayerbook is titled *With Jesus: Prayers and Instructions for Youthful Catholics* (1922); the author is "A Sister Servant of the Immaculate Heart of Mary," that is, an Immaculate Heart nun. The teaching that we should obey human authority *as if it were God's* appears a number of times in this short book, but I will quote only examples of the most startling logical leaps.

> God sees you always and everywhere. Do not displease him. Try to be obedient to parents and teachers. (Prayers during the Day)

Have I disobeyed my parents, my teachers, or any one who takes Thy
place, dear Lord? (Examination of Conscience)

How can I show my thanks, dear Jesus? Help me to try to do always just
what I am told. (Prayer during the Epistle)

Have I been disobedient to my parents, teachers, or anybody I ought to
obey? (Examination of Conscience)

Help me to be the child that Thou wouldst want me to be, obedient,
reverent at my prayers, ready to help in the house or in school, just like
Thou wert when Thou wert my age in the Holy House of Nazareth to
Our Lady and Saint Joseph.

Always remember that you must be obedient, you must love your parents
more than anybody else in the world, and you must rejoice their hearts
by the countless "little things" they love so dearly.[88]

These quotations may explain some of the unusual degree of parent-centered-
ness in the autobiographies under examination. Mainstream readers will find
all this surprising, I think, just as Louisa Field was astonished by Kathleen
Norris's enthusiasm for motherhood.

The language employed in their early religious training has affected Catholic women permanently, and, as adults, they sometimes echo that language,
consciously or unconsciously. An example of this appears in *Mémoires d'une
jeune fille rangée,* when Beauvoir explains how she moved beyond the temper
tantrums of her infancy over commands given without rational explanation.
When she grew older and had begun school, she was "able to ask why, and to
discuss the matter." If her parents gave only the reasons, "It's not done," or
"When I say no I *mean* no!" she notes, "I was sure that my parents were only
trying to do their best for me. And besides, it was the will of God their lips
gave utterance to: He had created me; He had died for me; He was entitled to
my total submission."[89] When Catholics look at authority, they see double.
This elision of human and divine authority is distinctively Catholic. In at least
some other cultural traditions, authority does not attempt to inspire so much
awe. The ecclesiastical role assigned parents may explain, too, why Catholic
autobiographies often begin with adulthood, for one can hardly evaluate figures representing God himself.

Consistently, the prayerbook has a message about criticism, which contributed to a partial paralysis of the analytic process in Catholic women's autobiographies. "Have I spoken badly about my parents and teachers or deceived them
in any way? Did I tell anyone's secret faults? Did I listen to unkind talk, or lay

the blame on others, or have I thought and said what was unkind of another without cause?" (Examination of Conscience) In case a child might doubt some of this, the biggest gun is brought in. "I am sure [Jesus speaking of his crucifixion for the sake of the child] you will not think of making the wounds deeper, will you, dearest child?"[90] The prohibitions so tenderly taught in prayerbooks for children explain in great part the puzzling concealments, the silences and half-silences of Catholic women in their autobiographies. These women have analytic ability, as other women do, but unfortunately they have learned to think of analysis as a breach of love.

Although chapters 21 and 22 of *Baltimore Number One* ask only for participation in the Church, and not appreciation, the Church provides much that makes its members love it: a philosophy with which to approach the randomness of life; a yearly calendar to fill time; emotional support from the imagery, bodily involvement, and symbolism of its prayer life; knowledge of historical periods not explained in the public schools;[91] an ethical system which, if used selectively, can help develop individual strength; and regular social contact, however cool and carefully distant. These benefits meant so much to me in the melancholy of youth and made me love the Church so deeply that I find it difficult to admit its faults, even to myself. However, Catholic ethical training has also brought me to the point of wanting not to lie to myself any longer. Even though the Church gratifies and heals some women, it disappoints and damages others. Both groups of women should be respected and their experiences studied.

When autobiography is what Catholic women want to write, they may be hampered by their catechetical training to such an extent that they cannot explain themselves in a natural way. If the surfacing of their memories aroused old hurts and angers, the trouble they would naturally have in putting them into words would be aggravated and the phraseology distorted by their ecclesiastical education. Any negative memories of parents, teachers, priests, and Church could not be recounted in a simple manner, but must be tossed to and fro by conflicting ethical desires: to suppress the critical and to tell the truth.

In all cases the Catholic women autobiographers of the twentieth century take some position on a scale between acceptance and rejection of Catholic censorship; thus, one distinguishing feature of this group of writers is that they respond to the rule not to criticize the Catholic Church. Their strategies vary, thus establishing simultaneously that they belong to a definable subclass among women and that uniformity in any human class or subclass is impossible.

When a Catholic woman attempting to write autobiography finds that some of her thoughts are critical, she has approximately five alternatives. First, she can tell the truth, as the teaching of the eighth commandment requires, carrying this directive even to telling the whole truth—that is, she can present her memories of unpleasant as of pleasant moments in the Church with the same calm thoroughness. Among the women studied in chapter 1, Repplier, in spite of her tolerance of flaws in the Church, comes closest to attaining this level of analytic honesty. She might have been educated in such a way as never to have applied the prohibition against criticism to her writing. Second, the nascent autobiographer can refrain from including any critical thoughts about "God's representatives." Matute achieves this where the nuns were concerned by writing only about the summer vacations. Autobiographers who were nuns seem to write more in this spirit than the laywomen do, yet all the nuns criticize Catholic authority figures for one thing or another. Third, a Catholic woman autobiographer can criticize but defend, excuse, or praise the Church, as Carroll and Farrell do. Fourth, the autobiographer can tell the truth incompletely, as Mellish does. In such works, readers can observe structures or processes of concealment and resistance to concealment. These devices show that the topography of an autobiographical text may look pleasant, while in actuality it is heaving, folding, and cracking. These sequences can fairly be said to have expanded the possibilities of autobiography as an art form. Fifth, if a Catholic woman decides to reject the requirement not to criticize, she can make her struggle to overcome censorship a valuable part of her autobiography. The autobiographer can camouflage her critical thoughts by a disciplined abundance of literary devices. Matute, Repplier, Colette, Janés, and other Catholic women autobiographers use this indirection to communicate forbidden attitudes. The variety of strategies used by the literary writers—particularly symbolism, the omission of explicit comment, and fragmentation of narrative argument—inevitably affects the surface or topography of their writing just as significantly as does the anger that erupts uncontrollably into the work of less skillful writers. The struggle between truthfulness and the prohibition of criticism affects the autobiographies on the formal level.

Catholic women autobiographers have as a result of their training in charitable speech an extra handicap. Their reluctance to criticize their parents and teachers interferes at times with their obligation as autobiographers to reflect on their lives and their relations with society. Yet desires to tell the truth, to avoid or conceal criticism, and to avoid looking into their anger constitute much of the interest and value of these texts, whether their thoughtfulness is hidden under mildness or under lyricism and symbolism. The Church intended to form girls to a single, well-defined mold, but differences in their responses confirm the impossibility of uniformity. Because women have reason and are heterogeneous, they have the possibility of writing autobiography, and these writers have accepted or, in some cases, attempted to accept, the challenge the genre sets.

chapter two

Unexpected Frustration and Grief

*A*s soon as I completed the exploration of writers who portrayed their Catholic girlhoods as positive, I began to find autobiographers who were candid about the negative side of their relationships with Catholic parents, nuns, and clerics. Some twentieth-century Catholic women have been able to express negative judgments openly, and consequently have not had to side-step remembered exchanges with Catholic authority figures as they traverse the past. Beauvoir, Schoffen, Benoist, Delarue-Mardrus, Noël, Jouhandeau, Chacel, McCarthy, Mullen, Pillay, Fontenot, Asquerino, Janés, Wong, Rose, Conway, Brave Bird, and Menchú all assume that some unpleasantness is necessary to find truth or that criticism of harmful practices is a social duty.

Beauvoir goes over Catholic girlhood more thoroughly than any other author discussed here, in her *Mémoires d'une jeune fille rangée* (1958). A thorough person by nature, she attended a school run by the Madams of the Sacred Heart and completed the course of study. She came out of it with a disciplined mind, and she knew that sector of the Catholic world well. Thus it is not surprising that her account of Catholic femininity training is logically complete, giving due consideration to all its important aspects. Though she writes with wit and insight, love and sometimes lyricism, Beauvoir was not aiming at a pleasant surface as the women referred to in chapter 1 were. In *The Second Sex* Beauvoir complains of women who write prettily; she feels that women cannot attain equality with men by doing inferior, "feminine" work, and she praises Colette for having avoided this.[1] Like the Spanish writer León, Beauvoir seems deliberately honest about the Church, a choice I see as a rejection of Catholic femininity training.

In general, the writers of this more honest and larger group sometimes felt that demands were being put on them to behave in bizarre and irrational ways because they were girls, as when Beauvoir's reading was more curtailed than that of the cousin she calls Jacques, and when Benoist and her female cousin were not allowed to swim unless the boys in the family were there to protect them.[2] The issue of why the girls felt these demands were irrational will be discussed in chapter 4. For now it is enough to consider what their candor reveals about the Catholic feminization program. Their sorrow and anger cluster around just a few issues: abuses of authority, opposition to their intellectual development and their occupational hopes, classifications of their sexual desires as unconnected to love, distress about the situations of their mothers and diminutions of the dignity of women as such. As the autobiographers recall their exasperation and anguish over these difficulties, they locate themselves in memory in the context of unwelcome feminization, that is, of assaults on their humanity.

Although their education stressed the children's side of the relationship with authority figures—that is, obedience—the girls were offended when authority was used in a way they felt was unjust. Perhaps they thought justice is a duty of adult Catholics; it does occupy a place among the virtues listed in Scripture, the catechism, and examinations of conscience. Three styles of authority are characterized by Agnes Repplier, one good, two less than good. She praises a nun she calls Mme. Rayburn for her respect for Agnes's innocence and privacy.[3] But Repplier freely criticizes Mme. Dane for imposing uniformity and exalting the trivial.

I will not be giving many discrete examples of this demand for uniformity, which tends to permeate other demands made of Catholic girls. It appears in the first panel of Varo's triptych—"Toward the Tower" (1961)—which shocks graphically by the identical faces, heights, dresses, and vehicles for all seven convent students.[4] All their dresses are full-length, gray with long, wide, monastic sleeves and high white collars. All their faces are pale and wan with staring eyes and expressionless mouths, all their temples are covered by thick wings of blonde hair, all their heads have been forced a little forward. Thus she recalls "the anonymity of being one among an indistinguishable many." Bernhardt also identified the erasure of individuality as the aspect of convent life most to be rejected.[5]

The pressure for uniformity is explicitly mentioned in *Memoria de la melancolía* (1970) by María Teresa León (1904–1988) and *Lakota Woman* (1990) by Mary Brave Bird (1953–). Brave Bird, a Native American artist who had attended a nuns' school in South Dakota, complains, "I did not take kindly to the discipline and to marching by the clock, left-right, left-right." León, a surrealist writer who had attended a nuns' school in Madrid, complains that the "reticent nuns . . . [would] give the signal to rise or sit all in unison, with two little pieces of wood stuck together."[6]

León's anger at these details may seem incongruous to readers who have never lived under the wooden clapper or the bell or under rules of not crossing the legs or laughing aloud. The cause of her anger seems to be the steady compression of one's individuality hour by hour. If a girl cared to survive as a personality, she would begin to fight back, as Brave Bird did, or to evade uniform schedules, uniform dress, uniform behavior, as Repplier did. In 1869, at about the age of ten, Repplier found herself expelled by the Madams for being a leader in mischief, though she was actually a follower; her integrity in negotiating with the other girls was apparently not known to the nuns.[7] One of the intentions of her book seems to be to tell the other alumnae of her convent school exactly how wicked she had been.

In addition to the spiritual Mme. Rayburn and the mechanistic Mme. Dane, Repplier introduces a Mme. Bouron (French for "the torturer") to characterize a third style of authority, one that operates by insult. This nun one day summoned Agnes and her friends for circulating within their group a poem about the young seminarian who had been serving Mass. Mme. Bouron implied that they might try to contact the young man outside Mass, that the poem had an impure quality, that he would have to be sent away because of their crush on him. These insinuations—all false—disturbed the girls; making matters worse, the nun admitted that "she had never entertained a good opinion either of our [ethical] dispositions or of our intelligence."[8]

Repplier comments that the girls believed that they must have been guilty of something; their uneasiness came from not knowing exactly what it was.[9] Since they had not actually committed any sin, their gloom after the scolding must have come partly from Mme. Bouron's saying that they had harmed the young man and partly from the idea that it might be possible to sin accidentally. Disorientation may therefore result from incorrect accusations of sin. Here I think also of Marie Noël (the pseudonym of French poet Marie Mélanie Rouget [1883–1967]), whom Pope John XXIII praised in these terms: "She had the purity of heart, purity of mind and purity of style of a medieval artist."[10] In her autobiography, *Petit-Jour: Souvenirs d'enfance* (1951), Noël objects as strenuously as she is able to the way her parents prepared her for her first confession.[11] When Marie tried one day to deceive her parents about the location of a mouthful of boiled beef she hadn't eaten, they put a red spot on her nose while she was asleep. She was told it was a result of her dishonesty and made to wear it all day. Her father also attached a kind of verbal red spot to her by calling her "the embroiderer" and "the tale-teller."[12] The association of sin with her face and identity caused a hurt that seems to have burdened her all her life.[13] Moreover, the storytelling for which Noël was punished was an imitation of the women in her home: her grandmother, her mother, and the cook.[14] To be told that their speech was dishonest rather than imaginative attacked her identification with them; that is, she was assaulted, not only in her behavior and person, but in her relationship with older women.

Sheelagh Conway (1952–   ), born and reared in Ireland and now a Canadian citizen, reports a similar experience in her autobiography, *A Woman and Catholicism: My Break with the Roman Catholic Church* (1987). She was old enough to attend catechism class, and one day she knew she would be punished for not having learned her lesson by heart. When the time came to recite, panic caused her to invent "bits that I knew sounded ridiculous the moment I said them." In her desperation she insisted to Miss FitzPatrick she had learned the catechism. To that, Miss FitzPatrick answered, "Now, my lady, do you know that when people lie the Devil puts a big black spot right in the middle of their tongues?" Sheelagh believed this dramatic notion, and so would not open her mouth even though she was whipped across the fingers with a ruler till she cried and sobbed.[15]

Perhaps the idea of these colored spots came from the Latin for spot or moral spot, *macula*. The words *immaculate* and *spotless* are often applied to Christ and to a child's soul, in preparing children for first communion. The anomaly is that Miss FitzPatrick did not try to make the words *spirit*, or *past*, *present*, and *future* graphic for the children. Very probably she drove home this particular word because sinfulness had been stressed in her own religious education.

Mary Brave Bird had to board at the Catholic mission school at St. Francis, South Dakota, where the boys were taught by Jesuits and the girls by

Madams of the Sacred Heart from Bavaria. The school was built about 1900 and had been "a curse for our family for generations." Here too the exaggeration of sinfulness was common. If several girls huddled in bed together for comfort, as they did at home, the dormitory nun would come in and say, " 'What are the two of you doing in bed together? I smell evil in this room. You girls are evil incarnate. You are sinning. You are going to hell and burn forever. You can act that way in the devil's frying pan.' She would get them out of bed in the middle of the night, making them kneel and pray until morning."[16] Brave Bird points out that the girls hadn't the faintest idea what the nun was talking about; the nuns probably did not realize that the girls were still in the latent stage sexually. As with Repplier's reprimanded children, these girls ended in gloom, partly because of hurt and partly because they did not understand what wrong they had committed.

Brave Bird's religion teacher once reproached her publicly (in an all-girl class) for holding hands with a boy. "Sister Bernard singled me out for some remarks, pointing me out as a bad example, an example that should be shown. She said that I was too free with my body. That I was holding hands which meant that I was not a good example to follow. She also said that I wore unchaste dresses, skirts which were too short, too suggestive, shorter than regulations permitted, and for that I would be punished. She dressed me down before the whole class, carrying on and on about my unchastity."[17] This language distorted Brave Bird's character, for these minor offenses were not, of course, offenses against chastity. The nuns simply did not know enough about sex to know what was and was not chaste.

Other women who attended convent schools report that bed-sharing, signs of affection, cherished friendships were attacked there, sometimes because the nuns feared sexual activity, sometimes because the girls had teamed up against them.[18] Even more basically, horizontal bonding probably disturbed the devotion of the nuns to hierarchy as such. The latter was apparently the reason the Madams who taught Simone de Beauvoir decided not to allow her to sit with her best friend, Zaza Mabille. Mabille's girlhood story parallels Beauvoir's except that Mabille failed repeatedly in her efforts to broaden her life and establish her personal autonomy. Mabille's desires—whether to attend the Sorbonne, choose her own husband or even her own friends, plan her schedule on a summer day, read, practice the piano seriously, or play tennis—all were blocked by her parents, and the comprehensive quality of her frustration eventually resulted in depression, illness, and death. When Simone was assisting at lectures at the Sorbonne, the Mabilles discouraged the friendship, but while the girls were still studying with the Madams, it was the nuns who opposed it.

Beauvoir mentions that tears stood in her eyes when she heard the nuns inform her mother of this punishment, giving as their reason that Mabille was not a good influence on her. Beauvoir felt the loss more than the insult, it seems, for she never minded being "influenced" by a worthy person. In addition, and perhaps out of a desire to be fair, she includes in her anger and sadness a vague realization that her increasing liberty of decision was bringing her childhood relationship with adults to an end.[19] The only relationship she was to be allowed with the nuns was unquestioning obedience.

A more vague diapproval from the Madams assisted Mary McCarthy's decision not to stay with them for high school, as she explains in *Memories of a Catholic Girlhood* (1957). McCarthy (1912–1989), an American novelist and drama critic, employs comic techiques to good effect in this autobiographical work. The Madams at Forest Ridge Convent in Seattle rewarded good conduct with wide moiré ribbons that the girls wore bandolier-style. For eighth graders these were pink, and McCarthy wanted very much to wear one, but she never did. "I was not bad; I did not consciously break the rules; and yet I could never, not even for a week, get a pink ribbon, and this was something I could not understand, because I was trying as hard as I could. . . . The nuns, evidently, saw something about me that was invisible to me."[20] Although she did not understand at the time, elsewhere in *Memories* McCarthy gives the probable cause. She says she had made critical, even cruel, remarks about her rival for a part in the seventh-grade play. The nuns no doubt thought this was envious. Ironically, the reason Mary could not understand their disapproval of her sniping might have been a belief that truthfulness or a competitive spirit justified her.[21] Either she was not able to understand her fault or the nuns were unable to clarify it. She describes the subtle discounting that followed. "Just as I felt I was beginning to belong to the convent, it turned me into an outsider, since I was the only pupil who was not in the know. I liked the convent, but it did not like me. . . . By this, I do not mean that I was actively unpopular, either with the pupils or with the nuns. . . . It was just that I did not fit into the convent pattern."[22] Under disapproval of a trait that was never clearly identified for her and a demand for a virtue perhaps too advanced for her level of moral development, McCarthy felt uneasy, hopeless, and shut out.

In a group of adults working with younger people, disapproval sometimes leads to unwarranted damage to a child's reputation. Abbé Martin had been Beauvoir's confessor for seven years when, one day before he began the ritual, he said to her, " 'It has come to my ears that my little Simone has changed . . . that she is disobedient, noisy, that she answers back when she is reprimanded. . . . From now on you must be on your guard against these things.' "[23] She quickly inferred that the nuns had told him about her behavior toward them. His intervention was upsetting to Beauvoir, in part because in the confessional the priest does not normally initiate accusations; the patient accuses herself and classifies her wrongdoing according to a checklist of faults. Beauvoir notes that she would have classified the actions Abbé Martin reproached her for as "inconsequential chatter" (my translation), not sinful; he labeled them as morally wrong, offenses against the fourth commandment. The difference dismayed her.

She was taken aback, too, by his having accepted a detraction, which is a sin against the eighth commandment. Finally, he used a religious rite, the sacrament of penance, in an inappropriate way, to serve a school, a merely human institution. She must have realized this was a sacrilege and had cost her one of the protections Catholics have counted on against errors and tyrannies. She had trusted his knowledge of ethics enough to choose him as her confessor. Beauvoir now felt that a person she had taken for a representative of God was revealed as an impostor. She attempted to limit her horrified reaction to the priest, as she had been taught to do, but the shock sent ripples in the direction of God; if such a man represents God's character, then God cannot be very good. Soon she reexamined the examination of conscience; she concluded that if disobedience, impure thoughts, and earthly pleasures are sins, then sin and God are to be rejected as mirages.[24] In other words, if naturally good actions are condemned as sinful by the Church, the Church is presenting falsehood as revelation, and the whole Catholic system must be a sham. In Beauvoir's life, then, insult and disapproval were upsetting, but instead of allowing them to poison her self-esteem, she traced them to their origin, analyzed their characteristics, and removed herself from their reach.

Nearly one in five of the writers examined here—Brave Bird, Fontenot, Jouhandeau, Pillay, McCarthy, and Mullen—complain of physical abuse at home or at school. In addition to bodily suffering, they recall distress at the lack of justice, love, and charity. Some of them also object that violent punishment is associated with training animals, not humans. The usual view expressed in catechism classes at the time, for example, when children inquired whether their pets would go to heaven, was that animals had bodies but did not have souls. In theology class this distinction between animals and humans was refined to an extent; animals were thought to have animal souls but not to have rational souls. To be treated as an animal was therefore a deeply felt dishonor.

Elise Jouhandeau (1888–1971) received both blows and insults from her mother. Elise was only an unimportant girl then, not yet the dancer Caryatis, well-known between the wars, who danced in Eric Satie's ballet *Parade* (1917), not yet the famous target of the denunciatory novels of her husband, Marcel. But her vitality and natural happiness were so great that her mother tried to keep her from laughing and to quench her joy, saying that this exuberance was too much like her father or that it would lead her into sin.[25] Because Elise had been conceived before the wedding, it may be that her mother feared her daughter had inherited her own inclinations as well. Jouhandeau recounts the push and pull of their relationship in volume 1 of *Joies et douleurs d'une belle excentrique,* entitled *Enfance et adolescence d'Elise* (1952).

When her mother beat Elise, the child was covered with welts, but never had broken bones or damaged organs. The offenses that merited such punishment included looking out the window, breaking a candelabra, coming home late from work, and going dancing. Elise was whipped just as ferociously for imagined offenses as for real ones.[26] Her mother continually emphasized the daughter's obigations to her and warned Elise not to sin against chastity or associate with even the most benevolent men. Perhaps Jouhandeau had difficulty in deciding which aspect of her mother's attitude she should respond to. Would she be able to please her mother best by chastity, obedience, avoidance of men, or apathy?

The most stylish method of correction mentioned in this set of books is shock treatments. In 1918, when Mary McCarthy was six, her parents died in the flu epidemic. Her Catholic grandparents, also McCarthys, undertook to reduce the amount of money their son and his family had been costing them by imposing an austere lifestyle on Mary and her three younger brothers. Mary was treated as for a mental problem for remembering the cultured life they had led with their parents. At the doctor's office, she says, "every Saturday I screamed and begged on a table while electric shocks were sent through me, for what purpose I cannot conjecture." When people asked if Mary remembered or ever mentioned her parents, Grandmother McCarthy would say, " 'She doesn't feel it at all' . . . contentedly, without censure, as if I had been a spayed cat that, in her superior foresight, she had had 'attended to.' " Soon the senior McCarthys farmed out their grandchildren to members of their clan who would mock Mary for using "big words" or use a razor strop and hairbrush on her for winning an essay contest at school; thus she experienced both the most old-fashioned and the most modern methods of correction.[27]

Barbara Mullen, an Irish actress born in 1914, only two years later than McCarthy, was not given shock treatments to persuade her to abandon her loyalty to her absent father. Whereas the senior McCarthys had a fortune made from grain, Barbara's mother ran a speakeasy in Boston for a time and used the less expensive form: beating. Mullen's tale, *Life Is My Adventure* (1937), is better written than Jouhandeau's and differs from it also in focusing less on Catholic motherhood than on the quandaries of Catholic daughterhood. Barbara's father had returned to Ireland, and she wanted to write him letters, but her mother forbade Barbara to write to him or to speak of him unless it was to say how much she disliked him. Whenever the little girl voiced her wishes to contact her father, her mother beat her; Mullen objected to this treatment because it was applied in the spirit of training an animal.[28]

Gradually Mullen lost respect for herself on account of her excessive obedience to her mother. "Slowly I began to understand that I had been wrong to let my mother crush my beliefs and mould my character as she saw fit." Here Mullen must be referring to her work in the speakeasy, where she served customers or stood at the door watching for policemen; the Sisters at parochial school warned Barbara she would be damned for such actions.[29]

When Barbara wanted to correct what she thought was her deteriorating character, she wrote to her father again. He replied secretly, sending her a beautiful dancing costume. However, a family friend reported the exchange to the mother, who worked on Barbara for a week to write him "saying that I no longer wanted to hear from him, as I had no use for him and preferred my mother." Mullen adds, "My mother was trying by threats to make me obey her, to think as she wanted me to think, and that way only, to live as she decreed, and say only what she wanted me to say."[30]

Mullen's battle to prefer her father to her mother because of his ethical superiority resurfaced when she was eighteen and she and her mother were living in New York. That year her father and brother sent her the fare to come to Ireland, and Barbara told her mother she wanted to go. By her persistence and ingenuity in debate, Mrs. Brady got the fare away from Barbara, which according to my understanding of Catholic ethics, would make them both thieves and Barbara guilty of sinful obedience. This incident brought Barbara's frustration to unbearable intensity, because it made her moral weakness seem inescapable.

When Mrs. Brady went so far as to say that she would rather see Barbara

die than see her join her father in Ireland,[31] Barbara reacted as if she had been
sentenced to death by one who had the authority to do so; that is, she stopped
eating. Possibly the reason she took her mother's phrasing literally was that the
lifestyle Mrs. Brady had imposed on Barbara was already killing her socially
and psychologically. The mother had taught Barbara not to chat about men,
with the result that she could not make friends with the other elevator girls at
the office building where she worked. Barbara's mother had also made her
break her engagement with Jimmy Hines, perhaps because he had been the
one to forward the costume from Barbara's father. Whatever the motive, the
mother isolated Barbara from everyone but herself and Barbara's cousin John,
who, I assume, was on the mother's side of the family. When John married
and left town, Barbara had no social contacts left.[32]

Mrs. Brady interfered with all Barbara's natural inclinations. Mullen at
one time overheard her mother explain the beatings: "She's too much like the
Mullens, with her books, and reading, and queer notions. But I'll knock it out
of her."[33] Mrs. Brady must have thought books would either alienate Barbara
from her mother or would make her unwomanly. Like Mme. Toulé, Mrs.
Brady would not have wanted Barbara to have any genes from her father, if
she could have prevented it.

Other autobiographers were subjected to physical force. In Brave Bird's
experience, St. Francis School was not friendly to Indian children. The nuns
favored the lighter-skinned girls ("breeds," Brave Bird calls them) by letting
them wait on the faculty and giving them ham or eggs and bacon in the
morning while the "skins" (also Brave Bird's term) sorted dirty laundry,
scrubbed floors, washed dishes, and ate the usual cornmeal mush, oatmeal, rice
and raisins, or cornflakes. Inevitably this disparity fostered antagonism between
the two groups.[34]

Penalties were too harsh for children and were inappropriate to actions
that in Lakota culture would have been considered good actions, and they were
not important in any view. If the girls stopped to chat or rest while cleaning
the dining hall, the nun would slap their faces with a dish towel. "When I was
a small girl at the St. Francis Boarding School, the Catholic sisters would take
a buggy whip to us for what they called 'disobedience.' "[35] Mary soon learned
what was unacceptable behavior. "All I got out of school was being taught how
to pray. I learned quickly that I would be beaten if I failed in my devotions or,
God forbid, prayed the wrong way, especially prayed in Indian to Wakan
Tanka, the Indian Creator."[36] When she was thirteen, Mary got the "swats"
(the girls' name for twenty-five hits with a board wrapped in Scotch tape) for

refusing to go to Mass when she was not feeling well. Other actions for which the nuns used this punishment included not doing homework or being late to school. She and Charlene Left Hand Bull, a full-blood friend of hers, got the swats once for staying on the boys' volleyball court three minutes longer than the girls' team was allotted. The frequent swats "had such a bad effect upon me that I hated and mistrusted every white person on sight, because I met only one kind."[37]

In addition to abusive punishment and discrimination, Brave Bird found other injustices in the school. She reports that the nuns ate better and had better heated rooms than the girls did. Some sexual harassment took place too, for one of the priests made a pass at Charlene in the school's darkroom.[38]

Civilized people need a nonviolent means of controlling children, and they need some way of ascertaining what the children's misbehavior is and how important it is. Into these more peaceful methods of control, abuse can also creep, or, for that matter, march along quite openly. When Beauvoir ran out of Catholic educational institutions that admitted women and had to attend a secular university, her parents did not like what she learned there. Her father specialized in verbal harassment, apparently displeased that Simone did not treat her education as frivolously as he had his. Her mother attempted to protect Simone from harm to faith. Mme. de Beauvoir's method of protection could be called close surveillance, a method she might have derived from the convent school she had attended.[39]

Close surveillance is also portrayed in Varo's triptych in the first two panels. In the first, "Toward the Tower," the girls are led from a residence hall toward the tower by a man who looks like a Jewish peddler, perhaps a symbol of the Old Dispensation, and by a nun in a gray hat with a wide, flat brim like a cleric's, no doubt a representative of the New Dispensation as bestowed on girls in convent school. The girls are right behind the nun, and none of them are thinking of asking if they may go to the tower unchaperoned—no light appears in any of their eyes. In the second panel, "Embroidering Earth's Mantle," the girls are sewing at stations around the wall of a room at the top of the tower, with their backs to each other.[40] A lector or reader with large glasses stands in the middle of the floor, eyes on the book but also on the stairway down. This figure serves as the supervisor; the flutist playing in the niche at the rear merely sets the rhythm.

Close surveillance distressed the girls greatly, not because they wanted to hide evildoing, but because it discourages innocent activities. However worthy one's enterprises are, to be watched constantly can lead a girl eventually to abandon spontaneous actions, and with them, authentic development. Beauvoir observes that to be always with one's parents distorts perception. "Whenever I went out with my parents or the Mabilles, an impenetrable glass would be interposed between me and the world."[41] The cause was that these Catholic parents did not want their daughters to notice the world.

Year after year, Françoise de Beauvoir, Simone's mother, insisted on approving any book her daughters read. At best she let them select books in a bookstore where only conservative Catholic books were sold. She read their mail before they did until they were seventeen and nineteen years of age, and then they had to ask her to stop doing it. When Simone began to read and study suspect books in a room her mother did not often go into, her mother stopped heating that room. Instead, she selected a room she often passed through and set up a card table there for Simone's studies. She then continually interrupted her daughter, asking, "What's that you're doing? What's that book you're reading?" or even "What are you thinking about?" Then she would protest, "Of course, I'm only your mother, you won't tell me anything," an appeal related to the loss of her role as a Catholic Mother, the only social role she could ever expect to play.[42]

Mary McCarthy finds a different motive for surveillance. The guilty person was her Great-Aunt Margaret, who had been hired by the senior McCarthys to raise Mary and her three brothers.

> The basis, I think, of my aunt's program for us was in truth totalitarian: she was idealistically bent on destroying our privacy. She imagined herself as enlightened in comparison with our parents, and a super-ideal of health, cleanliness, and discipline softened in her own eyes the measures she applied to attain it. . . . To the best of her ability, she saw to it that nothing was hidden from her. . . . Our letters to Seattle [that is, to their maternal grandparents, who were not Catholic] were written under her eye. . . . And if we were forbidden companions, candy, most toys, pocket money, sports, reading, entertainment, the aim was not to make us suffer but to achieve efficiency. It was simpler to interdict other children than to inspect all the children with whom we might want to play. From the standpoint of efficiency, our lives, in order to be open, had to be empty; the books we might perhaps read, the toys we might play with figured in my aunt's mind, no doubt, as what the housewife calls "dust catchers"— around these distractions, dirt might accumulate. The inmost folds of consciousness, like the belly button, were regarded by her as unsanitary. Thus, in her spiritual outlook, my aunt was an early functionalist.[43]

Although McCarthy wittily compares her great-aunt's system to totalitarian efficiency and to functional design, the list of forbidden items seems particularly Catholic. It is reminiscent of convent life before Vatican II, when wide reading or even much reading was one of the principal casualties of Catholic supervision. Great-Aunt Margaret's system of surveillance seems particularly Catholic, too, in imposing asceticism on others. The basic frustration both McCarthy and Beauvoir felt in face of enforced minimalism has to do with its prevention of a fully vigorous life.

Of possible abuses of authority toward girls, then, these Catholic women report five major types: homogenizing regulations about morally neutral or trivial matters, insult and imputations of sinfulness, separating friends and turning children against one another, inhuman violence, and close surveillance, together with some dishonesty about the Church's requirements. Thus the frustration of the girls did not come from the usual discomfort between the powerless and the powerful; as girls, if the autobiographers remember correctly, they were upset by unnecessary excesses and distortions, and more upset by attacks on their individuality, friendliness, and other positive human characteristics. Moreover, they were distressed because authority that should have been exercised for their benefit was being used to teach conventionality and submissiveness, low self-esteem and false guilt, an exclusive focus on adult females, and a general absence of initiative, together with an avoidance of learning, of aggressive speech, of interest in potential sexual partners, and of friendship. In other words, power was employed to maintain the institution and its authority over women and to prevent the establishment of new selves.

In addition to mastering lessons in subordination and selflessness, Catholic girls were educated more formally, at least in the catechism, and sometimes attended Catholic or, less often, secular schools. About half of them think they were not well educated, and some of the others were not educated any better but did not discuss the matter. The girls detected the superiority of the schools boys and non-Catholic girls attended through talking with boys in their families, through meeting a rare educated woman, or through temporary attendance at public schools. They discovered that Catholic authority was being used to discourage them from learning much, as shown in episodes reported by Mullen, Schoffen, and others.

Many of the girls were baffled and bothered by this kind of deprivation. They did not see the interference as good, possibly because Catholic adults had so energetically insisted that they learn to read and memorize the catechism or even that they excel in the early grades. Once cognitive habits and desires had been established and the girls wanted to continue, they could not understand why that insistence reversed itself. They were too young to present arguments that wanting to learn is natural or that the Creator gave them their minds for a purpose or that Christ would not accept their burying their talents, but they must have absorbed these beliefs from their religious, civil, or familial milieu. Otherwise, why would they have been so taken aback when adults prevented them from following their intellectual bent? Schoffen, Benoist, Delarue-Mardrus, León, and Beauvoir say that they were refused access to good schools or to college; Mullen, to books; Repplier, Beauvoir, and McCarthy, to books that were too modern or were written by non-Catholics. León was punished for reading titles listed in the Vatican's Index of Forbidden Books. In the United States, the Index and the list of censored films were usually endorsed in pulpit and classroom, and Repplier, for one, reports that her school library and her family provided girls with silly, moralizing, boring books.[44]

Several women complained about inept catechetical instruction, more than one would expect had the group been hostile to the Church. Conway's account of her catechism class is a protest against poor teaching, that is, having children memorize abstract principles without explaining the terms. When she had to memorize the answer, "God is our Father in heaven who knows all things, past, present, and to come, even our most secret thoughts and actions," she had trouble because, "As a small child I had no idea what past, present, and to come meant. Heaven stumped me, too, as did secret thoughts and actions." Then, for "God is a spirit," Conway comments: "None of us knew what a spirit was. If Miss FitzPatrick had said that the banshee was a spirit, I would have understood right away. But she never explained the words, and they seemed like a foreign language to a small child. Not even the Gaelic stumped me as much as the catechism."[45]

Mary Hunt Benoist (1865–?), a St. Louis socialite, wrote a pamphlet auto-biography, calling it *Memories* (1930). Addressed to her children and grandchildren, the text mentions a number of past customs Mrs. Benoist knew the children would enjoy hearing about. In spite of her purpose of entertainment, her childhood frustration about some of these practices comes through strongly. She complains that, although their father heard the girls' catechism before their first communion, he explained nothing. Her assessment of the result was, "We were letter perfect, but never were two children more poorly prepared." Similarly, she relates that the girls were provided with rather poor governesses while the boys in the family were sent to the best schools and universities at home and abroad. "Our last governess came to us when I was seventeen and remained a year. Then our education was considered complete and school days were over."[46] The girls were taught to dance, play the piano, and ride; they were not taught to improve their natural abilities to read, write, speak, and persuade.

Mellish's description of her crisis in faith, discussed in chapter 1, although she attempts to make it colorful and entertaining, includes objections to the intellectual inadequacy and inconsistencies of Catholic religious instruction. At the time Catholic education made only feeble efforts to explain, for example, the connection between faith and science, and would tell a person at one time to respect her mother as an example of self-sacrifice but at another to expect her to spend long years in Purgatory.

In childhood, Rosa Chacel was at first taught religion and other subjects by her mother, but eventually her parents put her in school to obtain more help with her French. Her father, however, subverted the plan by choosing a Carmelite school where the other children were behind Rosa in knowledge, including that of religion. Chacel expresses unchanged the disgust she felt when one of her Carmelite teachers told her she was wrong to do physical exercises at home because the Blessed Virgin Mary had not done exercises. As a child Rosa felt the nun's remark was sacrilegious and trivial, and she disapproved of religion at that school because it was all pink and blue,[47] a reference, perhaps, to gender training.

María Teresa León, a Spanish patriot loyal to the Republic and a surrealist, called her autobiography *Memoria de la melancolía* (1970) because it is a lament over the sorrows and harmful effects of the exile and of her childhood in Spain. Though as an adult she actively supported the legitimate government of Spain against Franco's rebellion, her parents were not unlike him in some matters. Her father had been a colonel and her mother had been educated by ultra-Catholic French nuns. When her parents decided to send her to Sacred Heart Academy to be with other upper-class girls, she immediately felt discouraged. She had been comparing her mother, who had attended Sacred Heart, to her mother's sister, María Goyri de Menendez Pidal (1873–1954), the first woman in Spain to graduate from a university. Because her aunt could answer her questions and her mother could not, María Teresa expected that attending Sacred Heart would make her as ignorant as her mother.[48]

Even as a child María Teresa was alert to the characteristics of the school her cousin Jimena attended: the students could read any books they liked, no one taught the catechism, and the teachers did not lower their voices to speak of art or ignore the numerous nudes in the museums as the nuns did. Among her cousin's family and friends, when someone mentioned don Francisco Giner de los Ríos, the founder of secular schools, people listened with respect. When Giner de los Ríos died, the poet Antonio Machado wrote a poem expressing the common pain, but when she told the nuns at her school, they said he had not been buried in sacred ground.[49] This reaction implied to María Teresa that the nuns put partisanship ahead of knowledge.

The nuns taught her that secular study, unless done under ecclesiastical direction, was disloyal to the Church and dangerous to faith. This teaching was reflected in several months of paralysis that followed her playing a part in a nativity play at her cousin's school. She mentions that the nuns would probably think that the illness was a punishment for having participated in "blasphemous recreations that offend God," though in fact no one had blasphemed, and she had played an angel announcing Christ's birth to the shepherds.[50] Surely any element of punishment here was self-punishment in the thought of how the nuns would feel about her participation. Alternatively, the paralysis could be considered a protection, still self-inflicted, against the monstrous sins the nuns thought a child would commit if she entered a world or even a school without nuns and priests.

Eventually the nuns expelled María Teresa for having read Dumas. Most of his novels were on the Index of Forbidden Books, as the nuns knew, but León notes that they had to ask the confessor if reading Dumas was a sin. Pope Leo XIII had in 1897 decreed that reading forbidden books incurred ipso facto excommunication; but the nuns had evidently not given the children a list of forbidden books so they would know what to avoid. María Teresa's teacher did not blame the child alone, but rather her mother for scanty vigilance, her uncle for having allowed her to read his books, and her aunt for having studied at the university. María Teresa was infuriated and deeply wounded by these public insults to her family.[51]

Thus, some of the autobiographers saw a connection between educational deprivation and a kind of enclosure within Catholicism that prevented a girl from learning about other philosophies, philosophies favoring full human development in women. This evaluation was made not only by the literary León writing in Italy but also by the American nurse Elizabeth Schoffen (1861–?), who wrote only one work, a pamphlet autobiography called *The Demands of Rome* (1917).[52] When I first read this title in a bibliography, I thought it was a bogus nun tale, a subgenre of fiction. (Bogus nuns were women who gave talks and wrote books about their supposedly scandalous and miserable lives as nuns, when in reality they had never been nuns. They served in anti-Catholic organizations like the Know-Nothing Party and the American Protective Association.) Schoffen, however, was a real nun. She became a Sister of Providence in Vancouver, Washington, on July 31, 1881, and withdrew in 1912.[53] Thirty-one years did not provide her with episodes like one in the Maria Monk books, in which the pitiful young protagonist is forced by her superiors to dig graves in the rain. (Maria Monk was a bogus nun who wrote tracts such as "Awful Disclosure" [1836] and a series of novels revealing scandals about religious life that had never taken place. These books were well known among rural and small-town evangelical Protestants throughout the nineteenth and early twentieth centuries.) Schoffen's complaints have to do with her inadequate education, which at the time was a realistic complaint. Her narrative has a kind of restraint and everyday quality that make it believable.

Schoffen's father, a public school teacher in Minnesota, had left all decisions about the children to his wife, who, Schoffen feels, was completely under the domination of the parish priest in regard to the education of the children.[54] Her mother expected Elizabeth to act as her apprentice and often kept her home from school to help with the housework. This attitude was perfectly in line with official Catholic beliefs on gender (see chapter 3), but Elizabeth wanted to become a teacher.

In time Mrs. Schoffen insisted that Elizabeth change to the local Catholic school, where her education immediately went into decline, a cause of lifelong distress to her. Schoffen complains that at least one of the Sisters teaching there had not been to college. Schoffen did not exaggerate this problem. Correcting that situation was a project of the Sister Formation Program, which Sister Madaleva Wolff worked on. Schoffen objects to having been made to teach the younger children in the parish school the arithmetic she had learned in the public school, since this activity left her little time for her own studies. She expresses bitterness at the willingness of her mother and her nuns to sacrifice her for other children, which she may not have realized was their way of educating her for Catholic Motherhood. As a girl she was constantly frustrated, and at the age of fifty-six, when her autobiography was published, Schoffen was still upset about her lack of education. She says she entered religious life because a Jesuit promised her she would be educated as a teacher there.[55] In the outcome, she was assigned to hospital work, and in her judgment she never received adequate training for that either.

Simone de Beauvoir also objects to the insularity of Catholic education. Assessing her intellectual deprivation from childhood on, Beauvoir begins with her mother's membership in the Confraternity of Christian Mothers. The meetings of this group led her mother, among other things, to pray with Simone and her little sister daily, and to check Simone's homework from the time she started to school. When Simone was five and a half, the Beauvoirs enrolled her in *le cours Désir,* a Parisian school run by the Madams of the Sacred Heart, considered by the Beauvoirs' social set to be the best teachers available for Catholic girls.[56]

At first she was happy with the Madams, she says, because she was given such high marks, but once she learned that the world contained viewpoints other than the Catholic and royalist, she referred to the nuns as "derisory bigots" (my translation). Simone learned from her cousin Jacques that the Jesuits taught the boys at St. Stanislaus "knowledge . . . with all its pristine glory intact," whereas her teachers gave her only "an expurgated, insipid, faded version." As a girl, she did not want the nuns to delete parts of and dehydrate what they taught the girls. Like Schoffen, but better trained in antithesis, Beauvoir complains that the nuns "were more rich in virtues than in diplomas" (my translation). Beauvoir's father let her know that he thought it a serious defect for the nuns to end their discussion of French literature before Voltaire.[57] Clearly, any complete understanding of modern society, even of the postmodern rebellion against the Enlightenment, would be difficult without knowing Voltaire.

In adolescence, Simone and her friends thought the Madams were quite stupid "to attach importance to trifles, to persist in observing conventions and customs, to prefer commonplace and prejudices to facts," and especially to believe that the girls "swallowed all the righteous fibs that were dished out." She and her circle smiled and joked about the silliness of the nuns, but feared it as dangerous to their hope of experiencing true desires and pleasures. In this way Beauvoir linked the walled-in intellectual world of the Madams to their opposition to personal authenticity. Examples of customs the nuns imposed on them and to which the girls objected included kneeling to their mothers to beg forgiveness on the eve of their first communion, wearing ugly dresses (so as not to attract male attention), and avoiding close friendships.[58]

These practices seem nunnish, for they resemble a certain style of monastic life and were not oriented to the lives the girls could expect as laywomen. What Beauvoir dreaded was self-abnegation, which was diligently taught by the Madams, and which she recognized would damage her future. Beauvoir maintained an angry tone longer during her discussion of the Madams than in any other passage in the *Mémoires;* the anger drops away only when she begins to discuss her more emancipated years.

She methodically demonstrates that the Madams' care to narrow the learning of the girls was picked up and carried on for several years by her parents. When her father told Simone that she and her sister must prepare to support themselves by taking college degrees, she obeyed, choosing in consultation with him to become a teacher. Because he asked her to attend the university and had agreed that teaching would be practical, she expected her parents to provide emotional support and to discuss her studies with her; instead, she found that they could not bear observing her life as a university student.[59]

Their agitation was more painful for her because for years they had abundantly rewarded her for excelling in school. She experienced their new opposition to her studying as a sudden change toward herself. In fact, the change took place at two moments; the first had been at her menarche, when her father discovered that however literary, she was neither male nor beautiful.[60] In the second, her parents recognized that she considered her university education to be more than an ornament to her ladylike charms. At the first of these moments she suffered her father's sarcasm and contempt. From the second on, she had to endure and evade deliberate interference from both her parents. She attributes their opposition to the way her attendance at the university exposed their relative poverty. They were disappointed, perhaps ashamed, that they had lost their money and were not able to provide her and her sister with dowries to attract husbands. Because of their sensitivity to social status, her parents wanted Simone to pretend that her learning was only a social grace and that she did not need to study much. They wanted her to resemble pre-debutantes, who were "brilliant ornaments to their mothers' drawing rooms." Official Catholic aversion to the higher education of women precisely paralleled her parents' attitude, and at the least reinforced it. They were unable to admit that, had she obeyed them, she would not have passed her examinations or supported herself. As a result, they brought every force they could bear on her, even calling in their friends to denounce whatever writers and ideas she admired.[61]

Continual harassment by her parents exhausted Beauvoir emotionally. She felt she could have relaxed and recovered had they allowed her to go out with her friends in the evening, but they did not allow that until she had almost finished her studies at the Sorbonne. Though "bursting with health and youthful vigor," she was "confined to home and library." As a result, Beauvoir finally "lost all sense of reality: the streets, the cars, the passers-by were only so many shadows among which my own anonymous presence floated aimlessly."[62] This disconnection from identity and world brought her near the psychological and physical disaster that finally overtook her friend and alter ego, Zaza, whose parents exercised their authority even more extensively and rigorously than the Beauvoirs did. Beauvoir's *Mémoires d'une jeune fille rangée* presents mental health as the most important reason not to hinder girls who want an advanced education.

Perhaps having recently read Beauvoir and wanting to distinguish her own experience of the Madams, McCarthy praises those she studied under as "cool and learned, with their noses in heretical books." She seems to have loved them as "truly intellectual women"; however, she describes Forest Ridge Convent in Seattle as a world held over from early nineteenth-century France, where the society of the Madams of the Sacred Heart was founded.

> The quarrels of the *philosophes* still echoed in the classrooms; the tumbrils had just ceased to creak, and Voltaire grinned in the background. Orthodoxy had been re-established, Louis XVIII ruled, but there was a hint of Orleanism in the air and a whisper of reduced circumstances in the pick-pick of our needles doing fine darning and turning buttonholes. Byron's great star had risen, and, across the sea, America beckoned in the romances of Chateaubriand and Fenimore Cooper and the adventures of the *coureurs de bois*. Protestantism did not trouble us; we had made our peace with the Huguenots. What we feared was skepticism, deism, and the dread spirit of atheism—France's Lucifer.[63]

Thus a persistent anachronism affected the education of McCarthy and her age group in ways that seem unlikely in the 1920s and on the West Coast of the United States. While her objection to this is graceful, she did not want to stay in the Madams' school.

Another woman who learned to do minor mending in a Catholic school was María Asquerino (1927–   ), a successful actress of Spanish stage and screen, best known for her performance in *Surcos*. She notes in her *Memorias* (1987):

> A mania of my mother's was to put me into nuns' schools. It must have been the fashion of the day. In "Paidos," a school on Zurbano street, I was happy. It was a school that enchanted me, where I studied French and did gymnastics. Then nothing would do but my mother pulled me out of there and took me to a new school in Jordan street called "Christ the King." . . .
>
> In the short time I was there, I learned nothing. And I don't say so

because I was a slightly agnostic person—not slightly, totally agnostic. The truth was, they taught nothing more than to sew and pray, to do hemstitches and do them by the handful; as you might expect, these silly things have not helped me in any way in my life. And besides, I do not enjoy it.[64]

Asquerino was irritated by the limited world the Church foresaw for women because she had already participated in a wider world.

Varo made convent sewing lessons the main subject of her autobiographical triptych, the central panel of which is called "Embroidering Earth's Mantle." For her, sewing was not merely mending, but apprentice-level embroidery like that done for vestments. She has made it more, for the cloth pours out the tower windows down to the ocean, where the folds of the fabric become folds of the earth and embroidered pictures expand in height, becoming other towers, all built on Renaissance principles of symmetry and all looking empty and dark, with a few trees and people in appropriate places. These objects result from a description of them being read by the monastic reader in the center of the embroidery room, who thus becomes an overdetermined image of Catholic womanhood training as well as of a pattern-maker for stitchers. Kaplan correctly thinks of this situation—"faithfully recreating nature according to preordained rules"—as representative of a kind of art school.[65] The method of not allowing students to work on the modern period is also symbolic of Catholic education. Varo's objection to the dogmatic and hand-me-down origin of their cultural world is expressed by a picture one of the girls has done without having been asked to do so, a picture of two lovers, which she hides. Like León, Varo must have missed the absence of references to intimate human love in her convent education, and, like León, she objected to the reliance on one book—one world view—together with the imposition of silence and imitative thought on the students, as if their minds had nothing creative to offer.

Linda Marie Pillay (1943–   ) is the only one of the autobiographers in a position to evaluate a reform school, probably one of those run by the Good Shepherd nuns. According to her autobiography, she is a file clerk and housewife whose life-history, *I Must Not Rock* (1977), seems to have grown out of a women's consciousness-raising group.[66] She spent her childhood with her mother, who was a welder, and her Catholic stepfather, who raped Linda Marie repeatedly and frequently beat her, at least once with the buckle end of his belt. Sent to reform school by the California courts, she learned how much worse an education you can get in a Catholic reform school than in a parochial school. She has two basic complaints. First, reform school reduced her to an infantile level, for "The longer I lived in the convent the more dependent I became. And the more dependent, the more I grew to like it." Second, she could expect only a low level of employment. "One morning I woke up to a cap and gown and was told to get out and find a job. There wasn't any such thing for someone like me. I didn't know how to take care of myself; and they told me I had a low I.Q. . . . Potential employers didn't like the clothes on my back and they didn't like anything they'd heard about 'those girls from the convent.' "[67] She eventually realized she would never be able to get any job but that of a file clerk.[68] The girls in the reform school had been difficult to teach; but without doubt, they needed a better education than they received. Pillay takes a realistic attitude, but her rocking, which the nuns at reform school tried to prevent, was an expression of deep grief, not only for the loss of her family, but also, as she makes clear by the intensity of her academic satire, for the loss of the ordinary parochial school she had been attending.

When all these narrative laments or outcries about education and reading are taken together, flaws in the intellectual side of a Catholic girl's life sort into five types: the teachers were not well educated, the method of teaching was sometimes ineffective or harmful, the information was so limited to the Catholic view of things as to give a distorted picture of the world, personal talents and inclinations were disregarded in favor of preconceived models of what the good Catholic girl should know, and, finally, the content and skills taught would force the girls lower on the socioeconomic ladder than their parents were. Remarkably, these objections had already taken shape in the minds of the autobiographers when they were girls.

Similarly, they were distressed by refusals to provide helpful information about the subject of sex, and above all by the suppression of their natural affections through adult fear that affection could become sexual. In healthy circumstances, sexual expression enhances not only love but also general creativity and self-esteem.[69] Perhaps some people have a faint awareness of this great secret, for the Catholic women autobiographers report a distress over sexual suppression and distortion that would be quite different if celibacy led to a higher spiritual level. Mary Hunt Benoist found the erasure of sexual awareness and the failure to provide a cultural context for sex a source of grief. When as a child she asked her mother about sex, Mrs. Hunt replied that asking about it was to "talk like a strumpet." Benoist remembers, "I had no idea what the word meant, but I knew it must be something pretty bad to get Mama so excited. I never asked my Mother another question."[70] Thus, Mary generalized from sexual knowledge to all knowledge and gave up on all.

When Mary's first communion day was approaching, Mrs. Hunt had a seamstress make a beautiful dress for her. Unfortunately, on the day that Mary had been told would be the happiest of her life, her mother found that the dress no longer fit, because Mary had "developed." While the seamstress squeezed Mary's ribs, Mrs. Hunt closed the placket with a buttonhook, and told her daughter not to take a deep breath. Her chest hurt her all day "so I was ready to cry." This incident is the only one Benoist fully evoked in her girlhood narrative; all others she merely summarized or referred to. The reason for the importance of the tight dress to her may be that physical suffering was unusual in her life, or that she was hurt because her mother had not noticed such an important bodily change. Perhaps she felt that her mother would rather not have had to notice that Mary was a female as well as a soul. If Mrs. Hunt felt uneasy about female bodies, that may also explain why when Benoist married, she refused to go on a honeymoon.[71]

Lucie Delarue-Mardrus (1880–1945), a poet and writer of romantic novels, in *Mes Mémoires* (1938) reports with satisfaction that as a child she had rejected catechism class as more boring than school. She made no effort to pay attention in order to learn what was wanted of the children. However, she must have remembered something from the lessons, for at fifteen she thought her numerous fantasies about the wedding night were "impure thoughts," though she had no idea intercourse would take place. She says, "to think of these things was not good. But the more I repeated that to myself, the more I thought of them."[72]

The impossibility of ridding oneself of these ill-defined "impure thoughts," which were counted as mortal sins before the 1960s (committing a mortal sin means that one hates God and deserves hellfire), is a grievance often voiced by American Catholics as well. Again, the difficulty may be traced to beginning catechisms derived from the Catechism of Trent, which analyzes the sixth commandment, "Thou shalt not commit adultery," into two parts: "the one expressed, which prohibits adultery; the other implied, which inculcates purity of mind and body." *Purity,* a difficult term to pin down, is defined by the Catechism of Trent as not being "defiled [by] unlawful desire." In consequence of this interpretation, the 1863 *Catéchisme du diocèse de Paris* translated the sixth commandment in a verse decalogue as "Luxurieux point ne seras, de corps ni de consentement" (Never be lustful, either in body or will.") The ninth commandment, "Thou shalt not covet thy neighbor's wife," was translated as "L'oeuvre de chair ne desiras, qu'en mariage seulement" (Do not desire the works of the flesh except in marriage).[73] This translation changes the commandment as well as adding to it. *Baltimore Number One* also extends the commandments but does not present the additions as a stated part of the commandments themselves, as the French verse decalogue does. Instead, the extra obligations are added in other questions, such as "What does the sixth [or ninth] commandment forbid?"[74] The difference might have been of slight importance, but French children might have felt the prohibition of all extra-marital sex and sexual thoughts were part of the original decalogue, a heavy weight.

Elise Jouhandeau's education in sexuality was quite unlike that of Delarue-Mardrus. In the Vieux-Prieuré, Elise's teacher worked to awaken her from her erotic daydreams by tying a stick and bell to her belt, presumably so that she would pay attention in class.[75] Back in Paris with her mother, Elise had to listen to an incessant stream of chatter about how erotic her nature was. Her mother talked to Elise continually about the loose behavior she expected from her in the future. When she grew up and had been working full-time for a while, her resistance to her mother's drumming collapsed. She offered herself to a boyfriend, a kind of perverse if desperate submission to her mother's convictions.[76] For Jouhandeau, considerable guilt and depression followed.

When still a child, María Teresa León found that Spanish Catholic males already thought of her as sexual. From her early childhood they felt free to stare at her or make passes at her, causing her to throw up. Later she substituted washing off the spot where a male had touched her in a way that distressed her or where she felt she had been dirtied.[77] As an adult, she attributes her early reaction to her not having understood. (As a Surrealist, she may have meant that they were right about sex and she was not.) When she began school, she thought the nuns at Sacred Heart were too reticent, wrongly silent about relations between men and women. Looking back on it, she felt that only one nun had taught her younger self anything, and that was the one whose drooping head María Teresa thought of as sorrowing over a lost lover.[78] María Teresa was sure, from the nun's posture, that she must have had a child with a bishop. Like Noël and Mellish, León had not yet been taught the difference between statements in a factual context and statements in an imaginative or symbolical one. María Teresa was irritated by the very fact that the nuns taught the catechism,[79] which, with its offensive attitude toward human sexuality, may explain her disgust (see excerpt in chapter 3).

The girls were displeased when Catholic adults referred to sex as evil no matter what the circumstances, or taught that sexual desire was evil or as bad as adultery, or misread affection as sexual, or rejected all the questions and stories of children about sex as wrong. The disturbance in the girls came in equal parts from the degradation of sexuality and from the willingness of trusted adults to distort reality.

In adult women, childhood purity training may result in coldness, a lack of expressiveness, a lack of affection. The autobiographers remember this trait in a number of Catholic mothers and nuns, whose duty toward children, according to the Catechism of Trent, is to educate in virtue, not to provide warmth and encouragement. Mme. Delaure rarely touched her children, so that Lucie was overcome by delight when her mother once picked her up and hugged her.[80] Far less gentle than Mme. Delarue, Mme. Toulé, Jouhandeau's mother, never touched her children unless to strike them. She would push them away if they wanted a hug, and Jouhandeau remembers, "Often, my tears strangled me in the face of that firmness that didn't want to bend so as to give me a kiss."[81] Beatings and coldness in families could have developed as an overreaction to the danger of lust and incest, and canon law before the 1960s permitted the beating of children. I am not familiar with authoritative statements of other cultural groups so as to know how they regarded violent forms of punishment.

As a child Marie Noël used to imagine herself a tiny person searching through the snow palaces she saw in shrubs and trees for the fairy who had created them.[82] She never found her, nor admitted explicitly the identity of her Snow Queen, artful and generous, but physically cold and inaccessible.

When María Teresa León became paralyzed temporarily, her mother had time to nurse her malady, according to León, but no time for her; when she recovered, her mother did not find her perfect enough.[83] The implication is that her mother did not know how to relate to her on a personal level, and consequently used physical care and moralistic correction both to avoid intimacy and to express love in a safe, indirect manner. Her mother might have meant, "I'm afraid to show love" and "I love you," while María Teresa might have understood her to mean "I am doing my duty" and "I don't love you enough to overcome my fear."

Barbara Mullen remembers and describes best the moment after an illness when a usually cool mother may want to express affection but cannot bring herself to do so. Barbara had been injured, and her mother, who related to her by beating her, had been bringing up her meals, bathing her, and strapping her back with adhesive tape. When it was time for Barbara to get up from her bed again,

> She brought up my breakfast, and after asking how I was pulled up a chair close to the bed and sat down. I began to shake. I didn't know what she was going to say or do. She had never sat down beside me like that before. She cleared her throat. "Do you still want to go to the [jigging] contest?" she asked.
>
> "Yes, I do."
>
> "Well, I sent Puffy out to telephone the station and find out about the trains and how much the fare is."
>
> She was speaking in what I felt she meant to be a kind way, and I couldn't believe my ears. I wanted to throw my arms round her, but I didn't dare. I could only say "Thank you, I am very glad." There was a long silence. She moved about in her chair and let her hand fall casually on the bed. She wanted to reach over and pat my forehead I am sure, but, strangely enough, she who was able to cope with almost any situation didn't know what to do now, and finally with a sigh she took her hand away and folded both in her lap.[84]

Once when Ana María Matute expected a scolding for having lost her panties in the river while playing there with her brother and some village boys, she remarks that her mother was "serious, dry as a scythe; a scythe that threw stones with a shepherd's marksmanship and held words like nettles."[85] This mother's dryness and effectiveness in scolding might have been due to the Church's emphasis on the responsibility of the mother to raise virtuous children, but at the date of *El río* (1963) Matute would not have been allowed to print such a statement.

Wendy Rose (1948–   ), a poet, half Hopi, half Anglo-Miwok, wrote a telegraphic girlhood narrative in "Neon Scars," in *I Tell You Now: Autobiographical Essays by Native American Writers* (1987). Even in her elliptical style, she is able to indicate a withdrawn quality in both her sick mother and her teaching nuns.

> Facts: May 7, 1948. Oakland. Catholic hospital. Midwife nun, no doctor. Citation won the Kentucky Derby. Israel was born. The United Nations met for the first time. It was Saturday, the end of the baby boom or the beginning. Boom. Stephen's little sister. Daughter of Betty. Almost named Bodega, named Bronwen instead. Little brown baby with a tuft

of black hair. Baptized in the arms of Mary and Joe. Nearly blind for ten years. Glasses. Catholic school. Nuns with black habits to their ankles. Heads encased in white granite. Rosary beads like hard apricots— measuring prayers, whipping wrists. Paced before the blackboard. Swore in Gaelic. Alone. Alone at home. Alone in the play yard. Alone at Mass. Alone on the street. Fed, clothed in World War II dresses, little more. Mom too sick to care; brother raised by grandparents. Alone. Unwatched. Something wrong with me; everyone knows but me. They all leave me alone. No friends. Confirmation. Patron Francis of Assisi. He understands. Public high schools. Drugs, dropping out. Finally friends. Getting high, staying high. Very sick, hospital. No more drugs, no more friends. Alone again. Married at eighteen. Tried to shoot me. Lasted three months. Again at nineteen.[86]

"Granite," "hard," "measuring," "whipping," "paced," and "swore" describe a condition caused by the nuns' anxiety to control and by convent fear of sexuality, a fear that is allowed to spread to affection. The resulting coldness leads to isolation and pain for the nuns as for the children, and it calls into question the use of celibates as teachers.

Brave Bird, when her religion nun criticized her in front of the class for holding hands with a boy, stood up politely and corrected the nun on the grounds that the bodies of newborn white babies had been found in the convent water lines when they backed up.[87] Probably the nuns did not give birth to and dispose of dead babies, but the survival of this story among the girls at the mission school speaks of their suffering. They seem to have transformed their deep feelings of rejection by the nuns into this legend of dead babies left where the water of life should have been flowing. Maybe the Native American girls attributed the coldness and violence of the nuns not only to racism, but also to a death-oriented renunciation of motherhood.

Another devastating result of an unhealthy sexuality in Catholic adults is hostility to the female in girls. Linda Marie Pillay, Peggy Joan Fontenot, and Elise Jouhandeau experienced such hostility in an open and physical form: To show the hostility in her stepfather, Pillay writes, "Whenever Helda [her mother] wasn't around, Lester would have me blow him or he'd ball me in the ass or just jerk off in front of me or have me jerk him off. He'd whisper sweet things to me while he was doing this. When Helda was around, he'd beat the hell out of me in a strange display of anger and hate. When we were alone he'd tell me he had to do that so Helda wouldn't get suspicious. But it didn't seem like a game when he'd take off his belt and beat me like a mad man."[88] In Linda's situation, disapproval came easily, but disobedience was almost impossible.

Ironically, Linda would not have joined the Catholic Church or attended a Catholic school had her mother not married Lester. Because Linda did attend a Catholic school, she knew very well that she had obligations both to obey her stepfather and to avoid sexual activity, a confusing and painful situation. Lester did not allow her to have a will, a wish, or an independent life. After some years, she found him so oppressive, she separated from herself and from the world.

> I couldn't think straight. I wasn't able to concentrate on anything and was unable to read because the sentences would become words and the words, letters, which floated around and made no sense. I wasn't able to make friends because other children had trouble relating to a strange cripple child. I lived in a world vacant of feeling is what it all added up to. When people spoke to me, I'd focus on their mouths and watch their teeth moving together and know sounds was coming from them but could not follow the pattern of speech. I would start to speak but couldn't finish what I wanted to say—no matter how simple. My mind would draw a blank. I'd watch people's eyes squint while they waited for my next word; then I'd withdraw. Everything around me became one-dimensional—the trees on the street were paintings and the painting of a child I had on the wall in my room became a beast staring down at me from its frame. I was afraid to stand too close to the window in my room because I knew an unknown force would push me to my death.[89]

In addition to revealing her poor education and her outstanding intelligence, this paragraph offers other insights. Owing to his sexual hostility, Linda's emotions have been excluded in favor of Lester's. Because she was not allowed to finish sentences beginning "I want" or "I don't want," she lost her power to talk entirely. Like the one-dimensionality of her perceptions, her self-erasure was probably a defense against Lester's invasions of her body. But she did not choose such extreme selflessness on her own. The staring beast that had once been a child probably represents her self-concept at the time of Lester's most incessant incursions. She felt like an animal, but the reduction to passivity left her an even narrower, less vital identity. Her fear that she was about to be pushed to her death by an unknown force might have been a warning that her personality was on the verge of eradication. She must have felt, even if she could not have used such language, that Lester had an obsessive will to destroy her, that is, to be the only real person in the house.

Linda could not easily recover her confidence. After she had finally turned to a nun for help and had been to court, the Catholic boarding school she wanted to attend would not accept her because the nuns feared her premature emergence from latency might awaken a premature interest among other girls. In reform school the nun in charge of her age group, whom Pillay calls Mother Contrition, continually reproached her as responsible for the father's sins. The child's contamination by false guilt appears in her remark about visits from her family. "I was so afraid he'd touch me. I was afraid I'd freeze and be frozen in that awkward position because I didn't know how to say no."[90] Eventually, though her sexual yearnings were aroused only by women, Linda married, had children, and overcame her hesitancy about loving women sexually, but harmony with her husband, children, and lovers escaped her, at least during the years covered by her autobiography.

Cooperation with her stepfather's wishes harmed Linda, too, in spoiling her trust in God the Father. She transferred her hurt and anger from the head of her family to God, whom she saw as an old man and therefore hated.[91] This mixup is a response to constant Christian teaching that God is our father, and to Catholic teaching that our fathers represent God. When one's father or priest fails in love, God's love may then be doubted; as with Beauvoir, so with Pillay.

Unlike Pillay, Peggy Joan Fontenot was not raped but seduced. Her love for her young man was intensified when he was sent to prison for an unspecified crime. When he returned she consented to his demands and became pregnant. The priest, judging her passion to be merely carnal, refused to marry them, and he did not hesitate to tell her mother he considered Peggy Joan an animal. After a civil marriage and before the baby was born, when Fontenot was still fifteen or sixteen years old, her husband came into the bedroom one night, and because his friends had told him she was an "easy make," he threw her on the bed and started slapping her. From the time that liars had told him she had been seeing other boys while he was in prison, he insulted her, made her paranoic, beat her, and on her eighteenth birthday broke her nose [92]

The antagonism Fontenot and Pillay had to face, like that of Jouhandeau's mother and the lesser virulence of Beauvoir's father and Benoist's mother, seems to have been a reaction to the femaleness that is more apparent to some than to others. Continual insults or efforts to drive women to behave wrongly, like those of Jouhandeau's mother and Fontenot's husband, seem rather to originate in an inability to believe in or make mental room for good human beings.

Some Catholic adults denied the human dignity of the girls just because they were girls. An example of this occurred in Benoist's childhood, when she and her female cousin were not allowed to go barefoot lest they develop big feet, or to go without sunbonnets lest they develop freckles, and at a certain age were made to change to side-saddles.[93] All these interferences with the natural inclinations of girls to bodily activity and health offended the girls because such practices distinguish the genders sharply and impose physical disadvantages on females, thus tending to lower their social rank.

Without making rules, Marie Noël's mother used to train her children to expect females to be passive. Every night she would sing Marie and her brother a pair of songs. The little boy's song listed clothes and equipment he would have as a soldier. The little girl's song listed her doll's clothes, but no clothes for herself, no equipment that would have enabled her alter ego or herself to engage in any action. Noël may not have realized how she felt about these songs, for she reports without comment that both children asked their mother to sing them every night. The little girl's attitude comes out in her inability as an adult to recall the words to her own song, whereas she always remembered both the tune and words of her brother's.[94]

When an adult moves to reduce the human dignity and value of a female, either a wife or a daughter, an older girl who reacts is often told that disobedience should be reserved for major ethical issues, not trotted out over less grave incidents. For that reason, Rosa Chacel and her mother made no protest when Rosa's father would not allow them to touch an ashtray, the typewriter, or the duplicating machine he had borrowed, supposedly lest they get their hands dirty. Cleanliness and purity were merely his pretext; in reality these were gender markers for the father, and he did not want to share them with females. Rosa thought his prohibition was frustrating, depriving, and daft.[95]

María Teresa León complained vigorously about at least one gender custom related to the menarche, and that was being forced to change to a side-saddle. She was told, " 'A girl like you cannot mount so.' And they gave the little girl a skirt that reached to her feet and forbade her to mount like men, on those little leather saddles which she liked so much. . . . How difficult it was to leap hurdles with the two knees separated by those horns which made her dangle her legs at the same side of the saddle!"[96] An impoverished woman might think the side-saddle complaint trivial, but for María Teresa horses were a major and constant element of her life. In a normal approach, the knees of the rider are used to guide the horse. Moreover, the side-saddle, which prevented her from acting rational, natural, and skillful, was introduced only because she was a girl. León sensed immediately that, like the iceberg that sank the *Titanic,* the side-saddle was larger than it appeared to be. By distorting the rider's physical relation to the horse and throwing her off balance, it diminished her social status.

The morale of women suffers under a system that downgrades them. Matute notes this when she observes a caravan of tinkers passing through the village: "The men have the air of chief of tribe, the women are submissive and surprisingly tired, the children, happy and dirty."[97] The differences here raise the question of whether men channel and drain the natural diversity of women's energy.

When mothers are mistreated, their children often side with them, and Catholic girls are no exception. Many of these autobiographers, particularly the earlier ones, seem not to have noticed the effect of their parents' relationship on their mothers, probably because in those years parents carried on their internal diplomacy in private. But later in the twentieth century, more and more of the autobiographers note imperfections in the marriages of their parents. They recall shame or anguish at the submissiveness of their mothers or at the rudeness, cruelty, or indifference of their fathers toward their mothers.

Rosa Chacel was disturbed because of the financial anxiety her father caused her mother. They had lost their first child because the mother could not nurse him, and in winter she had to deal with shortages in the house. Poverty hung over them like a heavy cloud, for although her father was gifted, he was too proud to work for a salary or fee. Chacel words her opinion of this behavior strongly: "The only sweetheart that my father lay down for, the only one for whom he betrayed us—my mother, me, and Spain—was Mrs. Nothingness."[98] None of the writers discussed in chapter 1 would have made such a statement. As Chacel has written in a major set of essays, *Saturnal* (1972), "Long centuries of civilization *persuaded* humanity that wealth corrupts the human soul. Today we *know* that poverty destroys, annihilates, degrades the soul much more."[99] The poverty of Rosa's home created problems her mother could do nothing about; although she could have worked as a teacher, Catholic beliefs on marriage kept her from doing so. As chapter 3 will explain, she would have seen her working as usurping a responsibility of her husband, and working for a salary as competition with him for prestige and power in the home.

In addition, Chacel remembers listening to her parents carrying on a dispute while they were out for a walk. Rosa could hardly hear what they were saying, for she was slightly ahead of them, but from her father she could hear "cutting phrases that seemed to demand an answer." Because of his tone, she says, she "expected her mother to answer plain and forthright, but no; almost weeping, she said vague things, nothing decisive, and meantime she destroyed her fan, sinking her nails into the paper landscape and tearing it from the ribs." The father's attack was due to a jealousy he and everyone else knew was unfounded, but which he engaged in simply out of "a kind of need for psychic activity." While Rosa's expectation of her mother here showed solidarity, she found her mother's behavior inappropriate and even pitiable in such a splendid woman.[100]

Nevertheless, as a child Chacel admired many things in both her parents. In her mother's personality she found only two qualities she had to avoid imitating: her mother's excessive susceptibility to suffering and her submissiveness, whether to her husband or to her mother.[101]

María Teresa León notes with disapproval that her father allowed his adulteries to hurt her and her mother;[102] he might have done so to emphasize to them that his social rank as a colonel was superior to theirs. Similarly, María Teresa had learned that a certain priest had been grossly inconsiderate of one of her old aunts in Barbastro, a tiny cathedral town in Aragón. When the old lady told the priest that she wanted to marry, he objected on the ground of her age, until she said she was rich. Then he brought his nephew to court her. When she refused the nephew, for she thought him too ugly and forward, the priest insisted, and asked her for several thousand reales for the parish in exchange for his nephew. She laughed a great deal and sent them away. But when León met her, she was still a little hysterical over it, and would laugh at inappropriate times.[103] León might have been hurt herself by the implication that wives had value only reproductively or financially.

In early childhood, Simone de Beauvoir thought, and perhaps children whose mothers do not develop careers generally think, that "in certain respects Papa, grandpapa, and my uncles appeared to me to be superior to their wives. But in my everyday life, it was Louise [the nurse], Mama, grandmama, and my aunts who played the leading roles."[104] On the other hand, Simone noticed a deterioration in her father's treatment of her mother, and she strongly disapproved of that. Although her parents had been happy together during the early days of their marriage, after M. de Beauvoir lost much of his money, he lost some of his courtesy as well. "Whenever my mother asked him for housekeeping money, he made a violent scene." He also began to be unfaithful to her, and did not hesitate to excuse this behavior in debates with Simone, making no more effort to conceal his adultery than León's father did.[105] Beauvoir thought her mother was made vulnerable by her admiration and love for her husband and the belief "that the wife should obey the husband in everything."[106] Still living at home during her college years, Beauvoir was sickened by her father's unfairness, saddened by her mother's sorrow and loneliness.

McCarthy thought her Great-Aunt Margaret was shameless in her excessive gratitude for having a husband, and shameless in her injustices to the children for his sake. However, McCarthy could at least look back on a truly loving relationship between her own parents.[107]

Sheelagh Conway tells how she and her brothers and sisters could hardly avoid noticing the difference in power and status between their parents. Conway grew up in a cattle-raising society where the men drank up too much of the proceeds. After the cattle fair, her father would spend three days in bed recovering from his hangover and complaining. And then a colossal fight would develop.

> The money was gone and the hope dried to parchment. The fire was half lit at breakfast time, with a cake of brown bread on the table and the teapot settled on the coals to one side of the fire. The oak beams looked sootier than usual, and the smoke swirled ominously around the kitchen in great puffs. There was heavy silence interspersed with screaming, yelling, shouting, and insults. Cups and saucers went flying around the kitchen, to shatter against the whitewashed walls and fall in smithereens onto the clay floor. The Sacred Heart continued to smile serenely as tea streamed down the whitewashed wall beside him.
>
> Daddy always sat at the head of the kitchen table buttering the bread, spreading it slowly and thickly, and roaring at Mammy every time he paused in his task. Mammy stood and poked at the fire, trying to get it to light. After a bout of yelling, some deep insult was thrown, and they went for one another, Daddy punching Mammy in the face, once, twice, three times. The great muffled blows sounded like bags of wheat being thrown from the cart onto the ground. . . . Mammy held the tongs for protection, and when that failed she dropped her weapon and ran into the parlour, to emerge again with her coat on.[108]

She was going to the Church for help. "My mother then took to her bicycle, heading for Father O'Riordan's place, where the priest proceeded to tell her that she must be a good wife and listen to her husband. When the beatings were very severe he conceded that it was somewhat wrong; but she must still go home to her husband and children. Mammy usually stayed at some neighbour's house for a couple of days till the blackest part of the mood had passed."[109] Apparently the priest had read the Catechism of Trent and also canon law; for whatever cause, he accepted the father's behavior toward his family.

The children did not grow used to the fighting between their parents. "When the fights were in full swing I ran to Jack and Maggie across the boreen, imploring Jack to come quick before Daddy killed Mammy. I was always certain he would kill her in one of his violent rages, and the thought sent me into a spasm of fear that I was unable to contain." And when the fight was over, "There was no food, and the cows would roar at the gate to be milked and the calves to be fed. These were all reminders of the fight, the money, the poverty, the culture that underlined the dominance of men. I hated my father for it. I hated the way he humiliated my mother while all of us children cried in the ashes not knowing what to do."[110] Of course the Church did not keep Conway's loyalty. As she saw it, the parish priest prospered financially in symbiosis with men who drank excessively, engaged in violence, and neglected their families' physical needs.[111] The result was damage to all parties.

Not all Catholic fathers have failed to gain control of their lives. Some have traits worthy of emulation by any human being. One of the reasons Catholic women are considered relatively inferior is that they are discouraged from imitating these traits. If the girls followed the natural and usual path of imitating their mothers primarily, but their fathers in characteristics such as humor, interest in public life, and responsibility, they would attract more respect. Inconsistently with the Church's emphasis on giving good example, Catholic parents often suppress this form of filial piety in girls.

Some of the misery undergone by Colette, Beauvoir, and others was due to their parents' ruling out their partial identification with their fathers. Rosa Chacel is the one among these autobiographers who has written the most explicit account of this kind of ordeal. Her mother asked her to rid herself of uncharitable speech or sarcasm, which examinations of conscience often list as an offense against the eighth commandment and which was a habit both the child and her father had.[112]

Chacel writes in a flashback how her mother had one day asked her to correct her cruelty of speech. Rosa had thought a certain working man was named Parsley and addressed him that way, with the result that her mother "looked at me with an unaccustomed severity, took me into a corner and preached to me a long while on the extreme care one has to put into not offending ever a poor or an inferior person."[113] This story is presented as an aside in the narrative of the illness, not as a criticism of her mother.

Accepting her mother's request to give up sarcasm brought Rosa down with a high fever, one which took several months to get over. The gravity of the illness is what has led me to think Rosa's sarcasm was not a superficial mannerism, but a part of her identification with her father and his valor, an identification she formed before or outside the memories she includes in *Amanecer*.[114] Although Rosa accepted her mother's right to correct her, in effect the mother was rejecting a part of Rosa's personality. The mother was not just enforcing the eighth commandment; she preferred, in line with Trent, that her daughter identify totally with her and in no degree with her father.

Where the family was concerned, the girls accepted the Church's distribution of roles, and for this reason they resented certain deviations greatly. Conway, Chacel, and Norris recall anger at a father who did not provide for the family financially. Repplier, Schoffen, Benoist, Delarue-Mardrus, Noël, Jouhandeau, Mellish, Chacel, Beauvoir, McCarthy, Mullen, and Rose report hurt because of a mother or other female relatives or nuns who did not show them much or true love. These recollections reveal, in addition to injury to the self, that the children's religion teachers must have emphasized looking to one's parents as models of masculine and feminine moral behavior, the mother to represent God's love and the father God's providence. If the catechists had not done so, would the children have felt such shock and dismay at the neglect of precisely that task assigned each parent by the Church?

The autobiographers discussed in this chapter, unlike those in chapter 1, describe many injustices toward themselves. As a result of the gendered quality of these injustices, some of the girls felt a loss of hope and a diminution of the self, even a fear of having to become women. Noël's mother was generous with feminine symbols; for example, she sacrificed sleep to make Marie a little purse, yet she trained her by the doll songs to expect a barren and humiliated existence.[115] Noël used to imagine herself a tiny person searching through frozen foliage for the Snow Queen. Similarly, when she watched the fire, she saw a dwarf scaling a burning tower, hunchbacks rolling in hell with their humps scarlet, and queens with "maddened" hair.[116] I believe she was this dwarf, as well as the hunchbacks who were born deformed and the queens who had inexplicably lost their reason. Marie was kept small, made to feel deformed, driven to a kind of madness, yet she had been trying to move upward, to emulate adult women, and to serve order and beauty. Lucien Descaves, a Parisian journalist and member of the Académie Goncourt who visited her in 1932, reported that her hair was prematurely white, that she spent her time with her mother and the poor, and when he finally persuaded her to sing one of her songs for him, she sang weakly, with a voice "that raised itself with difficulty, like the chirping of a nestling, not wounded, but exhausted by the weight of its wings."[117] Thus, permanent damage had been done to her confidence and level of energy. What she might have achieved as a writer had she been unconflicted about her work, we will never know.

An equally grave reaction of young girls to gender beliefs imposed on them by Catholic adults is a loss of hope and a fear of the future that one would like to think were not the intention behind Catholic religious instruction. Beauvoir mentions this discouragement in her classmates at the cours Désir as they neared graduation. "The air of sadness that emanated from my other schoolmates was due less to their appearance than to their hopeless resignation." What they were accepting as unavoidable for good Catholic women was arranged marriages and relatively inactive lives.[118]

Among less affluent women, who lack servants, girls may gradually develop a fear of growing up because they know that adult Catholic women may face death, exhaustion, depression, or loss of health because of their faith. Catholic preachers do call on women to sacrifice themselves for love (see chapter 3). In *Nun: A Memoir* (1984), former nun Mary Gilligan Wong (1943–   ) recalls her growing awareness as a girl of the harm this practice was doing to mothers, their children, and their marriages.

> I began to question my girlish dreams of domestic bliss as I watched Mother. Sometimes it seemed that she simply dragged her body from one day to the next, fighting a war that could never be won. She would iron mountains of clothes, then just when she reached the bottom of the basket, there'd be another load from the clothesline. The baby would be sick, and as soon as she was well again, one of the other children would come down with the flu. Cooking dinner for seven took much of the afternoon; then within a few minutes all signs of the accomplishment would be erased, leaving only a stack of dishes to be washed. It went on and on with no relief in sight. Sometimes at night I would lie awake, listening through the vent that went from my bedroom to the kitchen: I would hear my parents talking and arguing late into the night, their voices fraught with tension and desperation. . . . I lived in fear of Mother ending

up like one of the parish women I had heard about: one had had a nervous breakdown and now lived on tranquilizers and shock treatments; the other had hanged herself with clothesline rope one gray winter morning as she hung out clothes in the basement.[119]

Conflicting demands to have more and more children, but not to work for a salary, can make life hard financially and physically, especially for a good Catholic. If mothers are worn out, driven mad, or die, their children suffer, and in particular their daughters.

Whereas Wong's parents could not afford servants, Menchú lived in an economy that forced her to become a servant. Hardship came to her family and neighbors because Catholic landowners misused their authority over the poor; they extorted money from the workers, ordered the foremen to fire anyone who took a day off to grieve over the death of a child, and had crops fumigated from the air while workers and children were in the fields. The starvation and poisoning that followed led Menchú to a conclusion similar to Wong's: "Always I had seen my mother crying, many times hidden. . . . But I always found her crying in the house or at work. I had a fear of life. . . . One of my brothers, my mother told me, died of poisoning [from the fumigation of crops] . . . and another of my brothers, I saw die of hunger, of malnutrition. I remembered all the times when I saw my mother sweat and work and never stop. She went on working. Many times she had nothing." Menchú's reaction, like Wong's was to decide not to marry, "because if you marry you would have children and to have children, it would cost you to see a child die of hunger or of suffering or of sickness."[120]

Those autobiographers who express frustration and grief openly are acknowledging remembered opposition to their natural inclinations from the very persons one would expect to be most supportive. The opposition they report had three principal aims: to obtain unexamined submission, to suppress their interest in sex and friendship, and to prevent their acquiring enough knowledge to pursue engrossing careers or to see through the Church's official teaching on females. The women remember themselves as disturbed by the danger these demands represented to their survival as persons; at the time when such gender rules were imposed they felt the interventions were destructive, irrational, and unjust.

When abuses of authority like those described earlier in this chapter result in incomplete self-development, autobiography may be expected to be impossible, but aggression from authority figures, especially when it has an institutional origin, provides very appropriate material for autobiographies because of the tendency of practitioners of the genre to describe relations between the individual and society.

The autobiographers of chapter 2, who express frustration and grief openly, are not merely more critical or more expressive than those of chapter 1. In reading autobiographical works by the second group of Catholic women, I have found that they are not asking, What charming memories have I? or How can I relieve the pressure to tell the truth in spite of the pressure not to? or What are the roots of my achievements and my fame? Their questions are, rather, Why did I suffer injustices? Why were my natural inclinations so interfered with? and Why was my initial enthusiasm for life so crushed?

No explanation can be adequate to the distress in Catholic girls, if by *explanation* we mean a list of reasonable causes or a classification that accounts for all these harmful behaviors logically. However, all the actions under discussion were caused by or aggravated by the Church's training for Catholic womanhood, as the next chapter will show. For girls, the extra emphasis placed on submission to authority, the aversion to providing much education, the attempt to prevent their ever enjoying their sexuality—all have come about because of the role the Church wants adult women to play, a role involving continual reproductive and domestic labor. Judging from the reactions of the girls, the proscriptions placed on their activities were unexpected. They saw the sudden appearance of gender rules in their lives as unnecessary obsacles to the emerging self. Consequently, children who had begun by loving their parents, nuns, and priests changed their attitude to some degree when required to make sacrifices that went beyond those we all have to make in order to become civilized humans. Even as young girls, these women felt the Church was asking them to give up innocent and good pursuits without a just cause. They sensed that the result would be at least partial destruction not only of their respect for adults, but also of their natural, positive personalities, which may explain their hurt and anger.

part 3

THEOLOGIES OF WOMEN

chapter three

The Message
of Subordination

JUDGING from the autobiographies of Catholic women, Catholic parents, priests, and teaching nuns often opposed girls' efforts to mature, that is, to become self-directing in spiritual matters. A few adults, adherents of the theology of equivalence, encouraged the girls to become completely human in their way of life, and I will describe their efforts in the following chapter. A probable cause why the theology favored by the majority of clerics dominated the lives of most of the girls is that Catholic adults wanted to train girls for lives that would not allow them much self-direction, however rational their self-direction was. When I first attempted to find out whether the Church was behind the suppression of self-government, vague memories came to mind of books I had read during the late 1950s on the topic of the Catholic Woman. However, Catholic college library collections no longer had them, and I had to comb second-hand and rare book companies to find several survivors of earlier enthusiasm for the subject, books written by priests and officially approved by ranking clerics. The first of these is *The Destiny of Modern Woman in the Light of Papal Teaching* (1950), by William B. Faherty, S.J., of Regis College in Denver.[1] The second, which I have already mentioned, is *Christ and Womankind* (1935; translated into English 1952), by

Peter Ketter, D.D., a seminary professor in Trier, Germany. The program articulated in these two books is traditional and explains many quandaries related to the girlhood narratives of Catholic women.

If we examine the tradition of Catholic femininity in more official sources—in the words of theologians who established its elements and popes who approved them—then it becomes apparent that the prohibitions, obstructions, and penalties that have caused Catholic girls so much distress were not just Victorian or Jansenistic or Puritanical or customary in the whole society of the late nineteenth and twentieth centuries, though overlapping occurs. The gender training of these girls was what it was because "God's representatives" intended it to be Catholic and made sure it was Catholic. The values and rules conveyed in this training might have come from secular society originally, but they have been maintained in the Church as characteristically Catholic and have reappeared in situations quite dissimilar from their culture of origin.

To clarify the contrast between Catholic and mainstream gender training, I will quote mainstream sources briefly. A 1992 secular psychology of women published in the United States describes childhood gender training in this country as follows: "Differential treatment is consistent with producing independence and efficacy in boys and emotional sensitivity, nurturance, and helplessness in girls."[2] As this chapter will show, Catholic girls are trained to helplessness and motherhood, but nowhere have I heard or read any mention of emotional sensitivity. Motherhood training will be in virtues that almost exclude forms of psychic nurturance, for example, in church attendance and self-sacrifice. The emphasis on sensitivity will be replaced by stress on obedience to mother or husband and guilt about the sexual dimension of the self. If mothers or husbands want sensitivity, they can require it; if they prefer stoicism, they can require that. They will probably not call for a natural, relaxed sexuality, or if the husband does so, he may not be able to obtain it, the change having come too late in the woman's life. Catholic demands on women corresponding to the demand for helplessness are for self-denial and subordination, which in time results in more or less helplessness. Thus, overlapping between mainstream and Catholic gender formation occurs and may give the impression of complete similarity, but differences between the groups are sharp.

Not only the content differs; methods of training do, as well. Bernice Lott in her 1981 secular psychology of women lists two methods of teaching gender behavior: (1) modeling by available and likable people, and (2) cueing behaviors as rewardable or punishable (by disapproval, ridicule, insult) whether directly or by verbal labels.[3] Chapter 2 indicates that Catholics have approved of and used a more extensive list of punishments than Lott gives, including close surveillance, physical violence, and isolation, and that the mother model in Catholic life is not necessary likable.

Catholic gender formation therefore should not be assumed to parallel that of other cultural groups, and should be studied both in its own theoreticians and in its own teachers.

Catholic feminists and Catholic antifeminists will surely agree that religious discipline of girls is grounded on definitions of the word *Woman,* and that these definitions have been preached in the Church to obtain a certain kind of behavior, on the assumption that the century of their origin does not alter their value or truth. To improve the chances that women will act out the definitions, the claim is usually made that God wills behavior in accord with them, though no claim is made that they were revealed by God. Of course, if God willed us to do so, a definition would have to be translated into habitual actions. A woman could turn her potential into reality through meeting the terms included in the definition. For example, if she were defined as one who listened and cooperated, she could develop her personality to perfection by not speaking and not initiating.

The most authoritative source of Catholic truth after the Scripture, in the opinion of some Catholics, is "the Fathers of the Church." The phrase refers to priests and bishops who wrote letters, sermons, and books during the first four or five centuries after Christ. Not made a part of the canon of Scripture, these works have nevertheless been accorded exceptional respect by Catholic theologians. Since theologians usually teach in seminaries and other Catholic colleges, patristic definitions of Woman have had an extended afterlife; that is, they are preached today on the parish level.

The Fathers of the Church are generally agreed by theologians to have made errors; for example, Gregory of Nyssa denied the soul's inherent immortality.[4] His denial would be rejected by Catholic anti-abortionists. Feminists are not unusual in thinking that some of the notions of the Fathers are false. Underlying many patristic mistakes about women is a lack of logic. Richard Robinson's book has been helpful in determining what constitutes a logical definition.[5] To me it seems illogical that the Fathers in general did not define *man* in a way symmetrical with their definition of *woman.* Usually distinctions between subclasses cover the same list of features, and I will be pointing out instances where the Fathers have not defined that way.

In the case of women the Fathers' views are not consistent with other Catholic beliefs, and certainly not with the Gospels. Apparently unconcerned by his lack of harmony with Christ's attitude, Tertullian (160?–230? C.E.) scolded women vigorously. "Do you not know that you are each an Eve? The sentence of God on this sex of yours lives in this age: the guilt must of necessity live too. *You* are the devil's gateway. . . . *You* are she who persuaded him whom the devil was not valiant enough to attack. *You* destroyed so easily God's image, man. On account of your desert—that is, death—even the Son of God had to die."[6] Among other errors in this definition of *all women,* Tertullian did not follow with an exhortation to men to consider themselves each an Adam and therefore morally flawed. In a further offense against logic, Tertullian's reproach reads as if he thought he had triumphantly summed up all the traits of all the women in the world in the name "Eve" or the phrase "the devil's gateway." A fundamental belief that all girls and women are inherently immoral appears in Repplier's Mme. Bouron, in Jouhandeau's mother, in Fontenot's husband, in Brave Bird's dormitory nun, and no doubt in others. One might think of their speech as uncharitable, but they were thinking in harmony with teachings repeated in the Church for centuries.

As Robinson has brought out, compressing all the facts about a thing into a short phrase "from which every truth about that object follows" is almost always impossible.[7] Yet like Tertullian with his "devil's gateway," Gregory of Nyssa (331?–395? C.E.) deduced from this word *Eve* an important rule for the behavior of all women. "The Eve-like frailty of women makes them unable to cope with the consequences of knowledge and therefore ill-suited for study."[8] Almost as if he were following a rule of unsymmetricality, Gregory does not mention the Adam-like frailty of men and their unsuitability for public debate. Perhaps because so many people have not noticed the omission, some girls who show a love for study have alarmed their parents and teachers. Schoffen, McCarthy, Mullen, León, and Beauvoir, but not Matute, Wolff, or Janés, describe opposition to their intellectual drive that they were not able to understand at the time. This disorienting obscurantism has often been voiced in language implying that intellectual life is somehow against religion and morality. Perhaps Gregory of Nyssa's influence helps to explain this non sequitur. Perhaps Catholic girls who love to study would have had an easier time had he noticed that Eve's intellectual curiosity was greater than Adam's. But even to praise women's intellectual vitality or beauty by reference to Eve is unwise. To define all women as resembling one woman, even the first, seems a sure path to error; women are sufficiently diverse as to make common traits difficult to identify, and especially so as cultures change and new human potentials are brought forward.

Not every definition of Woman given by the Fathers was as illogical as those of Tertullian and Gregory of Nyssa. Although it is repulsive and is embedded in a persuasive effort, I offer the following passage from Augustine (354–430) as including at least some analysis, as it were, of Woman into components:[9] "In the same woman a good Christian loves the being that God has created, and that he wishes to be transformed and renewed, while he hates the corruptible and mortal relationship and marital intercourse. In other words, it is evident that he loves her insofar as she is a human being, but that he hates her under the aspect of wifehood."[10] Thus Augustine follows the rule of logical analysis in identifying the human and religious component, on the one hand, including both body and soul, and the morally intimate and sexual, on the other. However, few men marry because they are disgusted with sex. Catholic women suffer some contempt from priests, for Augustine's beliefs about sexuality are still held by numerous clerics today. In the United States, aversion to human females as animal in their sexuality (like the hostility of Fontenot's parish priest) comes in part at least from Augustine's influence in seminaries, which is frequently mentioned in Catholic oral tradition to explain the hurtful attitude of priests toward women.

In the particular definition of Woman I am discussing, Augustine uses the words *hate* and *corruptible* to introduce a disapproval presented as objectively due such a repugnant reality as female sexual desire and attractiveness. Yet he has not presented any factual indications of baseness. Even though he laid down an analytic stratum in the definition, he invalidated the whole formula by assuming sexuality was for others what it was for him, in other words, that this revulsion at sexuality was a truth, not about himself, but about wives, and not just some wives. The Fathers generally defined the word *man* as a human person, religious and capable of renewal and redemption, but they did not add and perhaps even denied that male sexuality and the masculine role of husband introduced a corruptibility and despicability matching those of women. In fact, or so I hope, as many Catholic girls have hoped, the integrity and love in male sexuality may match those of women.

Along with Augustine's analytic definition of Woman as both human and wife, he also provides a synthetic definition (the discovery of a concept or pattern's place in a system of concepts or forms).[11] By speaking of Woman as a "creature of God" and a "human being," Augustine relates her to larger classes. Not every Catholic theologian has given women so much credit. Augustine's idea that the woman could run things when the man was out of the house shows that he also had a practical grasp of the competence of women, gained, no doubt, by the years he lived with his mistress before he negotiated a bishopric in the Catholic Church.[12] Mullen's mother might have been aware of this belief, for she did not mind her husband's absence in Ireland and clung to her unlimited power over her children. Augustine's refusal to allow wives equality in the home when the husband was present must have been based on other grounds than their ability, grounds almost without a doubt social. In spite of the limitations he placed on women, the acknowledgment of the humanity of human females and their creation by God has been taught to Catholics, along with his other, debasing ideas. The continued promulgation of belief in the dignity of women helps to explain why so many of the girls studied in these autobiographies have been horrified and resentful when representatives of the Church have attempted to prevent their fulfilling their lofty spiritual destiny.

An Augustinian disgust with sexuality has been expressed more confidently and publicly in Spain than in France or the United States in this century, perhaps because the Spanish audience included almost no members of religions other than the Catholic until 1975, when Franco died. A frank statement of ecclesiastical views on sex appears in the most voluminous and fatherly catechism I know of; published in Barcelona in 1927, it could easily have been taught in Matute's school. Among its illustrations of the sixth and ninth commandments, it presents a negative image of sex as perpetrated by males upon females.

> "Look at this rose-tree, my daughter," said Doña Francisca to her daughter Paquita. "What pretty roses it has!"
> The little girl wants to break off a branch, but sticks herself with the thorns.
> "Leave them there, silly, so they will be more fresh and luxuriant on the stem."
> The little girl notices another rose-tree with spotted roses whose petals are wrinkled. It makes her feel pity to look at them.
> "What's wrong with those roses, Mama?"
> "The slugs have travelled over them."
> "What are slugs?"
> "Here's one."
> The little girl sees a wretched little animal, like a snail without a shell, viscous and repugnant, that goes leaving drool wherever it passes, eating and dirtying everything.[13]

Now the attack is on male sexuality, but the shift would not necessarily please the girls. Inevitably, with such openness about the official view of sexuality, female Spanish autobiographers writing during Franco's regime object much more vigorously than the French or Americans to the Church's efforts to prevent women from enjoying sex. But everywhere Catholic women, especially now that they have opportunities to study biology, psychology, and sociology, disapprove of negative presentations of human sexuality.

One, at least, of the Fathers of the Church was concerned enough for women to want to help them rise above their low social condition. Jerome respected the intellectual ability of certain women and corresponded with them about Holy Writ. He promised that woman could find spiritual equality with man in this life by abandoning the female life cycle, which he felt drew her down. "As long as a woman is for birth and children, she is different from man as body is from soul. But when she wishes to serve Christ more than the world, then she will cease to be a woman, and will be called man."[14] Again one of the Fathers forgets to mention that men have bodies. Celibacy for women, commonly known in the Church as *virginity,* was urged widely from the fourth and fifth centuries C.E. until the rise of modern psychology, supposedly because it enabled women to attain equal glory with men before reaching heaven. Jerome's notion that motherhood may be the reason that women are not considered equal to men in this world, and his hope that celibacy might overcome the difficulty certain Catholic men experience when asked to accept women as their equals in Christ, had the political effect at the time of consoling some women for the loss of their public role in the churches. This policy damaged the morale of married women both then and later.[15]

The Fathers' attitude toward the animality and sinfulness of reproduction as entirely female helps explain certain aspects of other Catholic women's lives and life-stories as well. It probably accounts for the confidence of the nuns (Farrell, Wolff, and Carroll) and the ex-nuns (Schoffen and Wong). They are completely untroubled about not being married, quite unlike those single women who feel rejected, deviant, useless, unimportant, or disapproved. It may also be a factor in Beauvoir's avoidance of maternity, along with her strong desire not to repeat her mother's life.

After the Fathers, the theologian most influential in the Church has been Thomas Aquinas (1225?–1274), an Italian who lived in a Benedictine monastery from the age of five until he joined the Dominicans. Most of his remarks about women, such as his citation of Aristotle claiming that they are produced by a defect in the semen, or illness, or even "from some external influence such as that of a south wind, which is moist," are not from direct experience. In addition to being foolish, they conflict with his insistence on God's behalf that women are not defective for their role in reproduction.[16] These absurdities are not usually mentioned today, acknowledging the poor state of biology in his time or honoring his more useful ideas. Aquinas's less bizarre statements about women (though at least half of them, too, might better have been forgotten) have been made influential again in the twentieth-century Church through renewed teaching efforts of the Dominican Order and through the translation and publication of the *Summa Theologica.*

In the *Summa,* Aquinas writes three or four pages, out of a total of approximately three thousand, on the creation of woman, saying that although the Scriptures tell us she is necessary to man as a helpmate (here he cites Ecclesiasticus 17:5, a reference apocryphal for Protestants), the term *helpmate* does not apply to works other than reproduction and domestic life. In other tasks "man can be more efficiently helped by another man . . . [because] man is yet further ordered to a still nobler vital action and that is intellectual operation."[17] In our time, educated people may realize that Aquinas was in this passage taking the condition of uneducated women in the middle ages as inborn and the intelligence of educated men also as inborn. Although the great Dominican theologian referred to pagan philosophers frequently, he does not quote Rufus Musonius, who argued that since women are equal to men in their ability to think rationally about ethical issues, women should receive an education equal to that of men.[18] Without the rectifying influence of Musonius, and without direct relationships with women, Aquinas had no opportunity to discover the stage machinery behind his illusions. As a result, he deduces from what he thinks is the inborn intellectuality of man that woman is "naturally subject" to him.

At this point, however, Aquinas advances beyond many modern minds, for he first eliminates, as due to the Fall, the type of subjection in which the subjected person is used for one's benefit. However, if a person is subjected for her benefit, this subjection is natural, he thinks. His reason is that this state of affairs existed before the Fall and "because in man the discretion of reason predominates."[19] Aquinas's gratuitous assumptions about Eden and his premise that all men are reasonable have had damaging results for the education and treatment of women. In spite of his belief, now obviously untrue, but not neglected in the Church, that (all) women should be subjected to (any) male direction, he states that this subjection must serve the woman's welfare and not that of the man. I deduce from the man's monopoly on reason, however, that he would have to be the judge whether he was serving the woman's welfare.

In a later discussion of God's image in man, Aquinas with a jolly inconsistency acknowledges that women were created in God's image, too, and must therefore have an intellectual nature. Thus he contradicts all the harmful points above, but he has already planted them, both on paper and in numerous minds. In the brief passage on the image of God in woman, instead of deducing her equality, as he should logically do, he flees to Scripture for a way to deny it. He quotes 1 Corinthians 11:7 to argue that since woman was created for man, "man is the beginning and end of woman," a usurpation God might reasonably question. Then this devoted Dominican theologian reverts to his earlier idea that woman is mentally and morally weaker than man, as Eden supposedly proves. From the weakness of woman he deduces first that females could not become priests even if they were ordained, and then, again, that all females need male direction because males have "the discretion of reason."

A concise modern expression of Aquinas's attitude toward women is presented by José María Pemán, a member of the Spanish Royal Academy, in his book *De doce cualidades de la mujer* (On the twelve qualities of Woman) (1969). Pemán writes: "Woman: a being very much glued to Nature, very anti-intellectual by definition, totally constructed for communication with that other weak, submissive and irrational being that is the son. The dialogue of babblings and mysterious half-words between mothers and the child, as infantile in one as in the other, is a sweet compensation for the forced tension that the woman always has to submit herself to, in order not to disappoint in their table-talk the man."[20] The shocking, stinging power of this attitude goes a long way toward explaining the thorough study of spontaneous childhood intelligence in Spanish women's autobiographies written during Franco's regime by Chacel, Matute, and León.

In none of the girlhood narratives at hand is ordination or any desire for it ever mentioned. Just three among Aquinas's errors are active in these life-histories: that God did not create women to function intellectually, that women are useful to men only in reproduction and domestic life, and that women need male, rational direction. The first has sustained Catholic opposition to intellectual interests in girls and accounts for the enormous interest of Catholic women autobiographers in their reasoning in girlhood and maturity; the second has supported opposition to higher education and careers for women; the third has fed interference by fathers in the spirituality and inner life of young girls. A number of incidents in the autobiographies concerning fathers may startle readers from a different background, as when Bernhardt's father, who never married her mother, swept in from the Orient and installed Sarah in Catholic surroundings. Noël's father controlled her preparation for her first confession and presumed to rule on what her predominant vice was. Beauvoir's father, though an unbeliever, had begun life as a Catholic, and he attempted to control her opinions on ethical issues. Aquinas's theology of womanhood does much to unravel the knot of inexplicability retraced in chapter 2.

Ironically, the young Jesuit who pinned Brave Bird against the blackboard directed her not to act without reason. She had acted for a reason he neither recognized nor asked about, namely, that she wanted to see Native American students treated with respect.

Now that women are educated and can read the Gospels, Aquinas's notion that women are not rational and cannot make ethical decisions unguided seems peculiar, but it still commands compliance among Catholics. The conflicted manner of some autobiographers, pointed out in chapter 1, may be partly explained by Aquinas's reservation of intellectual operation and wisdom to the Catholic Man. For if at any time a Catholic girl heard or held beliefs that Woman is domestic and not intellectual, and for her lack of judgment must be subject to Man, she might later find difficulty in writing not so much in a rational manner as in a manner that revealed her rationality. To do so might be equivalent to admitting that she was less than a true Woman, and was a spiritual failure. Yet if she avoided writing rationally, she would be accepting definitions of herself as subhuman, and in that way disappointing her Creator, who has conferred on her his image as intellectual.

Aquinas does not hesitate to define *man* as "rational animal" without adding "and woman's helpmeet" (or helpmate, depending on the translation), whereas he defines *woman* as "man's helpmeet" without having first mentioned her genus: "rational animal." If a woman is defined as only "man's helpmate," then she can assist him only in reproduction. If she is defined as only "man's helpmeet," then she should limit herself to assisting men to meet the challenges of their lives. Perhaps preachers who repeat such definitions are aware that they are excusing men from helping women meet the challenges of women's lives, but these same preachers are less likely to be aware that the definition cancels a woman's obligation to meet the challenges of her own life. This call for a living death could by itself cause the dread of becoming women Catholic girls often feel, and could cause, in the rare total believer, the abdication of all responsibility.

Aquinas's fallacy here may be only that he is taking the relational definition for an analytic one, and failing to list all Woman's components, or Man's, for that matter. Some small fallacies, however, have large consequences. Underlying all the mistakes reported of local authorities in chapter 2 may be the one omission: that girls too are "rational animals," *rational*—in need of education—and *animals*—in need of a normal physical life.

Most of the catechisms and prayerbooks cited in this study seem to have been written for children, with resulting simplifications and exclusions of subject matter. A more authoritative catechism can also inform conclusions about Catholic gender belief. The *Catechism of the Council of Trent for Parish Priests: Issued by Order of Pope Pius V* was written to defend "the faithful" against Protestantism. It transformed Catholicism and remained the source of all modern Catholic catechisms, at least until 1992. Completed in July 1566, it was first translated into English in 1687 and has been retranslated a number of times.[21] A look at the Catechism of Trent is therefore necessary to ascertain the beliefs of the clergymen who taught all the Catholics referred to in the set of autobiographies being discussed here.

In explaining the sacrament of matrimony, this catechism distributes duties to husband and wife. A husband has three obligations: "to treat his wife generously and honorably" because she was created to be his companion and to obey him, to be "constantly occupied in some honest pursuit with a view to provide necessaries for the support of his family and to avoid idleness, the root of almost every vice," and "to keep all his family in order, to correct their morals, and see that they faithfully discharge their duties."[22]

Wives must, first, be "subject to their husbands" and not adorn themselves externally; second, "train their children in the practice of virtue and . . . pay particular attention to their domestic concerns. . . . The wife should love to remain at home, unless compelled by necessity to go out; and she should never presume to leave home without her husband's consent"; and, third, "next to God they are to love their husbands, to esteem them above all others, yielding to them in all things not inconsistent with Christian piety, a willing and ready obedience."[23] Later, in treating the fourth commandment, the catechism states that both parents "are obliged to bring up their children in the knowledge and practice of religion, and to give them the best rules for the regulation of their lives. . . . The priest, therefore, should admonish parents to be to their children guides in the virtues of justice, chastity, modesty and holiness."[24]

Finally, at the end of its discussion of the fourth commandment, the Catechism of Trent asks the parish priest to warn the parents of certain too frequent transgressions, especially excessive severity. "In the first place, they are not by words or actions to exercise too much harshness towards their children. . . . For there is danger that the spirit of the child may be broken, and he become abject and fearful of everything. Hence [the pastor] should require parents to avoid too much severity and to choose rather to correct their children than to revenge themselves upon them."[25] These brief but powerful rules may explain why the girls became upset with their fathers for rudeness to their mothers or for not providing a decent income for the family. Yet the girls would become upset when their mothers were too obedient and deferent to their husbands, a distress the Catechism of Trent does not explain.

Jouhandeau's father treated his wife with some respect by attempting to persuade her to go to Russia with him, but he criticized her to Elise because of her figure, her way of dressing, her peasant customs, and her narrow interests. " 'Her pleasure is limited to polishing her ugly furniture from morning to night, and to questioning her neighbors and passersby from the window,' he said."[26] Ironically, his wife's interests are just what one would expect of a good Catholic woman who never leaves the house. On the one hand, the father as the mother's spiritual director had the right to judge her; on the other, he did not judge her by the same rules that gave him his power. Moreover, he did not have the right to undermine Elise's respect for her mother. Tangled behavior of this type comes, ultimately, from contradictions among Catholic rules about women.

We see in the admonitions of the Catechism of Trent that both parents were responsible for the moral education of the children. Yet all the father is really required to do is provide financial support and be faithful to his wife, neither of which relates personally and directly to the children. The catechism imposes the father's duty of moral governance more on the wife than on him, for if the wife trains the children in virtue he will not have to correct them. Only those fathers who depart from these few requirements are much resented by the autobiographers.

In contrast, many mothers are criticized by these autobiographers, not only because their contact with the children was more extensive, but, more important, because their duty, according to the Council of Trent, was not to love, but to train their children in virtue and to model for their daughters the kind of woman that admires and obeys her husband, and perhaps offers him nothing else. The children naturally looked to their mothers for love, and were chilled and troubled by the refusals they met.

The formal restrictions put on these mothers by the catechism—for example, to stay at home unless they had the husband's permission to leave the house—were unusual in the West except where Moslem influence was felt, and, by the twentieth century in urban settings and in certain countries, they had become socially abnormal. In addition to requirements that made the mothers seem eccentric, the Church expected them to model an out-of-date style of love for their husbands and be more subservient, less sexual, less companionable, less open to other social relationships, and more tolerant of adultery and abuse than their peers outside the Church. Sadly, the most Catholic of the mothers remembered in the autobiographies hurt and exasperated their daughters—Chacel, León, and Beauvoir—by modeling a marital love deficient in friendship, spontaneity, social contact, supportiveness, and warmth, and which the father spurned with impunity.

Finally, the relative moderation of the beatings given the girls is explained by the Catechism of Trent. That is to say, none of these cases involve broken bones or internal damage, as often happens in secular life. Nevertheless, familial beatings themselves are accepted by the catechism, as by canon law before the 1960s.

Fortunately, canon law has been rewritten, and the life of women in the Catholic Church has improved. But in the Catholic Church warped opinions are difficult to leave behind. The Catechism of Trent, for example, was translated into English by two Dominican priests for a 1934 edition that was reprinted eleven times by 1949 (the edition cited here). This history of the Catechism of Trent is given in part in the translators' introduction, in part on the reverse of the title page, and it shows how the Church has been teaching the same beliefs on marriage for four centuries, a period in which, among other changes, psychology was transformed from a philosophy to a branch of medicine. Certainly every woman autobiographer discussed here heard sermons based on this catechism, not only because of its reprintings but also because of the sermon program following the translators' introduction.

This program of sermons distributed the doctrines given in the catechism over the church year so that all topics would be covered annually.[27] No less a churchman than Cardinal Newman (1801–1890) recalls, "The Catechism of the Council of Trent was drawn up for the express purpose of providing preachers with subjects for their sermons; and, as my whole work [the *Apologia*] has been a defense of myself, I may here say that I rarely preach a sermon but I go to this beautiful and complete Catechism to get both my matter and my doctrine."[28] Possibly many priests have followed this plan, yet the Catechism of Trent has not been mentioned in more than one or two of the many thousand Catholic sermons I have heard.

Whether local priests actually followed the sermon calendar in the Catechism of Trent, one can consult a plethora of other clerical instructions. A useful example is *The Destiny of Modern Woman in the Light of Papal Teaching*, by William B. Faherty, S. J., which summarizes the teachings of the popes between 1900 and 1950. Before the issue of abortion drew papal intervention, through the agency of Catholic clergy, into our political process in the United States, I used sometimes to ask Catholic laypeople about the influence of the pope in the United States, and they generally thought the pope had very little if any influence on their lives. I agreed at the time, but now I realize he has more effect than any priest or bishop through his directives and instructions to the clergy under his rule. After the pope gathers opinions from clerics in whom he has particular confidence, he decides on a policy, informs bishops, seminary professors, and local priests, and asks them to teach it. Monks, nuns, and parents hear it at Mass and read it in Catholic newspapers and magazines, books, pamphlets, and devotional manuals. In their turn, as they are asked to do, they teach it to children. When these children grow up, some of them write autobiographies about their experiences with these teachings, though they may be unaware of the route by which the teachings reached them.

The popes who directed Church policy on women during the period covered by Faherty were Leo XIII (reigned 1878–1903, during the girlhoods of Benoist, Colette, Delarue-Mardrus, Norris, Noël, Wolff, Dussane, Jouhandeau, Mellish, Carroll, and Chacel), Pius X (1903–1914, during the girlhoods of Wolff, Dussane, Jouhandeau, Mellish, Carroll, Chacel, León, Beauvoir, and McCarthy), Benedict XV (1914–1922, during the girlhoods of Chacel, León, Beauvoir, McCarthy, and Mullen), and Pius XI (1922–1939, during the girlhoods of Beauvoir, McCarthy, Mullen, Matute, and Asquerino). Father Faherty's book does not examine in detail the teachings of Pius XII (1939–1958, during the girlhoods of Janés, Pillay, Wong, Rose, Fontenot, Conway, and during the early childhood of Brave Bird), on the ground that this pope did not greatly change the teaching of his predecessors. However, one can see the greater reach of his influence in the printing of his speech on women's domestic destiny in *Vital Speeches* in the United States, which enabled him to reach an audience that was not as accessible to earlier popes.[29] Faherty's book does not cover popes reigning during the infancy of Adam, Bernhardt, Farrell, Repplier, and Schoffen, all grown before Leo XIII was elected, nor during that of Menchú, born after Pius XII died, but the popes he discusses are relevant to twenty-four of the thirty lives. For earlier popes, no important differences would be found, unless it would be the absence of that determining influence on twentieth-century papal policy on women: recent popes have classified feminism as communist, and opposed it as such. In most earlier periods theologians nevertheless opposed the equality of women to men in this life.

Leo XIII never mentioned women's suffrage, though it was widely discussed during his reign. However, his condemnations of what he took to be four feminist ideas on women were repeated by later popes, namely, "that wives should not be subject to their husbands, that divorce would improve women's status, that women should be expected to do the same work as men, and that a low standard of morality should be allowed to women."[30] The ways in which the pope's ideas were out-of-date are fairly obvious. He did not realize that wives like Mrs. Schoffen had to be guided only because of their lack of education, that women who can support themselves do not need to remain with abusive, irresponsible husbands as Conway's mother had to do, that homemakers working exclusively inside the house are much more vulnerable to illness than women working both inside and outside the family circle, that the standard of morality recommended by feminists is not necessarily low.

Pius X based his policy on Woman on a relational definition of her nature. "After creating man, God created woman and determined her mission, namely that of being man's companion, helpmate and consolation. It is a mistake, therefore, to maintain that woman's rights are the same as man's. . . . Woman, created as man's companion, must so remain—under the power of love and affection but always under his power."[31] Pius X cannot have had any idea what an experience of being always under someone's power, even power accompanied by love, could do to a woman's soul. However, he conceded that women were going to participate in public life, even if the popes urged them not to, for he attempted to channel the energies of women into activities that he thought would help the Church and not compete with men, including "works of charity on behalf of the sick, the suffering and children; the fight against divorce, immoral literature, improper dress, and dangerous entertainment; the education of youth and the religious development of girls and young women . . . social work . . . against white slavery."[32] Pius X used to write letters to one Catholic woman's organization after another urging them to maintain and revitalize religious principles among Catholic women and in society as well. At the time, his calls for service from women were exciting and new, and Catholic women who had the opportunity responded to them. Beauvoir's mother, guided by the chaplain of the Sodality of Christian Mothers, did her best to prevent Simone and Hélène from reading immoral literature, wearing attractive clothes, and attending dangerous plays unchaperoned, and she devoted time and attention to their religious development.

Benedict XV praised and more or less followed *The Woman Question* (*Die Frauenfrage*, 1895), by Augustine Roessler, a Redemptorist professor of theology. Faherty comments on this choice of theologians as follows: "Though Benedict XV was neither writing to the whole Church nor presenting an opinion on faith or morals, he could hardly have used more definitive language in speaking of *Die Frauenfrage* of Father Augustine Roessler. He described it as 'a book on social affairs for those with an intelligent interest in the subject in which they might safely and thoroughly and clearly discover what they should think of the social position of women according to the laws of the Catholic religion.' "[33] Faherty notes a flaw in Roessler, namely, that he does not recognize the success of practical reforms in English-speaking countries.[34] Roessler was not an innovator himself; he simply gathered Catholic teachings and applied the opinions of earlier theologians, whether theological or social in origin, to the issues of the industrial era. Whether because of this or because of the pope's approval, he was invited to write the article "Woman" for the first *Catholic Encyclopedia*, which came out in 1912.[35] Roesslerism probably pleased Benedict XV both because it was not innovative and because it renewed the energy involved in Catholic suppression of women.

Roessler's ideas given in the entry on "Woman" can be summarized as follows:

1. *"Man and woman are equal in that they share equally in the redemption and in their eternal destiny."* (Perhaps the Madams taught Beauvoir this idea, which came from the Fathers, and which she upheld in debates with her father. Incontrovertible to a believer in Scripture, this conviction is of incalculable importance in the resistance of Catholic girls to their femininity training, for it enables them to resist with a good conscience.)

2. *Man naturally and by the will of the Creator has authority, leadership, physical and mental power, determination, and enterprise; woman has dependence, submission, moral influence, contentment, and active charity.* (Norris's parents, educated in monastic schools, were acting on this belief at least fifteen years before Roessler's book.)

3. *Man must head the family.* (One or two male heads of families delegated authority over the children to their wives along with the responsibility

for them, but most did not. Françoise de Beauvoir and McCarthy's Great-Aunt Margaret upheld the status of head of household for their husbands even though the men were nonbelievers.)

4. *Woman's "normal calling [is] to be wife and mother."* (This idea is reflected in the disorientation the Beauvoirs felt when they had to deprive their daughters of a dowry and ask them to prepare to support themselves, in short, not to marry.)

5. *If a woman must work, it must not be at the expense of her family, and therefore, regardless of her intelligence, she should not work as a public official, lawyer, judge, artist, scientist, or professor; she will never equal a man in university study because of the temporary character of her occupational future.* (Chacel's grandmother, the Beauvoirs, and others were upset by the prospect of higher education and significant careers for women. Their reaction may be understandable if Pius IX is taken into consideration. This pope was not discussed by Faherty because he reigned 1846–1878, but these years overlapped the girlhoods of Adam, Bernhardt, Farrell, Repplier, Schoffen, Benoist, and Colette. On one occasion Pius IX argued that French girls should not be given secondary schooling because it was a prerequisite for a college education, which "would make a woman a stumbling block of scandal in the home rather than a shining light of purity.")[36]

6. *If a woman must work, the work must be appropriate, like maid service, factory work if her health and purity are protected, sewing, selling, clerking, secretarial work, teaching in the elementary or secondary schools, nursing and even medicine, if she specializes in women's and children's diseases.* (In symbiosis with custom, this teaching explains why numbers of the girls found mending was important in Catholic girls' schools. Chacel's grandmother, although she herself had never worked, felt justified in her enthusiasm for service occupations for her daughters and granddaughters; Mellish's priest and Latin teacher liked the idea of a woman doctor, but her mother did not. Of all the manifestations of Roesslerism in these autobiographies, perhaps the most precise was made to Delarue-Mardrus. When she chose François Coppée as her mentor in poetry, to which she intended to devote her life, he advised her to take up sewing and home management instead.)[37]

7. *Women should be paid absolutely the same as men if the training required and the work performed are equivalent.* (This policy has no relevance to the girlhood narratives, in which it is never mentioned.)

8. Woman should be educated for an appropriate occupation; therefore, coeducational schools are a mistake. (The autobiographers do not tell us much about their experiences in this regard. Beauvoir mentions that the boys' school had a better course of study than the girls' school did;[38] Repplier and Brave Bird hinted at the longing that can result from segregating the sexes in high school; but none of these writers is much interested in the issue.)

9. Women should not have the vote: "Nature herself, unchangeable, remains as the chief objection to equal political suffrage." (This policy is related to leaving public life to men, as indicated in the feast day verses Repplier quotes, by means of which the nuns told the girls not to run for public office; Norris's mother told her daughters she did not want them to work for suffrage. Both these incidents took place long before Roessler wrote his book, however, which again brings out the traditional character of his ideology.)[39]

Perhaps because Roessler and Benedict XV were so thorough, Pius XI never brought up "the woman question" in any of his thirty encyclicals. He did mention it in speeches and letters. He recommended that if "the modern woman, the feminist" wanted to "be sufficient for herself, open her own path, and not be dependent on the egoism and domination of man," to "find a field for her own proper activity," she should enter the convent.[40] Farrell makes no comment on this advice in her girlhood narrative. Wolff and Carroll did experience a development of their ability and independence through their work in the convent. Wolff was encouraged to excel for the sake, no doubt, of her college. She was so concerned, however, to meet secular standards that—unlike the philosopher Julian of Norwich with her epistemology of hope[41]—she did not open her own path. Without a history of her mature philosophical or literary position, Wolff's autobiography is singularly uninformative. Carroll had already attended Pratt Institute when she entered, and she had already been allowed to set up a home economics department as she judged best. She does not mention any bishop coming around to check on what she taught, though bishops have at times interfered with the independence of groups of nuns. From these three autobiographies one can conclude that a girl may gain independence by entering the convent, but nothing is said about those nuns who lose it; Bernhardt observed such nuns in convent school. This balanced conclusion offers further support for Ruether's majority/minority theory about Christian gender beliefs (that is, subordination preached by the majority; equivalence of women to men by the minority).

Pius XI found that in spite of papal wishes, women were entering politics and the work force in ever increasing numbers; in response, he urged Woman to use her "influence to promote everywhere respect for family life, the care of the Christian education of her children, and the energetic protection of public morality."[42] He continued to repeat Roessler's ideas, often emphasizing woman's differences from man (he was not referring to biology); he seems to have been preoccupied by communist beliefs that women are like men.[43] He insisted that feminism has a Marxist context, though feminism has always been with us. He was also especially concerned about modesty of dress for women.[44] His concern was heard by Françoise de Beauvoir, the Parisian Madams, and the Madams who taught Brave Bird. I taught with a number of nuns in Chicago who, before Vatican II, used to have the girls kneel on the floor to make sure their uniform skirts would touch it. These girls might have said, "I was floored." Pius XI tended to bring down not only hemlines but also the hope of a feminist movement among Catholic women.

Pius XII, on whom Faherty does not give much information, in the 1945 address reprinted in *Vital Speeches* urged Catholic women not to work, but if they were already doing so, to devote their efforts to persuading other working women to return to the home full-time.[45] Of the autobiographers studied here, at least twenty worked outside the home or maintained careers, yet only three or four had mothers who also worked outside the home. The others had to find their way without models.

All twentieth-century popes have taught femininity beliefs and have worked to make sure Catholic women and girls heard or read them. We may wait a long time for a papal treatise on the Catholic Man. One of the communication channels running from the popes to women was a type of priest who wrote for women and led women's discussion groups. Adult Catholic women had been asking for spiritual help pertinent to them. Tired of listening to counsel inspiring and helpful only to men, such as advice to be more humble, Catholic laywomen who made retreats or joined Church organizations asked for spiritual direction they could use. They hungered and thirsted after righteousness and apostolic influence, for a function in the Church that would give as much meaning and value to their days as they expected from a religion that preached and promised the possibility of divine goodness in this life. A priest here or there, perhaps in large urban parishes, was asked to guide these women, especially since their requests surfaced while the popes were fighting both feminism and communism.

Father Peter Ketter, a seminary professor and chaplain of women's study groups, wrote *Christ and Womankind* to satisfy the spiritual aspirations of women, relying on Roessler as a source for ideas on what the Catholic Woman should be and do.[46] His book was published in Düsseldorf in 1935, and copies of the 1937 British edition were distributed in the United States. A translation from the second, enlarged German edition was published in the United States in 1952, and the publisher, one of the more intellectual Catholic companies in the United States, advertised the book as "one of the finest books ever published on the subject of women, their rights, privileges, responsibilities and their fundamental role in the Christian scheme of things."[47] The book probably provided material for many sermons. Ketter's book appeared at about the midpoint of the publication dates of the women's autobiographies studied here, and it represents fairly what devout Catholic women were reading during the whole period.

Ketter uses a number of definitions to delineate what he thought was the essence or nature of woman, so that the woman he imagined himself writing for would know how the Creator would like her to live. The motive of these definitions was persuasive and even pastoral, that is, intended to help a woman save her soul.

Ketter defines Woman's essential nature as "that self-surrender and entire devotedness that finds its most beautiful expression in the '*fiat*' of the Virgin Mary," that is, her acceptance of being the mother of the Divine Priest.[48] This definition is more polite than Tertullian's, but when Ketter says that all women are Mary's, he excludes at least Bernhardt, Colette, Delarue-Mardrus, Jouhandeau, Beauvoir, McCarthy, Pillay, Fontenot, and Brave Bird. None of these women were devoted to only one partner in their lifetime, and, in one sense, Ketter's definition excludes monogamous mothers, like Benoist, since they are not virgins. He is left with only the celibates, and then the definition excludes them because they were not mothers. When all women are defined as Marys, no women but Mary count.

Again, this rhetorically skilled priest writes, "To be permitted to serve, to be a handmaid, so to speak, is the natural craving of every woman."[49] The girls remembered in Catholic women's autobiographies were not craving to be handmaids; they were thinking of fun, of reading, of their friends or brothers and sisters, of their parents and other older relatives, of their future husbands. They could not know, though they might wonder, how Mary spent her time, but they did want to avoid the drudgery and sadness their mothers endured.

As out-of-touch with real women and girls as Ketter seems, he characteristically prefers the singular, *woman,* to *women,* as implying that women are all alike *in essence:* for example, "The soul of woman is by nature . . . particularly susceptible to religion."[50] And again, "The Creator has implanted in the nature of woman the desire to please. But the way in which this desire often overrides all natural feminine modesty and leads to disregard not only of convention but also the moral law, amounts to a relapse into paganism. For it is no longer the individual who looks for attention, but the female creature, the creature of sex, from the fetters of which Christ loosed woman."[51] An illogical switch is made here from the classes *woman* and *feminine people,* for which individuality is claimed, to the class *the female,* of which individuality is denied without explanation. Colette's erotic history was not like Bernhardt's, nor León's like Chacel's, nor was the history of interference with their love life the same for Mullen and Repplier.

An arbitrary association of some human trait like modesty with "femininity" does not really deserve to be called a definition, for although it expresses the definer's concept of an ideal woman, it does not ascertain which, if any of these traits, real women actually have. Similarly, when Ketter uses the phrase "the nature of woman," a claim is being made that women have certain virtues in common because of their gender, a claim that can be invalidated even without studying genetics, whether by recourse to Wittgenstein's concept of the family of resemblances, by observation of diverse women, or by noting the variations among autobiographers in a set like "Catholic women" or "Native American women."

Much of the zany logic in remarks like Ketter's no longer surprises Catholic women. What makes them roll their eyes and sigh as they chat after sermons and conferences is the assumption that women have the option of not being female. Priests have begged women hundreds and thousands of times not to be female, an attitude reflected in Simone de Beauvoir's parents, who were easily offended by any behavior revealing the female in women and who trained their daughters to avoid broadcasting such information. "These prohibitions were aimed particularly at the female species; a real 'lady' ought not to show too much bosom, or wear short skirts, or dye her hair, or have it bobbed, or make up, or sprawl on a divan, or kiss her husband in the underground passages of the Métro: if she transgressed these rules, she was 'not a lady.' Impropriety was not altogether the same as sin, but it drew down upon the offender public obloquy that was infinitely worse than ridicule."[52] Femininity is what was approved.

Ketter, after repeating that "the nature of woman is more deeply rooted in love than in sober understanding," a contrast that carries a delayed poison, somewhat incredibly claims, "it is not always sufficiently realized that the sex difference is as marked in the soul as in the body; indeed, it is more so."[53] This remark assumes an inborn difference in male and female souls, while contradicting absolutely a number of earlier passages he draws from the Fathers of the Church about the complete equality Christ bestowed on the souls of women. In this passage, Ketter is reviving an old notion, also from the Fathers, that woman was not created in the image of God, an involuted notion Aquinas denies, as I mentioned earlier.[54]

An outsider must wonder why a Christian, which Ketter indisputably was, would attempt to glorify the inequality of women in the Church; however, his argument has a practical intent. Ketter devotes long passages to the proposition that women would be masculine if they "tortured the ear, intended for delicate perceptions," by asking for their rights. His message is that women who try to lead, who refuse to obey, and who throw off modesty will alienate themselves even from their own selves, becoming godless and merely sexual.[55] In other words, they will be atheistic communists.

Not only Ketter, but numbers of priests in various countries produced a spate of books, sermons, pamphlets, prayerbooks, magazine and newspaper columns and articles during the anticommunist period, all explaining the exalted spiritual destiny awaiting the Catholic Woman. As a sample of the resulting local spiritual instruction as it reaches women, I offer this quotation from a Father Catoir writing in 1969 for the *Wyoming Catholic Register,* a paper subscribed to by many Catholic parents in that state. "You want to be a good mother, you love your children and yet something in you is raging, struggling to be free. You come to see that real love is a harsh and dreadful thing; that it brings pain, that it calls for sacrifice, restraint, a losing of one's own life. . . . What is required is a readiness to abandon your own ideas of self-fulfillment for the sake of these human beings entrusted to your care, not in a slavish way but freely and for the sake of love."[56] In view of this trickle-down system of spreading doctrine, the repeated and widespread reappearance of old attitudes on Catholic Womanhood seems inevitable. In Catoir's eloquent clichés we have an association between Woman and Sacrifice, Woman and Suffering that does not appear in the catechism and is not matched by calls to the Catholic Man for sacrifice and suffering, but that is considered and rejected by Adam, Repplier, Chacel, Beauvoir, Janés, and Menchú. Others of the women—Norris and Wong—do not discuss the association, but describe the suffering caused their mothers by the Catholic ideal of motherly sacrifice.

Unlike *Baltimore Number One,* the Paris catechism of 1863 twice suggests that Christ wishes his followers to suffer, and that we should do so willingly, but this *we* is ungendered.[57] Nevertheless, though the catechism itself does not teach that a woman is especially destined to suffer, Catoir is not alone in thinking she is. Ketter, writing in Germany, says as much, and Pemán, writing in Spain, devotes a chapter of his book on Woman to the proposition that while men are meant for pleasure, women are meant for suffering. The main argument he presents for this is that he can more easily imagine women in poses of suffering than in poses of pleasure.

The question raised by the remembered sufferings of Catholic girls as identified in chapter 2 above has been answered. These efforts to interfere with maturation come from teachings of the Fathers on sex and gender, of Aquinas on rationality and gender, of the Catechism of Trent on parental duties and gender, and of popes of the past hundred years on the proper subordination and domesticity of women. Their doctrines have been taught to girls all over Europe and the United States, in Catholic schools, from the pulpit, in Catholic publications, and at home. At this point I should like to examine verbal messages that were actually given the Catholic girls to find out how well local teachings represented the dominant theology of women.

Like the Fathers of the Church, some Catholic adults told girls in their care that they were inherently immoral, not by calling them Eves but by equating them with the devil. Perhaps these adults did not see much distance between Eve and the serpent. Sarah Bernhardt (1844–1923), a much-loved tragic actress, recalls in her autobiography, *Ma double vie* (1907), that as a child she was often told she was "a devil in disguise," a correction that was justifiable according to Tertullian, but seems disproportionate to temper tantrums.[58]

Repplier mentions a retreat preacher who apparently thought girls before the age of puberty could benefit from scoldings like Tertullian's. "The terrors of the Judgment Day were unfurled before our startled eyes with the sympathetic appreciation of a fifteenth-century fresco, and the dead weight of eternity oppressed our infant souls. . . . The third night's sermon reduced Annie Churchill to hysterical sobs; Marie was very white, and Elizabeth looked grave and uncomfortable."[59] Annie Churchill was the goody-goody of the convent, and the other girls were far from being criminal types, though once they stole a few straws from the manger of the Infant Jesus just to be naughty.[60]

Catholic beliefs about obedience in future wives were also conveyed to the girls in words they remembered. For example, at the mission school Brave Bird attended in South Dakota, the Bavarian Madams were concerned about obedience. Whenever the girls paused to rest, doodle, or converse during their scrubbing or potato peeling, "the nun would come up with a dish towel and just slap it across your face, saying, 'You're not supposed to be talking, you're supposed to be working!' "[61] In its insistence on domestic labor and silence, this remark can be taken as applicable to all workers, to those under a specific command to perform a task, or to the role of women as such, but the controlling idea of it is the phrase "supposed to be"; in other words, girls are meant to practice silent domestic work in order to prepare themselves for marriage or for jobs under male supervisors.

The interest of Catholic ecclesiastics in teaching femininity appears everywhere indirectly in the autobiographies; only on occasion is it mentioned directly. When Elise Jouhandeau arrived at convent school for a two-year stay, Sister Lucie, helping her change into her uniform, told her, "We're going to soften your angles! You need it, to refine your femininity." With that, she ordered Elise to say various prayers at dawn, noon, and night, to make herself more tranquil.[62] In this way a mental association was set up between femininity and tranquility or perhaps emotional flatness.

The underlying angelism (denial of bodily life or the value of bodily life) in much Catholic gender training results in some erasure of the physical in Protestantism as well, though lesser guns are trained on Protestant girls. Jouhandeau's mother, Mme. Toulé, exaggerated convent school lessons on purity when she taught them to Elise. Mme. Toulé warned Elise repeatedly that if she left home unmarried she would fall into a life of sexual sin. In addition to the insults and beatings mentioned in chapter 2, Mme. Toulé used exempla against men and diatribes on Elise's sexuality (both rhetorical forms learned from sermons) to keep Elise, once grown, at her mother's side. The mother called Elise's beauty, joy, and grace "sensuous" and "seductive." The staple topic of her oratory was Elise's "wicked personality," so that Elise became more and more afraid of her own sexuality and of her future.[63]

Brave Bird, as I mentioned in chapter 2, was once criticized in religion class as an example of impurity. Sister Bernard listed Mary's faults as including holding hands with a boy and wearing unchaste dresses with skirts that were "too short, too suggestive, shorter than regulations permitted."[64] Sister's speech, too long for Brave Bird to recall word-for-word, is all an indirect quotation, but, as McCarthy said of her memory of priests, this is the way nuns talked and these arguments are the ones they used. Apparently the idea of forbidding these innocent activities was to fight the battle to protect virginity at the perimeter. Perhaps the nuns, to divert the students' attention from the illogicality of imposing purity rules on asexual, neutral behavior, attempted to make obedience the issue around which resistance and debate would swirl.

McCarthy's Madams were eager to be thought modern, and so they exaggerated their lack of prudishness, as she indicates in the episode of her imaginary menarche. Again, McCarthy's panic when she incorrectly assumed she had lost her virginity, tells us that her Catholic education, beginning in a parish school and ending in the Madams' school, had given her no education on sexuality. In her day sex education given by nuns was mostly a matter of warnings and omission. Sexual activity was considered a danger rather than an expression of love, and very little mention was made of the Canticle of Canticles (the Song of Solomon), the principal Scripture praising erotic love. Overall, one may say that many Catholic adults fear the female in girls and would like to suppress it permanently. They expect Catholic girls to express their entire life-force in the forms and customs of femininity.

Numerous Catholic adults have attempted to keep girls away from universities. The nun who scolded María Teresa León at the same time scolded her aunt, though she was not present, for having attended the university, for the nun said, "By that path the devil enters."[65] This warning came from Gregory of Nyssa and told León not to emulate her aunt if she wanted to save her soul.

Similarly, the Madams in Paris warned Mme. de Beauvoir not to allow Simone to attend the Sorbonne. "They had given their lives to combating secular institutions and to them a state school was nothing better than a licensed brothel. In addition, they told my mother that 'the study of philosophy mortally corrupts the soul: after one year at the Sorbonne, I would lose both my faith and my good character.'"[66] The nuns did not mention the issue of gender on this occasion, but it is evident that they did not think Simone really needed to pursue a career. She says that the nuns supported the system of arranged marriages practiced in the families of the girls they taught.

On a more fundamental intellectual level, Mullen's mother, Mrs. Brady, was determined to break Barbara of reading books. " 'You're too much like your father, reading whenever you get the chance. As if it will ever do you any good. That's the trouble—too much like your father. Well, you better change, because if it's the last thing I ever do, I'll knock it out of you if I have to kill you! . . . You don't need to run at all. I'm not going to touch you,' she said. 'But from now on you'll give up your book-reading, and be said and led by me. Come downstairs when you're ready.' "[67] In one sense the message is not orthodox, for Catholic children were to love and obey both their parents. In another sense it is doubly orthodox, in that the daughter should be modeling herself on her mother and not on her father, and she should also not pervert her nature by an interest in the intellectual.

Juliette Lambert Adam (1836–1936), best known as founder of *La nouvelle revue* (1879–1926), recalls that her mother, Olympe Lambert, disapproved of Juliette's being able to judge authors whom Mme. Lambert scarcely knew, and disliked hearing her daughter praised. "If my father spoke of my intelligence, of my beauty, my mother would declare that I was as foolish as [I was] ugly." Mme. Lambert attempted on one occasion to persuade Juliette to stop trying to attract such "extravagant love."[68] These messages seem connected with the mother's fear of rivalry, but her complete opposition to the family's policy in regard to Juliette also reflects her harmony with Catholic teaching on the way a mother should raise her daughter. The Catholic ideal for girls would favor not only a lack of knowledge and judgment, but also a habit of centering on someone else, first the mother and later the husband.

Some of the autobiographers report interference with their preparation for careers they considered appropriate to their ability. Repplier's nuns encouraged the girls to serve men who had noble careers, and Beauvoir describes a kind of guerrilla warfare her parents kept up to prevent her from studying.[69]

Rosa Chacel's account of opposition to higher careers for women manifests excellent recall for the speech of traditional Catholics. Her maternal grandmother, Julia, wanted very much to persuade Rosa that she should not prepare for a higher profession. Julia had trained most of her daughters to a humble state. Clemencia gave piano lessons, Teresina taught a few neighbor children the basics, and Julieta had given up her art and her soul when she married a colonel—Rosa saw her as a suicide—to play the kind of subservient role the grandmother wanted. Rosa felt reinforced in her evaluation of her aunts when one of her uncles told her Julia had made idiots of her daughters, and Julieta was the worst, because she had so much potential.[70]

Julia was persistent and introduced a deceptive discourse into Rosa's life with the intention of bringing her to the same pass as her aunts. "My grandmother intensified her discourses on how *the woman* needed economic independence, on how the convenient thing is to exercise a profession that has a future, that gives security in life."[71] Rosa must have noticed the disparity between the two clauses modifying *profession* in this utterance, and she was subjected to more of these deceptive messages.

Her grandmother said that if *the woman* had a worthy career and economic emancipation, she would not have to be a slave or to depend on anyone. Rosa had mentioned studying medicine; Julia said that with a briefer program of study, Rosa would soon be able to buy clothes for herself, an appeal the Madams would have been appalled by. In an even worse insult, Julia argued that "with important degree programs *the woman* had of course to face the struggle for positions. A diploma would not be enough; to obtain an outstanding place, *the woman* would have to pay, etc."[72]

After Rosa's mother promised her that she could enroll in art school, Julia used the information as a manipulative device or lever. "One more thread in the spiderweb, one more stroke of the shuttle, recurrent, insistent, sometimes abrupt, other times an oblique, soft insinuation. The impracticality of an artistic career. If you are not a genius, as you know, you end a bohemian. And a woman, how can a woman open a path for herself? No one takes a woman seriously as an artist. . . . The theme sprouted at any moment; at the table, in conversations mixed with domestic doings, while one sewed or ironed; while one strung green beans or sorted lentils." Julia's theme flowed as she made and poured mayonnaise. "Triumphs, successes, *a woman?!*"[73]

The drive toward mediocrity expressed by Julia, the Beauvoirs, and Repplier's nuns reveals a dread of higher careers for middle-class females. Perhaps this fear covered another, that desirable men might not want to marry women who could equal them in conversation and productivity. Such a fear may also underlie efforts to eradicate sarcasm, irony, and wit in girls, a campaign that Chacel's otherwise encouraging mother carried out against her.[74] She might have thought wit would "give away" the presence of intelligence in her daughter. These nested terrors might have caused modern Catholics to accept the traditional and official opposition of the clergy to a superior education for girls. Because of fear, they taught girls to leave to men the enjoyment of sexuality, study, and careers involving intelligence. Girls were to content themselves with femininity—that is to say, mothering and mending.

The second most frequent religious theme in this set of autobiographies is bigotry. Warnings against Protestants or communists as godless and to be avoided have a connection with Catholic gender training in that Protestants and communists had a concept of women, their possibilities, and their proper role and treatment that contrasted to the Catholic concept. The clergy, with those laypeople who were close to them, at one time tried to fight off "non-Catholic" influence by keeping Catholic girls among Catholics.

McCarthy's Minneapolis grandmother talked frequently about Protestants, a habit McCarthy the autobiographer deplores. She reports that Grandmother McCarthy engaged in three topics of conversation: Protestants, whom she wanted to be converted; Protestantism, which she wanted to be extinguished; and the fourth commandment, which she wanted her grandchildren to obey. McCarthy puts it sardonically. " 'Honor thy father and thy mother,' a commandment she was no longer called upon to practice, was the one most frequently on her lips."[75] Somewhat inconsistently, Grandmother McCarthy found it convenient to demand that the children obey their Protestant Great-Uncle Myers Shriver as a way to keep them away from their mother's Protestant father, Harold Preston.

A very clear statement of parental opposition to outside influence comes from Beauvoir. When she began to read modern novels, some by quite conservative Catholics like Paul Claudel and François Mauriac, her parents disapproved.

> For months I kept myself going with books. . . . My parents cast black looks upon them. My mother divided books into two categories: serious works and novels; she considered the latter to be an amusement which, if not sinful, was at least frivolous, and blamed me for wasting on Mauriac, Radiguet, Giraudoux, Larbaud, and Proust time which would have been better employed studying the geography of Baluchistan, the life of the Princess of Lamballe, the habits of eels, *the soul of Woman,* or the Secret of the Pyramids. My father, having cast a rapid eye over my favourite authors, pronounced them to be pretentious, over-subtle, queer, decadent, and immoral: he was indignant with Jacques [her cousin] for having lent me, among other works, Marcel Arland's *Etienne.* My parents no longer had any way of censoring the books I read: but they often made explosive scenes about them.[76] (italics added)

One begins to wonder if the reason the Beauvoirs disapproved of the books Simone read was that they were intelligent books, examples of spiritual autonomy, that even the Catholic works she liked were not ostentatiously supportive of the Catholic and royalist set, whereas a book on the Princess of Lamballe would have to discuss Marie Antoinette. They sensed that her reading was somehow helping Simone cut the umbilical cord. Bigotry was a part of the gender training of girls in that it prevented their learning whether gender rules were identical in all religious and cultural groups.

The children or local representatives of the Church—that is, parents, teachers, and priests functioning in their ecclesiastical roles—may have misquoted or misinterpreted or even willfully distorted official Catholic teaching on the subject of Woman, as they often did the teaching on the subject of sin, though it seems less likely. But the possibility of distortion makes the printed words of theologians and popes of the period more important. By examining them, we can see that most of the Catholic adults remembered in these books were insisting on official Catholic femininity beliefs. The presupposition of immorality in girls, prohibitions against study, refusals to send them to good schools, prevention of career preparation, purity indoctrination, and subordination training were all considered orthodox attitudes, that is, parents had been taught them by the clerical, authoritative Church.

Some local authorities, however, did deviate from the teachings of the official Church. Bernhardt's Aunt Fauré should not have referred to Sarah's naughtiness as demonic possession. Noël's father was embroidering Catholic ethics when he equated fiction with lying. Repplier's disciplinarian, Mme. Bouron, was wrong to talk as if Catholic ethics includes rules against an asexual love poem or against admiring the beauty of another human being. Dussane's headmistress should not have tried to keep her from doing her best by equating excellence with pride.[77] Mullen's mother, as a mentor in the life of virtue, was wrong to oppose her daughter's love for her father, though she was within her rights as a Catholic mother to discourage Barbara from reading books. Pillay's stepfather was not being a good Catholic father when he ordered her to submit to him sexually or when he bartered her sexual submission to the landlord for rent. Jouhandeau's mother could not justify her telling her children that if they left home they would fall into sin.

But if the false, manipulative, and unjust arguments of certain parents are set aside, many messages remain which, though harmful to the girls, are approved teachings of the Catholic Church. When the girls were reproached for their tendencies to immorality, even when they were not conscious of any immoral desires, the parents, priests, and nuns involved were speaking within Catholic tradition, with its belief that Eve made all her female descendants seducers. When the girls were forbidden to study seriously or kept away from good schools or discouraged from occupational choices appropriate to their intelligence, the parents involved were entirely in tune with the popes and the clergy. When the spiritual autonomy of the girls was interfered with just because it was not under authority, that was correct upbringing for girls, according to the official Catholic position. Punishment of independent judgment or of acting on one's conscience, though not correct for all Catholics, was considered correct for Catholic girls, since the Catholic Woman's duty is submission to the rational direction given by a male authority figure or his female delegate.

Yet a Catholic could argue (and I do) against any correction as wrong, of tendencies that are in reality innocent or neutral: for example, self-government when carried out ethically, requests for information on sex, a love of outdoor play, reading, friendship, or storytelling. Though such reprimands accord with the official teaching on gender and can be presented as socialization, this teaching is not related to ethics and should not be described as carrying moral force, for by so doing, ethical rules are discredited. In addition, necessary components of human personality are suppressed, harming the mental and physical health of both individuals and society. Catholics may believe that certain traits are not feminine but are not justified in calling them immoral or wrong.

Those who attempted to extirpate these inclinations seem to have been motivated both by loyalty to Rome and by concern for the girl's future role as a woman. They seemed to think that fidelity to one husband would be encouraged if the wife lacked interest in sex, that her devotion to the care of one household would be enhanced if she refrained from learning about the outside world, and that her determination to keep her children Catholic would be protected if she discovered nothing about other churches or philosophies. The worst messages Catholic adults gave girls described them as evil, and some predicted that they would never be any better. The use of fixed answers, illogical reasoning, manipulative motivation, and dishonest concepts also shows a lack of respect for the child being addressed. Finally, the bigoted remarks that imprinted themselves on the memories of a number of the children, even though they were intended to maintain institutional integrity, gave a poor example of charity.

Because of the Catholic definition of *Woman,* and because the hierarchy so insists on it, a Catholic woman has difficulty fulfilling the natural desire of an autobiographer to tell and interpret her experience and her life. In Catholic women writing in the twentieth century, this desire has been interfered with, not only by old hurts and angers, not only by fear of criticizing the Church, but also by definitions and doctrines that discourage women from living in ways that could result in an authentic life-history.

This chapter has examined the official teaching of the Catholic Church on the nature of Woman, which amounts to a set of rules for women, rules derived from a theology of subordination. These rules have been imposed on girls by local authorities in two spirits: one of conformity to official teachings; the other of self-service and dishonesty or error. The Catholic Church is not responsible for the latter way of acting, but the validity of a theology of subordination is called into question by its vulnerability to abuse.

chapter four

The Message
of Equivalence

*T*HE attitude of the official or majority Church toward
women and girls may shock or surprise, and its repudia-
tion by even very young girls (described in chapter 5) may also surprise. In this
chapter I hope to explain an array of causes for their resistance. Aristotle held
that events have multiple causes: material, formal, final, and efficient. In more
modern terms, I should say that a person decides or acts at the last moment in
a process of assessing options and correlating data about the past, present, and
future. Though the girls we are thinking about have only a few years to remember, they are nevertheless able to consider conflicting influences, mutually exclusive demands, and contrasting hopes. Most of the girls resolve these discords
in favor of self-respect and love for the Creator—that is, the theology of the
equivalence of women to men.

An array of causes also explains why readers would not expect girls to resist
gender training. Catholics in the United States generally say that the character
of children is formed by the age of six. With girls, Catholic gender training
may be assumed to "take" early, insofar as it depends on the imitation of one's
mother. Then, too, some children are devout, as Beauvoir, Chacel, and Fontenot were. Chacel reports that she listened "with passion" when her mother

taught her Christian doctrine and sacred history.[1] When Beauvoir was seven or eight, she would read a chapter of the *Imitation of Christ* every morning and often raise her soul to God during the day; even in early adolescence, she remembers that "All nature spoke to me of God's presence."[2] As a girl, Fontenot, moved by the death of her older sister, would go out to the backyard and "sing praises to the Lord, and I would cry while I made songs and sang them to God." She recalls that "instead of fussing and fighting, I would give in to everyone."[3] Such piety could be expected to increase acceptance of secondary beliefs attached to the religion. Moreover, as shown in chapter 3, though the gender beliefs of the Church are contradictory and are not universally held or taught, still the idea of a limited Catholic woman has become dominant. In spite of all these circumstances, more of the Catholic girls were upset by their gender training than otherwise, and the majority placed countermoves against it.

The most salient cause of aversion to femininity demands at the time of girlhood was contact with at least one individual who did not share the dominant belief that the essence of "Woman" is or should be subordination to men. Adam was early summoned by her family to a higher plane than that. When her maternal grandmother kidnapped her from her more orthodox mother, the purpose was to raise Juliette for the life of a Parisian "savante."[4] Some of León's relatives and Pardo Bazán urged her to learn and to write.[5] Beauvoir's cousin Jacques and her friends at the Sorbonne discussed forbidden books and ideas with her.[6] Headmistress Mme. MacIllvra predicted McCarthy's career as a novelist.[7] These adults and others recognized that a girl might be intelligent and have whatever other qualities a professional life might require. Although these encouraging adults were sometimes minor characters in a predominantly traditional cast, they did open an escape for the girls by expecting them to be suns rather than planets.

A related influence was contact with someone who verbally undermined the Church, like Adam's father, Dussane's mother, Beauvoir's father, and Colette's mother.[8] Mr. Schoffen used to speak of "the teachings and superstitious practices of the church as 'priest foolishness.' "[9] In these cases, the girl did not always give complete credence to the negative voice, as Beauvoir reports of her reaction. "My father's individualism and pagan ethical standards were in complete contrast to the rigidly moral conventionalism of my mother's teaching. This imbalance, which made my life a kind of endless disputation, is the main reason why I became an intellectual."[10] Beauvoir took aspects of her belief system from each parent. In contrast to Beauvoir's situation, in Chacel's family a range of religious positions co-existed without debate—Masonry, rationalistic Catholicism, a devout and unquestioning faith (but wounded by *beatos*), and a modern or instructed faith. Moreover, Chacel's parents, who had taught her her religion, had not pressured her to take one attitude or another toward it.[11] As a result she assumed she could choose what was meaningful for her and still be acceptable. She felt free to reject Catholic femininity when it was demanded of her; she was in doubt of the outcome but not of the merit of her choice.

With some of the girls, an important force in their resistance was a drive arising from heredity or from identification in early childhood with a parental trait opposed to Catholic femininity. Bernhardt's theatricality, McCarthy's desire to resemble her highly verbal father, or Janés's longing for the artistic life of Barcelona dated from infancy and formed a more fundamental layer of personality than Catholic instruction did. A number of the girls wanted to develop their early inclinations, preferring them to the uniform femininity preached by the Church. In cases where such individual tendencies were opposed by feminizers, the result was usually a girl who consistently, valiantly, and successfully defended her freedom to live as a more complete human. Even the sad Noël, too stricken to make a valiant defense, did not allow all her poetic side to be burned away.

Paradoxically, when the girls rebelled against a uniform style of femininity they were obeying other, more central teachings of the same Church—for example, teachings that every Christian must practice courage and justice. When the girls came under attack, if they recognized the degree of danger they were in (as Benoist did not) and if they did not face overwhelming force (as Jouhandeau did), they refused to surrender. Somewhat ironically, perhaps the most frequent, if quiet, reinforcement of their tenacity about their own growth came in this way from early Catholic education. One of the underlying ideas taught in Catholic homes and schools is that women since Christ's redemption have the same opportunity for grace and eternal bliss as men. Even Roessler was careful to acknowledge this belief before he listed rules against its fulfillment in this world. None of the autobiographers includes passages on how she wanted to imitate the Mother of God; none of them mentions a prominent Catholic symbol of sacrificial love, the pelican that pierced his breast to be able to nurse his young on his blood, but some do recall the belief that girls are as much members of the communion of saints and the priesthood of the faithful as boys are. McCarthy mentions how her mother, an enthusiastic convert to Catholicism, used the religion as a gift to the children without distinction between Mary and her brothers. "Everything in our home life conspired to fix in our minds the idea that we were very precious little persons, precious to our parents and to God, too, Who was listening to us with loving attention every night when we said our prayers."[12] How could a person precious to God think she should submit, later on, to human scorn?

Beauvoir also speaks of her mother's having taught her that heaven's attention was focused on her as an individual without regard to her gender. "As soon as I could walk, Mama had taken me to church: she had shown me, in wax, in plaster, and painted on the walls, portraits of the Child Jesus, of God the Father, of the Virgin, and of the angels, one of which, like Louise [her nurse], was assigned exclusively to my service. My heaven was constellated with a myriad benevolent eyes." This beautiful figure of speech expresses the confidence the girls took from these teachings. Mme. de Beauvoir did not offer her lesson on her daughter's religious situation entirely of her own accord, but as a result of her membership in the Confraternity of Christian Mothers.[13] Mrs. McCarthy was also a member of a sodality of the Ladies of the Sacred Heart; in other words, these mothers were trained by Jesuit chaplains to convince their daughters of their spiritual value. When dealing with preschool girls, the dominant group in the Church believes in the theology of equivalence.

Even without Jesuit aid, nuns who want to help children develop sufficient self-respect to make moral choices and in this way prepare for their first communion often tell them God loves each one of them as if that child were the only one he had ever created. The parish priest, too, promotes individual self-respect when he tells the people that Christ would have died for any one of them, even if that were the only person that existed, a notion often brought into a Catholic religious service or devotion called the Stations of the Cross.

The belief that the souls of women and girls are the same as the souls of men and boys has been everywhere preached in modern times and even gloried in as one of the superiorities of Christianity over other religious and cultural systems. Catholic girls and women are very much aware of their equality with boys and men at the baptismal font, altar rail, confessional grill, and deathbed. They know that all will be judged by God on the issue of their care for those in need; Christ's story about this matter does not distinguish gender. As a result, and most relevant to autobiography, the Catholic path of spiritual development—good actions and habits, together with prayer and the love of God—is theoretically as open to women as to men.

Certain readings from Genesis and the Gospels, particularly the creation narrative and the parable of the talents, tend to promote self-development, to free people from inhibitions about maturation of their faculties. Reflection on the creation story, which is read and preached frequently in the Catholic Church, may give children the idea that the Creator would not have given them a mind and a body if he did not want them to be used, and used to the best advantage. Similarly, Christ told a rather threatening parable on not burying one's talents but investing them to make them grow. Most of the Catholic women I have asked about this parable have taken the word *talent* as applying both to the money of the time and to their personal talents, so that other interpretations come as a surprise to them. Christ's personal treatment of women, as reported in the Gospels, also builds up in girls and women a deep-seated expectation of similar treatment from his male followers.

But Catholic socialization of women, as mentioned in the Introduction, has been flawed by a fundamental contradiction. After first teaching girls and women to take their individual lives seriously, to develop their moral and spiritual characters to the highest degree possible to humans, and to defy social convention when it differs from Christ's teaching, the official Church and its representatives on the parish level will at one time or another ask the same women and girls to conform to conventions of femininity that make a mockery of these noble ideals. The contradiction probably explains much of the distaste many orthodox Catholic women and girls feel for Catholic femininity training.

Theology aside, Catholic feminization programs pose an insurmountable practical problem for girls. The girls are facing a lifetime as Catholic women, and they often experience their nature (all the attributes given them genetically or in infancy, realized or potential, stable or changing) as more inclusive than or even antithetical to the definition they are being told they must accept. They had perhaps assumed, for example, that the duties of love and self-fulfillment would not conflict with one another, but as indicated in chapters 2 and 3, prohibitions and penalties in late childhood or adolescence attempt to teach them they are from then on to view love as requiring the renunciation of self-fulfillment.

When this change of tune occurred in the lives being discussed here, the girls usually held firm, at least where their internal convictions were concerned, and I attribute their steadfastness to belief in God's regard for them, no doubt by that time internalized. Because of the early encouragement the Church gives to individuality, later prohibitions interfering with self-development shocked the girls. Their reaction was usually to reject the new and, to them, irrational rules, which appeared to be in jarring disharmony with the religion of spirituality and loving-kindness they had been taught. As girls, all the Catholic autobiographers, not only Noël, felt hurt if significant Catholic figures tried to stop their becoming "original and vigorous personalities."[14] Those who, like Farrell, express no dismay at the Church's demands for self-renunciation also report no such demands. Most of those who do were quite upset at the time and threw them off or disapproved of them, in this way not allowing any implicit message to prepare them for Catholic Womanhood. The imposition of Catholic femininity rules might have seemed like attempts to enlist the girls in a church within a church, a subgroup whose ethics they did not share.

Under pressure, their minds seem to have moved all the way back to "Who made us? God made us." From this first question and answer, a child's mind would not have to be sophisticated to deduce that a loving Creator must desire her life and fruition. In the early years the girls had been repeatedly taught the primary theology of women, more in harmony with Christ's treatment of women, namely, that women are or should be equal to men in the eyes of God; consequently, they could not accept the official gender teaching. To do so would have been disloyal to their Creator, to Christ, and to sacred Scripture. In addition to the scriptural passages Ruether lists, and which I mentioned in the introduction, I will quote four theologians to sketch in the components of the theology that women are equivalent to men. The first theologian is Aelred of Rievaulx, a much-loved Scottish Cistercian abbot of the twelfth century; the second is Luis Pueyo y Abadía, a Spanish Carmelite of the seventeenth; the third is Denis Kenny, an Australian priest publishing in 1967; and the fourth is a California Dominican publishing in 1988, Matthew Fox. Aelred notes in his treatise on spiritual friendship that "as a clearer inspiration to charity and friendship [God] produced the woman from the very substance of the man. How beautiful it is that the second human being was taken from the side of the first, so that nature might teach that human beings are equal and, as it were, collateral, and that there is in human affairs neither a superior nor an inferior, a characteristic of true friendship."[15] Thus he finds in the tale of the first couple a significance quite unlike that found there by Tertullian and other priests between the second and fifth centuries C.E.

Of the same Biblical story, considered archetypal by many Christians, the Spanish Carmelite writes, "What would Eve be, if God in Paradise had believed Adam? All the fault would have been hers, and Adam would have been innocent."[16] In fact, the Fathers of the Church could be understood as having answered the question, "What must Eve be, since we believe Adam?" Unfortunately, this intelligent Spanish priest was not typical of seventeenth-century preachers.

The two twentieth-century theologians (and many other theologians could be quoted) are sensitive to the way the dominant group in the Church had understood sinfulness as sexual and sexuality as sinful. They could have maintained one of the themes of the Bible against these traditional opinions, or they could have learned from modern psychology that sexual repression causes a loss or curtailment of creativity, compassion, and universal charity. Kenny and Fox have undertaken to defend the teaching of Genesis and the Canticle of Canticles (Song of Solomon), that fruitfulness and passionate love are in themselves, unless they are warped by their practitioners, good and even sacred. Kenny writes that "the communication of the self . . . needs to be expressed physically. . . . Sexuality is the ordinary way in which two persons give themselves to each other. The sexual act [like the sacrament of Holy Communion] is both a sign of love and a most important means of intensifying this love."[17] The teachings of Jerome and Augustine would have contained more charity and provided more pastoral assistance, had those authors realized and taught these simple truths.

Fox, assuming the immanence and love of God, and understanding that symbolism is a two-way street—that, for example, in the Canticle of Canticles, the sexual vehicle is not purely metaphorical but is relished for itself, and the religious tenor colors its sexual vehicle with the presence of the divine—has published five deductions:

(1) The Song of Songs praises our sexuality as part of the sacred gift of the Cosmic Christ whom lovers encounter in one another. All too many Christians have been led to believe that Christ is not present in lovemaking;

(2) Every time humans truly make love, truly express their love by the art of sexual lovemaking, the Cosmic Christ is making love;

(3) The living cosmology ushered in by the Cosmic Christ will do more than redeem creativity itself; it will propose creativity as a moral virtue—indeed as *the most important moral virtue of the upcoming civilization*;

(4) The cosmic Christ is the suffering one found in every person and creature who suffers unjustly;

(5) Listen to the Cosmic Christ, to Cosmic Wisdom calling all the children of God together: . . . "Praise one another. Praise the earth. In so doing, you praise me."[18]

In this doctrine, sexual and spiritual love dovetail, creativity is more virtuous than self-abnegation, injustice is worse than disobedience, and appreciation is better than insult.

Elements of the primary theology of women originating in Scripture and brought forward by all too few theologians include the principles that women are loved by God and have been created equal to men and, moreover, that women should be encouraged to learn and to be creative, to improve morally, and to enjoy sex as a form of love—exactly the things men are encouraged to do.

Fortunately for the girls, some local Catholic authority figures held to this theology, preferring beliefs closer to those of Christ, that is, orthodox by a higher standard than that of the Church Fathers. Encouraging words to the girls cluster in two areas: moral improvability and intellectual ability. No doubt this distribution reflects what the adults considered the greatest dangers to the girls, namely, corruption of their goodness and interference with their learning. Such teachers of faith evidently either thought Augustine and Jerome were mistaken in their attitude toward women or did not read the Fathers at all. In describing the natural goodness in Colette, her mother called her a jewel, not a devil.

Agnes Repplier's beloved Mme. Rayburn did not hesitate to let Agnes know, after the frightening sermon on hell, that hell was not her destination. "She was not given to caresses, but she laid her hand gently on my black-veiled head. 'Not for you, Agnes,' she said, 'not for you. Don't be fearful, child!' thus undoing in one glad instant the results of an hour's hard preaching, and sending me comforted to bed."[19] This nun knew enough about ten-year-old girls to realize that they are not all headed for a life of sin and need not be loaded with dread and undeserved guilt.

Simone de Beauvoir had a Latin teacher, Abbé Trécourt, who sided with her when one of the Madams accused her of cheating in his class. This good priest rejected the charge, announcing to the class that he had given Simone the highest mark for the most original translation.[20] His language here avoids uncharitable speech about the nuns and insists on charity to Simone, who had in fact done the literal translation but then copied a literary translation out of humility, as students sometimes do.

Abbé Trécourt again gave the girls the support of his authority against the worse side of the Madams when the end of their schooling approached. He met with each of the graduating girls, asking them not to let their hearts shrivel up as their schoolmistresses had done. He said that the nuns were saints, but it would be better not to follow in their footsteps.[21] Here he did risk uncharitable speech; however, the girls already knew what their schoolmistresses were like. The priest had little choice. If he wanted to undermine the nuns' poor example of charity, he had to ask the girls not to overapply the fourth commandment and the Church's request for respect for one's teachers.

Sister Andrésie, who had the main responsibility for Elise Jouhandeau when she was in convent school, planned to respond to the child's uncertainty and unrest about her future with "a formation that would thwart risk." This nun did not think, like Elise's mother, that Elise was doomed to an immoral life. If the girl acquired good habits, she could direct her own ethical progress. Mlle. Ombelline, a family friend engaged to the Marquis de Montamousse, once called on Jouhandeau at the convent school. Elise went to the parlor, but would not answer any questions, because she thought to converse with such a worldly woman would interfere with her preparation for first communion. As Mlle. Ombelline left the convent parlor that day, she had a tactful message for Elise, that "virtue is personal, but charity does not allow any exceptions."[22] Ombelline did not hesitate to administer moral correction, but this particular correction contained the message that Elise could do better.

Peggy Joan Fontenot quotes her father, who was an oil-rig worker, when he learned she was pregnant at fifteen. "After he had finished crying, he started talking to me. 'I don't want you to get married unless you are sure that is what you want to do. I'll give the baby our name and I'll support you and the baby,' he told me. I know that dad really wanted me to stay home with them, because I was so young."[23] Such kindness came in part from his belief that Peggy was not a bad girl, and would turn out all right, if she could have a better start. All these adults felt that "evil" is not the right judgment to make on female sexuality, that is to say, on females.

Colette tells several anecdotes to show the way in which her mother refused to impose rules on any living being, and especially on Colette, except those against killing and unkindness. By her behavior, Sido taught two rules to her daughter: respect the freedom of every living being, and care amply for any beings who live in your territory.[24] In sum, her message was that only the fifth commandment was important, for other commandments could easily interfere with it. Sido was in this way supportive of Colette both directly and as a model of beneficence.

Juliette Adam found herself able to play an active and prominent role in public life as an adult because her grandparents intended that she should, educated her as well as they were able, and were delighted with her efforts from the beginning. As an autobiographer she took pleasure in portraying forces that had enabled her to develop an exceptionally healthy ego: the first was her grandmother's refusal to let the child's mother train her in the theology of women's inferiority; the second was her grandparents' benevolent and nourishing style of authority. They gave her care, affection, and knowledge, asked only positive actions, provided models of female self-direction in the form of tales about herself and her mother, and presented their requests openly without concealing commands in them. Although her grandmother wanted her to be a monarchist, she praised Juliette's courage in upholding the cause of the workers and taught her that authority has obligations. Submissiveness, subordination, subservience, self-erasure, though consistently taught in the other Church, were never an option for Juliette in the Church she grew up in. Her grandparents and friends persistently rewarded her for self-expression, initiative, and originality.[25]

When Sarah Bernhardt was taken to the convent to be prepared for the sacraments, her first fear of the place (which began with her Catholic aunt's pious but punitive attitude to Sarah) was dissolved by kindness and the way the nuns talked with her about the small garden each child was allowed to have. The mother superior, Mother St. Sophie, had been informed of her temper and took the time to preach to her gently when she needed it, to read to her or tell her some instructive story. Mother Superior's answer to inner tumult was a rational answer. One day Sarah, who was over ten, saved a four-year-old from drowning. While Sarah was still in bed recovering she overheard the Mother Superior telling the doctor, "This child, Doctor, is the best we have here. She will be perfect when she has received the Holy Chrism" at confirmation.[26] This judgment would be memorable for anyone, but the more so by contrast with the messages Sarah had heard from her Aunt Fauré.

When Sarah did not get a part in the school play and was disappointed, Mother Superior explained to her that they had thought of her, but she had been too shy when questioned, a much different response from that of McCarthy's nuns. The watchfulness over an individual child, the care lest Sarah feel hurt, recommends this nun as loving and warm, not cold through fear of sexuality, and not anxious to make children suffer for the advancement of their souls. Finally, when Mother St. Sophie allowed a naughty Sarah to refuse to come inside when asked, so that she became chilled and almost died, the abbess kept saying, "I left her too long! . . . This is my fault! It's my fault!"[27] The humility, benevolence, and informative attitude of Mother St. Sophie far outweighed the religious training her Catholic aunt had given Sarah, not only because Sarah spent more time at the convent than with her aunt, but also because the aunt had just a single string to her fiddle. The nun could and did speak to the wealth of traits in the child, and not simply to her mischief or her temper.

Certain Catholic authority figures wanted the girls to study and to do well in school. Adam's grandparents and father, for example, tutored her and wanted very much to see her succeed. Although the level of schooling for Jouhandeau was much lower, the chaplain at her convent school expended some ingenuity to convince her that she ought to learn to write and spell French correctly. Colette reports that her father thought well of her power of criticism, and he used to discuss poetry with her rather than with her brothers. Though he flew into a rage and called her names on these occasions, she realized by this that he was treating her as an equal. McCarthy remembers, from her two years with the Madams in Seattle, one reproach that made her happy and proud. Mary's favorite teacher, Mme. Barclay, had "a bitter and sarcastic wit" that awed all the girls. Once when Mary seemed to be ignoring the nun's lesson on Byron, Mme. Barclay reproached her in an ironic way. "You're just like Lord Byron, brilliant but unsound." This remark gave Mary the happiest moment of her life, one mingling pride with the joy, unusual for her, of being appreciated by an authority figure.[28]

Like Adam and Colette, Delarue-Mardrus was fortunate in having an encouraging father. In primary school, she wrote poetry, drew, sculpted, and played the piano; her father's reaction was to nickname her "the Four Arts."[29] His attitude was as far from that of Noël's father as one can imagine. Similarly, Norris recalls that her father gave her support for her storytelling. "At another time some members of the home circle accused me of exaggeration. 'Let her alone!' said Dad. 'Any good story deserves a top hat and a stick!' "[30] This remark comes from a father friendly to literary imagination in women.

Mullen mentions one teacher, "one of the few who seemed to understand that school had become a place of torture for me," who kept her after class to persuade her to ignore the sneers and jibes of the girls and recover her earlier lead in her studies, and who offered to give her help.[31] But this one voice could not outweigh all the others. Barbara had given up, and she soon dropped out of school.

Chacel, on the other hand, never gave up on learning, because her parents were the ones who supported her; they brought her up in a totally positive atmosphere where knowledge was concerned. She quotes them more as conveyors of culture than as conveyors of commands. In early childhood they stood her on a table and had her sing, "I have a bicycle that cost 2,000 pesetas and covers more ground than the train."[32] In her infancy her father used to command her to look at the world and tell him what she saw. The result she says, is that she has known to do only that, all her life. By giving her the message that she should observe and represent her observations in words, he prepared her for her vocation as a novelist.

As Chacel got a little older, her parents would put on musicals, operas, or plays by Zorrilla for her. Her mother and father did not skimp, she says, on folklore, so that phrases from that realm affected her dreams. One of her father's sisters, Eloísa, talked out imaginary adventures with her, and while these included ladies' visits, they also included lion and tiger hunts. Her mother had taught her arithmetic and religion—a kind of devout history of religion, a little dry but never trivial—as well as some French. All these experiences enriched Chacel's intellectual life rather than limiting it.[33]

When Rosa was sent to the country to finish recuperating from an illness, she quotes a conversation about bee-eaters, a bird that "flamed yellow and a radiant blue like that of silk or metal."[34] These adults were emphasizing the natural and the beautiful, rather than diminishing them by comparison to God's glory in another world. Their attitude provides a link between the Creator and secular education, probably necessary for the Catholic minority who take a positive view toward human endeavor engaged in outside convents, rectories, and churches.

In Chacel's life two kinds of messages resounded. Her parents, Eloísa, the doctor, and the country people spoke to inform and nourish. Because of them, whenever young Rosa heard the opposite type of speech, she was horrified by it, whether it came from her mother's mother, Julia (discussed in chapter 3), from the Carmelites, or from the *beatas* (hyperCatholics who would not say anything but a hostile, fearful "Oh yes?").[35] In Rosa's childhood, commands and judgments were usually meant to negate her positive desires; affection and hope usually provided information and guided her as she constructed a positive attitude toward life.

Even Barbara Mullen's mother, who can hardly be classified with the benign minority, was not entirely negative toward her daughter. Mrs. Brady was supportive of Barbara as a competitor in jigging contests, for the nonverbal arts were considered feminine in her social group, and she herself had been a dancer. Thus Mrs. Brady did not find it difficult to say, "I hope you win," and when Barbara won the first-prize cup, her mother was truly overcome: " 'By God,' she said as she looked at it, 'it was worth letting you go.' " Only when she realized how much whiskey she would have to contribute to fill the cup did she hesitate about the celebration; still, she came through.[36]

Catholic adults who believed in the scriptural and theological view that women are equal to men in God's eyes looked on girls as worthy of every form of assistance. Their expressions of approval and affection were remembered and cherished. Is it possible that so many and such effective constructive messages have been conveyed by the minority of believers as to outweigh the destructive ones given by those with more ecclesiastical power? One can hope for a gradual increase of support, justice, and love for girls, until the old hostility and self-serving dominance fade away. But such a time had not yet come when these autobiographies were written. Still, many of the remembered words quoted here express respect for the girls, together with hope for their moral improvement or success in life. Others warn of true dangers, offer assistance with difficulties, or in a few cases commend a girl's human activities.

If the autobiographers had all attended college and studied theology and logic, they might say that the theology of equivalence, or following Aelred, the theology of friendship, is more orthodox than the papal theology of subordination. A theology of women that considers them equal or equivalent to men and capable of being their friends is based, first, on more important sources, including Christ's teachings and behavior; second, on more reasoned and less culture-bound interpretations of Scripture; and, third, on such higher duties as the obligation to complete the Creator's initiatives on one's behalf.

Because the girls felt that efforts to diminish them and prevent their using their gifts were wrong, they had an obligation under the fifth commandment to protect themselves, or at least to make a bona fide effort to do so. When the girls refused to accept a future in which they would serve as examples of the Catholic Woman, further manipulation, pressure, and force were often brought to bear. At this point, being outgunned, a number of the girls turned to strategy in their defense. In order to recognize the ways in which they shielded their personal development, I have in chapter 5 compared their behavior under attack to that described in the classic treatise on strategy, Sun-tzu's *Art of War*.

part 4

SPIRITUAL COMBAT

chapter five

Catholic Girls in Defense of Their Spiritual Well-Being

*M*OST of the female Catholic twentieth-century autobiographers when they were girls considered themselves under attack as persons. They thought adults were wrong to attack or defeat their eager efforts to educate themselves, to make ethical decisions, or to anticipate erotic happiness. The feeling of wrongness seems to have come from earlier Catholic teaching that the girls were important as persons and equal to boys in the eyes of God. As a result of this fundamental instruction, they must have felt that a failure to defend themselves from such assaults would be to fail their Creator, to ignore his will concerning their destiny, and to abdicate their human dignity. In studying the fifth commandment, they had learned that they had an obligation to defend themselves, especially against spiritual attack. If they could do so, that would prove their love of God, their courage, and their prudence. Those girls who were familiar with Aquinas's definition of *human* as a "rational animal," or with the way Catholic boys are brought up in consequence of the phrase, probably thought that as humans they had every right to their animality, which, after all, was stirred by the life of the mind and led to the full development of that mind. If they could defend these rights in a reasonable manner, that would doubly prove their right to be called *rational.*

As this chapter will show, all the girls rejected some part of the dominant view, and about 80 percent of them joined battle with the feminizers. In order to analyze the rationality of the girls' defense, I looked for terminology for social strategies. Since I do not know of a Catholic work on the spiritual combat that looks at the application of intelligence to social relations, I consulted a source more archaic even than the Fathers of the Church, Sun-tzu's Taoist work, *The Art of War*, which was written between 400 and 320 B.C.E.[1]

From this ancient treatise a list of strategies and tactics can be drawn up as a grid against which the girls' behavior in social conflicts can be assessed. In other words, *The Art of War* is considered here not as a source of the girls' behavior but strictly as a means of understanding what the girls were doing. Thinking about their responses and initiatives in Sun-tzu's terms will bring out the tactical character of some actions that might otherwise be considered instinctive or even wrong, and will show whether the girls were intelligent enough to come up with the best possible defensive strategies.

Of course, the circumstances of these young girls differed in several ways from those of the officers envisioned by Sun-tzu. First, because the girls were not military, my comparisons are all analogical. Second, Sun-tzu thought the leader of an army would have a plan that covered large distances as well as many years. The Catholic girls were involved in struggles that lasted several years, and consequently, although most of them laid no plans, they did develop sets of procedures or styles of conflict, so that they can be said to have manifested strategic intelligence; however, their wars were not fundamentally geographical, and their aim was not to seize control of a large populated area, so some of Sun-tzu's strategies do not apply.

Third, the girls' circumstances differed from those envisioned by Sun-tzu in that most of the girls, because of their youth or the type of education they had, did not fully realize that they were being opposed by the Church as an institution, and none of them knew that large numbers of girls were in the same situation they were. These girls remembered their struggle as small-scale, a conflict between themselves as individuals and one or two other people, or at most with a few nuns and a priest or two. Brave Bird's underground newspaper was suggested by a person she identifies only as a blond girl from the East.[2] The other girls studied here never thought of communicating with sister-sufferers on a scale larger than two or three friends. For them, "we" was a very small group. Even those of the girls who did not love the Church and had no positive experiences with it did not think they needed to formulate a plan of defense, much less attack, against it. In no case can I imagine their having wanted to take over the Church or even a school, nor could they have conceived of such a possibility. Since most of the girls never undertook a full-scale offensive, they would not have found much value in Sun-tzu's advice to lure attackers to strong points by making these seem weak or to attack by setting fires at any opportunity.

Moreover, the girls were unable to control the length of any battle, so, although they might have liked to, they could not take Sun-tzu's advice to fight only brief skirmishes.[3] In only one case did a girl maintain an engagement longer than the opponent wished, and that was in McCarthy's challenge to the faith of the chaplain at Forest Ridge.[4] More typically the adults, as the aggressors and the more powerful, decided the length of all battles. The persistence of Adam's father and grandmother in their rivalry for her allegiance, the endlessness of the jealousy of Bernhardt's mother, the rootedness of Mrs. Schoffen's bigotry, the indefatigable craftiness of Jouhandeau's mother, the perseveration of the Beauvoirs, the recidivism of Pillay's mother and stepfather as abusers—all resulted in prolongation of conflicts the girls would have liked to bring to an end.

The great similarity of the girls' plight to that of Sun-tzu's intended audience is that the girls were dominated by opponents far more powerful, more numerous, and wealthier than they. Because of this resemblance, many of the strategies he recommends, such as exploiting the resources of the opponent and finding worthy allies, were appropriate to the girls' needs and resources. I am using the word *allies* to replace his military term *subordinates* because *allies* can include both friends and friendly relatives. If the girls used these strategies and others appropriate to their limited expertise, property, maturity, contacts, and opportunities, and did not use those more appropriate to a situation that called for planning a series of attacks, their intelligence, rationality, and prudence in regard to real-world situations are validated. Whether they intended to prove their merit in this way cannot be known, but their strategic intelligence can be demonstrated or falsified by sorting their behavior into Sun-tzu's categories.

From reading *The Art of War,* one can identify two kinds of strategies the girls acted on: those usable in many circumstances and those usable in particular circumstances. Five of their cumulative strategies can be stated as counsels: (1) gather allies who share your ideals and purposes; do not allow yourself to be isolated, lest you be ambushed or surrounded;[5] (2) surprise your opponents at all times and keep your plans secret;[6] (3) prepare; that is, build up your strength; develop your own store of principle, discipline, courage, logic, and decisiveness;[7] (4) maintain the flow of supplies, but instead of draining your own region, capture and use the opponent's equipment and soldiers (since in the girls' conflicts this rule was applied almost entirely for their own emotional sustenance, I will discuss it as a part of strategy three, self-strengthening);[8] and (5) gather the best possible intelligence on the opponent's situation and personnel; leak false information to the enemy; intelligence (in the sense of information) is the essence of strategy.[9]

Among moves Sun-tzu recommends for specific circumstances, the girls primarily used five: (1) avoid attack unless victory is certain or your destruction must otherwise follow;[10] (2) instead of attacking troops or cities, thwart strategies or alliances;[11] (3) vary methods of (counter) attack;[12] (4) adapt to circumstances: if opponents are calm, spirited, and organized, do not attack; if you are vulnerable to ambush, block openings and exits; if opponents retreat, do not attack, lest you make them desperate;[13] and (5) if you face overwhelming numbers and certain defeat, retreat.[14]

The results of applying these five universal and five circumstantial principles may be more substantive than a simple labeling of the girl's effective actions as strategic. Beginning with strategies applicable under a great many circumstances, we quickly find that the autobiographies say much more about the recruitment of worthy supporters and the development of personal strength than *The Art of War* does. That the autobiographers wrote so much on these two strategies implies that a girl in conflict with a major institution will find herself at first inadequate in both areas. That a young girl under pressure would look for allies is not surprising, but the girls labored equally hard to overcome their weaknesses of character and other personal vulnerabilities.

The search for allies was not the same for all the girls. Schoffen in her small midwestern town could not locate helpers, especially because her father, who was a teacher, allowed his wife to prevent Schoffen from becoming a teacher too. Jouhandeau and Beauvoir, who lived in Paris, were able to find several allies, even though their parents tried to prevent their doing so. What was almost always the same was that the girls made sure their helpers and allies shared their ideals and hopes.

Shared aspirations is the first requirement of wise strategy, according to Sun-tzu, yet he mentions discarding unworthy officers only once, and only according to one possible translation.[15] These young girls apparently found it of greater importance. Even before any attack had been made, girl after girl rejected one adult or another as an ally because that person's priorities and values did not match her ideals. For example, Chacel avoided those of her aunts who were envious of her Aunt Eloísa.

Although Sun-tzu claims that acting as a unified group will lead to triumph, he does not explain why. The autobiographers do. They recall that allies who were acceptable to the girls functioned either as models for self-improvement or as sources of practical help. McCarthy, for example, emulated a series of people, at first her father and mother, and later her mother's parents and Mme. Barclay, who taught her Romantic poetry.

A special form of alliance, one still frequently unrecognized in discussions of the lives of women, is formed with the girl's father or grandfather. Colette, Norris, Chacel, and others imitated their fathers to escape the limitations of the required identification with their mothers. Most often the girl needed the father in regard to the pursuit of a career, but sometimes he exemplified some virtue the mother lacked.

A number of the girls sought allies for emotional support in their loneliness; for example, because she had lost her father's affection and literary conversation when she reached puberty, Beauvoir had to replace him. She substituted a series of young male friends whose minds were more active than his or who believed in social justice, as he did not. This series of young men culminated in Jean-Paul Sartre, a kind of male version of herself also produced by the clash of Catholic formation with modern life. Sartre's ambition and industry, his personal warmth, his spirit of fun and adventure, and his encouraging attitude filled precisely the set of absences her father's deterioration in morals, manners, enterprise, and intellectual activity had left in her life.[16]

Before she met Sartre and driven by her parents' abhorrence of her life as a university student, Beauvoir took the initiative to keep and find other allies, not so much out of loneliness as for the practical assistance they could give. The friends she made at the Sorbonne were helpful to her in discussing ideas, exchanging advice, improving her personality, and learning to develop relationships.[17] In the hope of moving her acquaintance with another student, Herbaud, to a friendship, she approached him in the restaurant of the Bibliothèque Nationale. Her success with him expresses perfectly the spiritual help a friend can give. "When I got to know Herbaud, I had the feeling of finding myself: he was the shadow thrown by my future. He was neither a pillar of the Church, nor a book-worm, nor did he spend his time propping up bars; he proved by personal example that one can build for oneself, outside the accepted categories, a self-respecting, happy, and responsible existence: exactly the sort of life I wanted for myself."[18] As a university student Beauvoir thus found friends who precisely countered her parents' disapproval.

In cases where unsolicited help was offered, the girls readily embraced it. Jouhandeau responded positively to the men around her, for they urged her to learn, to study dance, to enjoy life and the arts, and to escape her mother's blows, insults, and repressions.[19] Béatrix Dussan (1888–1969), the cultured, "smiling and luminous" actress "Dussane," at the Comédie Française and in later life a radio personality, could almost be characterized by her appreciation of everyone who shared literary and other cultural knowledge with her, especially her mother and her godfather. When a defensive headmistress attempted to discourage her, Dussane was present during her mother's counterattack and responded by holding to the path her mother had opened for her.[20]

Sometimes, sadly, the girls wanted to ally themselves to people who would not have them: Bernhardt's mother preferred Sarah's sister; an upper-division student rejected Repplier's crush on her; Schoffen's father did not support her against the parish priest and her mother; a baroness opened the heart of De-larue-Mardrus but refused to carry through (she said out of respect for the authority of Lucie's parents); and Jouhandeau's mother. Beauvoir's father re-peatedly scorned her efforts to recover their friendship. The Madams seemed to rebuff McCarthy's attempts to win their approval.

The nuns Linda Pillay knew marginalized her and her companions in reform school because they were incest victims and potential lesbians. Linda asked a friendly nun if she too could enter the convent, so as to get away from her abusive stepfather and all other men as well, but the nun, no longer friendly, replied that a girl who hated men could not be included in the com-munity of loving souls. In reform school, the psychology teacher thought she was encouraging normalcy in the girls by being "a firm believer in Freud and in all of us as potential mothers of male children."[21] Linda felt this attitude showed a lack of solidarity with the girls, all of whom had been female chil-dren, many of whom were incest victims, and any of whom might give birth to daughters.

When allies could not be had or could not be contacted, some of the girls, like Mullen, were able to resort to writers or to stories for company, informa-tion, and inspiration.[22] After François Coppée spurned Delarue-Mardrus as a poetic disciple, she substituted Théodore de Banville (1823–1891) in the form of his *Petit traité de poésie française* (1871).[23] When Beauvoir's parents turned against her, she was bitterly surprised and disappointed, but she resorted to young writers for mental companionship. She notes that she read all the novels and essays of her older contemporaries precisely because "we were all in the same boat"; that is, they were all breaking away from the class in which they had grown up. She felt that they resembled her or she them, in that they were unwilling to "use hollow words, false moralizing and its too-easy consolations."[24] By this internal bonding Beauvoir was able to defeat her parents' efforts to isolate her.

Another kind of distant ally some of the girls relied on was accessible to them through their thoughts alone. Repplier believed as a child that if she was punished, the Blessed Mother sided with her.[25] Bernhardt confided one of the roots of her tragic genius when she wrote that during her stay at the convent, "the Mother of Seven Sorrows [became] my ideal."[26] Well into the twentieth century, Wendy Rose, who sums up her life so briefly that one would think she had no space to indicate strategies of resistance, notes of her confirmation, "Patron Francis of Assisi. He understands."[27] The word *understands,* taken with the ten times she has just said she was alone, implies that no one else did understand. She seized on the idea that a saint assigned to her would be aware of her and her inner feelings. In these three instances and in probably thousands of others that have not been recorded, an isolated little girl under attack has turned to a religious figure for comfort and dignity, thus capturing a resource of her opponents and using it in her own defense.

Perhaps because of the odds against the success of girls involved in a spiritual conflict with the Catholic Church, alliance was one of their strongest needs, accounting for much of the charm of their autobiographies, as well as for the impression some of the books give of being mere reminiscences. In reality, the role the girls played in their alliances and relationships creates a self at the center of their histories.

Secrecy and surprise are prominent elements of Sun-tzu's philosophy of strategy,[28] and, though often discouraged in children, they are sometimes necessary to survival in social conflicts. Catholics are taught not to deceive anyone and are not taught to deceive hostiles as much as possible. Yet secrecy is characteristic of convent schools. Repplier and her friends veiled from the Madams an imaginative underground life full of forbidden feasts, play-romances, play-funerals, passionate friendships, and cliques governed by the code of loyalty.[29] Their desperation to escape constant surveillance did not come from a desire to hide sinful behavior; one must conclude that the girls limited the influence of their nuns so as to create a space and time in which they might develop in their own way. Their escapes freed them to initiate personal changes that bore no relation to convent rules and reproaches, not even that of rebellion. By

Repplier's account of events, "the iron hand of discipline" caused growth only to the degree in which the girls evaded it.

In Varo's central panel on convent school, the girl who has secretly embroidered a pair of lovers is able to hide them by embroidering leafless trees as a screen not so much of them as of her supererogatory stitches. Janet Kaplan explains the implications of this concealment: "In a masterful variant on the myth of creation, she has used this most genteel of domestic handicrafts to create her own hoped-for escape. Unlike Rapunzel and the Lady of Shallott, Varo's young heroine imprisoned in the tower is not merely a metaphor for confinement, but also an agent of her own liberation."[30] That is to say, what we can imagine we can carry out, when the right time comes. Varo's convent girl is like Beauvoir planning her relationship with Sartre long before she met him. The extra-large glasses of the sewing room supervisor do not catch the presence of lovers because the supervisor has to read, stir the pot, watch the exit, and stay aware of any odd movements in the girls. In the sewing room, setting stitches is not an odd movement. The strategy of this girl is not only astute; it represents the imagination of any student, which, though expected to focus on instruction, may be doing certain embroideries on its own account.

Reversing the locations of harassment and secrecy, McCarthy and her brothers were allowed to do their homework, but had to find a secretive way to read, for their foster parents were anti-intellectual. The only way the young McCarthys could find books was in condensed form in the *Book of Knowledge*. They would tell each other stories when their foster parents were not present. McCarthy did not find in this underlife a marvelous and imaginative world like that of Repplier, but a rather scrawny substitute for full culture. Yet it kept the children going until they could find something better.

Admissions of girlhood secrecy as a defense against one's parents occur in numerous places in these autobiographies. As Beauvoir matured, her parents began to interpret whatever she said in such a way that she could not recognize her ideas, and "as soon as I opened my mouth I provided them with a stick to beat me with." To defend the integrity of her mind and the sovereignty of her conscience, Beauvoir became more and more silent, that is, more and more secretive.[31]

In spiritual combat, trust is suicidal. To show the dangers of living under traditional Catholic authority without secrecy, Beauvoir compares herself to her best friend in girlhood, Zaza. From late childhood Beauvoir disobeyed her parents selectively and secretly, particularly in order to get access to a wider range of books and social contacts, and to a very small extent, to learn something about her erotic possibilities. Her secrecy came from wisdom. By exploring various paths, she was able to choose among them, without having to battle her parents before she knew enough about the world even to know which paths she wanted to fight for. In the shelter of secrecy, she was able to build up her strength. Then when she began advanced study and her parents began to harass her, she was disconcerted but was able to be resolute. Secrecy allowed her to familiarize herself with books and friends so that she knew what she would lose if she gave them up and, incidentally, where the real dangers were.[32]

Beauvoir's friend Zaza failed in her struggle against Catholic femininity training because she did not utilize the strategic principle of secrecy. She would confide to her mother that she planned to play tennis with Simone and a couple of young men or that she wanted an advanced education or that she was fond of one young man or another, in this way letting her mother know what to oppose or prohibit.[33] Zaza's mother used her daughter's confidences against her by filling her days with shopping, canning, and superficial socializing. Zaza allowed her mother to usurp all the time the young woman could have used to establish adult friendships, to work toward a diploma, and to allow the unfolding of an adult intimacy with a man her mother had not chosen for her.[34] Defeated in more and more important matters, Zaza lost her mental and physical health. Her story brings out by contrast what secrecy did for Beauvoir's personal development.

Other girls were more prudent than Zaza. Jouhandeau refused to tell her mother the name of the young man with whom she had gotten herself pregnant, because her mother meant to use the information for vengeance, by forcing them into an undesirable marriage like her own.[35] For a long time Pillay kept her stepfather's incestuous behavior a secret from her mother. In reform school she kept her friendships secret from the nuns, and then in public school she kept her aversion to sex with boys a secret from the other students.[36] All these silences were necessary to her safety.

Partial identification with one's father is often protected by secrecy, by avoiding display or speech on the subject, and sometimes by keeping silence even toward oneself, as Chacel did.[37] Colette focuses on her love for her mother throughout *Maison*, not admitting her identification with her father until she passed the age of fifty and was writing *Sido*.

Deceit and the creation of illusion about oneself combine as a form of secrecy Sun-tzu recommends heartily.[38] Probably because the catechism forbids deceit, fewer of the girls used this strategy, at least deliberately, than used simple secrecy. Carroll persuaded her father that she was a poor driver and could not learn to drive better, and worse, led him to think she was serious about a Protestant boyfriend. Her father broke off the romance and forbade her to drive again, apparently not realizing that she had been managing him.[39] She herself might not have recognized, and he certainly did not, that he was helping her to escape his control by entering the convent.

Apparent submission is so common as not to seem deceitful, but it is. Among these girls, false and temporary surrenders took place frequently. Mullen submitted to her mother's orders not to write to her father and, later on, to break her engagement.[40] Although the mother believed she could beat Barbara's preference for her father out of her, and for that reason thought that her daughter had changed, she never changed; she had merely learned to keep silent. After some years passed and she had enough money to go to Ireland, she asked again to go to her father, and this time she succeeded in getting away. In general, if the girls engaged in deceit, it was to protect vulnerable resources from destruction. When antagonism was overwhelming, they surrendered soon enough to avoid collapse, and then waited till they grew up or had the financial means to act on their consciences.

Secrecy and deceit in Sun-tzu's recommendations serve the tactic of surprise. From the rule of surprise he derives another: keep moving. He instructs his readers to move their soldiers continually, to send them wherever they are not expected, and to conceal their location.[41] Readers may not expect the girls' tactics to be mercurial, since they still had to live at home. But some of the girls needed geographic mobility to counteract their isolation (cultural and social) or, in Jouhandeau's more Catholic frame of reference, their enclosure, which leads to a deterioration in one's strength. Aggressive adults in the lives of Adam, Bernhardt, Schoffen, Jouhandeau, Beauvoir, and Pillay could get at their victims too frequently. As a result, changes of location made crucial differences for these girls, with the exception of Schoffen, who was unable to get away until she left home. León and Matute, though they did not complain of frequent attacks, also used the tactic of geographical mobility, which may imply that they felt themselves to be under permanent siege.

Adult allies provided some of the necessary moves, as when Bernhardt's father suddenly reappeared and enrolled her in convent school, a change that ultimately defeated her mother's efforts to compete with and defeat Sarah.[42] The girls made changes of location during adolescence on their own. For example, León found her way to her uncle's library and her aunt's secular school, places that gave her an alternative to the deprivation she faced at the convent school. Beauvoir located a number of places in Paris where her parents did not expect her to go, including the Jockey Club and various theaters.[43] In other words, in the life of a beleaguered Catholic girl, as well as that of a Chinese soldier, quick or secret shifts of location can be necessary for survival. For Chinese soldiers, the advantages of unexpected changes of position were to hide one's intended targets and to prevent attacks on one's own units.[44] For Catholic girls, who were not planning attacks on anyone, the basic reason for staying on the move was defense.

To build up her store of goodness,[45] Pillay respected the spiritual autonomy of other girls. Even in bed in the dormitory with a friend her own age, Linda always stopped short of imposing sexual contact on a girl who did not want it.[46] She might have shown the same respect had her Catholic stepfather not raped her over and over, but she may have developed it in reaction to his deficiencies.

Rosa Chacel took the responsibility of curing herself of sarcasm and of moving from the anal phase to the genital phase, to use the autobiographer's Freudian frame of reference for this episode. Rosa carried out her project by alternating between fantasies about her own cruelty toward soft, nourishing persons and newer fantasies exercising her admiration for noble, beautiful persons—in other words, ideal adults.[47]

The Catholic girls in these narratives had to keep their supply lines open, just as Sun-tzu's army did. Whether for defense or attack, supplies are never sufficient for the completion of a war, but anyone who fails to stay supplied will lose.[48] In the spiritual combat that engaged the girls, supplies meant information about the outside world and emotional support to counteract their isolation. The best McCarthy was able to get from any of the older McCarthys was a copy or two of forbidden magazines such as *Extension,* a lowbrow Catholic periodical.[49] But as soon as Mary appealed to her mother's parents for relief, they moved her to their home, where her grandfather's library and good private schools were made available to her.

When a supply line has been cut or dries up, as when McCarthy's parents died or the Beauvoirs lost their income, or when the available level of Catholic culture is no longer stimulating, a girl may feel herself in danger of dwindling intellectually. Beauvoir took responsibility for preventing this decline. In the Jesuit milieu in which she grew up, she had derived sustenance for her mind, or at least comprehensible activity and a sense of order, from spiritual reading and prayer. In her early college years, she substituted secular reading, but she read in the manner she had been taught for religious reading. "Literature took the place in my life that had once been occupied by religion: it absorbed me entirely, and transfigured my life. The books I liked became a Bible from which I drew advice and support; I copied out long passages from them; I learnt by heart new canticles and new litanies, psalms, proverbs, and prophecies and I sanctified every circumstance in my existence by the recital of these sacred texts. . . . For months I kept myself going with books: they were the only reality within my reach."[50] Thus Beauvoir cast about for a means to survive and found Catholic procedures ready to hand, already a part of her system of coping with reality. Had she been rebelling for the sake of rebellion, she would not have been willing to adopt them.

Beauvoir's use of familiar Catholic discipline to appropriate fresh intellectual material demonstrates the way the girls characteristically fused the strategy of supply with self-strengthening. They could either give up and conform, or they could recycle certain elements of Catholicism. In general, their transformations of this material supplemented their emotional strength or turned some other element of their faith against Catholic femininity training.

Sarah Bernhardt appears to have appropriated the idea of being number one from Mother St. Sophie, head of her convent school in Versailles. At fifteen, waiting for the family council that would decide her career, Sarah imagined herself sacrificing pleasures, kings, and jewels in order to occupy Mother's chair.[51] The fantasy helped her keep her morale up, and in time Sarah did sacrifice pleasures, kings, and jewels, but she did so in order to be the queen of tragic theater.

In an inspired redirection of Catholic teaching, Elise Jouhandeau promptly obeyed her mother's command: "Bird of ill-omen, fly away quickly, that I may no longer see you!"[52] That very afternoon Elise went to her boyfriend's apartment, the first action she had taken that committed her to leaving her mother. One of the most repressive Catholic concepts Elise reoriented was that reproduction is a woman's only duty.[53] The idea might have sounded limiting to another girl, but for Elise it was a source of hope. To reproduce would enrich her life beyond its level at home with her mother. Again, Elise used Genesis to prove to a certain young man that sexual love originated with our divine Creator.[54] This quite undeniable argument turns the minority belief against the majority's, to follow Ruether's terminology. Finally, Elise relied on a mental list of her mother's vices to build up her resolve to leave home; Elise had culled the list from the catechism and examinations of conscience.

Chacel took from the Church whatever would help her become a strong woman. To the devotion of the Way of the Cross, which she said was impossible for her to apply, she preferred the notion of the spiritual path, the one road through life best suited for each unique person. To Our Lady of Sorrows she preferred Our Lady of Mount Carmel and Our Lady of Victory; Our Lady of Mount Carmel was pictured as reigning above the flames of Purgatory, and Our Lady of Victory as reigning above her name.[55]

Fontenot took great delight in filling the concept of complete devotion to God with love for her boyfriend Tony. "At this point in my life I would never even think about God. . . . Now Tony was in my life, and there wasn't room for anyone or anything else in my life. . . . Everything revolved around him. I gave myself to him with no reservations."[56] Fontenot's language about her first love for Tony—"I gave my whole self to him with no reservations"—is devotional, prayerbook language. Although in her persona as repentant autobiographer Fontenot condemns her love as an exclusion of God, at fifteen she dealt with Tony through a transformation of her love for God. Like God, Tony made it possible for Peggy Joan to pour out her entire self as a libation, holding nothing back, ready to submit in everything. She had almost certainly been taught by her Church that her future offered her such an option in the form of marriage and motherhood. Because she had been a religious child, Peggy easily moved into this attitude and found in it an ecstasy. Because she made her love for Tony sacred in this manner, she always believed that, although "some people said it wasn't love," it had been.[57]

The girls managed to turn Catholic worship to their personal advantage, weathering difficulties with the help of the emotional language of prayers, either by reminders that they were loved or by the outlet for love otherwise choked off. When Farrell joined the Charities and the priest did not carry out the ceremony well, she nevertheless found a way to take advantage of the liturgy, in that her "heart was singing the Canticle of the Three Children." She felt that her years as an orphan were over, that she had been "transported to some wonderful country of beauty and peace."[58] After Beauvoir no longer prayed, she would sometimes hide in a church so as to be able to weep in peace.[59] In other words, the girls saw the Church of their opponents as their Church as well, and felt at ease in exploiting its resources.

Sometimes the girls survived under pressure by secularizing other methods of the inner life. When Bernhardt's mother ruined Sarah's hairdo just before the acting school competitions, Sarah fell apart and performed poorly in the tragedy contest. She recovered before the comedy contest by creating an interior dialogue that reconstructed her ego. "I awarded myself . . . all the gifts necessary to the blooming of my dream: to become the first, the most celebrated, the most envied [of actresses]. And I enumerated on my fingers all my merits: grace, charm, distinction, beauty, mystery and piquancy. "Oh! Everything! Everything! I found that I had all that. And when my logic and my integrity raised a doubt, or a 'but' . . . to this fabulous nomenclature of my good points, my combative and paradoxical 'Me' found an apt response, decisive and unanswerable."[60] She credits this inner dialogue, which is simply a form of meditation or examination of conscience, with her winning the second prize in comedy that day. The dialogue transposed the examination of conscience into a positive key for a new function, namely, to liberate her mind from excessive subjection to her mother; like a number of the girls, Bernhardt secularized her Catholicism to free herself of it.

In the Catholic Church people learn to visualize dramatic moments in Christ's life and the lives of persons close to him. These skills too can be secularized or personalized. Pillay includes more of her fantasies as a girl than did any of the other American autobiographers. While incarcerated at what she calls Holy Terror School, she had a fantasy about a male alter ego that helped her endure. Jake was an armed robber with two motorcycles, one for her. "I was Jake, tough and free. I took what I wanted and didn't beg, or wait for someone to give it to me. I was louder and taller than most people, so no one pushed me around. Most of all, this Jake, who was me, took care of Linda who needed someone just then to take care of her."[61] In his strength Jake was like Pillay at eight, before her mother remarried. The Jake fantasy enabled Linda to combine that earlier strength with her adolescent warmth, so that she began helping children, instead of beating them, as she had done when she was little, or ignoring them, as she had done while she was a victim of incest.[62]

The girls also diverted Catholic dogma to their spiritual defense. Beauvoir did this best, gathering elements of dogma she could detach and recombine to form a strong personality. Particularly interesting among her modifications are those she made to beliefs in the resurrection, vocation, and free will. The first of these, the archetype of resurrection, she applied to herself on the verge of finishing her schooling at *le cours Désir.* "I smiled to myself at the adolescent who would die on the morrow only to rise again in all her glory."[63] A second idea that she liked and used in defining her future was the Catholic ideal of service and vocation. She thought that if she could write novels like *The Mill on the Floss,* she could help others to weep or to live in their turn.[64] This vision of extending a hand to others helped her through the most difficult years of academic work. Third, the idea of *free will,* which she calls *choice* (possibly because of her existentialism), was crucial to her in late adolescence. Inspired by the optimism and commitment of Robert Garric, a lecturer at the Institut

Sainte-Marie, she was repelled by the nihilistic despair of her cousin Jacques, and told him, "One had to consecrate one's life to a search for its meaning: meanwhile, one must never take anything for granted but base one's standards on acts of love and free-will that were to be indefinitely repeated."[65] She wanted to convince him to adopt a lifestyle based on the Catholic concept of freely given love.

The transformation of the Catholic Woman's self-sacrifice, however, was a more challenging task, for it is so often preached as an imitation of Christ's love. The desirability of sacrifice is taught to all Catholics, but it is intended to be taken up much more by girls than by boys, as indicated in chapter 3. As a group, the girls can be said to have realigned the idea of self-sacrifice, so that it was no longer a religious synonym for their feminine role. Bernhardt was never willing to sacrifice herself in the sense of forgoing her human sovereignty, her individuality, or her future greatness as an actor, but she was very prompt, even at the age of ten, to risk her life to save that of a smaller child.[66]

Living under nuns who promoted the practice of small ritual sacrifices, Agnes Repplier refused to join in. For example, she once ate a chocolate pudding another girl was giving up for Reverend Mother's farewell card, and she refused her friend Elizabeth's suggestion that she should talk with an unpleasant girl as a sacrificial act.[67] But Agnes gave up her doll when her friends asked her to, apparently because they wanted to help her mature. The sequence of sacrifice and maturation inverts the Catholic plan for the women's self-sacrifice, which was designed so that she would consecrate her inner life to someone else.

When the girls rejected sacrifices that promised no assistance to another person and no self-expression, they were at the same time rejecting recommendations that they should suffer. Both as a child and as an autobiographer, Noël gently evaded messages that she should accept crosses. Perhaps she did so because the penance and pain her parents introduced into her childhood did not help her. The same belief system that sees suffering as God's will for us also considers that God removes our guilt by his love without needing the crucifixion. At the time of her first confession, her depression had been cured, not so much by the sacrificial death of Jesus, although she made her verbal curtsy to that doctrine, but by "a look from very high resting on me. . . . so pure, so salutary, so mercifully attentive, that on raising my eyes toward him all my spots were washed away."[68] The doctrine of mercy is the one Noël preferred and immersed herself in.

Later on, when the nuns offered her a choice of holy cards portraying

Jesus, she chose one of "My Savior who climbed a steep path among briars, his lamb—myself—across his shoulders."[69] She preferred a Christ who would save her from suffering to one who would impose it. In her family she also chose a model of love that did not suffer but spread pleasure: her grandmother. Marie spent hours every day of her infancy with her grandmother, listening to tales from Aesop, history, her father's life, or the Gospels, or tagging along while her grandmother performed innumerable services for the parish, none of them sacrifices. In addition to sewing for the poor, she made jams and lottery prizes, and she provided flowers and flowering plants for the sanctuary of the Auxerre cathedral on the great summer feasts. She was a joyful woman, not because she repressed her inclinations, but because she used her skills for others. Hers is the style of devotion to the Church that Noël elected to follow.[70] Because of her grandmother, Noël understood that she could serve by writing religious verse and need not abandon the world for the convent.[71]

A different way to shun sacrifice is to reinterpret those occasions on which sacrifice is typically recommended and turn them to one's advantage. In Catholic schools and churches, major illness is often presented as an opportunity to identify with Christ on the Cross, offering the pain in payment for one's sins or those of others. Adam, Bernhardt, Delarue-Mardrus, and Chacel, all of whom went through grave illnesses, saw affliction instead, as their families did, as a situation to escape from and a challenge to human resources of ingenuity, medicine, solidarity, and courage. In Chacel's relatively lengthy narrative of her mental process during illness, no word or phrase refers to any religious value she thought her suffering might have had.

Beauvoir as a university student developed a variety of antidotes to depression, indicating that she did not view sorrow as a gift from on high. The slide toward despair came from the disapproval and nagging of her parents, resulting in loneliness, isolation, hurt, and low self-esteem. Beauvoir on her nineteenth birthday fought off the defeatism and nihilism that were consuming her father and her cousin Jacques by writing a dialogue between the voice of futility and a voice that affirmed that "life, even a sterile existence, was beautiful." At other times, she would counteract her dejection by making a decision about her future: to write, to be happy, or to come to Jacques's or Zaza's aid. In letters to friends she would ask their approval of her desire to become a writer. This kind of self-assertion had the merit of overcoming, at least for a time, both the fear of uncertainty and the fear that her parents might recover their control. Sometimes she made a direct attack on gloom by visiting an art gallery or garden, gazing at a beautiful view of the city, or attending a play, film, or concert. Sometimes Simone had no way to compensate for the loss of her parents' support and affection except by resolving "I shall love myself enough, I thought, to make up for this abandonment by everyone. . . . In my diary I had long conversations with myself."[72] Because she was willing to try a variety of comforts, Simone was able to keep her morale healthy until she could find better friends and establish a better home; her versatility would have dazzled Sun-tzu.

These writers did not adopt the general view that voluntary pain makes a worthy offering to God, yet when pain was inflicted on them, they used it to grow in courage, sometimes thinking of Catholic martyrs as models. Martyr stories are often told in Catholic catechesis to add interest and to let children know that earlier Catholics valued their religious beliefs more than personal survival. Beauvoir implies that she was being narcissistic in childhood by imagining herself as one or another female martyr.[73] But McCarthy once gave herself very necessary comfort, after a severe and lengthy beating, by the thought that she had behaved like the martyrs.[74] Conway thought of the martyrs when her catechist abused her verbally and whipped her hand with a ruler. "It was then that I understood the power and strength of martyrdom. I understood Kevin Barry and the saints who went to their deaths for a principle. A seed was firmly planted that day in Miss FitzPatrick's class that would grow and serve me well in later years."[75] The reason was practical and not related to narcissism; once she "petrified" herself and refused to obey, her panic and pain vanished.

Pillay notes that the nun who was friendly to her could not understand the reason for Linda's "interest in St. Maria Goretti, who was stabbed to death by a rapist."[76] Pillay's history implies that she identified with Maria Goretti in her goodness, victimization, and danger. Thus Pillay, Conway, and McCarthy reoriented the Church's gift of martyr stories to steel themselves against wrongfully used authority.

A third type of sacrifice taught in the Church—in addition to imposed sacrifices and prayerful sacrifices, whether of pain or pleasure—is entrance into the convent. But instead of sacrificing the self, Farrell and Carroll seem to have taken the veil as a way of emotionally rejoining their dead mothers.[77] Farrell wanted to be with a group of nuns her mother had loved, while Carroll wanted to act out her identification with her mother as a homemaker. She could have continued teaching home economics for the Mercies without entering the community, but Carroll had always wanted to be on the inside of any circle of females. Surely this desire too came from her longing to continue her deep identification with her mother.

The autobiographers in this study who were nuns did not want their readers to think convent life had been a sacrifice for them; their intention by rejecting that argument was to praise religious life and the Church that made it possible for them. As Carroll wrote, "Anyone who follows the path he wishes despite all obstacles is selfish. And when you go to the Convent, you are not sacrificing. Your parents and those responsible for you are. Why do people think it is difficult to leave the world? It's the easiest thing after you once are sure."[78] One could hardly say more against the idea that religious life is a sacrifice.

By revising the idea of self-sacrifice and reversing the flow of energy in a number of other Catholic beliefs, devotions, and practices, the girls fortified and invigorated themselves, thus utilizing the resources of their opponent.

Chacel and Beauvoir were able to combine parts of Catholic culture with parts of secular culture to come up with syntheses or new philosophies for the lives they intended to live. Chacel, when she was preparing for the sacraments, must have been determined to prove to herself that she had reached the age of reason, that is, that she knew good from evil and could commit herself to the good. She saw the choice of a secondary school and her advance to the age of reason as intertwined. She thought it would be evil to choose an occupation that would prevent further spiritual development, and she began to realize that she would have to defend any higher choice from her grandmother, who was a devout churchgoer.

Rosa decided on art school as a path that she was capable of following successfully and that would lead her above the servile level. A most methodical girl, at the age of nine she worked out a three-legged philosophy or mental attitude to support her choice. The first leg was a self-concept reinforced by memories of her family's love in Valladolid and by a ceremony in which she dressed her three-inch jointed doll in golden silk from a cocoon she had been keeping. She sang herself the birthday song her mother used to sing her, thus becoming her own mother. She remembered that, when she had been allowed to attend an art class in Valladolid, the boys had praised her work. She reminded herself that she had always disliked the idea of abasing herself, whether religiously, socially, or economically. All these thoughts helped her choose a more dignified type of work.[79] The second leg of her philosophy was an analysis of her grandmother that would keep the need for resistance in the forefront of Rosa's mind. She formed this concept partly by comparing her Madrid grandmother's faults, both in Spanish grammar and in charity, to the virtues of her Valladolid grandmother and her Aunt Eloísa.[80]

The third leg of her philosophy was a concept of art that would inspire conviction and dedication in herself. To assure herself that art was not in itself masculine, she mentally transformed a Gaudí house into an image of "a woman-house; a nymph-house adorned with flowers." She had already found art to have three phases—"the artisan's work," an erotic phase, and a phase of mystic vision. This wholeness, she judged, would allow her to absorb herself in it completely. She had always thought of art as a form of communication; to strengthen this idea, she now defined it as a form of love, like the mutual look between a patient and a doctor, in which the patient gives confidence and the doctor removes "the pain, the danger, death." In art the gaze of the artist indirectly meets the gaze of the one viewing a work of art. Their loving gaze conveys a secret light like the tranquil love between herself and a peasant she had known in the country, or the light between two stars, so that through art Rosa would be able to communicate transport and to transport others (this wordplay is hers) "from the place where they were to a better [one]."[81] In this way, Rosa at nine put together a philosophy of art derived from earlier experiences, a philosophy that related art to charity and the sacred, thus making it feminine in a deeper sense than that conceived by her grandmother or the clerics quoted in chapter 3.

The deliberate decision of this depth—supported by a new, conscious self-concept, a clear analysis of her opponent, and a complete spiritualization of her profession—more than proves that the child was rational. She was so intelligent and creative that she restored humanity where it had been destroyed.

Beauvoir's synthesizing power appears in her account of the period when she was fifteen and about to leave the Madams' school. For her future, she did not want the traditional Catholic blueprint, which dehumanized marriage. She drew materials for her own plan from experience and observation. What she rejected in traditional Catholic arranged marriage was the lack of choice, to which she attributed her father's infidelity; the absence of unpredictability and therefore of joy; and with all that, the absolute hierarchy of power and knowledge on which she blamed the spiritual deterioration of Catholic married people in their middle years.[82]

To assemble a new concept of intimacy she began with a film image of a joyful couple and a couple of French phrases—translatable as "two hearts as one" and "a man made for me."[83] From her experience she drew a concept of superiority in one of the partners as inspiring rather than domineering. One of her sources was her convent-school friendship with Zaza Mabille (whom Simone believed to be more intelligent than she); the other was her earlier relationship with her father as teacher. She felt that some superiority in her future partner would be necessary in order for her to progress continuously.[84] At the same time, the other person must want her to advance and must also respect her sovereignty and her ability to teach him in her turn. "Doubtless it was my friendship with Zaza which made me attach so much weight to the perfect union of two human beings; discovering the world together and as it were making a gift of their discoveries to one another, they would, I felt, take possession of it in a specially privileged way; at the same time, each would find a definite meaning in existence in the other's need."[85] The next sentence—"To give up love seemed to me to be as senseless as to neglect one's health because one believes in eternal life"—must represent Simone's contemplation of the nuns and of her mother, as well as stating her judgment on arranged marriages like that of her parents. The sentence could hardly occur in a non-Catholic girl's autobiography, for non-Catholics are not normally taught to renounce sexual love for the sake of marriage, as if there were somehow a contradiction. The grand negative value of a Catholic education is brought out, for the notions of religious celibacy and of marital coolness or detachment work as boundaries or borders, assisting Simone in clarifying her ideas and defining the type of intimate life she prefers.

Religious terminology—"the spiritual ascent," "predestination," and "overcoming the world"—also appears in the original concept of marriage, which can be read also as heterosexual companionship, with which she concluded her synthesis. "The picture I conjured up in my mind was of a steep climb in which my partner, a little more agile and stronger than myself, would help me up from one stage to the next. . . . A life in common would have to favor and not stand in the way of my fundamental aim, which was to conquer the world." At the end of this brief history of her thinking on intimacy Beauvoir incorporates secular language drawn from psychiatry, philosophy, and politics. "The man destined to be mine would be neither inferior nor different, nor outrageously superior; someone who would guarantee my existence without taking away my powers of self-determination."[86]

Although Beauvoir's parents did not provide her with a practical model of Catholic marriage, she was able to incorporate part of their belief system in her own model. She had experienced a different function of superiority from the one envisioned by Catholic ideas of matrimony, and this distinction led her to a happier and more spiritual intimacy than her parents' had been. One of Beauvoir's most important strategies as a girl was to be alert for the slightest trickles of light from outside the family tower and ready to integrate these with whatever seemed desirable and useful from within it. Thus Beauvoir, like Chacel, defended and fortified herself in the ordeals she experienced using whatever resources were available.

One would think that espionage, which "armies depend upon in their every move,"[87] would be one strategy the girls would not use, since serious spying does not seem to be a characteristic pursuit of girls. If the girls had inside knowledge of their opponents, they probably collected it inadvertently. In convent schools and Catholic women's colleges, where information and deduction were relayed from each girl to her friends, the intelligence network was not deliberately organized.[88] Jouhandeau unintentionally accumulated more evidence than she wanted that her mother was adulterous, violent, vindictive, uncharitable, and proud of all but the first of these traits.[89] Her mother's insinuations that life in her apartment was morally superior to any life Elise could live on her own could never have sounded true.

Although accidental espionage cannot be counted as a proof of strategic intelligence or prudence, awareness of the strategic value of information and the intelligent application of it confirms the presence of tactical thought. The girls were skilled at using information about their opponents. Benoist and Beauvoir learned rapidly not to ask their mothers about sex, because their mothers were horrified at their first question. Schoffen decided to enter the convent because she could not obtain her mother's permission to leave home and become a teacher in any other way. She knew, because she had observed her mother's habit of ranking the parish priest higher than her husband and children. Thus the girls quickly recognized how to apply their inside knowledge of the Catholic system.

But in more instances than one might expect, the girls set out deliberately to gather information. To ascertain the historical role of the Princess of Eboli, a laywoman whose portrait hung in the convent school though she was not a saint, León wrote a note to a classmate whose father was in the Spanish Royal Academy. Elise Jouhandeau went to her boyfriend's apartment partly to investigate "the life of sin." As a result she learned some truths her mother had not told her about a sexual life: it might be disappointing and not especially pleasant, lacking the exhilaration and drama of Sin, but at its worst it would be far better than living with her mother.[90]

In another example of gathering intelligence directly, Simone de Beauvoir, like Jouhandeau, called on a potential sexual partner, her cousin Jacques. In this case nothing sexual occurred, but by getting him to reveal his views when older relatives were not present, Simone in time understood that he was committed to despair.[91] This information saved her from wanting to marry him or, probably, any of his peers.

Mary McCarthy acquired from living among her father's relatives a habit of closely observing people's approval or disapproval of her and adapting her behavior accordingly. Once when her foster father and great-uncle Shriver had framed her for a theft, and he and his wife were beating Mary to get her to admit it, she did not fully understand what he was up to, until he let his satisfaction in his triumph show prematurely. "The sight of him, sprawling in his leather chair, complacently waiting for this, was too much for me. . . . As I looked straight at him and assessed his ugly nature, I burst into yells. 'I didn't! I didn't!' " The Shrivers resumed their beating, but this time Mary fought back so fiercely that they gave up.[92] Had she done what Shriver wanted, her reputation with her great-aunt and her brothers would have suffered; worse, she would know that she had lied, thus ruining her self-respect. But she would not have realized the danger and would not have persisted in her own defense had she not looked at Shriver and seen how much her confession would please him.

When she arrived among the Madams in Seattle, McCarthy watched for signs of their approbation. When she found signs of disapproval and misunderstanding, she concluded that Forest Ridge would not be a healthy environment for her. Had McCarthy not noticed signals of the nuns' reaction to her, she would not have been aware of her situation.

When Matute was away from the supervision of her mother or the nuns, she would gather intelligence on the "masculine" world (for which we can read "human" world), from which Catholic gender rules excluded her. By doing so she learned, among other things, that forbidden fruit may be delicious and not harmful. Matute and her brother climbed a mulberry tree on the rectory grounds, a parallel to the forbidden tree in God's original garden. The children ate as much of the luscious fruit as they could. The priest, like God in Genesis, was unaware of their presence. Their only opposition came from birds who had wanted the mulberries (in Spanish, *morales*). Matute describes the children's joy as coming more from eating the fruit than from doing the prohibited. She mentions vengeance, but it was the vengeance of the juice itself; that is, excess has natural consequences.[93] This version of Genesis refers to her childhood investigation of adult deceptions, for it topples them one by one. She repeated this process of discovery when she saw the village boys crucify a bat and learned what gratuitous violence is.

In a sense, the girls leaked false information to their enemies when they appeared to surrender but remained faithful interiorly, a move I have discussed under the head of deceit.

The process by which knowledge gained through espionage becomes a guarantee of victory is represented in several incidents. Jouhandeau freed herself of excessive allegiance to her tyrants by observing the unworthiness of the lives they wanted her to share; in this way she found the independence to become an adult and take up a career. Chacel as a girl used her knowledge of her grandmother's strong and weak points subtly, never debating with her, but building up internal arguments against her program of diminution.[94] Beauvoir protected herself from inner defeat and did not insist on more external victory than necessary. McCarthy used her understanding of the conscious and unconscious enmity around her to shield her self-respect, and to find her way, like Beauvoir, to a superior education and a fulfilling career as a committed writer. In this way the girls based their defense of their spiritual health on their observations of people and decisions that could harm them.

Sun-tzu's five universal strategies or policies, then—worthy alliance, secrecy, capturing, self-reinforcement, and espionage—might as well have been studied by Catholic girls. Under attack from institutional teachers of gender beliefs, the girls approached the problem of self-defense in ways so similar to his recommendations as to suggest that the human mind will generally come up with analogous solutions to analogous difficulties. However, strategic wisdom does not guarantee tactical skill. Although the girls used long-term strategies well, their inexperience might easily have kept them from tactical alertness—that is, from successful defense, counterattack, and attack. In reality, most of the girls followed tactical principles similar to those put forth in *The Art of Warfare,* differing only where they were overpowered or where circumstances such as being in reform school kept them in ignorance of alternatives.

The attacks made on the girls as described in chapters 2 and 3 included discounting, harassment, exclusion, unethical persuasion, abuse, and cultural deprivation. When the girls could, they defended themselves without counterattack, even if the attack on them was physical. For example, Schoffen says that she had to exert all her physical and moral strength to resist the advances of the priest who was escorting her to the convent, but she does not report any counterattack—no effort, for example, to hit him with a hotel lamp or with a

Gideon Bible. Pillay sometimes defended herself from trauma by anger or other internal distancing.

Under attack for their "rebellious" plans to become women not quite like the Catholic Woman, the girls often defended themselves by logical reasoning, even though this choice meant that they sheltered mostly their inner convictions. After it was decided that Dussane would compete for the conservatory at the Comédie Française, the head of her old neighborhood school warned her that a career in theater would endanger her morals. Béatrix, then thirteen, answered immediately that the flesh is weak everywhere, but within a year she had a better defense, that "the same persons who seemed disappointed would have fully approved if I had become a literature teacher. . . . At the Comédie Française, I will play masterpieces, in that way I will help make them known and loved."[96] She does not indicate that she presented the second answer to anyone but herself.

Against prohibitions they considered inimical, including those that damaged their individuality, the girls defended basically by secret disobedience, as in sneak reading, disguise (as when Beauvoir attended a Catholic institute for a year in order to carry on the forbidden friendship with Mabille), or in some cases what may be called *edging* (when Colette or Brave Bird stayed just a little bit longer than they were supposed to).

Open counterattack has been as acceptable to Catholic girls as serious attack is unacceptable, probably because catechism lessons usually say in discussing the fifth commandment that self-defense is permissible and may be a duty. When María Teresa León pulled off the veil of a nun, she did not do so without provocation, for the nun had insulted her family.[97] One might not consider such a counterattack effective, especially after reading that the child was expelled as a consequence. But she had used the tactic best suited to liberate her from a school she had dreaded attending. Sun-tzu would have predicted her success, for he says, "If you . . . seize something he cannot afford to lose, he will do your bidding."[98] A nun's veil, conferred in a public and ancient ceremony, traditionally signified her spiritual marriage to Christ, her consecration to God, her dedication to the works of mercy (in this case, education), and the gender neutrality or equality recommended by Saint Jerome. Tactical intelligence appears in the intuitive way León used her knowledge of nunly values and in the resulting success of her move.[99]

In late adolescence Brave Bird also took a nun's veil off, when Brave Bird and her friend Charlene Left Hand Bull were whipped once too often. Brave Bird told Charlene, "We are getting too old to have our bare asses whipped that way. We are old enough to have babies. Enough of this shit. Next time we fight back." Her first retaliation was in defense of a little girl who was too shy to take her panties off in the shower. The nun was getting her swat to threaten the child, and Brave Bird stopped her. "I went up to the sister, pushed her veil off, and knocked her down. I told her that if she wanted to hit a little girl she should pick on me, pick one her own size. She got herself transferred out of the dorm a week later."[100] On another occasion Brave Bird bloodied the nose of a priest because he had shoved her against the blackboard and twisted her arm.[101] She apparently never took in the notion that one must accept authority even if it is misused.

Simone de Beauvoir obeyed her parents as much as she could, but when their harassment had reached an intolerable level, she finally counterattacked. She would read at meals and neglect her grooming. Forced to leave her books to entertain her mother's friends, she would sit on the edge of her chair, teeth clamped shut, looking so angry her mother would send her out again.[102] Her tactical style, simple rudeness, seems odd, but it worked, being perfectly adapted to the opponent. Soon Simone was allowed to pursue her studies and to spend her socializing time as she chose.

Life was a little different among the Boston Irish during the days of the Catholic Temperance movement. Barbara Mullen once defeated a girl in a fistfight because she had "cried in front of the class that my mother had been arrested."[103] Also in a less affluent class than Beauvoir, Pillay was caught up in a life of counterattack. She brought the nun, the social worker, and the courts down on her stepfather, though she did so only when she began to fear for her sanity and her life. Against the less physically invasive dominance of the re-form-school nuns she resisted with naughty symbolic actions, carving her initials on the skin of her arm with a piece of broken glass or drawing a moustache on the statue of the Blessed Virgin Mary.[104] When she returned to the reform school voluntarily as a high school senior, she observed that the nuns worshipped any and all males, with a consequent lack of support for victimized girls. This time around, she resisted them—more deliberately, but again mostly through mischief, a kind of guerrilla warfare that upset them without revealing her identity.[105]

The girls did not tend to fix on one form of counterattack, but seemed to realize that versatility would make them unpredictable,[106] or perhaps they were responding to shifting forms of assault. Repplier, in opposing Mme. Dane's drive to uniformity, once switched everyone's laundry around; another time she and her friends had a party after hours. The nuns could not possibly anticipate every form of deviation from rules that the younger girls could think of.

In twentieth-century girls' schools, underground newspapers appeared, though because of the universal discipline of the Church these publications were rare and short-lived. In Paris Beauvoir contributed to one published by her younger sister, Hélène, with her friend Anne-Marie Gendron, called the *Cours Désir Gazette*. Beauvoir says they "turned out some bloodthirsty numbers." Their tactical effectiveness can be gauged by a new experience in their lives: bad conduct marks; in addition the nuns lectured them and complained to their parents, but M. Beauvoir laughed.[107] In St. Francis, South Dakota, Brave Bird put out an underground paper called the *Red Panther* with her friends Charlene Left Hand Bull and Gina One Star. Brave Bird says it had only one issue and she wrote the worst article in it. A denunciation of the priests, "it was the kind of writing which foamed at the mouth, but which also lifted a great deal of weight from one's soul." The *Red Panther* was sufficiently effective that Mary had to scrub six flights of stairs on her hands and knees every day and lost the usual permission to use the boys' gym and other facilities, even though her mother stood up for her with the nuns.[108]

Unique among the girls' replies to oppression was Bernhardt's invention of a comic episode when a soldier's shako blew over the cloister wall. When the soldier followed, the nuns hid behind the trees, and Sarah gave herself and the other little girls ineffable joy by keeping the hat away from the soldier and prolonging his stay.[109] The underlying point of the merriment was that the cloister walls, the hiding, and the habits were completely unnecessary. The girls knew the soldier was chasing only his hat.

Like Sun-tzu, the Catholic girls of this set of autobiographies preferred thwarting the strategies or alliances of their opponents to launching attacks that might be costly.[110] They were not, after all, backed by large armies, unless one could call the heavenly host a large army. Repplier and her friends crossed up the Madams' efforts to make them all alike. Wong and Menchú thwarted the program of Catholic matrimony simply by not getting married.

The girls successfully adapted their defenses to variations in the behavior of their opponents. When a parent or chaperone was confident of the rightness of their rules or interference, the girls would back down.[111] If the Catholic girl was surrounded,[112] she would somehow keep a space for herself into which her opponents could not enter, yet from which she could escape if they did swarm in. Repplier and her friends did this by devoting their free time to parties and creative drama or games of imagination.

In general the girls responded with restraint to retreat and concession. When Mullen's mother finally said she could go to Ireland with her blessing, Barbara accepted without launching reproaches.[113] Carroll showed a similar forbearance toward Mother Catharine when the novice-mistress apologized for her efforts to keep Carroll from entering.[114] However, no other opponents ever retreated except in the sense of allowing their children finally to leave home.

The possibility of themselves retreating or taking evasive action,[115] not through cowardice but through necessity, has a special importance for the girls because of their material dependence. Catholic children know the story of the infant Jesus' flight into Egypt well, and they are taught a reason that it was no blot on his courage that he fled from soldiers intent on murdering him: God did not wish to lose him just then. In great danger, physical or spiritual, Catholic girls have been known to flee without the least qualm of guilt and in perfect confidence that they are not cowards. When McCarthy and her brother ran away from their foster parents and hid all night in the art museum, and when Brave Bird's sister Barbara and Barbara's friends ran away from the South Dakota Madams, they had a precedent in the behavior of Christ himself.

Wong, Schoffen, Bernhardt, and Jouhandeau left home as the only way to survive. The strategy of surprise also came into some of their retreats. When Schoffen joined the convent her mother may have been startled, because Elizabeth had been unhappy with the nuns who taught her.[116] Jouhandeau also took a route her despotic mother did not expect, leaving home by climbing down some scaffolding that happened to be outside her fifth-story window.

These flights from cultural and affective deprivation are paralleled and illumined by ''The Escape'' (1962), the third panel of Varo's girlhood narrative in oils.[117] In this picture, the convent student who embroidered the lovers is shown to be a magician, for the picture she stitched has come true.[118] She is now standing behind a young man dressed in pale red in a small boat under a cloudy sky headed through reddish foam for some rough crags. He is using his cloak as a sail; she, still in convent attire but with her skirt billowing up around her knees, is steering the boat with a fanciful rudder. The two are looking at a rather narrow cleft through which they hope to sail. Beyond it and behind the cliffs, the sky is bright. The painting universalizes a flight into unknown reality, including, but not limited to, Varo's rocky marriage at the age of twenty-one in 1930 to Gerardo Lizarraga, one of her fellow students at her art school in Madrid.[119]

But some of the girls, when they could not retreat and faced death, madness, or other severe personal defeat, would fight so desperately as to triumph.[120] McCarthy, Chacel, and Mullen were pushed to the brink of death—moral, psychological, or physical—and in that extremity finally took up the battle they had been evading. The ensuing victories met their personal ethical standards and ensured their survival.

The girls usually succeeded by means of their strategic intelligence. However, sometimes a girl had to surrender to some degree. Even though she knew adults were striking at her spiritual and ethical autonomy and integrity, her retreat was blocked and the force against her was overpowering. Mellish, Chacel, and Noël had to surrender sectors of their lives; Benoist and the nuns surrendered all but one or two sectors of life. Chacel gave up a part of her arsenal to her mother, whom she respected, but she was able to hold her own against her grandmother, whose character was weak. Schoffen, Asquerino, Repplier, and León had to accept unwelcome decisions of adults with regard to their education. Similarly, as young children Bernhardt and Benoist were unable to protect their playtime from adult invasion and the imposition of penalties for breaking gender rules. Even if the girls had recognized the importance of those apparently trivial interferences, they were too small to stop the adults. Similarly understandable is the submission to extreme physical violence made by Jouhandeau, Mullen, Pillay, Fontenot, and Brave Bird. All five took a long time finding a way to escape from physical abuse, in part because Christ's resignation had been preached to them, in part because civil law trapped them with abusive individuals.

Mellish and Noël saw their loss coming but did not have resources adequate for their defense. Mellish was just as submissive at eighteen or so as Noël was at nine. The would-be singer did not look for a way to attend the conservatory without her mother's money and enrolled in teacher's college as her mother wished. Some of the girls surrendered more, but they seem to have done so unconsciously. Benoist did not recognize during her girlhood that she was under attack as a person or that her losses would affect her the rest of her life; as a result, she did not attempt to prevent or modify her mother's femininity training, nor did she try to counteract her parents' sending only the boys to school. The only path Benoist thought of was the one her parents offered her, namely, to divert her energy into activities they accepted as feminine. She probably submitted to her parents' program because of the pleasant lifestyle they were able to provide for her, less a bribe than a distraction. The restrictive gender rules and discrimination she was subjected to must have seemed to her nothing but flashes of bitterness in long periods of sweetness. For example, she always regretted and claims not to understand why, when she married, she refused to go on a honeymoon. She says this even though she mentions her mother's aversion to sexuality. In short, Benoist allowed herself to be deceived in the short and the long run.

In another defeat, Carroll's parents so dominated her as to make her dependent and weak, continually pleading for acceptance, yet she worked out the logistics to fulfill her imperious need to belong. The dominance of her parents might have been the reason Wolff attended the University of Wisconsin in Madison only one year before writing to St. Mary's asking to be rescued, thus inadvertently giving the impression that she could not bear solitude, independence, and a certain kind of responsibility. Nevertheless, with the support of monastic structures, she became a scholar and a firm administrator, a writer and a poet.

Sometimes the girls failed to act strategically and therefore defend themselves successfully because, like Fontenot and Carroll, they could not bring themselves to admit the danger posed by people whose love they wanted. Occasionally, girls used poor strategies because of their rashness or their lack of knowledge of the world. Bernhardt jumped out the window to stop her aunt from leaving her any longer with her nurse. The child was moved to her mother's apartment, but the resulting injury to her leg was too heavy a loss to count the strategy a triumph. In later childhood, however, and quite unaided by any teacher, Bernhardt developed a repertory of strategies that did work. For this reason, she can be credited not only with strategic intelligence, but also with exceptional self-direction.

Though love, danger, and other circumstances may somewhat excuse the defeats and submissions listed above, the girls did not always employ strategic intelligence because their reasoning power was flawed or had not yet matured. Through a lack of courage or knowledge, a lack of strategic imagination, an absence of adequate escape routes, or a lack of other necessary resources, some of these Catholic girls in some situations were unable to imagine or locate a way to defend their integrity or personal development.

Of course, these defects are not surprising in girls trained to be obedient above all else and who lived in a society that provided no practical alternatives to their situation. Some of the girls accepted much of the Catholic Woman program. The Catholic feminization system, taken with the power delegated to parents and nuns, seems to have caused their losses. Authority figures who asked girls to abandon morally good or neutral activities as unfeminine must have resolved the contradiction in Catholic instruction of women by preferring Roessler's view (see chapter 3) or by assuming that his is the only Catholic view. Girls who accepted requirements posited by definitions of the Catholic Woman chose, to that extent, to disregard earlier catechetical instruction they had been given about their lofty destiny. They retained the virtues of piety, humility, and obedience; they discarded all ideas of advanced study and service in the public sphere, together with whatever pleasures men rely on in public life.

Girls who behaved in cowardly or less than prudent ways can be judged with some lenience in accord with their youth and the principle of family resemblances; for example, a girl lacking in ingenuity might have counterattacked vigorously. As a group Catholic girls show much more tactical intelligence than would be possible if by nature women were not capable of intellectual operations. In a group dominated by a theology of the lesser rationality of women, what is surprising is the number of instances in which the girls moved adroitly forward. Their selection of allies, their lack of arrogance, their nonviolence, and their ingenuity show how advanced in rationality and prudence they were.

The actions of the strategically successful girls also met ethical standards imparted in their early catechesis. Perhaps they were not conscious of living up to those teachings, but their behavior is consistent with them. For example, they preferred defense to aggression, and they cared for their own physical and spiritual health and that of their attackers (attitudes required by *Baltimore Number One* in its explanation of the commandment not to kill). Furthermore, the girls were humble in recognizing their vulnerability and their need of self-strengthening and of allies. Their pre-eminent motive was hope, the theological virtue closest to courage, in which they excelled, being for the most part neither rash nor pusillanimous, nor were they unnecessarily cruel. In Catholic terminology, their strategic decisions were acts of prudence, the virtue by which a person chooses the best means to an end. In the sense of *rational* that requires the *content* of our choices to be good, Catholic girls are shown in these texts to make more virtuous choices than vicious ones. In the sense of *rational* that requires the *manner* of our choices to be good, the girls are shown here to excel in prudence—the intelligent design of means to an end, and this can be said, more often than not, even without taking into account their material dependence and the limitations of their knowledge of the world.

Above all, they practiced the moral virtue of creativity, which Matthew Fox prophesied will be the most important of the coming civilization.[121] Repplier and her friends, like Bernhardt, put on spontaneous dramas; Bernhardt and Beauvoir composed dialogues that moved them forward in life; numerous girls spun illusions or carried out other strategic processes to alter their situations; finally, they did much to create new selves, the very thing a belief in a Creator most requires us continually to do.

Incidentally, the strategic and tactical intelligence of the girls affects autobiographies about them by removing them from the category of observers. They remembered their younger selves as centers of activity and responsibility. They were not only under attack, not only to be captured or lost, not only observers or potential war correspondents. These girls took up the good fight, engaged in the conflict, and almost always decided its outcome. As a result, they have life-histories and provide adequate subject matter for autobiography.

These tales can play a role in the reading lives of people not belonging to the Catholic Church. Mainstream readers or readers from other minority groups may be surprised by the forms gender discrimination has taken in the lives of Catholic girls. Feminist readers from other backgrounds might not have appreciated the struggle their Catholic sisters have had to undertake just to get hold of some books and friends and to acquire a college education, a moderate sex life, and the opportunity to make ordinary decisions. No doubt other feminists have had difficulties of which Catholic women are unaware. Spelman argues in *The Inessential Woman* for inclusion of black and other minority women in feminist study so that we will not homogenize women even in thought. Catholic women too can guarantee the variety of women, both by writing autobiography and by reading autobiographies from groups unfamiliar to them.

The spectrum of behavior among Catholic girls shows that no minority group is monolithic either, thus expanding our concept of women on a second level. The prescription of Catholic femininity rules has sometimes produced women who submitted through faith or wounded love, accepting the Catholic Woman's lie of constantly manifested femininity, domesticity, or spiritual motherhood, carried on without much intellectual activity, without serious achievement, without independence and intentionality, or without expression of sexual energy. In other instances, Catholic gender requirements have produced women who cling so fiercely to simple human things like education, sexuality, and personal judgment as to reject motherhood or hyperfemininity altogether for their sake. Between these extremes, combinations are possible: a little obedience with a lot of independence, for example. Differences between the challenges faced by Catholic girls and by other girls, diversity among Catholic girls, and the model of strategic intelligence Catholic girls offer make Catholic girlhood narratives an exotic yet useful part of the new library of women's books.

chapter six

Catholic Women Autobiographers Keep Up the Good Fight

*I*F Catholic women can be said to define themselves through
autobiography, or if the readers of their autobiographies were
to define the self of women by analyzing these texts, the definitions would not
read quite the same as clerical definitions. In the following description of herself as an infant, Chacel gives an implied definition of the mature self: "My
illuminations marked the road, but between its brilliant points was the Cloudy,
where sheltered infantile fear, indecision, abandonment to the will of others,
the suspension of one's own judgment."[1] Her childhood history is one of
deliberately moving beyond these weaknesses to maturity, a human condition
she must therefore have seen as involving the virtues of courage and decisiveness or independence of judgment, a personal autonomy arising in my view
from our each having a separate brain. These autobiographers can be said to
define their girlhood selves as persons developing toward a life of intelligent,
resourceful justice to self and others, or as endowed with a full range of human
potentials, some of which they developed by opposing the Church's efforts to
stop them. Speaking negatively, they would define themselves as not having
been interested in a life of embroidery, with all the futility such an ideal suggested to them.

These narrative definitions imply approval of the earlier self, but an autobiographer could repudiate her younger self, and if she did, a narrative about earlier resistance to the Church's gender training would deplore that behavior. Autobiography is a genre whose revelation of the present is more significant than its recollection of the past.[2] Lejeune distinguishes among attitudes of the autobiographical self toward the narrated self. The remembering "I" may write about the remembered "I" from a stance of identification (either cerebral or emotional), of amusement, of nostalgia, or of shame.[3] After studying Catholic women autobiographers, I would add to these four stances two others: those of self-effacement and unshakable determination not to be effaced. When the writers of this study are examined against this grid, some fall into every category, but only Mellish blames her younger self in any serious way. She is ashamed and disturbed by the wrongness in her remembered self, but it is not a wrongness originating with Eve or the nature of Woman; the wrongness she regrets comes from growing up a Catholic girl, bigoted and, she feels, narrow-minded.[4] Fontenot, who formally repents of her sins in her autobiography, when she looks into their causes rather approves of the generous love of that young girl. Self-effacement afflicted the women in various degrees, to the greatest extent in Carroll and Norris. Wolff seems most out of touch with, or least interested in writing about, her younger self, with the result that readers may wonder if her superiors commanded the composition. Some of the others—Carroll, for example—regard the earlier self with grandmotherly affection; a few find their early dramas and excesses amusing.[5] But a larger number are interested in their memories of girlhood as the source of the later personality: for example, Bernhardt of her theatricality, Beauvoir of her existentialism,[6] McCarthy and Conway of their attitude toward the Church, Menchú of her social activism. All the autobiographers approve of and identify with the remembered self, insofar as she refused to be made a bigot, diminished, or effaced. In other words, the feeling of the narrating voice (which for convenience I shall refer to as the autobiographers) favors the girls in their fight with Catholic isolationism and femininity training.

The attitude of the autobiographer may be the best way of ascertaining whether she still supports the resistance of the young girl she once was. But semantic or other linguistic clues may also save a reader from mistaking the voice or distorting the intention through a personal bias. When Rose says that on her birthday Citation won the Derby and both Israel and the United Nations were born, most readers would attribute these associations to an adult reflecting on the past. Similarly, few readers would think McCarthy in a 1920s parochial school in Minneapolis would have learned much about totalitarianism, the characteristics of institutions, or less famous Greek myths. Yet she writes of that period, "The basis, I think, of my aunt's program for us in truth totalitarian. . . . Aunt Margaret strove purposefully toward a corporate goal. Like most heads of institutions, she longed for the eyes of Argus."[7] Statements that are cognitively impossible for even the brightest child can be attributed to the autobiographer.

A second sign of the autobiographer's voice is a judgment the child could not have made, like Mellish's remark that she had been bigoted. At the time, she might have known the word and its meaning, but she did not know that it described her and her teachers. A third sign that the autobiographer is distinguishing between present and past views of events are phrases like McCarthy's "what interests me now" or "it now seems to me."[8] In addition to these three kinds of signal of the autobiographer's voice, readers who have noticed or are familiar with Matute's system of evading censorship, as described in chapter 1 above, can apply that knowledge to see the messages hidden in or near instances of symbolic disguise, omission, allusion and hypertext, or iteration.

If these signals of the autobiographer's attitude are taken into account in reading the autobiographies of Catholic women, it becomes clear that maturity did not soften the rebellion against Catholic femininity. Most of the autobiographers are more strongly opposed to Catholic gender training as adults than they had been as children. Among the prominent differences between the women writing and the girls speaking is a greater understanding of who their opponent is. Many of the autobiographers indicate in one way or another that they now see the opponent as the Church itself. In childhood they experienced the Church as their family, school, or parish; now they have a better idea of its size and missionary attitude. For that reason they write not letters to their bishop calling for local reform, but works addressed to the public. When they write for a general audience about the limiting effects of Catholic femininity, they are composing entries in a cultural debate.

Even though as women many of them had to struggle with some form of censorship, most of them lived at some distance from their former opponents. Farrell, Carroll, and Wolff, of course, lived and worked in the same building or plant with their superior and near a chaplain or parish priest; the nuns still sound as orthodox as when they were children. As far as I know, only Conway has deliberately engaged a member of the hierarchy at a public meeting in order to bring official Catholic views on women into the open; this courageous action led to ecclesiastical retaliations against her children.[9]

For examining the autobiographers, Wittgenstein's principle of family resemblances can help clarify the overall tendency of their arguments. Some of the women remember the Church's having acted against them in particular areas of life; others in quite different areas. Consequently, their arguments and countermoves against the concept of the Catholic Woman vary. If all the arguments and countermoves of all the autobiographers are considered successful, however, nothing of the official definition of Woman or the traditional way of teaching it to girls is left standing.

The values and causes argued for include: girlhood exploration of this world, wide reading and nonsectarian education, the existence of reason in girls, the sacredness of the secular, participation of women in public life, a life of providing beauty and charity to people outside the family, secular careers that involve autonomy and even glory, friendships, encouragement of athletic, intellectual, or artistic inclinations and ambition in girls, an ethics based on the natural rather than the ecclesiastical, self-respect and a healthy egoism, laughter, artistic activity, the possibility and even probability of moral improvement in girls, the right to prefer or imitate one's father to some degree, the right to direct one's spiritual growth, a synthesis of sexuality and love, the natural variety and goodness of heterosexuality, homosexuality, and bisexuality, convent life, judicious rebellion in the young, freedom to keep silence about one's opinions if self-defense requires it, the value of criticism when institutional reform is possible, a realistic assessment of the abilities and virtues of girls and women.

Similarly, one or more of the autobiographers oppose: expressions of contempt and discouraging remarks to girls, inappropriate or disproportionate punishments, gratuitous violence toward or exclusion of innocent people or animals, enclosure in a purely Catholic milieu or mental world, sectarian narrow-mindedness, voluntary unimportance, programming women to be immoral because they are female, perverted ideas on sex, compulsory and lifelong monogamy, compulsory heterosexuality, avoidance of the topic of sex in society, prudery, declaiming against sexuality or an interest in sex as lustful, conferring divinity on parents and parenthood on nuns and priests, making the mother the only model for girls, making an exclusive relationship with one's mother a form of training for matrimonial fidelity, uniformity of values and manners, a life of sacrifices imposed by others, unnecessary and excessive sorrow due to interference with the personal development of women or with their children, helplessness in women, being expected to obey unworthy people or people who abuse their authority, the trivial envy and malice induced by convent life, and exclusive assignment of certain virtues and intellectual or cultural pursuits to men and boys.

A Catholic woman writing an autobiography is already a subversive. Just by writing and publishing she proves that she would be unable always to wait for direction from a superior, even one appointed by the hierarchy; when she criticizes the Church, she disproves again that she is by nature deferent to males. Catherine of Siena, Hildegarde of Bingen,[10] and Teresa of Avila expressed their criticism of certain clerical decisions and actions without softening the force of their words; the high standard they set has not been everywhere abandoned.

In other words, taken together, the autobiographers reject Catholic gender training entirely. Their interpretation of the experience of growing up "in an institution" is not favorable, overall, to the institution. Autobiography can present a version of the past and work to persuade readers to accept that version, as Starobinski suggests.[11] These narratives are not neutral eyewitness accounts of the way Catholic gender theology has been applied to girls and women between 1835 and 1990; these texts are persuasive, using four narrative strategies to convince readers of their version of events: (1) constructing a plot or overall structure that doubles as a demonstration of a thesis; (2) reversing or transforming devices often deployed in narrative, such as example, classification, causal analysis (most frequently in pointing out harmful results of Catholic gender training), process analysis, definition, comment, maxim, summary, or contrast, or changing more general literary devices or modes like association, tone, metaphor, or description, so that instead of supporting the church as a traditional Catholic reader would expect, episodes and small narrative units contradict or otherwise undermine the official program; (3) camouflaging one's criticism while revealing its presence to sympathizers through affinity signals; (4) describing alternative, better paths in the outside world or in the part of the world that keeps escaping Catholic control. This last form of argument, which occurs frequently in the texts, makes the autobiographers visionaries as well as critics.

Because the autobiographies show marks of having been composed (for example, changing the order of incidents from the chronological), they prove that although the Catholic Woman as an abstract, clerical concept may be naturally and inevitably subrational and sexually dangerous, real Catholic women can think, are disciplined, and work in a creative way. Overall, as I will show in the second part of this chapter, innovations in these autobiographies, while not abandoning a fundamentally realistic narrative, have tended to expand the genre into realms of the imaginative, intertextual, witty, and symbolic.

First, some examples of autobiographers' narrative arguments or cases seem necessary. Marie Noël makes a point of not accepting her parents' insistence on her sinfulness. She reasons that because she had not been sinful, to suggest that she had been was unjust, especially in its devastation of her self-respect, her confidence, her joy. Their treatment of her lying had trapped her in sadness about herself that she was unable to overcome without help from Christ himself. She denies that an artificially induced misery was necessary to convince her of Christ's mercy. The feeling of having been deliberately wounded by her beloved parents explains her cry as autobiographer: "Grown-ups, what have you done?"[12] What may seem an intrusive comment from a novel's narrator becomes in autobiography the heart of the narrative. Noël's criticism of her parents in print, especially of their zeal in preparing her for the sacraments, may shock a traditional Catholic believer. However, in her text she is fair to her parents, describing their merits and affection as well as their mistakes. Noël's emphatic objection to sinfulness training (for by sifting her behavior every day for sins, her parents were teaching her to believe she was a sinful person), taken together with her love for other elements of her religion, indicates that she probably wrote *Petit-Jour* in an effort to obtain an improvement in Catholic religious education; in other words, autobiography can provide loyal criticism.

The date of *Petit-Jour* (1951) places it in the stream of a general movement in Catholic education to remove the threat of hellfire from the education of very young children, a threat that may be more terrible for girls than for boys, as it was in Noël's family. Noël in her maturity thinks her father should not have blamed his merciless, punitive attitude on Jesus, who relieved her of guilt and accepted her offerings. Judging from her examples of what she was punished for, she believes children should not be taught to feel guilty about actions that are morally neutral or trivial. If Noël and others had concealed the excessively discouraging impact of the old way, it would never have been changed. What she avoids, as an orthodox and exceptionally devout Catholic, is grounding her objections on any philosophy other than the Catholic, or criticizing her father for any other behavior.

Several autobiographers contend that girls are good in that they are capable of moral improvement. Barbara Mullen's narrative is designed to show how she at first lacked the courage to resist her mother's pressure to live at a low level of spirituality but over time built up her courage and finally did leave her mother.[13] The coherence of the book comes from the steady, gradual change in Barbara's character as she grows in independence; thus, the formal narrative progression reinforces her message that women can make spiritual progress. In this way she constructs a text whose remembered story and whose autobiographical voice combine to form a single argument.

When girls are believed to be good at heart and, if flawed, capable of improvement, persuasive effort shifts to ridding them of discouraging sermons. Dussane opposes disapproval and hellfire education first by relating how her mother pulled her out of a Catholic school after she began having nightmares about hell. This recollection seems meant to be acted on by clerical readers and parents. Second, Dussane praises the virtues she was taught in the neighborhood school and the positive encouragement she was given there. Mme. Dardaillon and Mlle. Gouélin, instead of training the children in obedience, humility, and mildness, trained them in "virile virtues: physical and moral courage, solidarity, frankness, sense of responsibility, taste for initiative, war on pettiness, sneakiness and informing, respect only for those hierarchies established on authentic value." These secular teachers also fostered intellectual virtues: concentration, initiative, and enthusiasm. Dussane notes and commends their vigilance against her disorders an inattentions; she also praises them because in their school she was "always induced . . . to go forward" in whatever direction she attempted to test her new energies.[14] Dussane's description of what a good secular education can do disables the rationale for educating girls only in religious subjects and for urging women to devote themselves completely to the religious education of children. She might have enjoyed Asquerino's joke about her Catholic school: "The outcome of knowing how to sew on a button and turn up a hem doesn't seem to be, on the face of it, otherworldly."[15] Dussane proposes by her example that women move as complete persons into public life.

Taking the defense of the moral educability and goodness of human females to a higher level of abstraction, where she was more likely to get a hearing, Colette presents a case against the idea of a uniform moral code that applies to both women and men. In her description of the (certainly Catholic) village in which she grew up, Colette does not discover the moral uniformity envisioned by the catechism. She matter-of-factly describes as natural a range in the independence and sexuality of people and a variety in their social roles. She never judges the goodness of anyone's position along this range; the point she makes is that reality is more complete than the Church's picture of it.

Several autobiographers—especially Schoffen, McCarthy, and Beauvoir—

make a case against Catholic isolationism or cultural enclosure, which applied mainly to women in Mediterranean countries after the filtration of Islamic influence between the eighth and thirteenth centuries. Schoffen's text answers an implicit questionnaire originating with Protestants during the nineteenth and early twentieth centuries, when Protestants and Catholics in the United States were warned to avoid each other: Why did you join the convent? Do Catholics really think Protestants are going to hell? Why didn't you attend the public school? Why didn't you run away from home? How did the priest deceive you into joining the convent? Did the priest molest you? In what ways were you mistreated in the convent? Her answers are not those of a bogus nun, but they add up to a condemnation of the sacrifice of the educational opportunities of Catholics to prevent their mingling with non-Catholics at school.

McCarthy recalls how her Grandmother McCarthy had been preoccupied with the evils of Protestantism, and how she wanted to keep Mary and her brothers away from their Protestant grandparents. As a girl, McCarthy soaked this up. When her Protestant grandfather came to rescue her at her request, she told him that all Protestants deserved to be burned at the stake. She quotes the hate chant she used to recite against Jews under her breath, even at a time when she felt considerable awe of her Jewish grandmother. But the adult McCarthy recognizes in those Catholics who have written insulting letters to her the spirit of her bigoted grandmother McCarthy, and, as an autobiographer, she follows the data to a conclusion different from what the child had been capable of. Her introduction closes with a disavowal of the kind of God invoked in the letters: an exclusive and condemnatory deity. As a result of her firsthand experience of the results of bigotry and anti-intellectualism, both in the past and in the present, she states that "the Catholic religion, I believe, is the most dangerous of all, morally (I do not know about the Moslem)."[16]

A number of women write their autobiographies as an argument for a certain type of egoism. In all the autobiographies by women I have read, even the poorest, when the self is not the direct subject it is always the true subject. The main character recounts her remembered self's internal responses to the other characters as models, allies, or opponents and often analyzes her external actions in regard to them. One of many examples of a woman's autobiography that portrays others not as separable beings but as relating to a central remembered self is Barbara Mullen's *Life Is My Adventure*. This work presents a full account of a dominant mother, but always and only in relation to the main narrative, namely the story of Mullen's resistance to her mother.

When Wolff entered the convent she felt she had little to offer; she did not think so in retrospect. "When a young person, in a short, succinct formula, gives to God by vows pronounced in public, her whole life with all its promise, all its possibilities, little room is left for commentary. I had done this. I had given away everything that I had, or ever could have or be. I had come to the final answer. I had found out why God had made me. For Him and His reasons I had begun to be." To many nuns, this gift of themselves to God and to the Church meant to refrain from shining in this world, to hide their glory until the next. To Wolff, and no doubt to other modern nuns as well, it meant to shine as brightly as possible, like a diamond on his watch fob, to add to his credit with strangers. She titled one of her chapters "It Pays to Advertise," referring to the St. Mary's ad that had attracted *her*.[17]

Adam defines *egoist* as a person who does not live for others, and she goes on to say that she has always lived for others.[18] This statement could not be made by a self-deprecating woman. For her autobiography, which was written to explain how she came to surpass other women, Adam defines *egoist* more narratively; that is, she relates only those incidents from her girlhood that describe her happy and healthy confidence in her goodness and ability. The virtues she attributes to herself are those of public life, not those of domestic enclosure.

Delarue-Mardrus frankly wanted to be "something and even someone," and she reverses the Church's classification of pride as a capital sin. "I have never been able to attain vanity, a capital lack from which I have suffered and suffer still—vanity, indispensable light which for me has never illuminated the dark corners."[19] By observing that excessive humility has damaged her life, she discredits Catholic gender training as a system.

Inevitably, significant arguments are leveled by the autobiographers against the excesses of Catholic teachings on parental authority. The most basic point made is that parents are not divine but human. Delarue-Mardrus notes that her parents were not especially Catholic—"with us, [Catholicism] did not play much of a role"[20]—and did not feel they had a duty to represent God's wishes or authority. As a result, Lucie was able to respond to her parents with a sensitivity that does not necessarily appear in efforts to carry out ethical principles, even sound ones. Her bond with them was based not on catechesis and duty, but on affection.

For several autobiographers the crux of their difference with the Church is that parents should not have exclusive power over their children, not only because some parents are vicious, but because others of a child's contacts may be benevolent and beneficial.

In reacting against another branch of the teaching on parental authority, Rosa Chacel argues for imitating the good in one's mother, and against imitating what the Church thinks is good in her. Rosa adopted only those traits the Church did not promote in women: knowing how to look at beautiful things and desiring to realize one's ideas. She kept nothing of her mother as a Catholic mother. She rejected her mother's lack of courage, her openness to suffering, and her submissiveness to her husband and her mother.[21] Rosa absorbed from her father his interest in the world, his courage, his satirical tendency, and his talent for writing.[22]

Norris, Beauvoir, Delarue-Mardrus, Brave Bird, and Menchú investigate the influence of siblings and friends in a girl's formation, an influence not envisioned by the catechism. Delarue-Mardrus devotes considerable space, playing off Genesis, to establishing the complex role her five sisters played in her progress. In the family garden, which she refers to as a paradise, her sisters called her into this life from her absorption in former centuries, especially those of the pharoahs and ancient Greek writers. She completes the story of her personal Genesis by telling how her sisters used to frighten or ridicule her, calling her stupid or a great worm, possibly in reference to the snake of Eden. In later childhood the sisters observed together the sex lives of animals. In her late adolescence, the older sisters began to give Lucie approval and to find cultural opportunities for her.[23]

Elizabeth Fishel in her book *Sisters* gives attention to blood sisters and to other females who function as a girl's sisters.[24] Repplier and Beauvoir in particular maintain the ethical value of such bonds. Repplier repeatedly tells how her friend Elizabeth liked to urge her upward and sometimes prevailed. Repplier describes herself and Elizabeth as walking happily together in the garden during retreat, and mocks them a little for having used their examination of conscience as a means to gossip about other girls.[25] Their friendship qualifies as a spiritual friendship, if only in its beginning phase, by the standards of St. Aelred of Rievaulx, the greatest English Cistercian, a Father of the Church, and the best Catholic authority on the subject of friendship. He recommends that friends should enjoy their natural affection for one another, and on that foundation the sharing of higher goods will develop naturally. "Spiritual friendship among the just is born of a similarity in life, morals, and pursuits, that is, it is a mutual conformity in matters human and divine united with benevolence and charity."[26] Agnes repented the defect in charity after her gossip with Elizabeth. In reforming her behavior with her friend she took a step toward benevolence.

Although spiritual friendships are not recommended or discussed in the catechism, some girls had the good fortune to experience such relationships. Simone de Beauvoir comments on the spiritual benefit of her friendship with Zaza Mabille: "Henceforward my self-sufficiency was tempered by feelings inspired by someone else outside my family. I had had the good fortune to find a friend."[27] This judgment measures friendship against the standard of social justice. One of the fruits of this relationship was a strong conviction in both girls that marriage or its equivalent should be based on a personal bond and should not be contracted because two strangers are found by their parents to have equal social status.

In addition to maintaining that parents are not divine and that their influence (or the mother's influence) should not be the only one allowed, a third consideration the autobiographers have in mind—particularly McCarthy, Jouhandeau, and Mullen—is that the Church is wrong to assume that all parents use their authority for the spiritual good of their children. A few of these women deplore the teaching of the Church that women must be directed by men on the ground that not all men are worthy of the task. McCarthy describes her great-uncle Myers Shriver as unworthy of heading a family because he was gluttonous and anti-intellectual, actively promoting "everything sour and ugly."[28]

Again, the Church's extension of maternal authority to nuns and paternal authority to priests sometimes improves a child's lot, as it did with Bernhardt, but more numerous autobiographers—León, Beauvoir, Brave Bird, Pillay, and others—report an opposite result. León, by including all the circumstances of her expulsion from school by the nuns to show how unjustified it was, stands with that girl and refuses to condemn her. She also identifies with her by a comment near the end of her book, to the effect that she hopes her grandchildren will not think her ignorant of life, not feel the same rage she had felt toward the nun who insulted her.[29] Her *Memoria de la melancolía* is not a forgiving book; León is not willing to sugarcoat or conceal injustice.

Norris takes a different tack, not criticizing anyone she knew for abuses of authority in the enforcement of the femininity program, but maintaining that a program of complete subordination for women has disastrous results. She demonstrates the weakness of Catholic femininity in the person of her aunt, who was unable to function without a male at the head of the family and therefore unable to act justly and charitably. "My aunt was the timidest and least practical of nervous little women. She had been reared to play the piano, arrange flowers, and be gracefully helpless. In the catastrophe that had befallen us, and under the fearful blow of seeing her beloved brother's daughters 're-duced,' she succumbed to invalidism. She never quite recovered, although she lived for many years. "Under her plaintive mismanagement, we did everything wrong. There was no system to us."[30] Norris must have felt that these results implied that her aunt must have been asked in adolescence to sacrifice her expressiveness, sexuality, courage, competence, and adaptability.

Almost all these women, including the nuns, reject the cult of self-sacrifice. Writing her autobiography at the beginning of the twentieth century from a position of cultural importance as founder of a respected Parisian journal, Adam distinguishes between worthy self-sacrifice as devotion to others or to principle and abominable self-sacrifice as renunciation of self-development or life-enhancement. She thought such abdications could not have an adequate ethical motive.[31]

In the entire *Roman de mon enfance et de ma jeunesse,* Adam describes no sacrifice made for a theoretical result, like those made by Catholic schoolchild-ren when they sacrifice candy to help a soul escape from purgatory. Speaking of these juvenile rituals, Repplier comments that " 'making an act' was the convent phraseology for doing without something one wanted, for stopping short on the verge of an innocent gratification. . . . It will be easily understood that the constant practice of acts deprived life of everything that made it worth the living."[32] Her humor does not interfere with her precision; these little sacrifices were not made to deepen any virtue, but only to develop the habit of voluntarily doing without innocent pleasures. As I mentioned in chapter 5, Repplier repudiated this formation and no doubt believed every reasoning Catholic woman would do likewise, preferring to perform sacrifices, as she did, only for love.

In addition to seemingly pointless renunciations, Beauvoir's training in sacrifice did call for acts of virtue. But she mocks these childhood practices for their contribution to her conceit and the far-fetched results that were promised the children. "It had been explained to me that if I were good and pious God would save France [from the Germans in World War I]. . . . Abbé Martin distributed to us at the beginning of Advent pictures representing the Infant Jesus: whenever we did a good deed, we had to prick with a pin the outline of the figure, which was drawn in violet ink. On Christmas Day, we had to go and place our pictures round the crib at the end of the church, where the light played through the pin-prick holes. I invented every kind of mortification, sacrifice, and edifying behavior in order that my picture might be richly be-dight with pinpricks."[33]

Some Catholic women writing autobiography have no complaint about the reticence or suppression of information in their sexual training.[34] However, what the clergy teach on female sexuality is almost universally disturbing to good Catholic women. By Mary McCarthy's account, the Madams of the Sacred Heart wanted so much not to be repressive, that they fictionalized the major elements of her female life cycle. Under them, Mary had a bathetic menarche that was really nothing but a cut on the leg; she experienced the awakening of the abstract intellect because of their discussion of atheism; and, because of their teachings, she thought she had lost her virginity when she had only fallen asleep in the arms of a sentimental man also satisfied to fall asleep.[35]

McCarthy makes a graceful case for free and healthy female sexuality with her memories of her beautiful and dignified Grandmother Preston. In early adolescence McCarthy's scrupulosity and prudery appeared in her disapproval of her grandmother's "mature sensuality," as manifest among other ways in her love of being courted. Mary's wishes as a girl that they might talk more, her naughty invasion of her grandmother's cosmetics, her observation of her grandmother's sensuous enjoyment of downy fruits predict "the real dame" McCarthy became. As an autobiographer McCarthy compares her own adult love of apricots with her grandmother's, reassuring readers that she would eventually escape her Irish Jansenism. By means of her later realization of how desirable her grandmother was, McCarthy confides in us one of the mysterious values of her heritage, namely, a rich sense of her own femaleness.[36] McCarthy's adult approval of female sexuality is far from unusual in this group of writers. (Although the nuns in the group do not much discuss the subject, they do not voice any disapproval.)

León wanted sexual love considered equal to the highest good, for it enables one generation to pass its vitality, courage, and culture to the next. When she is lamenting her exile because of the loss of cultural continuity, she expresses her sorrow with a striking image of loss. "I sometimes see around myself a pool of blood. I cannot put back in my veins what I go on losing. Now my imagination doesn't function enough and memory is forgotten."[37] This attitude is a development of surrealist monism, but her disapproval of the Church's low opinion of the sexuality and intelligence of women preceded and opened the way to her surrealism. In childhood she objected violently to the prohibition of books and pictures that could inform children about sex in art, story, and history. She maintains that the Church is wrong to conceal sexual love as if it were evil. She calls evil the Catholic cardinal who withheld approval of her love for Rafael Alberti, the Catholic government that exiled practitioners of love for country, and the Catholic bombardier who destroyed the symbols of love in children's nativity scenes.

Simone de Beauvoir as autobiographer considered that Catholic belief about and practice of purity had harmed her as a girl; at seventeen she did not recognize how completely she had been trained in prudery.[38] By *purity* the Church has ordinarily meant freedom from all sexual activity outside marriage and freedom from all sexual desire and enjoyment, even while endeavoring to reproduce, or, as in Beauvoir's Thomistic definition, which lasted most of her university career, complete control of sexual desire by reason: "All is well if the body obeys the head and the heart, but it must not take the first step."[39] Perhaps owing to this idea of desirable sexual activity, Beauvoir's girlhood erotic history deals with advances upward toward zero.

To begin with, the rule of never discussing sex created a breach between Beauvoir and her otherwise affectionate mother. Her mother associated sex with evil and danger and was quite frightened when she found Simone looking at one of her father's novels. Beauvoir notes that, among less desirable results of this maternal model, her mother did not provide needed information; she did not tell Simone that she would menstruate, what it would be like, or how to cope with it. When Simone and her younger sister Hélène asked about childbirth, their mother gave them the impression that babies emerge through the anus and without causing pain. Once, standing in the back of a movie theater, Simone put herself in danger by thinking that molestation by a strange man must be the unsuccessful efforts of a pickpocket. In other words, Beauvoir is pointing out that girls need information on sex in order to be able to protect themselves when they no longer have chaperones. In another needless and emotionally exhausting error because of her lack of information on sex, she wasted years courting her cousin Jacques, a man for whom she felt no physical desire and from whom she actually recoiled, because she did not realize that her repulsion was a signal not to marry him.[40]

The ignorance cultivated by the Beauvoirs was not only neutral. Their disapproval of modern dress, bobbed hair, and so on, was made to seem to Simone and Hélène a disapproval they shared with everyone.[41] In fact, it is the Catechism of Trent that states explicitly, "Too much display in dress, which especially attracts the eye, is but too frequently an occasion of sin. . . . As women are given to excessive fondness for dress, it will not be unseasonable in the pastor to give some attention to the subject and sometimes to admonish and reprove them."[42] The drilling Simone had received in prudery affected her for some time after she began university life. She would shrink, "shrivel up," or "go rigid with disapproval" if her new acquaintances attempted to explain men to her or mentioned that a couple "were together."[43]

Her own avoidance of sexuality generalized into an avoidance of physical activity except for walking. Her lifestyle at the university was hampered by an imbalance in favor of the cerebral. Her too continuous attention to study for a time deprived her body to such an extent that she slipped out of contact with reality, experiencing life as a desert of misery and abstraction. During most of her university career, Simone's concept of human nature excluded the body. "I was a soul, a pure, disembodied spirit; I was only interested in people's souls and spirits."[44]

In addition to analysis, another strategy she uses against a Catholic upbringing in chastity is to report similar priggishness in her male peers. She mentions two young Catholic males who were so frightened when their fiancées kissed them passionately that the young women lost patience with them and ended their relationships.[45]

After Simone had been at the university for a time, she made a friend, André Herbaud, whose person opened her eyes to the human body. "It would have been impossible to reduce Herbaud's face to a symbol; the jutting jaw, the broad, liquid smile, the blue irises set in their lustrous corneas; his flesh, his bone structure, and his very skin made an ineffaceable impression and were self-sufficient. Herbaud had more than a face: he had an unmistakable body, too. . . . I would watch him come striding through the gardens with his rather awkward grace; I would look at his ears, transparent in the sun as pink sugar-candy, and I knew that I had beside me not an angel, but a real man."[46]

Beauvoir's use of the word *angel* may indicate that she had been ignoring her friends' bodies, aware of them only as conversational partners or thinkers. In hindsight, Beauvoir thought angelism led to biases and failures of understanding precisely because of its denial of police brutality, pimps, "poverty, crime, oppression, war."[47]

Beauvoir's text reveals a literary result of angelism, one damaging to autobiography. In characterizing her friends, she recalls their merits and flaws, their ideas, their ways of relating to life and people, and occasionally a detail of their appearance above the neck.[48] She very seldom indicates any bodily gesture they made, and she never mentions what their physical condition was on a given day.

Finally, she does not refer to any sexual feeling she might have had in the first months of their relationship for Jean-Paul Sartre, her lifelong love and lover, an omission that may indicate a very strange degree of sexual suppression. However, as I mentioned earlier, she says she was not afraid of sex if it followed a rational decision. In addition to the influence of Aquinas on this attitude, she might have escaped the fear of sexual consummation itself partly because of the happy intimacy her parents seem to have enjoyed during the early years of their marriage.[49] Perhaps her prudery at the Sorbonne was concerned only with conversational references to sex. Moreover, Beauvoir's readers all knew that she had a sexual relationship with Sartre, and perhaps she could tell them nothing as surprising about that as the incidents in which they two had celebrated the joy of their first love at bookstalls and sidewalk cafés or driving with their friends.[50]

Nevertheless, paradoxically, Beauvoir does not omit her erotic history, dealing with this challenge by telling the history of her desexualizing education instead. In place of giving a history of her awakening sexual feeling, she relates incidents in which sexuality was disapproved of by her parents and teachers or the knowledge of sexuality was withheld or her behavior reflected these earlier incidents.

Catholic repression of sexuality in young girls can be complex, related to protectiveness toward young girls, to a firm intention that they are never going to allow themselves to enjoy their sexuality, and to wish that we had no bodies. Among these autobiographers vigorous objections are found to all that, and also to Catholic aversion to individuals who engage in serial marriage, lesbian bonding, or the imitation of masculine virtues. Colette makes a case against compulsory and lifelong monogamy. She finds no fault with her mother for having divorced her first husband and married another. She praises her mother's devotion to her financially unsuccessful second husband and her passionate care for her children, for animals even when they ate her food, for her flowers, and for literature. Of these forms of love, the Church asked Sido to practice devotion only to her husband and children; moreover, she would have been considered on the road to hell because of the divorce and remarriage. Colette herself when grown imitated her mother in all her loves, for Colette divorced and remarried twice, cared deeply for cats, devoted herself to literature and to the assistance of a financially unsuccessful husband, her third. All these actions were outside and some were opposed to the Church's definition of the Catholic Woman. Therefore, in her autobiographical works eulogies of her mother serve to defend Colette's life by reversing Catholic descriptions of the kind of mother a daughter is to imitate.

Colette makes a case, too, against compulsory heterosexuality, in a rather daring passage that compares her mother's love for her with that of a young man for a young girl he is kidnapping.[51] In *La maison de Claudine* Colette did not write a direct statement on the acceptability of human bisexual character. She knew human nature is not considered by the Church to be a moral guide and that Catholics have no sexual choice other than the one between monogamy and celibacy. But through this and other episodes of *La maison de Claudine* and *Sido,* she defends the co-existence of bisexuality and homosexuality with heterosexuality in human society.

Delarue-Mardrus defends her lesbianism by recounting its prehistory. Without knowing of the existence of other lesbians, she had learned from three kisses what moved her. The kiss of a young man she had decided to marry did not; a kiss from a woman who was visiting her sister Charlotte did. But she was distracted by wondering whether the second kiss had been intentional or accidental, so that she did not ask herself what the implications of her intense reaction were for her future. What finally taught Lucie that she would prefer a woman as a sexual intimate was a kiss given her by a cultivated baroness who was visiting the family. Delarue-Mardrus comments that though from that moment she was "marked, lost," she had only then been born, because "for such a passion one could kill, dishonor oneself, risk prison, death."[52] Such a narrative is no doubt told to prove that she was a lesbian not because of deprivation of male attention, rebellion against the Church, or a love of fashion and notoriety. In other words, her sexual orientation was natural for her.

The history of Delarue-Mardrus's unfolding consciousness of the erotic illustrates how she responded most to Catholic ethics at the time of her menarche, when she was absorbed in what she thought were sinful fantasies of the wedding night; when she experienced real attraction to real people she thought much less about Catholic ethics. Thus, erotic history as an element of autobiography is not classwide or generic, as Father Ketter implied in speaking of female sexuality.

The final argument to be identified on sex and gender is the argument of several autobiographers that girls can develop "masculine" virtues and that they should be taught to do so, if these are in reality human virtues.

One Catholic laywoman who heard about this study urged me to emphasize the sexual problems the Church creates for women, but many of these difficulties surface after girlhood. The texts themselves seem more concerned about the old, persistent accusations that women are inherently not rational and not good. The personal history or cultural situation of women growing up Catholic has given them a reason to insist on their rationality. Matute, Chacel, and León make a narrative case for the intelligence of girls. The Spanish argument is that if the writer reasoned before "the age of reason" (which in some times and places the Church has considered to be ten, in others, seven), then women in general must be naturally rational. In other words, if an infant reasons before she has been schooled, this is nature, not nurture. Matute, by telling how she used to name the creatures of her world, is answering the common Catholic argument that men are more intellectual or rational than women because in Genesis it was Adam who named the animals. Matute makes the major contention of *El río* her power as a little girl to educate herself in direct relation to the world and her parallel power as an autobiographer to derive ideas from her experiences.

Speaking of her infant self, Rosa Chacel states explicitly that her decision to wean herself was conscious; by so doing, she begins to interpret her childhood as a history of intelligence. "Around all those acts that can be executed in the beginning of life . . . I manage to distinguish an attempt of consciousness that, later, I came to formulate to myself and that manifested itself in struggle—a struggle for life, similar to that of the shipwreck or better than that of someone who is drowning in a marsh—against my infancy."[53] Her desire to move from infancy and nonexistence into consciousness was one of the most important drives of her childhood. Thus, Chacel argues that even before she was five, she wanted to attain consciousness and control.[54] This claim denies that males monopolize rationality and should monopolize education. In the rest of her book Chacel recounts the types of thinking she did as a girl and the sound results she achieved. In her turn, León relates how she had wanted to learn and how she fought the nuns because they were not giving her the intellectual freedom enjoyed by her aunt, María Goyri.

Against the argument that women lack the capacity for higher study, Delarue-Mardrus employs the historian's strategy of periodization. In describing the way she provided her own higher education, she divides the process into the study of, first, the novelists and poets, second, the fixed forms of French verse, and, third, Latin and Greek grammar, philosophy, heraldic art, Plato, Epictetus, Plotinus, Greek tragedies, Aristotle, the German philosophers, Lao-Tsu, and so forth.[55] In this case, periodization confers a seriousness and a resemblance to higher education. When she undertook these studies, Delarue-Mardrus was fighting exclusion from the university; as an autobiographer she is claiming that a person who could complete such an education on her own is doubly intelligent.

McCarthy, to express her continuing disapproval of those who attempted to suppress her intellectual interests, used the grotesque mode to characterize her vulgarizing great-uncle, the ironic mode to describe her great-aunt Margaret's anticultural disciplinary style; comedy to critique the out-of-date education given by the Ladies of the Sacred Heart; and satire to deplore the rote religion of their Jesuit chaplain. All these characters are shown working against intellectual excellence in the young; whether the Madams and the Jesuit did so deliberately is impossible to say.

Beauvoir approaches the issue of intelligence in Catholic women differently, arguing that in order to acquire a truer and more complete knowledge of the world, she had to leave the Church, that the Madams' supposedly excellent education had not prepared her well for the Sorbonne, that the school subjects she was taught were not only narrow but distorted, and that most of the churchgoers she knew were uneducated women.[56] In sum, her analysis finds the incapacity for higher study not in women but in the Church.

Repplier, Delarue-Mardrus, and others argue against limiting women to servile or nonintellectual occupations. Entering the convent has permitted some poor women in the United States to attain careers or at least middle-class work; however, all the occupations permitted nuns are oriented more toward service than toward achievement. Bernhardt, surprisingly, comments on this matter most definitely. Her convent narrative at first obscures her critique of monastic life by the joy of certain memories, her gratitude to other girls, and her love of Mother St. Sophie.[57] But when she tells how her family insisted she become an actress rather than an abbess, she brings out the other side. "True life began for me. Cloister life is a life for the whole: whether one numbers a hundred, whether one numbers a thousand, one lives a life that is the same, single life for all; sounds from outside shatter on the heavy door of the cloister. Ambition consists in chanting louder than the others at Vespers; in taking up a little more of the bench; in having the end of the table; in being in the tableau of honor."[58] Bernhardt had not kept her eyes on the floor when she was boarding at the convent. Like Chacel, she favors occupations that humanize.

Several autobiographers pursued careers themselves, for the most part as actors or writers. Today these are not considered unusual occupations for women, but, as chapter 3 above makes clear, the Church would still prefer that all women either marry or join the convent. Therefore, those autobiographers who let it be known in the text that they have engaged fully in demanding careers establish their opposition to the official gender teaching. Delarue-Mardrus defends her career as a writer against beliefs that women should not publish in part by relating how her parents set up the momentum for her profession. A second way she defends her career is by claiming poetic inspiration. "Perfected by diverse generations, I have received the portion of vibrating antennae, which from earliest infancy have not ceased to collect the waves that pass."[59] This claim answers two objections: that she is a woman and would offend God by writing, and that she does not have the education of men and for that reason would not be able to write well. Inspiration transcends and can compensate for educational deprivation; moreover, inspiration could not come to her against God's will, as education could. Yet the Catholic church concedes the status of *inspired* to no writer since the completion of the New Testament.

Delarue-Mardrus found a solution by turning to religions that do not deny living women the possibility of inspired work. She devotes considerable space in her autobiography to her paganism, defending her value as a writer and her loyalty to civilization as she understood it. She repeatedly states that she never had any faith to lose, so her preference for paganism was not disloyal or a rebellion, but a position in a debate.[60] She could have omitted all reference to psychic experiences in her life-history so as to protect her reputation in Catholic eyes; she did not do so. She wrote about her psychic experiences to help define her individuality, to defend herself against beliefs that a woman could not become a poet, and to establish for her readers the worldview in which her works had been composed.

Of Delarue-Mardrus's pagan recollections, the one that most reinforced her career as a writer must have been her dream of the world tree, the more-than-tree that links the earth to the stars and provides the route of diviners and shamans in ecstasy, enabling them to explore the underworld, this world, and the skies.[61] The dream of the cosmic tree came when she was about eight and a half years of age, still "the somnambulist little girl," before she would be considered at the age of reason by the church in France at that time.[62] In the dream Lucie was embraced by this tree and alternately lifted to heaven and put down on the earth. In addition to connecting her with the rhythm of the universe—very useful for poetry—the dream must also have established in her mind that one does not have to give up heaven or earth to have the other. Catholic gender teaching is that women are to be equal to men in heaven, but not on earth, unless, as Jerome advises, they give up femaleness, in much the same way as anorexic women cease to menstruate. By its swinging, Delarue-Mardrus's unifying tree made belief in a destructive concept of gender impossible. At the same time, by including this dream, she is taking a stand for the mind as poetic, not merely as the locus of ethical decision.

The brain is also the locus of autobiographical decision. A person who engages in an autobiographical project by that action demonstrates her attention to the present and the past, together with her intention for the future; remembering, perceiving, planning are what indicate the presence of a person.[63] As autobiographers write, they continually consider choices in presentation. When they turn some established feature of the genre of autobiography to the purpose of describing their own history more deftly, when they use an element of their past to realize an unused or little used potential of the genre or to find a path into a viable future, their brains are functioning in creative ways. These autobiographers may tend toward imaginative behavior because of their childhood belief that they themselves originated out of a creative divine act. In girlhood they refused to tamp down their originality at the request of wrong-minded institutions and their representatives. In maturity, too, they exemplified creativity, an irrefutable demonstration of their capacity for intellectual operations. My argument is that the number of instances of creativity in these texts reflects their determination to prove their rationality.

The professional writers among these autobiographers show a feeling of confidence about the art of writing. They have studied other authors, and they choose forms appropriate to the design they want to create; for example, Repplier chooses the narrative-essay cycle; Matute, the prose-poem cycle; McCarthy, linked comic sketches; León, the surrealist lament, which she may have invented. Reason is apparent in a text that does no more than observe well. The action of reason on the text is more evident, however, when the writer has done something beyond merely registering events and, in autobiographical texts, has done more than transcribe memories just as they come to mind. None of these writers merely records remembered observations, and almost all introduce design into their work. Design and care are a kind of present-tense pervasive assertion of the writer's merit, of the belief that she is capable of fine work. Perhaps in this way some of them found an application for their convent sewing-room lessons after all.

The New Critics have convinced many people that an author's intention cannot be identified in a text; nevertheless, unless he or she tries to mask it, traces of the writer's intention do appear. An example is Repplier's creation of the nuns' names Rayburn, Dane, and Bouron. If these were actually the names of the nuns in question, then a higher artist, the genetic code, was at work, for the nuns carried out, respectively, three types of authority: to praise, to herd, and to humiliate. Like this unlikely occurrence of symbolic names, a number of other textual features probably result only from thought and choice. Such properties are evidence of rationality if they serve the cognitive discovery, persuasive purpose, or narrative form of a particular autobiography. Among these proofs of the intelligence of women I will briefly examine seven types: (1) features of surrealism employed for insight and emotional force; (2) acts of creative imagination, such as figuration, engaged in to bring out some quality of a life-story; (3) paratextuality, that is, relating the title to the text for insight into the meaning of the whole;[64] (4) formal similarity across differences in scale, or "repetition of structure on finer and finer scales" as a revelation of the distinguishing features of a particular writer;[65] (5) narrative forms that model the writer's personal history; (6) genericity or architextuality, that is, reworking themes, models, forms, and so forth already in the genre[66] (in this case, in the pool of Catholic women's autobiographies) in a way that serves the new text; and (7) hypertextuality, that is, transforming one entire text into another quite different one,[67] as Delarue-Mardrus transposes the autobiography of Saint Thérèse of Lisieux into a secular key.

Among the impressive achievements of this group of writers I would count their original applications of surrealism. As Catholic women eager to recover their forbidden humanity, they would have agreed with the surrealists on the restoration of autonomy and sexuality but disagreed on the restoration of rationality, which surrealist men wanted either to diminish in themselves and their work or to fuse with wise irrationality.[68] Surrealism was well suited to the emergence of the new selves of twentieth-century women, especially if they had grown up with the thoroughly repressive Catholic gender training.

Remedios Varo became a surrealist, impelled by her desire to escape Catholic suppression of the female and creative nature of girls. In her convent triptych romantic love replaces socialization in dreamlike imagery. Both Colette and Chacel included dreams told in a surrealist manner. León wrote as a surrealist throughout her works and throughout her autobiography. Read without reference to surrealism, the text would seem more incoherent than Colette's and perhaps as randomly composed and incompetent as Mellish's. Read as surrealist, the text is unified and imaginative, especially in its associational manner of narration, its emphasis on surrealist objects and images, and its references to spiritual forebears.

León's memories are brought to mind by her everyday life in exile, and she relates these linked pairs of realities without explanation. She uses what may be called found objects and images, odd items memory has turned up; for example, toward the end of the *Memoria,* León is reminded by the phrase "femme des lettres" of the alphabet soup at Sacred Heart School. "Letters that float pursued by the spoon, where they were going to die. Did they sometime compose my name in the soup plate? 'Femme des lettres.' Never have I felt more lettered, never have I felt more reverence by means of my inquietude, by means of that daily beginning in my own flesh that gives me writing."[69] I interpret this recollection-speculation, written in the shifting manner of a message in one's soup, as a reiteration of surrealist beliefs that writing is an act of love and that children, like the mad, may be living in Freud's "oceanic experience," that is, they may be open to all things. As a surrealist object, León's alphabet soup was monist in regard to its unifications of opposites: its machined alphabet, its material spirituality, its modern antiquity. Femmes de lettres would also seem an oxymoron, if not an impossibility, to Catholic machismists.

León also brings up two portraits she remembers from the Sacred Heart convent school. The first was of the Princess of Eboli, wearing a black patch over her right eye. The king had exiled her because she had been unfaithful to him with the prime minister. The second was of María Teresa, the princess of Lamballa, Spanish widow of a Bourbon prince. During the French Revolution she was guillotined because of her friendship with Marie Antoinette. María Teresa León, guilty of living with poet Rafael Alberti all her life after the Church would not dissolve her first marriage, and exiled by Franco for her activity in the Spanish communist party, elects these two women as her surrealist forebears. Her narratives about them create an overlay effect like that Freud discovered in dreams. The stacking of pictures of women who were made to suffer for their love compound María Teresa León's autobiographical image, intensifying her personal story. Thus, the meaning of this created dream she has written is that sexual love is wronged by the punishments inflicted on it in our hyperrational society. León thus uses surrealist objects to support her life-long belief in erotic passion and her will to write.

León could have written a consecutive, coherent autobiography. By choosing a surrealist mode of narration instead, she denies the superiority of reason, an attack from the rear on the Catholic male's monopoly of reason.

These surrealists are women capable of participating in public life in the form of a cultural movement while doing intelligent and original work. In so doing they defy the ideal of Catholic womanhood.

While surrealism may be the most subversive of art movements, the imagination has other resources. Even those of the writers who were unfamiliar with surrealism include fantasies, original figures of speech, or symbols in their work, thereby manifesting not only the artistic potential of the genre but also their creative imagination. McCarthy gives a self-portrait in the subjunctive mode, a brief comic fantasy of her life had her parents lived and had she remained Catholic.[70]

Noël fantasizes a death for herself that is not precisely orthodox and does not refer to a priest administering guidance and extreme unction, pallbearers, or gravediggers. "Then, having crossed from world to world without knowing it, I will find myself elsewhere, newborn on a new road, just barely a little girl who does not have her eyes open yet and whom older souls, nurse-souls, mother- and grandmother-souls, already accustomed to the other country, will take by the hand in the night and lead from darkness to semi-darkness, through the uncertain first light of a freshly beginning Dawn [Petit-Jour] to the radiant morning where will brighten in a safe place the full light of Paradise."[71] By imagining a death so much like birth and infancy, surrounded and assisted by loving women, Noël finally heals the wound her father had inflicted when he demanded that she abandon not only lies but also the imaginative speech she had learned from women.

Like fantasy, figures of speech manifest in a clear way the power of the mind to recombine.[72] When they are given an autobiographical character, the author is using also the skill of integration. What I call *autobiographical figures of speech* serve an autobiographical purpose and may also use materials from the writer's life-story for the vehicle or tenor of the figure (vehicle being the "red red rose," tenor being "my love," and meaning being all that this rose implies about "my love" and vice versa). Technically speaking, three possible types come to mind: in the first, the tenor is autobiographical; in the second, both tenor and vehicle are; in the third, either tenor and meaning or vehicle and meaning are.

The best example of an autobiographical figure of speech in this set of works, in my judgment, is Mary McCarthy's. "My own chief sensation was one of detached surprise at how far I had come from my old mainstays, as once, when learning to swim, I had been doing the dead-man's float and looked back, raising my doused head, to see my waterwings drifting, far behind me, on the lake's surface."[73] The beauty of this figure comes not only from the apt and alliterative style, the imagery, the emotion, but also from the correspondence between two experiences she had had in different realms, the one an athletic endeavor, the other a theological debate, for the tenor of the figure or subject of the comparison is her girlhood dispute with a Jesuit over the basis of faith, in which she suddenly began to do her own thinking.[74] The reader's realization that the vehicle of the metaphor comes as much from McCarthy's life-story as the tenor does adds to the delight of reading, for the comparison reveals on a small scale the presence of a pattern on the large scale, namely, that Mary's maturation involved learning to act without familiar supports. The mutual illumination of tenor and vehicle, vehicle and tenor is a source of beauty.[75] Surplus information created by this metaphor[75] includes the partial lack of deliberation in Mary's move toward independence, as well as her happiness at her success in the debate with the priest. The figure reverses all the usual emotional associations readers have with atheism, adding another shock of discovery: McCarthy considers atheism a sound position and superior to Catholic belief.

Delarue-Mardrus, though unimpressed by the Church, draws on Catholicism as a source of figures of discourse in her autobiography. She fills four Catholic allusions, to "the real presence," "tables of the law," "the little benedictine," and "jesuitism," all empty for her as an unbeliever, with autobiographical meaning. In her youth "the real presence" had not meant Holy Communion but the presence of Eros in a lover's kiss.[76] As far as her life-history is concerned, the "tables of the law" turned out to be Banville's treatise on French poetry. "Jesuitism" for her was keeping silence about having broken things: "the jesuitism of a frightened little girl." Benedictinism was her studiousness during her preparation for a career as a writer. For Delarue-Mardrus, to be a Benedictine was to study pagan texts and to write in a religious spirit. These four metaphors are autobiographical, then, not only in their vehicles and their tenors, but also in their affirmations of her values, her worldview, and her concept of the self (as less an entity than the locus of receptivity).

Varo too uses metaphor in her triptych, in the mantle above all, but also in the tower that isolates, the book that indoctrinates, and the rocks that challenge, among others.

Thus, the autobiographers have brought the imagination to bear on problems of this genre, especially of writing about events that have not yet occurred or personal traits and longings that were unrealized during the time covered by the narrative or characteristics that might escape ordinary narrative by their abstractness, like autonomy or spirituality.

Titles of these autobiographies sometimes merely indicate the genre, like *Memories* or *Mes mémoires* or *Memorias,* or the topic, like Repplier's *In Our Convent Days,* or the message, like Farrell's *Happy Memories of a Sister of Charity.* But ten or eleven of the titles relate to their texts in a way that calls attention to some major insight of the life-history. Paratextuality offers the writers another way of playing creatively with the genre of autobiography. Some of the titles bring out a deeper meaning of their life-history only when the title is reread after having finished the work. In this way, too, art helps express an interpretation of experience, making autobiography more than an objective record. Brave Bird's title *Lakota Woman* asserts that her identity is not assimilated to European culture.

"Neon Scars" refers to neither neon nor scars, except that Wendy Rose recites some scarring experiences and speaks of herself as having been alone in the street. Perhaps the scars resemble tubes of neon pink; perhaps they came from urban neighborhoods lit by neon signs where a Native American woman may feel threatened or be assaulted on various levels. The title is therefore metonymic, unlike the other titles in the set.

Matute's title *El río* refers to a specific river, village, and way of life, all ruined when Franco's government built a dam just downriver; at the same time the title refers to the river of life. Matute's work points out a number of ways in which our lives can be dammed up and turned into unnatural, relatively dead or deadly lakes, or can be released to run into the future.

Colette's title *La maison de Claudine* is sometimes taken to be simply a link to the child she had written about in the Claudine novels, as a way of bringing her readers along to a more truthful picture of that child. But the text of *Maison* presents the theme of sexual variability again and does not renounce it.

Memoria de la melancolía is León's lament over exile from Spain, but we learn that she is mourning also the unnecessary sadness of her life there before the exile, her passion for forbidden truth, and the prohibition of her love. The text adds meanings as it progresses, converting the title into a dreamlike pun: Memoir of a Sorrowing Country, Memoir of a Country That Grieves Its People, and Memoir of a Sacred Heart, that is, the Spanish heart, León's heart. The melancholy is that of thwarted love, a theme León brings up more than once in the text; the Spanish woman's love for country is thwarted by Franco just as the Catholic Woman's love is thwarted by the unnecessary renunciations the Church imposes on her.

I Almost Burned in Hell: A Confession, Fontenot's title, contains the sad, proud phrase *I Almost Burned.* If Tony had loved her the same way she loved him, that is, with trust and generosity, she believes their marriage would have taken fire.[77] She was not able to win Tony for love, but, as she writes her confession, Fontenot still believes in love and works, however politely, against warnings that damnation may follow immoderate, unrestrained love. In spite of her concessions to the idea of more rational human love like that of her second marriage, she holds to the constancy of her identity as one who has loved without measuring and calculating.

McCarthy's title, *Memories of a Catholic Girlhood*, is among the finest puns of the set in its subtlety and import. In this title "Catholic" refers literally to the contrasting Catholic situations she experienced in childhood. McCarthy shows that she did not entirely join any one Catholic group in her family. Her mother and father identified with the loving and festive Church, her grandmother Lizzie McCarthy with the sectarian Church, her great-aunt Margaret Shriver with the totalitarian or disciplinarian Church, and the Madams of the Sacred Heart in Seattle with the Romantic and infallible Church (using their power to elect and damn).[78] McCarthy herself identified, however gradually, with the eclectic Church. The word *catholic* also refers to the universality of McCarthy's experiences of Catholics, Protestants, and Jews. In spite of the prejudice she carried away from her Catholic grandmother, McCarthy became a willing student of Protestantism and Judaism in her mother's family. Finally, we see that when she "lost her faith" she took on the ambiguity of ex-Catholics, not active in the Church but marked by it in innumerable ways. Her narrative of her Catholic girlhood could not end with her departure from Forest Ridge convent, and not only because her perceptions were still influenced by Catholicism, as Barbara McKenzie has pointed out.[79] McCarthy's actions were still Catholic actions; she had simply chosen to act on different sermons from those her Grandmother McCarthy liked.

Dussane entitled the first volume of her autobiography *Premiers pas dans le Temple*, asserting that theater is religious. After concluding her girlhood narrative Dussane moves into what seem at first to be memoirs of actors she met when she was fifteen and sixteen, just beginning her long career. She especially praises the tragic actor Mounet-Sully as a person who brought a religious spirit to the stage. She describes him as dedicated to calling down the divine,[80] and in describing him she alludes often to a variety of religions by phrases like "impassioned pilgrims," "holy of holies," "Olympian calm," "desired *fantôme*," "marvelous light." These allusions change the memoir section, not of itself autobiographical, into an indirect characterization of Dussane, for she too had brought the divine into the theater. The descriptions of other actors in this way become self-portraits.

Simone de Beauvoir's title *Mémoires d'une jeune fille rangée* must have been modeled on the title *Mémoires d'un jeune homme rangé,* a 1918 fictional study of adolescence by Tristan Bernard, with which it contrasts at every point. The main character of Bernard's parody of heroic autobiography follows masculine conventions slavishly, insincerely, and unsuccessfully.[81] The young Simone chose what she wanted from both masculine and feminine conventions, lived her choices ardently, rejected whatever conventions she could not carry through sincerely, and invented modes of her own to replace them. Her title thus renders "rangé" or "in line" ironic, showing that Catholic discipline may instruct a girl thoroughly as to which points she should deviate from when she can. Several of these titles condense the life-history, not in summary, but in insight. The more meaning-laden titles vary in what they emphasize against the Church, but authenticity, creative secular work, sexuality, warm affection, non-Catholics, internal vitality, and pagan tradition are all affirmed as good. Catholic demands on the girls had varied, but in the creative titles, the women claim sacredness for realities the Church disapproved or despised.

Not every work of art uses formal similarities across differences in scale, and not every autobiography exhibits this degree of sophistication. Chacel provides a particularly interesting example of autobiographical reiteration along a graduated series. In *Desde el amanecer* she frequently uses micro-expressions like "más bien" (better) and "o, más exactamente" (or, more exactly), which permit her to revise while retaining the unrevised sketch of an idea. Very frequently, too, she writes in denial-affirmation-combination structures like "Y no delectable, sino fulminate: el extasis al rojo blanco" (And not delectable, but explosive: ecstasy to white-red).[82] These small units advance the same way her autobiography does, by the process of synthesis.

More than once, blending opposites gives Chacel an unusually beautiful description of a situation or event. In the anteroom of the doctor who cured her, she combines the impotence of glass eyes in lifeless lion and tiger hides with the real force of the doctor's eyes and his manifest vitality, African energy with European science, discipline with affection, the hypnotic power of danger with the liberating power of love. By Rosa's "yes" to him, she said "no" to inner death.[83] On the microscale (phrases), the middle scale (incident and episode), and the macroscale (the overall work), Chacel is a synthesizer. On the macroscale the work combines the visual and the verbal, the scholarly and the artistic, the psychic and the social, the unconscious and the rational, her memories of the child who regained and improved her health (whom she calls the Phoenix) and the child who defended her right to further maturation (whom she calls the Griffin). Chacel's determination to synthesize the best of what both parents had to offer produced an autobiography that is the work of a thinking woman who cares about beauty, who is discerning, who narrates with warmth, style, and a fearless rationality.

Similarity across differences in scale is not allowed to occur in every literary or artistic school, but it does reflect a quality of nature, as Benoit Mandelbrot found of vast and small portions of a coastline and in the fractal pictures of the Mandelbrot set.[84] If these similarities, when they come to mind, are included in a text, they show a sensitivity to pattern indicative of aesthetic intelligence.

McCarthy and Beauvoir engaged in the type of literary realism that looks for new forms in our lives, which I will call *formal realism*. Mary McCarthy links her autobiographical episodes in part by a kind of syncopation appropriate to the 1920s. In each of the essays, Mary learned something or acquired some trait she did not use until the next. By the time McCarthy traveled east again on her way to Vassar she had developed a complex, rich personality, carrying along the aesthetic orientation of her parents, the bigotry of her Grandmother McCarthy, the skepticism of the persecuted, the competitive spirit of her parochial school nuns, the justice of her Grandfather Preston, the learning of her West Coast teachers, the beauty and erotic quality of her Grandmother Preston.

Simone de Beauvoir constructs her autobiography in a spiral, which while a traditional and even an ancient form, is not usually employed for this genre. Like McCarthy's syncopation plot, the spiral is a process form, thus harmonizing with the character of the life-story. Beauvoir's ascending and widening trajectory approximates that of her life after she discarded her faith. Her outward and upward motion was resisted by Catholic authority figures, because of their habit of urging girls to narrow and lower their expectations in the belief that they would thereby rise and become great in their holiness. Fortunately, criticism could not deceive Beauvoir into thinking down was up and inward was outward.

As a way of symbolically representing or indicating the spiral she traced by the way she lived, her memoir spirals up in loops, each loop devoted to a period of time, and each passing through certain topics, such as her feelings toward nature, reading, acquaintance with death, female friends, male friends, reaction to the Church. Often she flings a line back in time, down to the corresponding experience on a lower loop of the spiral, as when she writes, "The fluorescent blue of neon signs reminded me of the convolvulus of my childhood" or "Sartre corresponded exactly to the dream-companion I had longed for since I was fifteen."[85] These comparative sentences, by referring to the past, call the reader's attention to change and growth in Simone.

The topicality of her sequences is appropriate for the autobiography of a dutiful and for many years a docile student, since many of the topics might have been assigned in French composition class. Her autobiography becomes a model of the person it reconstructs because she arranged the topics on a trajectory led through the years by her love for the authentic and her will to live fully.

One of the more intangible properties of her upward spiral—namely, the constant danger it evaded—might have been more difficult to perceive had she not contrasted her life to that of her alter ego, Zaza Mabille. The second, narrowing spiral of Beauvoir's *Mémoires* is the one Catholic adults wanted her and Mabille to follow, and which Mabille did follow, to her destruction. Simone was able to take an expanding and rising path only by choosing unapproved experience. Her search for what she considered desirable forms of life established her survival course.

The spiral plays the part of an informing intelligence or an artistic organizing principle in *Mémoires,* for it serves equally well to express Simone's ascent to full adulthood and to symbolize the increasingly inclusive character of her narrative. An important form in nature and the occult, the spiral was probably not emphasized at *le cours Désir.*[86] Its consignment to cultural oblivion, like that of the tree of life or the world tree of Delarue-Mardrus, may be due to its perfect accord with expansion of experience, the very drive that the Church and the Catholic Mothers' Sodality fought in Simone and Zaza. Unlike the realism that condemns the evils of life in society by means of exhausting detail, the realism of Beauvoir and McCarthy opens up a more active relationship with perception, one that selects the most communicative details and searches among the data of memory for narrative forms that can symbolize experience.

Most of these writers have reworked the generic tradition in a manner that enhances their work. McCarthy seems to have studied Repplier and Beauvoir as a preparation for writing. Before Delarue-Mardrus completed her autobiography, she read autobiographical narratives by her friends Bernhardt and Colette, who were approximately as Catholic, artistic, and well-known as she was.[87] Had Colette not introduced the motif of writing paper provided by her father, Delarue-Mardrus would probably not have mentioned the scratch paper M. Delarue used to hand her, yet this topic gave Delarue-Mardrus the opportunity to discuss specific features of her life that distinguished it from Colette's.[88] She utilizes *Ma double vie* in the same manner. Had Bernhardt not told about herself as a child of ten saving the life of a drowning charity student or mentioned that mysticism took hold of her at about the same age, Delarue-Mardrus would probably not have denied this particular heroism of herself or would not have used the clause "no mysticism had flowered in me" of her first communion, because no one would expect heroism or mysticism at that age.[89]

Most important, Delarue-Mardrus brings the tradition of Catholic women's autobiography to the level of hypertext; that is, she writes a girlhood narrative that transforms another text, thus including it and commenting on it, while at the same time providing a continual contrast that illumines the new stream of narrative. In 1926 she had published *Sainte Thérèse de Lisieux,* for which she had studied the *Histoire d'une âme* (1895–97).[90] Chacel had developed motifs from this work for the most meditative phase of her girlhood account. But from the saint's life Delarue-Mardrus took the outline of her own girlhood narrative, playing her entire girlhood off against hagiography.

In her book on the saint, Delarue-Mardrus mentions that both she and Thérèse were Normans, the youngest of a group of sisters, and famous in some field. Moreover, she notes that the public image of Saint Thérèse is false ("the official genteel houri") and would not have been, had *Histoire d'une âme* been carefully read.[91] Delarue-Mardrus feels she too has suffered from misinterpretation. Owing to her interest in a disparity between reputation and one's self-knowledge, Delarue-Mardrus read the *Histoire* carefully, taking the trouble to decipher its conventual phraseology for a deeper meaning.[92] She found a usually unnoticed overall pattern and was able to subsume it into her own autobiography, written about forty years later.

Delarue-Mardrus's autobiographical pact for her own *Mémoires* shows that she valued *Histoire d'une âme* as the work of a human being rather than of a mere recording machine. "My intention is not to recount in detail. What I want is, in an ocean of forgetting, to let emerge some islets, to group this archipelago of memories in a way that establishes my truth, to survive, once dead, not entirely, but essentially. . . . Facts? Dates? Rather, shocks, charms. In a word, beatings of the heart. The distance being granted between a saint and a profane person, these memories, like the book of the little sister Thérèse de Lisieux, could be titled *History of a Soul.*"[93] For Delarue-Mardrus, the best way to construct an autobiography is to use as material the most emotionally alive, necessary, or individuating traits of a person. Although some other artistic principle might have caused it, her allegiance to Romanticism on the nature of the soul is why she does not write a heavy mass of indigestible Zolaesque minutiae, or a formless flow of perceptions, or a memoir about her famous acquaintances. As if to emphasize the value she places on form, her autobiographical pact is the only one among the French autobiographies to appear on a separate page with a separate title and date.

The mild witticism of comparing herself, known for her lesbianism, to a canonized saint emphasized another similarity in their autobiographies. Both women believed in their souls and also, as good Romanticists, in the history of their souls. They divided their histories into periods by looking for contrasts in their inner experience, enabling them to show progression. Changes are often marked in the text by tiny contrasts of a temporal character, such as, in Delarue-Mardrus, "Installed now in his apartment, we lived much closer to our father," or in Thérèse, "I poured out very bitter tears. I did not know then the joy of sacrifice."[94] Remarks differentiating between early and later conditions analyze change over time and phases of personal transformation.

Compared to temporal contrast, Delarue-Mardrus's adoption of motifs from Thérèse might seem trivial, had she not chosen so many, and had she not employed them to create an implied comparison of her girlhood to that of the saint. This comparison allowed her to round out the generic task of self-analysis. When she examined her ecclesiastical and academic history in relation to Thérèse's, she found, first, that Thérèse, under the influence of her family, responded favorably to both church and school, whereas Lucie's response was at first minimal to both, and even in that she was discouraged by her family. During the years when Thérèse felt increasingly unhappy in convent school but more drawn toward prayer, Lucie's response to the Church remained null, while her participation in school grew irregularly more positive. The comparison also revealed that Lucie's responses to the less institutionalized areas of life (nature, non-Catholic books, and sexual love) expanded and became full emotionally at the very age when Thérèse narrowed her field of response to religious thoughts about nature, one or two religious books, and passion for Jesus Christ.[95] Reading about the narrowing spiral of Thérèse's experience, knowledge, activity, and emotion must have made Delarue-Mardrus grateful that her family had freed her to move up an expanding spiral, one of relatively natural growth. She had lived her own story; Thérèse had lived as the surrogate of an institution or, at best, of her pious parents and her sister Pauline.

Delarue-Mardrus studied the contrast between her life and Martin's also in regard to their girlhood relationships with their sisters. The results were nearly the same as in the comparison of their relationships with institutions. For Thérèse, Pauline's encouragement was religious, Marie's affectionate scorn was religious, Céline's infant companionship was religious. Thérèse joined the convent to be with Pauline and did not differentiate herself from this older sister until she was near death. Lucie's sisters played no religious roles in her life. Charlotte's and Marguerite's encouragement was cultural, the affectionate scorn of all her sisters came over intellectual and ethical issues, Georgina's infant companionship is mentioned in regard to some animals they saw copulating and again in regard to harassment they suffered from their older sisters (far from a religious experience for them).[96] In childhood, Georgina defied the older girls only to be tormented more vigorously; Lucie watched the sequence and renounced defiance. Later, Lucie could have defeated her sisters, as Georgina did, by rejecting their values and joining a convent. Instead, she continued to embrace them and their values, defying only their scorn toward her.

Because Thérèse's overall point was that Christ's grace had meant a growth in her courage, this theme attracted Delarue-Mardrus's attention, and she looked for an increase of courage in her own youth. This evolution provides a climactic, glorious period for her girlhood narrative. In infancy Thérèse had begun more bravely than Lucie, by confessing her faults to her mother, but her goal was to lessen her punishment; Lucie refused to confess her faults because she hoped her guilt would not be discovered. Her highest attainment in this line was once to confess to Charlotte that she had broken something.[97] Thérèse's highest attainment in connection with guilt was to stop confessing things she hadn't done. As children, then, Thérèse and Lucie were apparent opposites, but both represented themselves in their autobiographies as cowardly girls who wanted only love. Both had to struggle for years to be able to face disapproval or punishment.

Courage during illness provided a sharper definition of both girls too. Lucie's lung ailment came at sixteen; Thérèse was about twenty-three when she contracted tuberculosis. Lucie had far better care and nourishment and recovered rapidly, yet she had been in danger of death, so the episode could serve as a comparison. She recalls that she was not overjoyed at the idea of going to heaven, but she would have liked to die in order to avoid adult life, possibly a feeling that formed a part of Sister Thérèse's joy at the prospect of death. Delarue-Mardrus attributes her lack of fear of sickness and death not to Catholic philosophy or to personal courage, but to a courage she and her sisters received from their mother. She makes it clear, however, that had she had to endure a long illness, as Thérèse did, her courage would probably have dissolved.[98] Delarue-Mardrus indicates that she found suffering less glamorous than its reputation. In contrast, Thérèse believed she attained maturity, courage, and joy the day she decided to desire pain rather than to avoid it. All the same, she lets it be known that tuberculosis is an ordeal not to be sought after.

In adolescence, Lucie too had thought she wanted to suffer, not as a way of loving Jesus, but as a poetic experience. When great suffering struck, however, on the day of the baroness's rejection of their relationship, Lucie did not find it beneficial. "Suffering . . . had come, secret and without tears, devouring, and it destroyed me slowly, at least, the first being that I was, before becoming this other that resembled her so little. I did not suspect, when finally I tried to react, that I was entering the era of solitary courage, and that it was for my whole life."[99] When Pauline abandoned Thérèse, Thérèse found a way to live with her, though the cloister allowed them little direct contact. Lucie did not have such an option, and since she had never believed in the Catholic faith she was baptized in, she could not substitute a passion for Christ crucified for a real relationship with her beloved baroness.[100] The baroness was a cultured person, however, as Lucie was, which may explain how the younger woman was able to redouble her investment in the life of the arts. In Lucie's grief, using "death in the soul" to steel her will, she addressed herself to study and writing, to organizing literary conferences, to attending gatherings of the artistic elite in Bernhardt's dressing room or the salons of Mme. de Herdia or of Hélène Vacaresco.[101]

Thérèse decries such a path as worldly, self-indulgent, egocentric, but she had glimpsed it only from a distance.[102] When Lucie walked it, she found it dark and painful. She later regretted, as I have said, that she had never had the vanity one needs in dark hours.[103] She was astounded, when she read the *Histoire,* at the number of Saint Thérèse's vain remarks, and she lists ten of these in her *Sainte Thérèse.*[104] Even with "vain thoughts" to console herself, by following Pauline into the cloister Thérèse had in effect reduced her activity to an unhealthy degree; Lucie's inability to follow the baroness, plus her decision to survive in any manner she could ("to live whatever"), led her to creative actions that increased her health.[105]

The contrast in their range of possible actions came from the difference in their education. Thérèse's solution to abandonment was dictated by what Delarue-Mardrus calls her "ultra-religious education."[106] The evaluation is fair enough when one realizes that Thérèse's father would not allow his children to read a newspaper or any other secular material. Lucie's education had given her access to a number of viable lifestyles and had left her free to pursue her cultural drives—which Thérèse had also possessed, as the historical method of her autobiography demonstrates, but which she could permit herself to follow only when they had religious content or were commanded by religious authority. A more personal cause of the difference, one Delarue-Mardrus does not identify in her autobiography, was her constant drive toward action and direct contact with reality. This energy would have made the spiritual, theoretical, or conceptual love so important in the convent impossible as a solution for Lucie. Perhaps after entering the cloister, Thérèse Martin developed the same need for reality and action, and once conventual rejection of her innocent human activities and traits became clear to her, she found the cloister equally impossible to support. Her request to go to the missions supports this hypothesis.

Delarue-Mardrus used the tradition of women's autobiographies as a grid of comparison in order to analyze her ethical and cultural history. Her brave reaction to the loss of the baroness provided her girlhood narrative with the last island of its archipelago. If she had named her islands the Isle of Yggdrasill (the world tree), the Isle of Five Sisters, the Isle of Three Kisses, and the Isle of Poets, then the final jewel of the diadem could have been called the Isle of Defiant Love. When Coppée repulsed her as a poet, she embraced Banville and became her own tutor; when the baroness did not take her up as a lover (thus putting social rules ahead of Lucie's needs), Lucie assumed the baroness's place in her life, providing herself with the approval she needed in order to go ahead with her career. Dealing with rejection by redoubled love, she became truly mature.

By relying on the autobiography of a woman saint, Delarue-Mardrus is able to put her lesbian heart in a setting not of lurid vice but of all the virtues. In her decision to transpose *Histoire d'une âme* for her comparative analysis of courage and commitment, she has found "something to hook onto."[107] Behaving on the verge of a later maturity (for she was fifty-eight when she wrote *Mes mémoires*) as she had done on the verge of first adulthood, Delarue-Mardrus counters rejection with solidarity, nullity with vitality, and the amorphous with form. She expresses the intentionality not only of her remembered self but of her writing "I."

The innovative acts of Catholic women autobiographers of the twentieth century, in addition to the seven types just analyzed, also include textual secularization in Janés, rehumanization of art in Chacel and of marriage in Beauvoir, and original insights into childhood. I argue that one of the origins of their creativity is their desire to prove their value not only in the past but also in the present. Although indirect, such acts make their strongest assertions of Self. The determination to prove themselves rational distinguishes this set of writers form those who are rational without having endured years of pressure to abdicate their rationality.

A subgroup of autobiographies manifests artistic defects corresponding to Catholic prohibitions for women; for example, Carroll devotes a disproportionate amount of space—about 15,000 words—to her parents before her birth, and she sometimes creates confusion by referring to herself as "she."[108] Adam, Bernhardt, Dussane, Rose, and Conway omit all mention of their girlhood erotic history, and Wolff omits her intellectual history though not her career history. Thus, Catholic gender training like ancient fields leaves marks on the Earth invisible or unnoticed at ground level but visible from the different point of view provided by genre study.

I refer to the autobiographers at times as a group, but repeatedly I have indicated the activity of a shifting minority that favors one facet or several facets of Catholic gender theology or that defends the Church just as if it had not imposed artificial limitations on them. One or two women who oppose the Church almost entirely nevertheless defend certain aspects of it. Perhaps as a concession, McCarthy extols the charitable priests and nuns she met over the years and the liturgical and intellectual Catholicism they shared with her.[109] Her gratitude for the loving part of the Church does not negate in any way the criticism she offers later in the text, but her appreciation may explain why her criticism of repressive and malicious sectors of the Church is presented in a comic manner.

Some, like Noël, serve the Church but complain of one or two aspects of it; Farrell, Carroll, and Wolff are writing primarily to defend the Church. Because the opportunity to live in a convent has been of such benefit to them personally, they may feel too grateful to the Church ever to understand how harmful it can be to other women. These nuns write protectively of the Church, thus occupying one end of a spectrum, yet they also defend a more modern view of women than the one the clergy promotes, especially the nuns' belief that women are rational. In this matter the nuns do not conceal their disagreement with Gregory of Nyssa and Thomas Aquinas. Wolff and Carroll were college professors, and even though they were allowed to teach "only girls," they certainly prove that women are capable of completing college and are suited to study, and even that God did intend women to devote themselves to intellectual operations.

While many features reappear in various of these autobiographers, this one stand is taken more often than any other, appears in many of their refusals to cooperate in their own destruction, motivates many of the arguments they construct as writers, and drives the formal excellence of their autobiographies. This particular resemblance demonstrates irrefutably that all these writers were deeply concerned about the Church's teaching that women are not as rational as men. They fought against this belief not superficially but at a profound level. The strategic quality of their responses to ideas of Catholic femininity both as girls and as autobiographers demonstrates how fully human they are. Catholic women have written personal histories rather than mere reminiscences or memoirs that lack selves at the center. As a result of their struggle to live authentically in spite of opposition from Catholic feminizers, these women developed life-stories and wrote true autobiographies.

n o t e s

_____

INTRODUCTION

1. Elizabeth V. Spelman, *Inessential Woman: Problems of Exclusion in Feminist Thought* (Boston: Beacon, 1988), 178.

2. Spelman, *Inessential Woman,* ix.

3. Ludwig Wittgenstein, *Philosophical Investigations,* trans. G. E. M. Anscombe (Oxford: Basil Blackwell, 1953), 31ᵉ–32ᵉ.

4. Gérard Genette, "Introduction à l'architexte," in *Théorie des genres,* edited by Gérard Genette and Tzvetan Todorov (Paris: Seuil, 1986), 142, 150.

5. Spelman, *Inessential Woman,* 132.

6. Thomas Aquinas, O.P., Saint and Doctor of the Church, *Summa Theologica,* trans. Fathers of the English Dominican Province, 5 vols. (Westminster, Md.: Christian Classics, 1981), 1:466.

7. Remedios Varo, *Embroidering Earth's Mantle,* private collection.

8. Jacques Franck, "Simone de Beauvoir a traité les problèmes de son temps," *La libre Belgigue,* 15 April 1986, abstracted in Joy Bennett and Gabriella Hochmann, *Simone de Beauvoir: An Annotated Bibliography* (New York: Garland, 1988), 445; Paule Melot, review of *Mémoires d'une jeune fille rangée* in *Présence et revue de Suisse* 9 (1959): 135–38, abstracted in Bennett and Hochmann, 312; Winthrop Sargeant, "Books," *New Yorker,* 26 September 1959, 186, 189, 190, abstracted in Bennett and Hochmann, 317; Anna Von Salomonson, "Fiktion als Rache: Zu den Werken Simone de Beauvoirs," *Hochland: Monatsschrift für alle Gebeite des Wissens* 52 (1960): 426–31, abstracted in Bennett and Hochmann, 106.

9. Suzanne Lilar, *La malentendu du "Deuxième sexe"* (Paris: Presses Universitaires de France, 1969), 254.

10. Roy Pascal, *Design and Truth in Autobiography* (Cambridge: Harvard University Press, 1960), 9.

11. Pascal, *Design and Truth,* 13–16, 17.

12. *Diccionario de literatura española,* 1972, s.v. "Rosa Chacel."

13. Liz Stanley, *The Auto/biographical I: The Theory and practice of feminist auto/ biography* (New York: Manchester University Press, 1992), 64.

14. Mary McCarthy, *Memories of a Catholic Girlhood* (New York: Harcourt Brace Jovanovich, 1957), 19–21.

15. Philippe Lejeune, *L'autobiographie en France* (Paris: Armand Colin, 1971), 74–75.

16. Jacob Stockinger, "The Test of Love and Nature: Colette and Lesbians," in *Colette: The Woman, the Writer,* edited by Erica Mendelson Eisinger and Mari Ward McCarty (University Park: Pennsylvania State University Press, 1981), 75.

17. Obituary of Sister M. Madaleva [Wolff], *New York Times,* 26 July 1964, 57.

18. Simone de Beauvoir, *Mémoires d'une jeune fille rangée* (Paris: Gallimard, 1958), 342. English edition: *Memoirs of a Dutiful Daughter,* trans. James Kirkup (New York: Harper & Row, 1959), 247.

19. Milton J. Esman and Fred C. Bruhns, *Institution Building in National Development: An Approach to Induced Social Change in Transitional Societies* (Pittsburgh: Graduate School of Public and International Affairs, University of Pittsburgh, 1965), 5.

20. Sun-tzu ping fa, *Sun-tzu: The Art of War: The First English Translation Incorporating the Recently Discovered Yin-ch'üeh-shan Texts,* trans. Roger T. Ames (New York: Ballantine, 1993).

21. Rosemary Radford Ruether, "Christianity," in *Women in World Religions,* edited by Arvind Sharma, 207–33 (Albany: State University of New York Press, 1987).

22. Stanley, *The Auto/biographical I,* 100–101.

23. Ruether, "Christianity," 207–9, 215.

24. Ibid., 208–9, 210–12, 214, 216.

25. Ibid., 221.

26. Ibid., 209, 210, 221.

27. Barbara Mullen, *Life Is My Adventure* (New York: Coward-McCann, 1937), 203–4.

PART 1. AUTOBIOGRAPHY AND THE CATHOLIC WOMAN

1. Saint Jerome, *Commentary on the Epistle to the Ephesians,* 3 Ephesians 5:28, trans. Mary Daly, in *The Church and the Second Sex* (New York: Harper & Row, 1968), 43. The original Latin reads, "quandiu mulier partui servit et liberis, hanc habet ad virum differentiam, quam corpus ad animam. Sin autem Christo magis voluerit servire quam saeculo, mulier esse cessabit, et dicetur vir," from S. Eusebius Hieronymus, "Commentarius in Epistolam ad Ephesios," *Opera Omnia,* vol. 7, in *Patrologiae Latinae,* vol. 26, edited by J.-P. Migne, 267–590 (Paris: Garnier Fratres, Editores and J.-P. Migne Successores, 1884).

2. Pascal, *Design and Truth,* 96; Georg Misch, *A History of Autobiography in Antiquity,* trans. E. W. Dickes, vol. 1 of 2 vols. (Westport, Conn.: Greenwood, 1907; revised, 1973), 15; Stephen A. Shapiro, "The Dark Continent of Literature: Autobiography," *Comparative Literature Studies* 5 (1968): 451.

3. Misch, *Autobiography in Antiquity,* 18; Arthur Melville Clark, *Autobiography: Its*

Genesis and Phases (London: Oliver and Boyd, 1935; reprint, Darby, Pa.: Darby, 1969), 21; Pascal, *Design and Truth*, 19; Lejeune, *L'autobiographie en France*, 10, 14.

4. Isocrates, *Antidosis* (354–353 B.C.E.), in vol. 2 of *Isocrates*, Loeb Classical Library, 1928, 7.

5. Pascal, *Design and Truth*, 9; Georges May, "Autobiography and the Eighteenth Century," in *The Author in His Work: Essays on a Problem in Criticism*, edited by Louis L. Martz and Aubrey Williams (New Haven: Yale University Press, 1978), 323–26; C. Hugh Holman and William Harmon, *A Handbook to Literature*, 5th ed. (New York: Macmillan, 1986), 43; Georges Gusdorf, "Conditions and Limits of Autobiography" (1956), trans. James Olney, in *Autobiography: Essays Theoretical and Critical*, edited by James Olney (Princeton: Princeton University Press, 1980), 35.

6. Pascal, *Design and Truth*, 3; H. Porter Abbott, "Autobiography, Autography, Fiction: Groundwork for a Taxonomy of Textual Categories," *New Literary History* 19 (1988): 597–615.

7. Jon Saari, "The Printed Word: Graham Greene," review of *Ways of Escape*, by Graham Greene, *Tucson Citizen*, 13 June 1981, Weekender, 15.

8. Linda Tschirhart Sanford and Mary Ellen Donovan, *Women and Self-Esteem* (New York: Penguin, 1985), 161, 162.

9. Sanford and Donovan, *Women and Self-Esteem*, 162.

10. Ibid., 161.

11. Ibid., 165, 168–69.

12. Ibid., 169.

13. Ibid., 174.

14. Karen Horney, *Self-Analysis* (New York: W. W. Norton, 1942), 290–91.

15. Stanley, *The Auto/biographical I*, 9, 12.

16. Elaine Showalter, "Introduction: The Feminist Critical Revolution," in *The New Feminist Criticism: Essays on Women, Literature and Theory*, edited by Elaine Showalter (New York: Pantheon, 1985), 14.

17. Domna C. Stanton, "Autogynography: Is the Subject Different?" in *The Female Autograph: Theory and Practice of Autobiography from the Tenth to the Twentieth Century*, edited by Domna C. Stanton (Chicago: University of Chicago Press, 1984), 14.

18. Hélène Cixous and Catherine Clément, *The Newly Born Woman* (Minneapolis: University of Minnesota Press, 1986; originally published as *La jeune née* [Paris: Union Générale d'Éditions, 1975]), 90.

19. Biddy Martin, "Lesbian Identity and Autobiographical Difference[s]" in *Life/Lines: Theorizing Women's Autobiography*, edited by Bella Brodzki and Celeste Schenck (Ithaca, N.Y.: Cornell University Press, 1988), 82–83; 102.

20. Shari Benstock, "The Female Self Engendered: Autobiographical Writing and Theories of Selfhood," *Women's Studies* 20 (1991): 13.

21. Misch, *Autobiography in Antiquity*, 3–4; Francis R. Hart, "Notes for an Anatomy of Modern Autobiography," *New Literary History* 1 (1970): 485.

22. William L. Howarth, "Some Principles of Autobiography," *New Literary History* 5 (1974): 364–65.

23. Carmen Martín Gaite, "La búsqueda de interlocutor," in *La búsqueda de interlocutor y otras búsquedas* (Barcelona: Destino, 1973), 21.

24. Simone de Beauvoir, *Le deuxième sexe*. Vol. 1, *Les faits et les mythes*, vol. 2, *L'expérience vécue* (Paris: Gallimard, 1949); English edition: *The Second Sex*, trans. and ed. H. M. Parshley (New York: Knopf, 1957), 714.

25. Lucie Delarue-Mardrus, *Mes mémoires* (Paris: Gallimard, 1938), 7.

26. Thérèse [Martin] de l'Enfant-Jésus, Saint, *Histoire d'une âme* (1895–97; Lisieux: Calvados, 1946), 61, 99; Rosa Chacel, *Desde el amanecer: Autobiografía de mis primeros diez años* (Madrid: Revista de Occidente, 1972), 316–18.

27. Wendy Rose, "Neon Scars," reprinted from *I Tell You Now: Autobiographical Essays by Native American Writers*, edited by Brian Swann and Arnold Krupat, 254–55; McCarthy, *Memories*, 225, 135–36.

28. Misch, *Autobiography in Antiquity*, 15.

29. Ibid., 96–97.

30. Isocrates, *Antidosis*, 189.

31. Jean Starobinski, "The Style of Autobiography," trans. Seymour Chatman, in *Literary Style: A Symposium*, edited by Seymour Chatman (New York: Oxford University Press, 1971), 288.

32. Teresa [Cepeda y Ahumada] of Avila, Saint and Doctor of the Church, *La Vida*, in vol. 1 of *Escritos*, vol. 53 of *Biblioteca de autores españoles desde la formación de lenguaje hasta nuestros días* (Madrid: Los sucesores de Hernando, 1923), 43, 75; Vicente de la Fuente, "Introducción al libro de la Vida de Santa Teresa," in Teresa, *Escritos* 1:2–5; Helmut A. Hatzfeld, *Santa Teresa de Avila* (New York: Twayne, 1969), 104.

33. Misch, *Autobiography in Antiquity*, 3–4.

34. Lejeune, *L'autobiographie en France*, 28.

35. Olney, *Metaphors of Self*, 45–46, 50.

36. Amy Katz Kaminsky and Elaine Dorough Johnson, "To Restore Honor and Fortune: 'The Autobiography of Leonor López de Córdoba,'" in *The Female Autograph: Theory and Practice of Autobiography from the Tenth to the Twentieth Century*, edited by Domna C. Stanton (Chicago: University of Chicago Press, 1984), 70.

37. Misch, *Autobiography in Antiquity*, 15.

38. Ira Progoff, *At a Journal Workshop: The Basic Text and Guide for Using the Intensive Journal* (New York: Dialogue House, 1975), 133–39; Stephen Crites, "Storytime: Recollecting the Past and Projecting the Future," in *Narrative Psychology: The Storied Nature of Human Conduct*, edited by Theodore R. Sarbin (New York: Praeger, 1986), 163.

39. Martin, "Lesbian Identity," 98.

40. Elizabeth N. Evasdaughter, "Autobiographical Closure in the Future: Women Constructing Hope," *a/b: Auto/Biography* 9 (1994): 119–30.

41. David Wiggins, *Sameness and Substance* (Oxford: Basil Blackwell, 1980), 171.

42. Rigoberta Menchú, with Elizabeth Burgos (oral historian), *Me llamo Rigoberta Menchú y así me nació la conciencia* (Barcelona: Seix Barral, 1992).

43. Elizabeth W. Bruss, *Autobiographical Acts: The Changing Situation of a Literary Genre* (Baltimore: Johns Hopkins University Press, 1976), 172.

44. Shapiro, "Dark Continent of Literature," 437.

45. Peggy Joan Fontenot, *I Almost Burned in Hell: A Confession* (Hicksville, N.Y.: Exposition Press, 1978).

46. Lynn Z. Bloom, "Promises Fulfilled: Positive Images of Women in Twentieth Century Autobiography," paper delivered at the annual meeting of the Midwest Modern Language Association, Chicago, November 1975, 1–2.

47. Crites, "Storytime," 164, 167–69, 172, 171.

48. Clara Janés, *Jardín y laberinto* (Madrid: Editorial Debate, 1990), 148.

49. Peter Ketter, *Christ and Womankind*, trans. Isabel McHugh (Westminster, Md.: Newman Press, 1952; originally published as *Christus und die Frauen* [Düsseldorf, 1935]), 82.

50. James Baillie, *Problems in Personal Identity* (New York: Paragon, 1993), 159.

51. Crites, "Storytime," 170.

52. Agnes Repplier, *In Our Convent Days* (New York: AMS Press, 1905; reprint, 1969).

53. Sister Consolata Carroll, *Pray Love, Remember* and *I Hear in My Heart* (New York: Farrar, Straus, 1947 and 1949).

54. Starobinski, "The Style of Autobiography," 289.

55. Menchú, *Me llamo Rigoberta Menchú*, 71.

CHAPTER ONE

1. Misch, *Autobiography in Antiquity*, 15; Shapiro, "Dark Continent of Literature," 437.

2. Sister M. Xavier Farrell, *Happy Memories of a Sister of Charity* (St. Louis: Herder, 1941).

3. Ibid., 13–14, 19, 30, 28–30.

4. Ibid., 88–89.

5. Ibid., 4–5, 42–46, 65–72.

6. Carroll, *Pray Love, Remember*, 226.

7. Ibid., vii.

8. Ibid., 301–2.

9. Ibid., 255–56.

10. Paul Benson, "Autonomy and Oppressive Socialization," *Social Theory and Practice* 17 (1991): 386–87.

11. Stan Shively and Knud S. Larsen, "Socialization Attitudes and Social Authorities," *Journal of Psychology* 124 (1990): 276.

12. Carroll, *I Hear in My Heart*, 257–58, 266.

13. Ibid., 285, 291–92; 316.

14. Ibid., 31–32; 285, 291–92.

15. Ibid., 123–24; 186.

16. Benson, "Autonomy and Oppressive Socialization," 396–97.

17. Sister M. Madaleva Wolff, C.S.C., *My First Seventy Years* (New York: Macmillan, 1959).

18. Louis O. Mink, "History and Fiction as Modes of Comprehension," *New Literary History* 1 (1969–70): 541–58.

19. Wolff, *My First Seventy Years*, 3–4, 9–10, 12, 14, 16.

20. Ibid., 16.

21. Ibid., 3, 10.

22. Ibid., 5–6, 46.

23. Kathleen Norris, *Noon: An Autobiographical Sketch* (New York: Doubleday, Page, 1925).

24. Obituary of Kathleen Norris, *New York Times*, 15 July 1966, 17.

25. Louise Maunsell Field, "Kathleen Norris Smiles Back at Life: 'Noon,' an Autobiographical Sketch, Has a Happy Ending and No Disagreeable People" (review), *New York Times*, 25 January 1925, sec. 3:6.

26. Norris, *Noon*, 3.

27. Kathleen Norris, *Family Gathering* (Garden City, N.Y.: Doubleday, 1959).

28. Norris, *Noon*, 10–13.

29. Ibid., 17.

30. Ibid., 19–23, 29–31.

31. Ibid., 29–31.

32. Ibid., 13–14.

33. Norris, *Family Gathering*, 25.

34. Deanna Paoli Gumina, "The Apprenticeship of Kathleen Norris," *California History* 66 (1987): 48.

35. Obituary of Mary Mellish, *Musical America*, 15 February 1955, 297.

36. Mary Mellish, *Sometimes I Reminisce: Autobiography* (New York: G. P. Putnam's Sons, 1941), 32.

37. Ibid., 9.

38. Ibid., 30, 31.

39. Mary McCarthy, *How I Grew* (San Diego: Harcourt Brace Jovanovich, 1987), 12.

40. Mellish, *Sometimes I Reminisce*, 31.

41. Ibid.

42. Confraternity of Christian Doctrine, *The Official Revised Baltimore Catechism Number One*, with Study Lessons by Ellamay Horan (New York: W. H. Sadlier, 1944), 52.

43. Mellish, *Sometimes I Reminisce*, 31–32.

44. Ibid., 32.

45. Ibid.

46. Ibid.

47. Ana María Matute, *El río* (Barcelona: Editorial Argos, 1963).

48. Leo XIII, "The Prohibition and Censorship of Books: Apostolic Constitution Officiorum ac Munerum" (25 January 1892), in *The Great Encyclical Letters* (New York: Benziger, 1903), 414.

49. Janet W. Díaz, *Ana María Matute* (New York: Twayne, 1971), 41, 54, 62.

50. Marie-Lise Gazarian Gautier, "Ana María Matute," in *Interviews with Spanish Writers* (Elmwood Park, Ill.: Dalkey Archive, 1991), 193; Matute, *El río*, 144, 172.

51. Matute, *El río*, 94.

52. Díaz, *Ana María Matute*, 25.

53. Matute, *El río*, 144.

54. Ibid., 52, 58–59, 107.

55. Ibid., 104, 139–41.

56. Paul MacLean, *A Triune Concept of the Brain and Behavior* (Toronto: University of Toronto Press, 1969), 8–18, 42, 58.

57. Matute, *El río*, 43, 172; 49–52; 104.

58. Colette, *La maison de Claudine* (1922), vol. 3, *Oeuvres* (Paris: Flammarion, 1960), 214–16; Dussane, *Au jour et aux lumières*, vol. 1, *Premiers pas dans le Temple* (Paris: Calmann-Lévy, 1955), 104–5, 127.

59. Repplier, *In Our Convent Days*, vii, viii.

60. Lejeune, *L'autobiographie en France*, 72, 80.

61. George Stewart Stokes, *Agnes Repplier: Lady of Letters* (Philadelphia: University of Pennsylvania Press, 1949), 32.

62. Repplier, *In Our Convent Days*, 227; 232.

63. Ibid., 228.

64. Nancy A. Walker, *A Very Serious Thing: Women's Humor and American Culture* (Minneapolis: University of Minnesota Press, 1988), 166–67.

65. Repplier, *In Our Convent Days*, vii–ix; McCarthy, *Memories*, 3–27.

66. Repplier, *In Our Convent Days*, ix.

67. Colette, *Sido* (1929), vol. 3, *Oeuvres*, 253–97 (Paris: Flammarion, 1960); Lejeune, *L'autobiographie en France*, 21, 25; Joan Hinde Stewart, *Colette* (Boston: Twayne, 1983), 105.

68. Claire Dehon, "Colette and Art Nouveau," trans. Abigail Siddall, in Eisinger and McCarthy, *Colette*, 105, 110; 108.

69. Colette, *Maison*, 222; see also Danielle Bouverot and Chantal Schaefer, "De la lexicologie à la sémiotique: Le vocabulaire de la végétation dans *Sido*," in *Colette: Nouvelles approches critiques. Actes du colloque de Sarrebruck (22–23 juin 1984)*, edited by Bernard Bray (Paris: A.-G. Nizet, 1986), 131–38.

70. Dehon, "Colette and Art Nouveau," 110.

71. Colette, *Maison*, 162.

72. Ibid., 159, 181, 212, 214, 265.

73. Christiane Milner, "Le corps de Sido," *Europe: Revue littéraire mensuelle* 631–32 (November–December 1981): 75.

74. Colette, *Maison*, 214–16; Colette, *Sido*, 268.

75. Janés, *Jardín y laberinto*, 10–11.

76. Ibid., 41–42.

77. Ibid., 103–5.

78. Ibid., 135–36; 35; 124–25; 43–44; 38–39; 379; 148.

79. Ibid., 15–17, 147–48; 43, 74.

80. Confraternity of Christian Doctrine, *Baltimore Number One,* 59.

81. *Catéchisme du diocèse de Paris* (Paris: Adrien le Clere, 1863), 63; 88–90.

82. Valerie Malhotra Bentz, *Becoming Mature: Childhood Ghosts and Spirits in Adult Life* (New York: A. de Gruyter, 1989).

83. *Catechism of the Council of Trent for Parish Priests: Issued by Order of Pope Pius V,* trans. John A. McHugh, O.P., and Charles J. Callan, O.P. (New York: Joseph F. Wagner, 1949), xx, xxii.

84. Ibid., 411–12.

85. Ibid., 413, 414.

86. Confraternity of Christian Doctrine, *Baltimore Number One,* 61–62.

87. Ibid., 108.

88. A Sister Servant of the Immaculate Heart of Mary, *With Jesus: Prayers and Instructions for Youthful Catholics* (Milwaukee: Milwaukee Church Supply, 1922), 24; 28; 49 ff; 104; 121; 226–27.

89. Beauvoir, *Memoirs,* 11–12, 31.

90. A Sister Servant, *With Jesus,* 105–6, 206.

91. McCarthy, *Memories,* 24–25.

CHAPTER TWO

1. Beauvoir, *The Second Sex,* 706.

2. Mary Hunt Benoist, *Memories* (n.p., 1930), 13.

3. Repplier, *In Our Convent Days,* 81–82, 103, 254.

4. Varo, "Toward the Tower," first panel of *Embroidering Earth's Mantle,* in Kaplan, *Unexpected Journeys,* pl. 11, p. 19.

5. Kaplan, *Unexpected Journeys,* 21; Sarah Bernhardt, *Ma double vie: Mémoires de Sarah Bernhardt* (Paris: Charpentier et Fasquelle, 1907), 58.

6. Mary Brave Bird [Mary Crow Dog] with Richard Erdoes, *Lakota Woman* (New York: HarperCollins, 1991), 32–33; María Teresa León, *Memoria de la melancolía* (Barcelona: Bruguera, 1979; originally published Buenos Aires: Losada, 1970), 74.

7. Stokes, *Agnes Repplier,* 31–32, 37; Repplier, *In Our Convent Days.*

8. Repplier, *In Our Convent Days,* 28.

9. Ibid., 30.

10. John XXIII quoted in "Marie Noël est morte," *Le Figaro,* 25 December 1967, 7.

11. Marie Noël, *Petit-Jour: Souvenirs d'enfance* (Paris: Stock, 1951).

12. Noël, *Petit-Jour,* 155–56.

13. Lucien Descaves, "Au pays de Marie Noël," *Les nouvelles littéraires,* 16 July 1932, 1.

14. Noël, *Petit-Jour,* 64–65.

15. Sheelagh Conway, *A Woman and Catholicism: My Break with the Roman Catholic Church* (Toronto: PaperJacks, 1987), 46–48.

16. Brave Bird, *Lakota Woman,* 29, 31, 35.

17. Ibid., 38–39.

18. Elise Jouhandeau, *Joies et douleurs d'une belle excentrique,* vol. 1, *Enfance et adolescence d'Elise* (Paris: Flammarion, 1952), 51; Beauvoir, *Memoirs,* 123.

19. Beauvoir, *Memoirs,* 124.

20. McCarthy, *Memories,* 136.

21. Ibid., 108–9; 18.

22. Ibid., 135–36.

23. Beauvoir, *Memoirs,* 134.

24. Ibid., 135, 137.

25. Jouhandeau, *Enfance,* 112.

26. Ibid., 80, 83–84, 86, 131, 149–50, 188.

27. McCarthy, *Memories,* 13; 36; 38–39; 44; 62, 63.

28. Mullen, *Life,* 10.

29. Ibid., 9, 15.

30. Ibid., 124; 142–43.

31. Ibid., 305.

32. Ibid., 295, 303; 297–98; 124.

33. Ibid., 19.

34. Brave Bird, *Lakota Woman,* 38.

35. Ibid., 34; 4.

36. Ibid., 32.

37. Ibid., 34, 37.

38. Ibid., 34; 39.

39. Beauvoir, *Memoirs,* 37.

40. Remedios Varo, "Embroidering Earth's Mantle," second panel of *Embroidering Earth's Mantle,* in Kaplan, *Unexpected Journeys,* pl. 13, p. 21.

41. Beauvoir, *Memoirs,* 243.

42. Ibid., 51, 70, 83, 108; 251–52; 226–27; 106.

43. McCarthy, *Memories,* 70–71.

44. Repplier, *In Our Convent Days,* 149–50.

45. Conway, *Woman and Catholicism,* 42.

46. Benoist, *Memories,* 24; 18, 29.

47. Chacel, *Desde el amanecer,* 66–68, 80–81; 103–4.

48. León, *Memoria,* 24–25.

49. Ibid., 24; 75.

50. Ibid., 76.

51. Ibid., 66–68.

52. Elizabeth Schoffen, *The Demands of Rome* (n.p., 1917).

53. Mary Gleason, S.P., letter to author, 17 January 1980.

54. Schoffen, *Demands,* 15.

55. Ibid., 16, 18.

56. Beauvoir, *Memoirs,* 21, 38.

57. Ibid., 122.

58. Ibid., 123; 106; 151; 124.

59. Ibid., 175–77.

60. Ibid., 36, 52, 121–22, 141, 101, 107.

61. Ibid., 178; 225.

62. Ibid., 192–93, 227; 287; 260–61.

63. McCarthy, *Memories,* 4; 93; 104.

64. María Asquerino, *Memorias* (Barcelona: Plaza & Janés, 1987), 32.

65. Kaplan, *Unexpected Journeys,* 21.

66. Linda Marie [Pillay], *I Must Not Rock* (New York: Daughters Press, 1977).

67. Ibid., 86, 87.

68. Ibid., 115.

69. Patricia Garfield, *Creative Dreaming* (New York: Simon and Schuster, 1974), 128–29.

70. Benoist, *Memories,* 29.

71. Ibid., 24–25; 38.

72. Delarue-Mardrus, *Mes mémoires,* 51; 71; 67.

73. *Catechism of the Council of Trent,* 432, 434; *Catéchisme,* 63, 78.

74. Confraternity of Christian Doctrine, *Baltimore Number One,* 60, 65.

75. Jouhandeau, *Enfance,* 44; 54.

76. Ibid., 198–99.

77. León, *Memoria,* 67.

78. Ibid., 11, 13–14; 74–75; 65.

79. Ibid., 75.

80. Delarue-Mardrus, *Mes mémoires,* 19.

81. Jouhandeau, *Enfance,* 196.

82. Noël, *Petit-Jour,* 48–49; 39–40.

83. León, *Memoria,* 119–20.

84. Mullen, *Life Is My Adventure,* 20–21.

85. Matute, *El río,* 52.

86. Rose, "Neon Scars," 254–55.

87. Brave Bird, *Lakota Woman,* 39.

88. Pillay, *I Must Not Rock,* 31.

89. Ibid., 30–31.

90. Ibid., 58.

91. Ibid., 32.

92. Fontenot, *I Almost Burned in Hell,* 29; 35; 44.

93. Benoist, 15; 27–28.

94. Noël, *Petit-Jour,* 55–57.

95. Chacel, *Desde el amanecer,* 48.

96. León, *Memorias,* 28.

97. Matute, *El río,* 57.

98. Chacel, *Desde el amanecer,* 15, 23, 111; 205; 330.

99. Rosa Chacel, *Saturnal* (Barcelona: Seix Barral, 1972), 218.

100. Chacel, *Desde el amanecer,* 40.

101. Ibid., 100; 40, 280; 248, 262.

102. León, *Memorias,* 22.

103. Ibid., 69–70.

104. Beauvoir, *Memoirs,* 55.

105. Ibid., 37; 177; 189–90.

106. Ibid., 37.

107. McCarthy, *Memories,* 58–59; 10.

108. Conway, *Woman and Catholicism,* 31.

109. Ibid., 32.

110. Ibid., 32–33.

111. Ibid., 14–17, 70–71.

112. Chacel, *Desde el amanecer,* 41, 109, 210.

113. Ibid., 109.

114. Ibid., 76.

115. Noël, *Petit-Jour,* 158–59; 55–57, 48–49.

116. Ibid., 37–38.

117. Descaves, "Au pays de Marie Noël," 1.

118. Beauvoir, *Memoirs,* 151–52.

119. Wong, *Nun,* 12–13.

120. Menchú, *Me llamo Rigoberta Menchú,* 114.

CHAPTER THREE

1. William B. Faherty, S.J., *The Destiny of Modern Woman in the Light of Papal Teaching* (Westminster, Md.: Newman, 1950).

2. Rhoda Unger and Mary Crawford, *Women and Gender: A Feminist Psychology* (Philadelphia: Temple University Press, 1992), 264.

3. Bernice Lott, *Becoming a Woman: The Socialization of Gender* (Springfield, Ill.: Charles C. Thomas, 1981), 60–65.

4. *Oxford Classical Dictionary,* 2d ed., s.v. "Gregory of Nyssa."

5. Richard Robinson, *Definition* (Oxford: Clarendon, 1954; revised 1965).

6. Quintus Septimii Tertullianus, *On the Apparel of Women,* trans. Rev. S. Thelwall, vol. 4, *The Ante-Nicene Fathers* (Grand Rapids, Mich.: Wm. B. Eerdmans, 1956), 14.

7. Robinson, *Definition,* 162–65.

8. Gregory of Nyssa, paraphrased by Marina Warner, *Alone of All Her Sex: The Myth and the Cult of the Virgin Mary* (New York: Knopf, 1976), 186–87.

9. Robinson, *Definition,* 172–73.

10. Aurelius Augustine, Saint and Bishop, *Commentary on the Lord's Sermon on the Mount,* trans. Denis J. Kavanaugh, O.S.A., vol. 3, *Writings of Saint Augustine,* vol. 11, Fathers of the Church: A New Translation (Washington, D.C.: Catholic University of America Press, 1951), 61–62.

11. Robinson, *Definition.*

12. Augustine, *The Trinity,* trans. Stephen McKenna, C.SS.R., vol. 18, Fathers of the Church: A New Translation (Washington, D.C.: Catholic University of America

Press, 1963), 352; Augustine, *Confessions,* trans. E. M. Blaiklock (New York: Thomas Nelson, 1983).

13. Rev. Mercedario Manuel Sancho. *El catechismo de los niños: Explicado con parábolas y comparaciones,* vol. 2, *Lo que se ha de obrar (doctrina moral)* (Barcelona: Subirana, 1927), 167.

14. Saint Jerome [Eusebius Hieronymus], *Commentary on the Epistle to the Ephesians* (3 Ephesians 5:28.5), trans. in Daly, ed., *The Church and the Second Sex,* 43.

15. Patricia Wilson-Kastner, preface to *A Lost Tradition: Women Writers of the Early Church* (Lanham, Md.: University Presses of America, 1981), xx.

16. Aquinas, *Summa,* 1:467.

17. Ibid., 467, 466.

18. C. [or Gaius] Musonius Rufus, "That Women Too Should Study Philosophy," in *Visions of Women,* ed. Linda A. Bell (Clifton, N.J.: Humana, 1983), 69–71.

19. Aquinas, *Summa,* 1:467.

20. José María Pemán, *De doce cualidades de la mujer,* 2d ed. (Madrid: Prensa Española, 1969), 82.

21. *Catechism of the Council of Trent,* xxv, xxviii, xxxi.

22. Ibid., 351–52.

23. Ibid., 352.

24. Ibid., 418.

25. Ibid.

26. Jouhandeau, *Enfance,* 23.

27. *Catechism of the Council of Trent,* xxxix–lv.

28. Ibid., xxxv.

19. Pius XII, "Woman's Dignity: Political and Social Obligations" (21 October 1945), *Vital Speeches,* 1 November 1945, 42–45.

30. Faherty, *Destiny of Modern Woman,* 20–31.

31. Ibid., 41–42.

32. Ibid., 51.

33. Ibid., 63.

34. Ibid., 71–72.

35. *Catholic Encyclopedia,* 1st ed., s.v. "Woman."

36. Adrien Dansette, *Histoire religieuse de la France contemporaine: L'église catholique dans la mêlée politique et sociale* (Paris: Flammarion, 1965), 308.

37. Delarue-Mardrus, *Mes mémoires,* 87–88.

38. Beauvoir, *Memoirs,* 120–22.

39. Faherty, *Destiny of Modern Woman,* 64–71; Roessler, *Die Frauenfrage vom Standpunkte der Natur der Geschichte und der Offenbarung* (Freiburg im Breisgau: Herder, 1907), 3–6, 116, 120, 124–25, 127, 131, 138–39.

40. Faherty, *Destiny of Modern Woman,* 81.

41. Elizabeth N. Evasdaughter, "Julian of Norwich," in *A History of Women Philosophers,* vol. 2, *Medieval, Renaissance and Enlightenment Women Philosophers A.D. 500–1600,* edited by Mary Ellen Waithe (Dordrecht: Kluwer, 1989), 191–222.

42. Faherty, *Destiny of Modern Woman,* 87.

43. Ibid., 86–106.

44. Ibid., 93–95.

45. Pius XII, "Woman's Destiny," 43, 44.

46. Ketter, *Christ and Womankind,* 191.

47. Ibid., book jacket.

48. Ibid., 82.

49. Ibid., 85.

50. Ibid., 69.

51. Ibid., 79.

52. Beauvoir, *Memoirs,* 82.

53. Ketter, *Christ and Womankind,* 84; 88.

54. For a discussion of this willful muddle, see Sister Albertus Magnus McGrath, O.P., *Women and the Church,* 2d ed. (Garden City, N.Y.: Doubleday, 1972).

55. Ketter, *Christ and Womankind,* 85–95.

56. Rev. John Catoir, " 'Love Is a Dreadful Thing,' " *Wyoming Catholic Register,* 26 October 1979, 8.

57. *Catéchisme,* 63, 123–24, 140.

58. Bernhardt, *Ma double vie,* 22; 14.

59. Repplier, *In Our Convent Days,* 81–82.

60. Ibid., 75–77.

61. Brave Bird, *Lakota Woman,* 34.

62. Jouhandeau, *Enfance,* 48.

63. Ibid., 107; 151–52, 159; 196; 149, 189.

64. Brave Bird, *Lakota Woman,* 38.

65. León, *Memorias,* 66–68.

66. Beauvoir, *Memoirs,* 160.

67. Mullen, *Life Is My Adventure,* 21–22.

68. Juliette Lambert Adam, *Le roman de mon enfance et de ma jeunesse* (Paris: A. Lemerre, 1902), 254, 348; 270.

69. Repplier, *In Our Convent Days,* 203–4; Beauvoir, *Memoirs,* 178–79, 187, 192–93, 226-27.

70. Chacel, *Desde el amanecer,* 262-63; 22, 250, 258, 350–51; 274.

71. Ibid., 275.

72. Ibid., 338-39.

73. Ibid., 349-50.

74. Ibid., 95, 109.

75. McCarthy, *Memories,* 33–34.

76. Beauvoir, *Memoirs,* 187.

77. Dussane, *Premiers pas,* 56–57.

CHAPTER FOUR

1. Chacel, *Desde el amanecer,* 32.

2. Beauvoir, *Memoirs,* 29, 73, 133.

3. Fontenot, *I Almost Burned in Hell*, 14, 20.

4. Adam, *Le roman de mon enfance*, 2, 7; 52–55; 90, 96, 103–4, 143, 341.

5. León, *Memorias*, 69, 70, 72; 25.

6. Beauvoir, *Memoirs*, 184–86, 246, 281–82, 284–85, 314–15.

7. McCarthy, *Memories*, 136.

8. Colette, *Maison*, 214–16; *Sido*, 263–64.

9. Schoffen, *Demands of Rome*, 15.

10. Beauvoir, *Memoirs*, 41.

11. Chacel, *Desde el amanecer*, 32–33.

12. McCarthy, *Memories*, 13.

13. Beauvoir, *Memoirs*, 9, 38.

14. Dussane, *Premiers pas*, 49.

15. Aelred of Rievaulx, Saint and Abbot, *Spiritual Friendship*, trans. Mary Eugenia Laker, S.S.N.D., Cistercian Fathers Series no.5 (Kalamazoo, Mich.: Cistercian Press, 1977), 63.

16. Rev. Luis Pueyo y Abadía, *Analogias de pulpito, y cathedra: Proporciones panegiricas, y escolaticas*, 2d ed. (Zaragoza: Viuda de Iuan de Ybar, 1677), 247.

17. Rev. Denis Kenny, *The Catholic Church and Freedom: The Vatican Council and Some Modern Issues* (St. Lucia, Queensland: University of Queensland Press, 1967), 204–5.

18. Matthew Fox, O.P., *The Coming of the Cosmic Christ: The Healing of Mother Earth and the Birth of a Global Renaissance* (San Francisco: Harper, 1988), 164; 172; 202; 234; 244.

19. Repplier, *In Our Convent Days*, 82.

20. Beauvoir, *Mémoires*, 153.

21. Ibid., 221.

22. Jouhandeau, *Enfance*, 54, 74.

23. Fontenot, *I Almost Burned in Hell*, 30–31.

24. Colette, *Maison*, 167, 214; Colette, *Sido*, 265; 269, 263, 268; *Maison*, 177; *Sido*, 265.

25. Adam, *Le roman de mon enfance*, 56; 64, 75, 126, 127, 143, 202–3, 370; 5–26; 91, 324–25; 95, 317; 57, 63, 68–77, 346; 90, 94, 100–101, 130–31, 164–65, 234, 341, 343–45.

26. Bernhardt, *Ma double vie*, 23, 25–27; 31; 34.

27. Ibid., 38; 57.

28. Adam, *Le roman de mon enfance*, 92, 96, 139, 324–26; Jouhandeau, *Enfance*, 58; Colette, *Sido*, 271–72; McCarthy, *Memories*, 92–95.

29. Delarue-Mardrus, *Mes mémoires*, 58–60.

30. Norris, *Family Gathering*, 10–11.

31. Mullen, *Life Is My Adventure*, 80.

32. Chacel, *Desde el amanecer*, 22; 52.

33. Ibid., 45–47; 50; 58, 62–66.

34. Ibid., 124.

35. Ibid., 128–31.

36. Mullen, *Life Is My Adventure*, 24, 38, 39.

1. Roger T. Ames, introduction to Sun-tzu, *Art of War,* 24.

2. Brave Bird, *Lakota Woman,* 35–36.

3. Sun-tzu, *Art of War,* 120; 165; 107–9, 125, 162.

4. McCarthy, *Memories,* 119.

5. Sun-tzu, *Art of War,* 103, 111–13, 155; 135, 141.

6. Ibid., 105, 119, 125, 126; 157, 159, 161–62.

7. Ibid., 104, 157; 149.

8. Ibid., 108, 130; 108–9.

9. Ibid., 130, 169–71.

10. Ibid., 111–13, 115, 125, 155, 166.

11. Ibid., 111.

12. Ibid., 119–20.

13. Ibid., 105, 160, 162; 131; 160; 132.

14. Ibid., 112, 149.

15. Ibid., 103; 283; Ames in Sun-tzu, *Art of War,* 283n.118.

16. Beauvoir, *Memoirs,* 36; 128–30, 176–78; 335, 340–43, 339–45.

17. Ibid., 235, 237, 239–40, 282, 284–85, 289, 296.

18. Ibid., 310; 314.

19. Jouhandeau, *Enfance,* 7, 21, 58, 86, 91, 101, 113–14, 122–26.

20. Jean-Jacques Gautier, "L'adieu," *Le Figaro,* 4 March 1969, 30; Dussan, *Premiers pas,* 11, 16–17; 32–36; 58.

21. Pillay, *I Must Not Rock,* 32; 85.

22. Mullen, *Life Is My Adventure,* 9–10.

23. Delarue-Mardrus, *Mes mémoires,* 87–88.

24. Beauvoir, *Memoirs,* 194–95.

25. Repplier, *In Our Convent Days,* 16.

26. Bernhardt, *Ma double vie,* 34.

27. Rose, "Neon Scars," 254–55.

28. Sun-tzu, *Art of War,* 125, 126, 157, 159, 161–62; 105, 119, 126.

29. Repplier, *In Our Convent Days,* ix, 19, 137.

30. Kaplan, *Unexpected Journey,* 21.

31. Beauvoir, *Memoirs,* 192.

32. Ibid., 100, 108–10, 163–67, 194, 161, 274.

33. Ibid., 277, 286, 332–33.

34. Ibid., 222, 276–77, 352, 353–54.

35. Jouhandeau, *Enfance,* 217–18.

36. Pillay, *I Must Not Rock,* 31; 49, 83–84; 74–75, 79.

37. Chacel, *Desde el amanecer,* 110–13.

38. Sun-tzu, *Art of War,* 104.

39. Carroll *I Hear in My Heart,* 122–23; 186.

40. Mullen, *Life Is My Adventure,* 297–98.

41. Sun-tzu, *Art of War,* 127, 159; 105, 157, 159; 115, 125.

42. Bernhardt, *Ma double vie,* 15, 20–21.

43. Beauvoir, *Memoirs,* 271.

44. Sun-tzu, *Art of War,* 135, 141, 147.

45. Ibid., 104, 149.

46. Pillay, *I Must Not Rock,* 49.

47. Chacel, *Desde el amanecer,* 95; 109–10.

48. Sun-tzu, *Art of War,* 107, 130.

49. McCarthy, *Memories,* 72.

50. Beauvoir, *Memoirs,* 187.

51. Bernhardt, *Ma double vie,* 60–61.

52. Jouhandeau, *Enfance,* 198.

53. Aquinas, *Summa* 1:466–67.

54. Jouhandeau, *Enfance,* 189; 167.

55. Chacel, *Desde el amanecer,* 111; 99.

56. Fontenot, *I Almost Burned in Hell,* 26–27.

57. Ibid., 14, 17–18, 68; 21.

58. Farrell, *Happy Memories,* 88.

59. Beauvoir, *Memoirs,* 232.

60. Bernhardt, *Ma double vie,* 109–10.

61. Pillay, *I Must Not Rock,* 56.

62. Ibid., 15, 62–63.

63. Beauvoir, *Memoirs,* 147.

64. Ibid., 140–42, 181, 191.

65. Ibid., 259.

66. Bernhardt, *Ma double vie,* 34.

67. Repplier, *In Our Convent Days,* 189; 205–6.

68. Noël, *Petit-Jour,* 63; 162–63.

69. Ibid., 78.

70. Ibid., 65–67; 64, 77, 79.

71. Ibid., 36–37.

72. Beauvoir, *Memoirs,* 231; 242, 265, 282; 252; 227, 263–65; 191.

73. Ibid., 57–58.

74. McCarthy, *Memories,* 78.

75. Conway, *A Woman and Catholicism,* 48.

76. Pillay, *I Must Not Rock,* 26–27.

77. Farrell, *Happy Memories,* 4–5, 12, 14; Carroll, *I Hear in My Heart,* 338.

78. Carroll *I Hear in My Heart,* 311.

79. Chacel, *Desde el amanecer,* 59–62, 204–8, 214, 308–11, 341–43, 357–58.

80. Ibid., 244, 326–28, 339–40, 343, 349.

81. Ibid., 84–85, 125, 217–18, 332, 353–56.

82. Beauvoir, *Memoirs,* 37–38, 103–4.

83. Ibid., 144.

84. Ibid., 144–45.

85. Ibid., 202-3.

86. Ibid., 146.

87. Sun-tzu, *Art of War,* 171.

88. Repplier, *In Our Convent Days,* 31, 217–18; Carroll, *I Hear in My Heart,* 241.

89. Jouhandeau, *Enfance,* 30, 182, 184, 194–96, 217.

90. Ibid., 201–3, 205–6.

91. Beauvoir, *Memoirs,* 217, 219.

92. McCarthy, *Memories,* 77.

93. Matute, *El río,* 139–41.

94. Chacel, *Desde el amanecer,* 351–55.

95. Pillay, *I Must Not Rock,* 18.

96. Dussane, *Premiers pas,* 63–66.

97. León, *Memoria,* 169.

98. Sun-tzu, *Art of War,* 157.

99. Ibid., 171.

100. Brave Bird, *Lakota Woman,* 37.

101. Ibid., 40.

102. Beauvoir, *Memoirs,* 106; 181–82.

103. Mullen, *Life Is My Adventure,* 80.

104. Pillay, *I Must Not Rock,* 43.

105. Ibid., 85.

106. Sun-tzu, *Art of War,* 119–20.

107. Beauvoir, *Memoirs,* 123.

108. Brave Bird, *Lakota Woman,* 36–37.

109. Bernhardt, *Ma double vie,* 52–56.

110. Sun-tzu, *Art of War,* 111.

111. Mullen, *Life Is My Adventure,* 124–25, 134–38.

112. Sun-tzu, *Art of War,* 160.

113. Mullen, *Life Is My Adventure,* 309.

114. Carroll, *I Hear in My Heart,* 307.

115. Sun-tzu, *Art of War,* 47, 112, 131, 158.

116. Schoffen, *Demands of Rome,* 16.

117. Varo, "The Escape," third panel of *Embroidering Earth's Mantle,* in Kaplan, *Unexpected Journeys,* pl. 15, p. 22.

118. Whitney Chadwick, *Women Artists and the Surrealist Movement* (New York: Thames and Hudson, 1985), 195.

119. Kaplan, *Unexpected Journeys,* 22.

120. Sun-tzu, *Art of War,* 157–58, 160–61.

121. Fox, *Coming of the Cosmic Christ,* 202.

CHAPTER SIX

1. Chacel, *Desde el amanecer,* 77.

2. Pascal, *Design and Truth,* 10.

3. Lejeune, *L'autobiographie en France,* 74–75.

4. Mellish, *Sometimes I Reminisce,* 32.

5. Repplier, *In Our Convent Days,* 91–92, 102–3; Beauvoir, *Memoirs,* 59, 73.

6. Beauvoir, *Memoirs,* 161.

7. McCarthy, *Memories,* 70–71.

8. Ibid., 51, 124.

9. Judy Gerstel, "She's a Long Way from Galway," *Windsor [Ontario] Star,* 14 November 1987, Lifestyles.

10. Elisabeth Gössmann, "Hildegard of Bingen," in Waithe, ed., *History of Women Philosophers,* 50.

11. Starobinski, "The Style of Autobiography, 288.

12. Noël, *Petit-Jour,* 156–57; 156; 162–63.

13. Mullen, *Life Is My Adventure,* 142–43, 267–68, 297–98, 305–8.

14. Dussane, *Premiers pas,* 49.

15. Asquerino, *Memorias,* 32.

16. McCarthy, *Memories,* 17, 39, 48, 53, 55, 61, 63–64, 66–70; 79–80, 88; 211; 23.

17. Wolff, *My First Seventy Years,* 36; 43; ix; 24–25.

18. Adam, *Le roman de mon enfance,* 166.

19. Delarue-Mardrus, *Mes mémoires,* 116; 10.

20. Ibid., 50.

21. Chacel, *Desde el amanecer,* 29, 53; 40, 100, 112, 248, 262, 280.

22. Ibid., 46, 47, 112.

23. Delarue-Mardrus, *Mes mémoires,* 12, 18; 28, 38, 51, 56, 99; 44–45; 71–72, 78–79, 87.

24. Elizabeth Fishel, *Sisters: Love and Rivalry inside the Family and Beyond* (New York: William Morrow, 1979).

25. Repplier, *In Our Convent Days,* 85–99.

26. Aelred, *Spiritual Friendship,* 54, 60–61.

27. Beauvoir, *Memoirs,* 91.

28. McCarthy, *Memories,* 17, 58–59.

29. León, *Memoria,* 379.

30. Norris, *Noon,* 18.

31. Adam, *Le roman de mon enfance,* 166.

32. Repplier, *In Our Convent Days,* 188.

33. Beauvoir, *Memoirs,* 29.

34. Repplier, *In Our Convent Days,* 43; Mellish, *Sometimes I Reminisce,* 35.

35. McCarthy, *Memories,* 132–34; 114–124; 181–82.

36. Ibid., 219, 225; Brock Brower, "Mary McCarthyism," *Esquire,* July 1962, 67, 113; McCarthy, *Memories,* 226.

37. León, *Memoria,* 102.

38. Beauvoir, *Memoirs,* 308.

39. Ibid., 290.

40. Ibid., 40; Yolanda Astarita Patterson, *Simone de Beauvoir and the Demystification of Motherhood* (Ann Arbor: UMI, 1989), 153; Beauvoir, *Memoirs,* 83; 38; 87; 161; 209.

41. Beauvoir, *Memoirs,* 82.

42. *Catechism of the Council of Trent,* 437–38.

43. Beauvoir, *Memoirs,* 244, 289.

44. Ibid., 260–61; 291.

45. Ibid., 235; 309.

46. Ibid., 313.

47. Ibid., 291.

48. Ibid., 235, 236, 246, 262.

49. Ibid., 6.

50. Ibid., 335, 339.

51. Colette, *Maison,* 161–62.

52. Delarue-Mardrus, *Mes mémoires,* 85–86; 97, 100, 106–7.

53. Chacel, *Desde el amanecer,* 18.

54. Ibid., 347; 77.

55. Delarue-Mardrus, *Mes mémoires,* 90.

56. Beauvoir, *Memoirs,* 121–23, 127, 168; 136.

57. Bernhardt, *Ma double vie,* 31–34, 41–42; 52–56; 67.

58. Ibid., 58.

59. Delarue-Mardrus, *Mes mémoires,* 15, 21, 46, 49, 58–59, 68, 100–101; 93.

60. Ibid., 15–16, 17–18, 24, 27–28, 45, 81; 52, 72–73, 75, 106, 109.

61. H. R. Ellis Davidson, *Gods and Myths of Northern Europe* (Baltimore: Penguin, 1964), 190–93.

62. Delarue-Mardrus, *Mes mémoires,* 21.

63. Wiggins, *Sameness and Substance,* 159.

64. Jean-Marie Schaeffer, "Du texte au genre," *in* Genette and Todorov, eds., *Théorie des genres,* 194.

65. James Gleick, *Chaos: Making a New Science* (New York: Penguin, 1987), 94–96, 100, 103, 110, 117, and plates following 114, 115, 117, 224.

66. Genette, "Introduction à l'architexte," 157.

67. Schaeffer, "Du texte au genre," 194.

68. Chadwick, *Women Artists,* 236.

69. León, *Memorias,* 331.

70. McCarthy, *Memories,* 16.

71. Noël, *Petit-Jour,* 172.

72. Samuel Taylor Coleridge, *Biographia Literaria* (1817; New York: E. P. Dutton, 1947), 146.

73. McCarthy, *Memories,* 123.

74. Ibid., 119.

75. Paul Ricoeur, *Interpretation Theory: Discourse and the Surplus of Meaning* (Fort Worth: Texas Christian University Press, 1976), 47–50.

76. Delarue-Mardrus, *Mes mémoires,* 85; 88; 90; 27; 69.

77. Fontenot, *I Almost Burned in Hell,* 27.

78. McCarthy, *Memories,* 90–91, 93, 108–9.

79. Barbara McKenzie, *Mary McCarthy* (New York: Twayne, 1966), 47.

80. Dussane, *Premiers pas,* 117–41.

81. Tristan Bernard, *Mémoires d'un jeune homme rangé* (Paris: Fasquelle, 1918).

82. Chacel, *Desde el amanecer,* 113.

83. Ibid., 84–85.

84. Gleick, *Chaos,* 96, 117.

85. Beauvoir, *Memoirs,* 315; 345.

86. Paul Waldo-Schwartz, *Art and the Occult* (New York: Braziller, 1975), 22–25.

87. Delarue-Mardrus, *Mes mémoires,* 105; Michèle Sarde, *Colette, libre et entravée* (Paris: Stock, 1978), 240, 418.

88. Colette, *Sido,* 284; Delarue-Mardrus, *Mes mémoires,* 59.

89. Bernhardt, *Ma double vie,* 34, 45; Delarue-Mardrus, *Mes mémoires,* 24; 52.

90. Lucie Delarue-Mardrus, *Sainte Thérèse de Lisieux* (Paris: Fasquelle, 1926).

91. Ibid., 89, 116; 9.

92. Ibid., 47, 71.

93. Delarue-Mardrus, *Mes mémoires,* 7.

94. Thérèse [Martin], *Histoire d'une âme,* 30; Delarue-Mardrus, *Mes mémoires,* 58; Thérèse, *Histoire d'une âme,* 52.

95. Delarue-Mardrus, *Mes mémoires,* 36, 51; 58, 71, 79; 53, 60; 71, 90; 62, 66, 70, 86, 106–7; Thérèse, *Histoire d'une âme,* 38, 78; 48, 65; 63–64.

96. Delarue-Mardrus, *Mes mémoires,* 83–87; 38; 44–45, 56.

97. Ibid., 26–27; 47.

98. Ibid., 74.

99. Ibid., 106–8.

100. Ibid., 109.

101. Ibid., 108–10, 112.

102. Thérèse, *Histoire d'une âme,* 49–50, 54, 75.

103. Delarue-Mardrus, *Mes mémoires,* 10.

104. Delarue-Mardrus, *Sainte Thérèse,* 92–93.

105. Delarue-Mardrus, *Mes mémoires,* 109.

106. Delarue-Mardrus, *Sainte Thérèse,* 89.

107. Delarue-Mardrus, *Mes mémoires,* 109.

108. Carroll, *Pray Love, Remember,* 255; *I Hear in My Heart,* 98.

109. McCarthy, *Memories,* 26–27.

works cited

Abbott, H. Porter. "Autobiography, Autography, Fiction: Groundwork for a Taxonomy of Textual Categories." *New Literary History* 19 (1988): 597–615.

Adam, Juliette Lambert. *Le roman de mon enfance et de ma jeunesse.* Paris: A. Lemerre, 1902.

Aelred of Rievaulx, Saint and Abbot. *Spiritual Friendship.* Trans. Mary Eugenia Laker, S.S.N.D. Cistercian Fathers Series no.5. Kalamazoo, Mich.: Cistercian Press, 1977.

Ames, Roger T. Introduction to Sun-tzu, *Art of War,* 3–99.

Aquinas, Thomas, O.P., Saint and Doctor of the Church. *Summa Theologica.* Trans. Fathers of the English Dominican Province. Vol. 1 of 5 vols. Westminster, Md.: Christian Classics, 1981.

Asquerino, María. *Memorias.* Barcelona: Plaza & Janés, 1987.

Augustine, Aurelius, Saint and Bishop. *Commentary on the Lord's Sermon on the Mount.* Trans. Denis J. Kavanaugh, O.S.A., 19–199. Vol. 3 of the *Writings of Saint Augustine.* Vol. 11 of *The Fathers of the Church: A New Translation.* Washington, D.C.: Catholic University of America Press, 1951.

———. *Confessions.* Trans. E. M. Blaiklock. New York: Thomas Nelson, 1983.

———. *The Trinity.* Trans. Stephen McKenna, C.SS.R. Vol. 18 of *The Fathers of the Church: A New Translation.* Washington, D.C.: Catholic University of America Press, 1963.

Baillie, James. *Problems in Personal Identity.* New York: Paragon, 1993.

Beauvoir, Simone de. *Memoirs of a Dutiful Daughter.* Trans. James Kirkup. New York: Harper & Row, 1959. Originally published as *Mémoires d'une jeune fille rangée.* Paris: Gallimard, 1958.

———. *The Second Sex.* Trans. and ed. H. M. Parshley. New York: Knopf, 1957. Originally published as *Le Deuxième Sexe.* Vol. 1, *Les faits et les mythes;* vol. 2, *L'expérience vécue.* Paris: Gallimard, 1949.

Bennett, Joy, and Gabriella Hochmann. *Simone de Beauvoir: An Annotated Bibliography.* New York: Garland, 1988.

Benoist, Mary Hunt. *Memories.* N.p., 1930.

Benson, Paul. "Autonomy and Oppressive Socialization." *Social Theory and Practice* 17 (1991): 385–408.

Benstock, Shari. "The Female Self Engendered: Autobiographical Writing and Theories of Selfhood." *Women's Studies* 20 (1991): 5–14.

Bentz, Valerie Malhotra. *Becoming Mature: Childhood Ghosts and Spirits in Adult Life.* New York: A. de Gruyter, 1989.

Bernard, Tristan. *Mémoires d'un jeune homme rangé.* Paris: Fasquelle, 1918.

Bernhardt, Sarah. *Ma double vie: Mémoires de Sarah Bernhardt.* Paris: Charpentier et Fasquelle, 1907.

Bloom, Lynn Z. "Promises Fulfilled: Positive Images of Women in Twentieth Century Autobiography." Paper presented at the annual meeting of the Midwest Modern Language Association in Chicago, November 1975.

Bouverot, Danielle, and Chantal Schaefer. "De la lexicologie à la sémiotique: le vocabulaire de la végétation dans *Sido.*" In Bray, eds. *Colette: Nouvelles approches critiques,* 131–38.

Brave Bird, Mary [Mary Crow Dog], with Richard Erdoes. *Lakota Woman.* New York: HarperCollins, 1991.

Bray, Bernard, ed. *Colette: Nouvelles approches critiques. Actes du Colloque de Sarrebruck* (22–23 juin 1984). Paris: A.-G. Nizet, 1986.

Brodzki, Bella, and Celeste Schenck, eds. *Life/Lines: Theorizing Women's Autobiography.* Ithaca, N.Y.: Cornell University Press, 1988.

Brower, Brock. "Mary McCarthyism." *Esquire,* July 1962, 62–67, 113.

Bruss, Elizabeth W. *Autobiographical Acts: The Changing Situation of a Literary Genre.* Baltimore: Johns Hopkins University Press, 1976.

Carroll, Consolata, Sister. *I Hear in My Heart.* New York: Farrar, Straus, 1949.

———.*Pray Love, Remember.* New York: Farrar, Straus, 1947.

Catechism of the Council of Trent for Parish Priests: Issued by Order of Pope Pius V. Trans. John A. McHugh, O.P., and Charles J. Callan, O.P. New York: Joseph F. Wagner, 1949.

Catéchisme du diocèse de Paris. Paris: Adrien le Clere, 1863.

Catholic Encyclopedia, 1st ed., s.v. "Woman."

Catoir, John, Rev. " 'Love Is a Dreadful Thing.' " *Wyoming Catholic Register,* 26 (October 1979), 8.

Chacel, Rosa. *Desde el amanecer: Autobiografía de mis primeros diez años.* Madrid: Revista de Occidente, 1972.

———.*Saturnal.* Barcelona: Seix Barral, 1972.

Chadwick, Whitney. *Women Artists and the Surrealist Movement.* New York: Thames and Hudson, 1985.

Cixous, Hélène, and Catherine Clément. *The Newly Born Woman.* Trans. Betsy Wing. Minneapolis: University of Minnesota Press, 1986. Originally published as *La jeune née.* Paris: Union Générale d'Éditions, (1975).

Clark, Arthur Melville. *Autobiography: Its Genesis and Phases.* London: Oliver and Boyd, 1935. Reprint, Darby, Pa.: Darby, 1969.

Coleridge, Samuel Taylor. *Biographia Literaria* (1817). New York: E. P. Dutton, 1947.

Colette. *La maison de Claudine* (1922). In vol. 3 of *Oeuvres*, 145–252. Paris: Flammarion, 1960.

————.*Sido* (1929). In vol. 3 of *Oeuvres*, 253–97. Paris: Flammarion, 1960.

Confraternity of Christian Doctrine. *The Official Revised Baltimore Catechism Number One,* with Study Lessons by Ellamay Horan, New York: W. H. Sadlier, 1944.

Conway, Sheelagh. *A Woman and Catholicism: My Break with the Roman Catholic Church.* Toronto: PaperJacks, 1987.

Crites, Stephen. "Storytime: Recollecting the Past and Projecting the Future." In *Narrative Psychology: The Storied Nature of Human Conduct,* edited by Theodore R. Sarbin, 152–73. New York: Praeger, 1986.

Daly, Mary. *The Church and the Second Sex.* New York: Harper & Row, 1968.

Dansette, Adrien. *Histoire religieuse de la France contemporaine: L'église catholique dans la mêlée politique et sociale.* Paris: Flammarion, 1965.

Davidson, H. R. Ellis. *Gods and Myths of Northern Europe.* Baltimore: Penguin, 1964.

De la Fuente, Vicente. "Introducción al libro de la Vida de Santa Teresa." In Teresa, *Escritos,* 1:1–10.

Dehon, Claire. "Colette and Art Nouveau." Trans. Abigail Siddall. In Eisinger and McCarty, eds., *Colette: The Woman, the Writer,* 104–15.

Delarue-Mardrus, Lucie. *Mes mémoires.* Paris: Gallimard, 1938.

————.*Sainte Thérèse de Lisieux.* Paris: Fasquelle, 1926.

Descaves, Lucien. "Au pays de Marie Noël." *Les nouvelles littéraires,* 16 July 1932, 1.

Díaz, Janet W. *Ana María Matute.* New York: Twayne, 1971.

Diccionario de Literatura Española, 1972, s.v. "Rosa Chacel."

Dussane [Béatrix] *Au jour et aux lumières.* Vol. 1, *Premiers pas dans le Temple.* Paris: Calmann-Lévy, 1955.

Eisinger, Erica Mendelson, and Mari Ward McCarty, eds. *Colette: The Woman, the Writer.* University Park: Pennsylvania State University Press, 1981.

Esman, Milton J., and Fred C. Bruhns. *Institution Building in National Development: An Approach to Induced Social Change in Transitional Societies.* Pittsburgh: Graduate School of Public and International Affairs, University of Pittsburgh, 1965.

Evasdaughter, Elizabeth N. "Autobiographical Closure in the Future: Women Constructing Hope." *a/b: Auto/Biography* 9 (1994): 115–33.

————."Julian of Norwich." In Waithe, ed., *A History of Women Philosophers,* 191–222.

Faherty, William B., S.J. *The Destiny of Modern Woman in the Light of Papal Teaching.* Westminster, Md.: Newman, 1950.

Farrell, M. Xavier, Sister. *Happy Memories of a Sister of Charity.* St. Louis: Herder, 1941.

Field, Louise Maunsell. "Kathleen Norris Smiles Back at Life: 'Noon,' an Autobiographical Sketch, Has a Happy Ending and No Disagreeable People." Review of *Noon* by Kathleen Norris. *New York Times,* 25 January 1925, sec. 3:6.

Fishel, Elizabeth. *Sisters: Love and Rivalry inside the Family and Beyond.* New York: William Morrow, 1979.

Fontenot, Peggy Joan. *I Almost Burned in Hell: A Confession.* Hicksville, N.Y.: Exposition Press, 1978.

Fox, Matthew, O.P. *The Coming of the Cosmic Christ: The Healing of Mother Earth and the Birth of a Global Renaissance.* San Francisco: HarperCollins, 1988.

Franck, Jacques. "Simone de Beauvoir a traité les problèmes de son temps." *La libre Beligique,* 15 April 1986. In Bennett and Hochmann, eds., *Simone de Beauvoir,* 445.

Garfield, Patricia. *Creative Dreaming.* New York: Simon and Schuster, 1974.

Gautier, Jean-Jacques. "L'adieu." *Le Figaro,* 4 March 1969, 30.

Gautier, Marie-Lise Gazarian. "Ana María Matute." In *Interviews with Spanish Writers,* 182–200. Elmwood Park, Ill.: Dalkey Archive, 1991.

Genette, Gérard. "Introduction à l'architexte." In Genette and Todorov, eds., *Théorie des genres,* 89–159.

Genette, Gérard, and Tzvetan Todorov, eds. *Théorie des genres.* Paris: Seuil, 1986.

Gerstel, Judy. "She's a Long Way from Galway." *Windsor [Ontario] Star,* 14 November 1987, Lifestyles.

Gleason, Mary, Sister, S.P. Letter to author, 17 January 1980.

Gleick, James. *Chaos: Making a New Science.* New York: Penguin, 1987.

Gössmann, Elisabeth. "Hildegard of Bingen." In Waithe, ed., *A History of Women Philosophers,* 27–65.

Gregory of Nyssa. *See* Warner.

Gumina, Deanna Paoli. "The Apprenticeship of Kathleen Norris." *California History* 66 (1987): 40–48, 72.

Gusdorf, Georges. "Conditions and Limits of Autobiography" (1956). Trans. James Olney. In *Autobiography: Essays Theoretical and Critical,* edited by James Olney, 28–48. Princeton: Princeton University Press, 1980.

Hart, Francis R. "Notes for an Anatomy of Modern Autobiography." *New Literary History* 1 (1970): 485–511.

Hatzfeld, Helmut A. *Santa Teresa de Avila.* New York: Twayne, 1969.

Holman, C. Hugh, and William Harmon. *A Handbook to Literature.* 5th ed. New York: Macmillan, 1986.

Horney, Karen. *Self-Analysis.* New York: W. W. Norton, 1942.

Howarth, William L. "Some Principles of Autobiography." *New Literary History* 5 (1974): 363–81.

Isocrates. *Antidosis* (354–353 B.C.E.), in vol. 2 of *Isocrates.* Loeb Classical Library, 1928.

Janés, Clara. *Jardín y laberinto.* Madrid: Editorial Debate, 1990.

Jerome [Eusebius Hieronymus], Saint. *Commentary on the Epistle to the Ephesians* (3 Ephesians 5:28), in the *Patrologiae Latinae,* ed. J.-P. Migne, 26:567, trans. Mary Daly, in *The Church and the Second Sex.* New York: Harper & Row, 1968.

Jouhandeau, Elise. *Joies et douleurs d'une belle excentrique.* Vol. 1, *Enfance et adolescence d'Elise.* Paris: Flammarion, 1952.

Kaminsky, Amy Katz, and Elaine Dorough Johnson. "To Restore Honor and Fortune: 'The Autobiography of Leonor López de Córdoba.'" In Stanton, ed., *The Female Autograph,* 70–80.

Kaplan, Janet A. *Unexpected Journeys: The Life and Art of Remedios Varo.* New York: Abbeville Press, 1988.

Kenny, Denis. *The Catholic Church and Freedom: The Vatican Council and Some Modern Issues.* St. Lucia, Queensland: University of Queensland Press, 1967.

Ketter, Peter, Reverend. *Christ and Womankind.* Trans. Isabel McHugh. Westminster, Md.: Newman, 1952. Originally published as *Christus und die Frauen.* Düsseldorf, 1935.

Lejeune, Philippe. *L'autobiographie en France.* Paris: Armand Colin, 1971.

Leo XIII. "The Prohibition and Censorship of Books: Apostolic Constitution Officiorum ac Munerum," 25 January 1892. In *The Great Encyclical Letters,* 407–21. New York: Benziger, 1903.

León, María Teresa. *Memoria de la melancolía.* Barcelona: Bruguera, 1979. Originally published Buenos Aires: Losada, 1970.

Lilar, Suzanne. *Le malentendu du "Deuxième Sexe."* Paris: Presses Universitaires de France, 1969.

Lott, Bernice. *Becoming a Woman: The Socialization of Gender.* Springfield, Ill,: Charles C. Thomas, 1981.

MacLean, Paul D., M.D. *A Triune Concept of the Brain and Behavior.* Toronto: University of Toronto Press, 1969.

Marie, Linda. *See* Pillay.

"Marie Noël est morte." *Le Figaro,* 25 December 1967, 7.

Martin, Biddy. "Lesbian Identity and Autobiographical Difference [s]." In Brodski and Schenck, eds., *Life/Lines,* 77–103.

Martín Gaite, Carmen. "La búsqueda de interlocutor." In *La búsqueda de interlocutor y otras búsquedas,* by Carmen Martín Gaite, 21–34. Barcelona: Destino, 1973.

Matute, Ana María. *El río.* Barcelona: Editorial Argos, 1963.

May, Georges. "Autobiography and the Eighteenth Century." In *The Author in His Work: Essays on a Problem in Criticism,* edited by Louis L. Martz and Aubrey Williams, 319–35. New Haven: Yale University Press, 1978.

McCarthy, Mary. *How I Grew.* San Diego: Harcourt Brace Jovanovich, 1987.

———.*Memories of a Catholic Girlhood.* New York: Harcourt Brace Jovanovich, 1957.

McGrath, Albertus Magnus, Sister, O.P. *Women and the Church.* 2d ed. Garden City, N.Y.: Doubleday, 1972.

McKenzie, Barbara. *Mary McCarthy.* New York: Twayne, 1966.

Mellish, Mary. *Sometimes I Reminisce: Autobiography.* New York: G. P. Putnam's Sons, 1941.

Melot, Paule. Review of *Mémoires d'une jeune fille rangée* by Simone de Beauvoir. *Présence et revue de Suisse* (Geneva) 9 (1959): 135–38. In Bennett and Hochmann, eds., *Simone de Beauvoir,* 312.

Menchú, Rigoberta, with Burgos, Elizabeth [oral historian]. *Me llamo Rigoberta Menchú y así me nació la conciencia* (1983). Barcelona: Seix Barral, 1992.

Milner, Christiane. "Le corps de Sido." *Europe: Revue littéraire mensuelle* 631–32 (November–December 1981): 71–84.

Mink, Louis O. "History and Fiction as Modes of Comprehension." *New Literary History* 1 (1969–70): 541–58.

Misch, Georg. *A History of Autobiography in Antiquity.* Trans. E. W. Dickes. Vol. 1 of 2 vols. Westport, Conn.: Greenwood, 1907; revised 1973.

Mullen, Barbara. *Life Is My Adventure.* New York: Coward-McCann, 1937.

Musonius Rufus, C. [or Gaius]. "That Women Too Should Study Philosophy." In *Visions of Women,* edited by Linda A. Bell. Clifton, N.J.: Humana, 1983. Pp. 69–71.

Noël, Marie. *Petit-Jour: Souvenirs d'enfance.* Paris: Stock, 1951.

Norris, Kathleen. *Family Gathering.* Garden City, N.Y.: Doubleday, 1959.

———.*Noon: An Autobiographical Sketch.* New York: Doubleday, Page, 1925.

Obituary of Kathleen Norris. *New York Times,* 15 July 1966, 17.

Obituary of Mary Mellish. *Musical America,* 15 February 1955, 297.

Obituary of Sister M. Madaleva [Wolff]. *New York Times,* 26 July 1964, 57.

Olney, James. *Metaphors of Self: The Meaning of Autobiography.* Princeton: Princeton University Press, 1972.

Olney, James, ed. *Autobiography: Essays Theoretical and Critical.* Princeton: Princeton University Press, 1980.

Oxford Classical Dictionary, 2d ed., s.v. "Gregory of Nyssa."

Pascal, Roy. *Design and Truth in Autobiography.* Cambridge: Harvard University Press, 1960.

Patterson, Yolanda Astarita. *Simone de Beauvoir and the Demystification of Motherhood.* Ann Arbor: UMI, 1989.

Pemán, José María. *De doce cualidades de la mujer.* 2d ed. Madrid: Prensa Española, 1969.

[Pillay], Linda Marie. *I Must Not Rock.* New York: Daughters Press, 1977.

Pius XII. "Women's Dignity: Political and Social Obligations." 21 October 1945. *Vital Speeches,* 1 November 1945, 42–45.

Progoff, Ira. *At a Journal Workshop: The Basic Text and Guide for Using the Intensive Journal.* New York: Dialogue House, 1975.

Pueyo y Abadía, Luis. *Analogias de pulpito, y cathedra. Proporciones panegiricas, y escolaticas.* 2d ed. Zaragoza: Viuda de Iuan de Ybar, 1677.

Repplier, Agnes. *In Our Convent Days.* New York: AMS Press, 1905. Reprint 1969.

Ricoeur, Paul. *Interpretation Theory: Discourse and the Surplus of Meaning.* Fort Worth: Texas Christian University Press, 1976.

Robinson, Richard. *Definition.* Oxford: Clarendon, 1954; revised 1965.

Roessler, Augustine. *Die Frauenfrage vom Standpunkte der Natur der Geschichte und der Offenbarung.* Freiburg im Breisgau: Herder. 1907.

Rose, Wendy. "Neon Scars." In *I Tell You Now: Autobiographical Essays by Native American Writers,* edited by Brian Swann and Arnold Krupat, 251–61. Lincoln: University of Nebraska Press, 1987.

Ruether, Rosemary Radford. "Christianity." In *Women in World Religions,* edited by Arvind Sharma, 207–33. Albany: State University of New York Press, 1987.

Saari, Jon. "The Printed Word: Graham Greene." Review of *Ways of Escape* by Graham Greene. *Tucson Citizen*, 13 June 1981, Weekender, 15.

Sancho, Manuel, Rev., Mercedario. *El Catechismo de los niños: explicado con parábolas y comparaciones.* Vol. 2, *Lo que se ha de obrar (doctrina moral).* Barcelona: Subirana, 1927.

Sanford, Linda Tschirhart, and Mary Ellen Donovan. *Women and Self-Esteem.* New York: Penguin, 1985.

Sarde, Michèle. *Colette, libre et entravée.* Paris: Stock, 1978.

Sargeant, Winthrop. "Books." *New Yorker*, 26 September 1959, 186, 189, 190. In Bennett and Hochmann, eds., *Simone de Beauvoir*, 317.

Schaeffer, Jean-Marie. "Du texte au genre." In Genette and Todorov, eds., *Théorie des genres*, 179–205.

Schoffen, Elizabeth. *The Demands of Rome.* N.p., 1917.

Shapiro, Stephen A. "The Dark Continent of Literature: Autobiography." *Comparative Literature Studies* 5 (1968): 421–54.

Shively, Stan, and Knud S. Larsen. "Socialization Attitudes and Social Authorities." *Journal of Psychology* 124 (1990): 275–81.

Showalter, Elaine. "Introduction: The Feminist Critical Revolution." In *The New Feminist Criticism: Essays on Women, Literature and Theory,* edited by Elaine Showalter, 3–17. New York: Pantheon, 1985.

A Sister Servant of the Immaculate Heart of Mary. *With Jesus: Prayers and Instructions for Youthful Catholics.* Milwaukee: Milwaukee Church Supply, 1922.

Spelman, Elizabeth V. *Inessential Women: Problems of Exclusion in Feminist Thought.* Boston: Beacon, 1988.

Stanley, Liz. *The Auto/biographical I: The theory and practice of feminist auto/biography.* New York: Manchester University Press, 1992.

Stanton, Domna C. "Autogynography: Is the Subject Different?" In Stanton, ed., *The Female Autograph*, 3–20.

Stanton, Domna, ed. *The Female Autograph: Theory and Practice of Autobiography from the Tenth to the Twentieth Century.* Chicago: University of Chicago Press, 1984.

Starobinski, Jean. "The Style of Autobiography." Trans. Seymour Chatman. In *Literary Style: A Symposium,* edited by Seymour Chatman, 285–94. New York: Oxford University Press, 1971.

Stewart, Joan Hinde. *Colette.* Boston: Twayne, 1983.

Stockinger, Jacob. "The Test of Love and Nature: Colette and Lesbians." In *Colette: The Woman, the Writer,* edited by Erica Mendelson Eisinger and Mari Ward McCarty, 75–93. University Park: Pennsylvania State University Press, 1981.

Stokes, George Stewart. *Agnes Repplier: Lady of Letters.* Philadelphia: University of Pennsylvania Press, 1949.

Sun-tzu ping fa. *Sun-tzu: The Art of War: The First English Translation Incorporating the Recently Discovered Yin-ch'üeh-shan Texts.* Trans. Roger T. Ames. New York: Ballantine, 1993.

Teresa [Cepeda y Ahumada] of Avila, Saint. *La Vida.* In vol. 1 of *Escritos*, vol. 53 of

Biblioteca de autores españoles desde la formación de lenguaje hasta nuestros días, 17–134. Madrid: Los sucesores de Hernando, 1923.

Tertullianus, Quintus Septimii. *On the Apparel of Women.* Vol. 4 of *The Ante-Nicene Fathers.* Trans. Rev. S. Thelwall, 14–25. Grand Rapids, Mich.: Wm. B. Eerdmans, 1956.

Thérèse [Martin] de l'Enfant-Jésus, Saint. *Histoire d'une âme* (1895–97). Lisieux: Calvados, 1946.

Unger, Rhoda, and Mary Crawford. *Women and Gender: A Feminist Psychology.* Philadelphia: Temple University Press, 1992.

Varo, Remedios. *Embroidering Earth's Mantle,* 1962. Private collection.

Von Salomonson, Anna. "Fiktion als Rache: Zu den Werken Simone de Beauvoirs." *Hochland: Monatsschrift fur alle Gebeite des Wissens* 52 (1960): 426–31. In Bennett and Hochmann, eds., *Simone de Beauvoir,* 106.

Waithe, Mary Ellen, ed. *A History of Women Philosophers.* Vol. 2, *Medieval, Renaissance and Enlightenment Women Philosophers, A.D. 500–1600.* Dordrecht: Kluwer, 1989.

Waldo-Schwartz, Paul. *Art and the Occult.* New York: Braziller, 1975.

Walker, Nancy A. *A Very Serious Thing: Women's Humor and American Culture.* Minneapolis: University of Minnesota Press, 1988.

Warner, Marina. *Alone of All Her Sex: The Myth of the Cult of the Virgin Mary.* New York: Knopf, 1976.

Wiggins, David. *Sameness and Substance.* Oxford: Basil Blackwell, 1980.

Wilson-Kastner, Patricia. Preface to *A Lost Tradition: Women Writers of the Early Church,* vii–xxx. Lanham, Md.: University Presses of America, 1981.

Wittgenstein, Ludwig. *Philosophical Investigations.* Trans. G. E. M. Anscombe. Oxford: Basil Blackwell, 1953.

Wolff, M. Madaleva, Sister, C.S.C. *My First Seventy Years.* New York: Macmillan, 1959.

Wong, Mary Gilligan. *Nun: A Memoir.* New York: Harper & Row, 1984.

index

Adam, Juliette Lambert, 20, 21, 140, 163;
conflicted gender training of, 65, 146,
170; harm done autobiography, 227;
and official theology of "Woman," 153–
54, 176, 200, 203; strategies as autobiographer, 32, 200

Aelred of Rievaulx, 150, 157, 201

"Age of reason," 145, 178, 209, 211

Alliance, 163–67

American Protective Association, 89

Angelism, 138, 206

Anger in autobiographers, 44, 45–46, 49,
52, 54, 63; and style, 53, 71

Animal nature, aversion to, 79–80, 101,
119; as disadvantageous to women, 121;
and full humanity, 125, 161. *See also* Femaleness

Anorexia, 8, 211

Antidosis (Isocrates), 26

Aquinas, Thomas: contradictions in,
122–23; gender theology of, 14, 121–25,
136, 137, 161; on sexual passion, 207

Art: Colette's emulation of, 59–60; as love,
179. *See also* Surrealism

Art of War (Sun-tzu): applicability of, 11,
157, 162–63; strategies borrowed,
163–64; strategies explained, 165, 169,
170, 171, 185, 186

Asquerino, María, 20, 21, 92; and authority, 188; and Catholic education, 92–93;

harm done autobiography, 227; strategy
as autobiographer, 32, 73

Attacks on personal bonds, 77–78, 80–81,
88, 101

Augustine, 119–21, 151, 152

Authority: abuse of, 74, 85; just use of, 65,
70, 74, 122, 126, 152–57; styles of, 74–75

Authority, Catholic beliefs on, 130–31,
205–6, 207, 210, 212, 213; critique of,
200–203; elision of human and divine,
69; extension of paternal, 66, 202; prohibition of criticism, 21–22

Authority, used against: ambition, 78,
139–41, 209–10; establishment of new
selves, 83–84, 85; forthright speech,
106–7; helpful relationships, 77–78,
80–81, 88, 101; individual differences,
57, 74–75; interest in men, 80; other religions, 82, 141–42, 199; reading, 82, 84,
88, 142; serious study, 85–94, 139–40;
vitality, 80

"Author's death": death of alter ego, 109,
169, 214; desire for death, 224; emotional death, 225; fantasy death, 215;
figurative death, 174; near-death, 42–43,
81–82, 107, 224; theory of, 27–28

Autobiographers, Catholic women, twentieth-century, xiii–xiv; authentic faith,
6, 15, 17, 212; critique of Catholic gender
training, 192–211; defiance of Catholic
gender training, 192–228; differences

from other women autobiographers, 4–5, 5–6, 11, 34, 70–71, 110, 144, 191, 227–28; rationality of, 15–16, 178, 208–9, 208–12, 227–28; reliability of, 35, 85, 138, 142–43; theoretical impossibility of, 19, 20–21. *See also* Variations among twentieth-century Catholic women autobiographers

Autobiographers, nuns as: advantages, 121, 132; critical judgment, 71, 227; faults of omission, 226–27; protectiveness toward Church, 178, 194, 227. *See also* Carroll; Farrell; Schoffen; Wolff; Wong

The Auto/biographical I (Stanley), 8

Autobiographies by twentieth-century Catholic women: artistic defects in, 226–27; artistic innovation in, 196, 211–26; attitude toward remembered self, 193–94; authorial comment through titles, 216–19; autobiographical metaphors, 215–16, 217; centrality of author, 28, 53, 61, 62–63, 81, 191, 199, 228; characteristics, 197; future orientation, 63, 178–81; original interpretation of experience, 32, 55, 58, 63, 178–81, 220–21, 222–26; persuasive intent, 26, 196–211; primary narrative subject of, 4, 6; self, implicit definition of, 55, 56, 192, 214, 220–21; serious analysis, 55, 58, 218, 220–21, 222–26; subgenres: anti-confession, 29, anti-development, 29, defiance, 32–33, feminine hope, 31–32, human hope or protest, 32, intellectual communication, 32. *See also* Censorship; Motifs

Autobiography, theory of: as art, 24–25, 211–26; continuity/discontinuity, 34; contribution of Catholic women's autobiographies, 4, 6, 7–8; conventions tending to exclude women, 20; conventions tending to include women, 24–28; distinction from reminiscence, 13, 41; future tense in, 27; interdisciplinary study of, 9–10, 10–12; present tense "I" in, 8, 9, 15, 34, 35, 193–226

Autobiography, value to readers: breaking up stereotypes, 3–5, 191; comparison to self, 8, 35, 191; understanding of author, 6; understanding of genre, 7–8

Autobiography, women's tradition, 25, 26, 29, 196, 221–22

Baillie, James, 31

Baltimore catechism. *See Official Revised Baltimore Catechism Number One*

Beauvoir, Françoise de, 84, 89–91, 104–5, 179, 205; and theology of subordination, 129–30, 130–31

Beauvoir, Simone de, xiii, xiv, 6; allies, 146; arguments for fully human girlhood, 108, 198–99, 202, 206, 210; artistry, 10, 28, 201, 218, 220–21; attempted cultural isolation of, 84, 90, 91, 139, 210; attitude toward remembered self, 193; autobiography of, as model of personal history, 220–21; and criticism of Church, 13, 73, 74; death of alter ego, 28, 221; desire for fully human life, 6, 32–33, 33–34, 174–75, 206, 210; desire for just life, 32, 174, 210; early piety, 146, 203; encouragement of, 89–90, 148, 152; and equality of women, 6, 74, 130; erotic anti-history, 29, 205–7; father vs. Church, 146; and "feminine" style, 74; friendships of, 165–66, 184, 202, 206; girlhood, study of, 7; harassment by parents, 84, 91, 142, 156–67, 165, 168; harm done to, 77–78, 84, 91–92, 205–7; hypertext, 218; interpretation of, 3, 6; irony of, 10, 203; literary prestige, 9; novels, desire to write, 174; portrayal of male authority figures, 78–79, 104, 146, 152, 176; portrayal of mother, 84, 89–90, 104–5, 179, 205; portrayal of nuns, 90, 139, 210; pre-Sartrean existentialism, 174–75, 193, 218; rehumanization of marriage, 179–81; rejection of sacrifice and suffering, 104–5, 136, 176, 203; and Sartre, 165, 206–7, 220; secularization, 33, 171–72, 173, 174–75, 176–77, 180; self-strengthening, 26, 33, 172, 176–77; spiral narrative form, 220–21; women's tradition of autobiography, 25, 74. *See also* Beauvoir, Françoise de; Beauvoir,

Simone de, Catholic influence; Beauvoir, Simone de, strategies as autobiographer; Beauvoir, Simone de, strategies as girl; *The Second Sex*

Beauvoir, Simone de, Catholic influence, 73; on behavior, 6, 161, 130–31, 205–7; on ideas, 73, 174–75, 210; language, 10, 69, 180; parents, 129–30, 130–31

Beauvoir, Simone de, strategies as autobiographer: anti-history of erotic development, 29, 205–7; closure, 28; death of alter ego, 28, 221; harmful results, 77–78, 84, 91–92, 205–7; irony, 10, 203; open criticism, 90, 179, 210; paratextual hypertextuality, 218; plot as argument, 220–21; process, 165; synthesis, 146, 178, 179–81; thoroughness, 73; tone, 90

Beauvoir, Simone de, strategies as girl: alliance, 164, 165–66, 166–67; counterattack, 185, 186; espionage, 181–82; geographical moves, 26; redirection of opponent's resources, 171–72, 174–75, 176–77; restraint, 183; retreat, 181; secrecy, 168–69, 170–71, 184; self-strengthening, 26, 171–72, 174–75, 176–77

Becoming Mature (Bentz), 65

Benedict XV, 130, 132

Benoist, Mary Hunt, xiii, xiv, 86; antipathy to female in, 95; femininity training of, 86–87, 94–95, 102; strategies as autobiographer, 32, 73, 95, 161, 188–89; strategies as girl, 181

Benson, Paul, 42, 44

Benstock, Shari, 24

Bentz, Valerie Malhotra, 65

Bernard, Tristan, 218–19

Bernhardt, Sarah, xiii, xiv, 137; attitude toward remembered self, 32, 193; criticism of convents, 210; early theatricality of, 147, 186; father of, 124, 128; humor of, 186; mother of, 166, 173; omission of erotic history, 227; opponents of, 137, 143, 173; portrayal of benign nun, 154–55, 202; preference for humanizing occupation, 210; strategies as

autobiographer, 7, 32, 210; strategies as girl, 172, 173, 175, 186, 187, 189

Betrayal of confidence, 79, 168–69

Bigotry, 52–53, 141–42, 193, 194, 199

Bipolarity, 23–24

Bloom, Lynn Z., 30

Brave Bird (Crow Dog), Mary, xiii, xiv, 21, 75; and abuse, 77, 82–83, 124, 184–85, 186; courage of, 124, 184–85; discrimination against, 82; femininity training of, 75, 82, 118, 132; friendship and, 83, 185, 186; justice of, 32, 124, 184–85; rejection of Europeanization, 217; strategies as autobiographer, 32, 73, 217; strategies as girl, 99, 124, 184–85, 186, 188

Brothers: as allies, 40, 47, 55, 98, 168, 182, 187, 199; parental injustice, 86–87, 102, 105, 182; parental justice, 147–48

Canada, Catholic Church in, 194

Canticle of Canticles (Song of Solomon), 139, 151

Careers: difficult beginnings of, 42–43, 45, 84, 89, 91–92, 94, 131, 140–41, 210; higher, 131, 178–79, 210–11

Carmelites, 87, 150, 156

Carroll, Consolata, xiii, xiv, 40; attitude toward remembered self, 193; authoritarian parents, 41, 44; avoidance of technological skill, 169–70; as college professor, 40, 41, 43, 132, 227; and convent, 43, 121, 132, 177–78; defeat, 189; defects as autobiographer, 40–41, 226–27; difficulty in portraying self, 40–41, 227; ego development, 41–43, 132, 189; excessive devotion to authority, 41–44, 63; false cheerfulness, 40, 43, 63; femininity training, 41–42, 44, 68; harm done to, 189; mother figures, orientation to, 41, 43, 177; orthodoxy, 42, 43–44, 194, 227; oversocialization, 42; quicksand pattern, 42–43, 44; rationality of women, demonstration of, 227; and sacrifice, 177–78; sartorial femininity, 41–42; self-negation in girlhood, 41, 42, 43, 193; sex education of, 43–44; strategies as autobiographer, 31, 43–44,

71, 193; strategies as girl, 41, 43, 169–70, 187; unintended criticism of Church, 29, 43–44; verbosity, 34, 40–41, 226

Catechesis: constructive influence of, ix; damaging to autobiography, 69–71; damaging to children, 64–69, 95, 100, 188–89; damaging to women, 136–37; disapproved by autobiographers, 45, 61, 64, 86–87, 208; disapproved by girls, 95; flaws of, ix, 201; unwarranted elaborations of Scripture, 64, 65, 66–67, 95–96, 120–21, 125–27; widespread, 64, 85, 127

Catechism of the Council of Trent for Parish Priests: Issued by Order of Pope Pius V, 14, 66–67, 95–96, 97, 106, 125–28, 137

Catéchisme du diocèse de Paris, 64–65, 95–96, 136

El Catechismo de los niños, 120–21

Catherine of Siena, 196

Catholic Church and autobiographers: assistance remembered, 70, 145–57, 190; criticized by most, 15–16, 195–96, 197; defended by few, 227; fallibility, 39; implied prohibition of autobiography, 12, 19, 20–21, 33; principal topic of, 4, 6, 11; prohibition of criticism of the Church's representatives, 13–14, 65–66, 67, 69–71, 197

Catholic Church and gender teaching of parents, 130, 136, 137, 142–44

Catholic Encyclopedia, 130–32

"Catholic Woman" concept: descriptive definitions, 4, 190, 191, 196; destructiveness, 3, 4, 6, 12, 144, 202–3; disproval of class consistency, 134, 135; illogicality, 11, 117; injustice, 3, 117; lack of unanimity on, 11, 14–15, 16, 22, 146, 150–52, 172; official (prescriptive) definitions, 19, 118, 119, 121, 130–32, 134–36; rejection by women, 5, 150, 175, 195, 228. *See also* Woman, official theology of

Catoir, Father, 136

Celibacy, 121, 134, 180

Censorship, ecclesiastical, 54, 69–70, 84, 86, 88, 194; evasion of, 54–55, 56, 61, 62–63, 227; internalized, 48–53, 55–56, 67, 70–71, 226–27

Chacel, Rosa, xiii, xiv, 7; artistry of, 7, 219; career for women, description of, 178–79; and Catholic authority figures, 87, 102, 103–4, 140–41; and Catholic femininity training, 102, 103–4, 140–41, 176, 179; cultural path, affirmation of, 155–56, 178–79; "death of the author," 28, 107; desire to live a just life, 32, 179; early piety, 145–46; and education, 87, 140–41, 147, 155–56, 185–86; femininity training of, 87, 102, 106–7, 140–41; goodness of, 179, 192, 209; harm done to, 28, 107; identification with both parents, 104, 107, 169, 219; literary prestige, 10; opponents of, 107, 140–41; parents, praise of, 155–56; rationality of women, argument for, 7, 123, 192, 208–9; rehumanization of career, 178–79; self, implied definition of, 192; similarities across differences in scale, 219; strategies as autobiographer, 24, 73, 208–9, 219, 316; synthesis, 172–73, 178–79, 207, 219; and theology of equivalence, 155–56; women's tradition of autobiography, 24. *See also* Chacel, Rosa, strategies as girl

Chacel, Rosa, strategies as girl: adaptability, 188; espionage, 183; redirection of opponent's resources, 172–73, 178–79; refusal, 176; supply, 165; surrender, 102, 165

Charitable speech, 49, 71, 106–7, 152–53

Cheerfulness, 63; and anger, 44, 45–46, 46–47, 49, 54, 63; and avoidance of analysis, 39–53; and style, 57–61

Christ, 22, 118, 136, 147; personal treatment of women, 149; retreat of, 187; and self-sacrifice, 175–76; and sexuality, 151; and suffering, 151; teachings of, 149; and theology of equivalence, 8, 16, 152, 157

Christ and Womankind (Ketter), 115, 133–37

Church. *See* Catholic Church

Cixous, Hélène, 23

Clément, Catherine, 23

Close surveillance, 83–85, 117, 167

Colette, Sidonie-Gabrielle, xiii, xiv, 59; artistry, 53, 59–61, 217; and catechism, 61; "Catholic Mother" in reality, 61, 153, 207; censorship evasion, 53, 56, 59–61, 71; desire for fully human life, 32; early encouragement, 152, 153, 155; father of, 61, 155; fifth commandment, 153; and human variety, 135, 198, 207–8, 217; identification with both parents, 61, 67, 165; and Philippe Lejeune, 59; mother of, 146, 153, 207; prose-poem cycle, 34, 59–60; self as true subject, 53, 61; strategies as autobiographer, 59–61, 153, 169, 207–8; strategies as girl, 169, 184; and theology of equivalence, 152, 153, 155; and uniform moral code, 198, 207–8, 217; women's tradition of autobiography, 74, 221

Commandments: first, 51; fourth, 64–68, 79, 125–26, 142, 153; fifth, 153, 157, 161, 190; sixth and ninth, 95–96, 71, 79, 106, 126–27

Communion, first, 76, 90, 95, 148, 153, 154, 197, 222

Communism, 129, 133, 136, 141

Confession (Sacrament of Penance), 76, 78–79, 124

Confessional autobiography, 29, 217–18

Confraternity of Christian Mothers, 89–90, 129–30, 148

Convent: as escape from parents, 170, 181; as independence from marriage, 132; not as sacrifice, 177–78; as rejoining mother, 177–78

Convent school: excessive discipline, 59; and secrecy, 167–68; and uniformity, 74–75, 85, 210; before Vatican II, 57–58, 85

Conway, Sheelagh, xiii, xiv, 76; abuse, 76; attitude toward remembered self, 193; desire to live a just life, 194; harm done to, 106; and male authority figures, 105–6, 107; mother's abuse, 105–6; objection to catechism, 86; omission of erotic history, 227; strategies as autobi-ographer, 32, 73, 86, 193; strategies as girl, 76, 106, 177

Coppée, François, 131, 226

Córdoba, Leonor López de, 27

Creation as validation, 5–6, 86, 145, 149, 150–51, 161, 168, 172

Creativity, 7, 16, 28, 151–52, 190–91, 212

Crites, Stephen, 30–31, 42

Criticism of the Church, 13–14, 39, 46–47, 50–53, 196; alternatives to, 70–71; and analysis, 69–70; of catechism, 61; for-bidden, 63–64, 69–71; and literary form, 46–48, 49, 53, 54–55, 64, 71–72; loyal, 45, 197; possible responses of au-tobiographers, 71; of traditional monas-tic discipline, 58–59

Crow Dog, Mary. *See* Brave Bird

Cultural and social deprivation, 82, 85–94, 198–99

De doce cualidades de la mujer (Pemán), 123

Death and autobiography, 27, 28, 55, 215; death of parents, 40, 42–43, 47, 62–63, 65, 80; death of remembered self, 42–43, 81–82, 107, 109, 169, 174, 214, 215, 224, 225

Deceit as strategy, 169–70, 183

Definition: exclusive definitions of "auto-biography," 19–20; "family resem-blance" and definitions of "women," 3–5; inclusive definitions of "autobiog-raphy," 24–28; illogical definitions of "Woman," 117–19, 122–23. *See also* Man; Self; Woman/women

Dehon, Claire, 59–60

Delarue-Mardrus, Lucie, xiii, xiv, 95; al-lies, 166, 216; autobiographical creativ-ity: 25, 216, 221, 222, 226; and catechism, 95; courage of, 224–25; and cultural path, 155, 209, 223, 225; defense of career as writer, 166, 209, 211; demy-thologizing of St. Thérèse of Lisieux, 223, 225; discrimination against, 131; early encouragement, 155, 210–11; ego-tism reclassified, 200; erotic history, 208, 224–25; humility of parents, 200; hypertext, 201, 222–26; literary experience, 9; mother of, 97, 224; paganism of, 200, 211; and rationality in women, 166, 209, 211; secularization, 213, 216, 223–26; self-direction, 209, 223, 226; sisters of, 201, 223–24; strategies as autobiographer, 73, 201, 208, 211, 216, 221–25; strategies as girl, 166, 201, 209, 223–24; women's tradition in autobiography, 25, 200, 221–22

Descaves, Lucien, 108

Design and Truth in Autobiography (Pascal), 7

Destiny of Modern Woman in the Light of Papal Teaching (Faherty), 115, 128–33

Le Deuxième sexe (Beauvoir), 6, 23, 25, 74

Dishonesty in authority figures, 75, 76, 77, 101; false or heterodox teaching, 76, 87, 143

Discrimination, 82–83, 131

Dominicans, xi, 121, 122, 127, 150

Donovan, Mary Ellen, 21–22

Dussan, Béatrix. *See* Dussane

Dussane, xiii, xiv, 166; affirmation of women, 198; allies of, 166; desire to live a just life, 184; maternal enrichment of, 166, 198; omission of erotic history, 227; opponents of, 143, 166; sacredness of secular arts, 184, 218; and secular education, 198; self as true subject, 56, 218; strategies as autobiographer, 198, 218; strategies as girl, 166, 184

Ecclesiastical support of violent parents, 65, 105–6

Eden, 122, 123, 182, 201, 209

Education of women, 122, 129, 131, 132, 139; discouragement of serious study, 91–92, 131, 143, 166; preschool training, 145, 147–48, 197

Educational deprivation of Catholic girls: in religious learning, 110–13, 126–35, 141, 142–50, 160–67, 169–73, 174–77; in secular learning, 157–58, 160–62, 165–66, 168, 169–70, 170–71, 173, 198

Educational reform, 16–17, 45, 83, 86–90, 92–94, 197–98

Egoism, 199–200

Embroidering Earth's Mantle (Varo), 17, 74–75, 83, 93, 187

Employment for women, 129, 131, 133, 140–41, 210–11; and subservience, 122, 129, 130–31, 137–38, 140–41

Equivalence, theology of, 14–15, 16, 54, 115, 145–57; and preschool, 147–48, 161

Erotic history: bisexual, 207–8; heterosexual, 43–44, 61, 62, 75, 80, 82, 90, 96, 101, 153, 168, 169, 172, 173, 179–80, 181, 183, 204–7, 213, 214, 217–18, 227; lesbian, 24, 99–101, 169, 208, 225–26

Espionage as strategy, 164, 181–83

Evangelical poverty, 47–48

Eve, 21, 118, 137, 143, 150, 193

Examination of conscience: as social control, 51, 69–70, 74, 106; used strategically by girls, 172, 174. *See also* Sin

Faherty, William B., 115, 130

Family resemblances, among twentieth-century Catholic women autobiographers, 5–6; 195–96

Family resemblances, concept of, 3–4, 5, 11

Farrell, M. Xavier, xiii, xiv, 40; attitude toward convent life, 31, 40, 121, 173, 177; defense of the Church, 40, 71, 173, 227; orthodoxy of, 194, 227; strategies as autobiographer, 31, 40, 53, 216; strategies as girl, 40, 173

Fathers: abusive, 76, 83, 99–101, 105–6; as allies, 140, 153, 155–56; duties of, 107, 125; financially improvident, 46–48, 103; flawed, 41, 44, 89, 91, 104, 143, 163, 197, 215; identification with, 107, 147, 165, 180, 201, 218; as models, 63, 67; opposition of, 87, 102, 215

Fathers of the Church, 117–21, 150

Femaleness, antipathy to, 95, 99–101, 119, 135, 139, 168, 181–85, 203, 207–8, 210

Femininity, defined, 141

Femininity rules, majority, 144; accept suffering as due punishment, 21, 118, 137; avoid bonding with nonfamily members, 77–78, 80, 82, 84, 90; be alike, 19, 20–21, 74–75; be neither female nor intellectual, 90, 118, 131, 135, 139; do domestic work only, 89, 125, 131, 138; dress modestly, 133, 205; enter only servile occupations, 131, 188; no equaling men in this world, 6, 90, 130–31; no expression of emotion, 138; no feminism, 129, 132, 136; no heading of families, 125, 129, 130; no higher careers, 131, 139, 133; no interest in sex, 20, 90, 135, 205–8; no leaving the house without permission, 125; no masculine activities, 6, 21, 55, 131–32, 141; no priesthood, 123; no self-direction, 21–22, 123; no suffrage, 132; obedience in small matters, 102; revolve around your mother, 67, 81–82, 90, 140; sacrifice yourself, 21, 62, 90, 134, 136, 137, 175–78; subordinate yourself to men, 20–21, 122–23, 129, 131; tolerate abuse and adultery, 104–6, 127; train your children in virtue, 125; volunteer instead of working, 129, 133

Femininity training, majority: contradictory, 14–15, 110, 117, 119–20, 121, 122–23, 147–50, 189–90; distinct from secular, 116–17; exclusion from masculine activities, 6, 21, 55, 131–32, 141; indirect, 138; little respect for girls, 137–41, 143–44, 266; orthodox/heterodox, x, 14–15, 115–37, 139–40, 143–44; strategies: see Authority, abuse of; Bigotry

Femininity training, minority: bolstering ego strength of girls, 147–48, 152–57; criticism of official Church, 61, 146; encouraging learning and achievement of girls, 146, 155–57

Feminism, 3–4, 29, 130, 133

Feminist theories of the self, 22–24

Field, Louise Maunsell, 46, 69

First communion. See Communion

First confession. See Confession

Fishel, Elizabeth, 201

Fontenot, Peggy Joan, xiii, xiv, 12, 29; abuse of, 79, 99, 101; attitude toward remembered self, 29, 218; confessional autobiography, 29; defeats of, 188, 189; early piety, 146; and male Catholic authority figures, 101, 153; opponents, 101, 118, 119; self-respect, 29, 153, 218; and

sexual love, 173, 217–18; strategies as autobiographer, 29, 153, 217–18; strategies as girl, 173

Fox, Matthew, 150, 151–52, 190

Fragmentation, literary, 54, 59–60, 61

France, Catholic Church in, 56, 131. See also Adam; Beauvoir; Bernhardt; Catéchisme du diocèse de Paris; Colette; Delarue-Mardrus; Dussane; Jouhandeau; Noël

Franco, Francisco, 34, 54, 62, 120, 121, 123, 217

Free will, 174–75

Friends: as cure for loneliness, 77, 176; happiness with, 57–58, 169, 180; inability to relate to, 82, 205–6; lack of, 82, 99, 100, 169; necessary to life-history, 58; respect for, 171; sharing struggle, 62, 65, 90, 163, 165, 186, 187; sharing suffering, 28, 75, 82–83, 162; strategic importance of, 163, 165, 167; support from, 43, 154, 163, 165, 175; as symbol of oneself, 28, 92; valuable, 55, 165, 167, 169, 176–77, 180, 181, 184, 206

Friendship, 150, 201–2; opposition to, 72–78, 84, 85, 90, 91, 144

Future, fear of, 108–9, 124, 138, 224

Gender theology. See Woman, official theology of

Gender training. See Femininity training

Genette, Gérard, 4

Girlhood, 7–8, 14, 17, 58

Girls, as narrated: defined, 192; family resemblances, 73–113, 137–43, 152–57, 161–91; imagination, 47, 95, 96, 97, 171, 172, 174, 178–79, 180, 211; opinions, 87, 90, 95, 104–5, 107, 108–9, 140, 149–50, 161–62, 174–83; preference for minority theology, 157, 161; self-development and the Church, 29, 167, 169, 171–81, 191, 192, 228; submission to feminization, 188–90

Girls, goodness of: authenticity (integrity), 167, 168, 171, 219, 220; courage/cowardice, 55, 147, 173–74, 182, 184–91, 197, 224–25; creativity, 62, 167, 170–81, 186,

190–91, 209; desire to be complete human individuals, 85, 147–50, 161; desire to live a just life, 89, 179, 184; faith in God's regard, 6, 149; false guilt, 8–9, 53, 101, 224; hope/despair, 42–43, 107–8, 190; justice, 55, 124, 154, 174, 179, 184–85, 190; obedience/disobedience, 41–42, 64–69, 80–82, 99–103, 147, 168, 172, 184, 185, 188–90, 197–98; piety, 69, 145–46, 175–76, 203; prudence/imprudence, 15, 161, 164, 188–91; rational self-direction, 15, 42–43, 161, 164–91, 209; self-education, 171, 209, 216; self-esteem, 172–74, 178–79. *See also* Identification
Gnosticism, 22
Good Shepherd nuns, 93
Gordon, Mary, 22
Goretti, Maria, 177
Gospels of St. Thomas, 22
Greene, Graham, 20
Gregory of Nyssa, 117, 118, 139, 227
Guatemala, Catholic Church in, 198–99

Hart, Francis R., 24
Helpmate or helpmeet, 122, 124, 129
Hildegarde of Bingen, 196
Histoire d'une âme (Thérèse of Lisieux), 222–26
Holy cards, 175–76
Hope and autobiography, 28, 30–32, 42, 108
Horney, Karen, 22
Howarth, William L., 24

Identification: with father, 106–7, 147, 169, 170; with mother, 177–78; with remembered self, 9, 76, 106–7, 192–93, 215
Illness and sacrifice, 176, 224–25
Index of Forbidden Books, 86, 88
Individuality, early encouragement/erasure: 74–75, 135, 148–49
Inessential Woman (Spelman), 3, 191
Inspiration and women, 211
Institution: and autobiography, 4, 6, 39, 109–10; defined, 11; and self-defense, 162–63, 194

Intellectuality, 118, 122–25. *See also* Rationality in Catholic women; Study
Ireland, Catholic Church in, 76, 105–6. *See also* Conway
Islamic influence, 127, 199
Isocrates, 26
Isolationism, cultural, 33–34, 82, 84, 89–91, 117, 170, 181, 198–99

James, William, 22
Janés, Clara, xiii, xiv, 61; artistry, 61–64; autobiography as search for path, 31; and "Catholic Woman," 62, 136; and death, 28, 63; early cultural orientation, 61–63; father as model, 62, 63, 147; and fully human life, 32–33; literary prestige, 10; prose-poem cycle, 34, 53, 61, 63; reminiscence as mask, 63; and sacrifice, 62, 136; self as process, 32; strategies as autobiographer, 28, 32, 62, 63, 73; textual secularization, 62, 63
Jerome, Saint, 121, 151, 152, 184, 211
Jesuits, 148, 171, 210, 215
Jesus. *See* Christ
Jewish women, 21, 199, 204
John XXIII, 76
Jouhandeau, Elise Toulé, xiii, xiv, 80; allies of, 153, 155, 164, 291; and cultural enclosure, 170, 183; and divinization of authority, 202; father's contempt for mother, 126; mother's abuse of, 65, 80, 143; mother's dishonesty to, 181; mother's hostility to, 80, 97, 118, 166; strategies as autobiographer, 32, 73, 81, 170, 202; strategies as girl, 164, 166, 169, 172, 181
Judaism, 21–22, 199, 204, 218
Julian of Norwich, 27, 132

Kaplan, Janet, 93, 168
Kenny, Denis, 150, 151
Ketter, Peter, 116, 133–37, 208

Ladies of the Sacred Heart. *See* Madams of the Sacred Heart
Language: analysis and protest, 61; allusion, 217, 218, 219, 221–26; figuration,

50, 215–16, 217; lyricism, 53, 59–60, 61; puns, 214, 217, 218; symbolism, 211, 220–21; reinterpreted religious terms, 172, 173, 174–75, 179, 180, 216, 218

Layteachers, 198

Lejeune, Philippe, 9, 26, 59, 193

Leo XIII, 54, 88, 128, 129

León, María Teresa, xiii, xiv, 75, 87; allies, 87, 146; attitude toward remembered self, 202; and catechism, 96; and Catholic education, 75, 87–88, 93, 96; defeats, 188; and female authority figures, 87–88, 97, 127, 202; and fully human life, 32–33, 87–88; harm done to, 88, 103; and insult, 88, 139, 202; and male authority figures, 104, 204, 217; and rationality in women, 87, 123, 139, 213–14; and sexuality, 96, 135, 204–5, 214, 217; strategies as autobiographer, 32–33, 73, 102, 204–5, 213–14; strategies as girl, 87–88, 170, 181, 184; surrealism of, 212, 213–14; title of work, 217; tone, 104, 202, 204–5; unwarranted expulsion of, 88, 202

Lesbianism, 24, 166, 208, 223, 226

Life (Teresa of Avila), 25, 29

Lilar, Suzanne, 6

Literary analysis, 10

Lott, Bernice, 116–17

McCarthy, Mary, xii, xiv, 78; abuse of, 80–81; allies of, 146, 155, 171; and anti-intellectualism, 84, 118, 168, 171, 198–99, 210; artistry of, 215–16, 218, 220, 221; and atheism, 216; attitude toward remembered self, 193, 199; autobiographical scrupulosity, 8; autobiographical simile, 215–16; belief in equality of women, 147–48; and Catholic authority figures, 65, 80–81, 84, 92, 141–42, 182; and Catholic bigotry, 65, 84, 141–42, 199; and close surveillance, 84; comedy as rhetoric, 78, 84, 199, 204, 209–10; concession, 155, 227; and convent school, 78, 92, 155, 204; and cultural enclosure, 84, 168, 171, 198–99; and disapproval, 78, 182; formal realism, 34, 220; and fully human life, 32–33, 147; harm

done to, 199; identification with relatives, 147, 204; and justice, 32; literary experience, 9; and marriage, 105; narrative essay cycle, 34; pluralism of, 218; rationality of women, 209–10; rejection of Catholic faith, 142, 216; self-affirmation, 26; and sexuality, 204; strategies as autobiographer, 73, 193–94, 215–16, 218, 220, 227; strategies as girl, 168, 171, 182, 183, 187, 188; and styles of Catholicism, 209–10, 218; women's tradition of autobiography, 221

McKenzie, Barbara, 218

MacLean, Paul D., 55

Madams of the Sacred Heart, 56, 73, 78, 90, 92, 137, 166, 204, 210, 218; not good models, 152–53

Man, definitions of, 119, 123

Mandelbrot, Benoit, 220

Marie, Linda. *See* Pillay, Linda Marie.

Marriage: arranged, 108, 179; authority in, 119, 122–23, 125, 130–31; fear of, 103–9, 179; husband's obligation in, 107, 125; low morale, 121; redesigned, 179–80, and remarriage, 207; and spiritual deterioration, 179; training for, 138, 144; wife's obligation in, 107, 124, 125

Martin, Biddy, 24, 27

Martin, Thérèse, 223. *See also* Thérèse of Lisieux

Martín Gaite, Carmen, 25

Martyrdom, 177

Mary, Virgin Mother of God, 134, 147, 167, 173, 185

Matute, Ana María, xiii, xiv, 7, 53; artistry of, 34, 53–54, 64, 217; censorship, 10, 53–55, 64–65; and divorce, 53; and enclosure of girls, 55; and exploitation of women, 103; and fully human life, 32–33, 55; hypertext, 54, 182; interpretation of, 53–54; literary prestige, 10; mother of, 98; prose-poem cycle, 34; and rationality in women, 55, 118, 123, 208–9; and sexuality, 54, 55, 120; strategies as autobiographer, 7, 34, 53–55, 123, 182, 217; strategies as girl, 55, 182; symbolism in, 54, 217; and violence, 55

Mellish, Mary, xiii, xiv, 65, 109; attitude toward earlier self, 193, 194; career ruined, 131, 188; femininity training of, 131; and religious education, 49–53, 87, 194; strategies as autobiographer, 12, 29, 49–53, 63, 71, 87; strategies as girl, 188

Memory and autobiography, 8, 9, 34–35, 62–63, 138, 193, 199

Menchú, Rigoberta, xiii, xiv, 35; attitude toward remembered self, 193; and Catholic motherhood, 109; desire for justice, 32, 109; and marriage, 109; and sacrifice, 109, 136, 186; strategies as autobiographer, 73; strategies as girl, 186; value of autobiography, 35

Milner, Christiane, 61

Misch, Georg, 25, 26, 27

Modeling unethical behavior, 126–27, 199

Monk, Maria, 89

Mothers and grandmothers, 5, 23, 61; antipathy of, 80, 101; authority of, 49, 67, 78, 80–82, 84, 89, 106–7, 163, 169, 197–98; coldness of, 97–99, 116, 126, 138, 166; cooperation with official Catholic femininity program, 41–43, 46, 84, 89–90, 92, 94, 96, 102, 108–9, 116, 118, 129–30, 131, 140–41, 143, 181, 182, 201, 205, 218; defense of, 18, 52; excessive focus on, 41–43, 90; as homebound, 125, 126–27; influence of, 61, 76, 127, 133, 139–40, 176, 224; organizations of, 89–90, 129–30, 148, 221; outsmarted, 187; and sacrifice, 108–9, 136, 175–76, 203; and self-development, 197–98; suffering of, 103–6, 108–9, 201; as supportive, 147–48, 152, 154, 156–57, 166, 176, 186, 198, 215

Motifs: awards for good behavior, 78; beauty of nature, 45, 146, 156, 204, 206, 211, 219, 220; bedsharing in dormitories, 77, 171; Blessed Virgin Mary, 87, 134, 148, 167, 173, 185; Christ, 54, 62, 105, 137, 148, 172, 175–76, 184, 188, 197, 203, 223, 224; Christmas, 63, 203, 205; exclusion from technology, 44, 102; hell and hellfire, 52, 81, 137, 197, 198, 199; illness, 88, 97–98, 107, 219, 224; menarche, 91,

95, 102, 204, 205, 208; questions on sex, 94–95; removal of nun's veil, 184–85; saints, 167, 177; Satan, 76, 77, 137; sewing lessons, 92, 93, 131; side-saddles, 102; sinner's spot, 76; underground newspapers, 186; Voltaire, 90, 92

Mullen, Barbara Brady, xiii, xiv, 81; anorexia, 8, 82; artistry, 197–98; encouragement/discouragement of, 81, 155, 156–57; excessive obedience, 65, 81–82, 187, 188, 197–98; femininity training of, 82, 118, 139–40; and fully human life, 32–33; justice of, 18, 32, 185, 197–98; longing for father, 81–82; mother's abuse of, 65, 79, 81–82, 139; mother's coldness, 98; and parish school, 81, 155; social deprivation, 81–82; strategies as autobiographer, 32–33, 73, 197–98; strategies as girl, 81–82, 155, 170, 185, 187–88, 197

Musonius, Rufus, 122

My Life (Sand), 23

Narrative form: 34, 196, 199, 212, 213–227; and unity, 48–49, 197–98

Native Americans, 17, 21. *See also* Brave Bird; Menchú; Rose.

New Critics, 212

Noël, Marie (pseud. of Marie Mélanie Rouget), xiii, xiv, 76; artistry, 28, 97, 107, 215; attitude toward remembered self, 197; and Catholic religious education, 76, 143, 197; and cultural alternative, 176; and death, 28, 215; femininity training of, 102, 107; harm done to, 47, 76, 108–9, 147; identification with women, 76, 215; John XXIII on, 76; literary inclinations opposed, 76; literary prestige, 10; parental dishonesty, 76, 143, 197; rejection of suffering, 175–76, 197, 215; self as true subject, 176, 197; self-respect, 215; strategies as autobiographer, 31, 73, 97, 107, 197; strategies as girl, 147, 175–76, 188; virtues as a critic, 197; and women's tales, 76, 215

Norris, Kathleen, xiii, xiv, 46; and Catholic parental roles, 46, 48, 65, 66, 125;

Catholic Woman, portrayal of, 202–3; courtship of, 47; disagreements with Church, 47, 49, 66, 136, 203; early encouragement of, 46, 155; false cheerfulness of, 46, 63; father's improvidence, 46–48; femininity training of, 46, 132; incoherence in *Noon*, 46, 48–49, 66; and justice, 46–48; literary success, 46; realism, 46–47; self, near-omission of, 46; strategies as autobiographer, 32, 46–48; strategies as girl, 47; textual traces of self-censorship, 46–49, 63, 66

Nuns as teachers: abusiveness, 75, 82–83, 99, 101, 184–85, 186; authoritarianism, 94, 218; authority, 66, 68–69, 152–53; coldness, 99, 152–53, 166, 218; disapproval of strong individuals, 150; disciplinarians, 56, 79, 83, 96, 153, 167; false blame, 75, 77, 81, 101; fear of sex, 93, 99, 139, 186; ecclesiastical femininity trainers, 75, 90, 118, 139, 141, 175; helpful, 101, 152, 154; hostility to affection, 77–78, 83, 90, 99, 169; hostility to education, 89, 90, 93–94, 139, 141; hostility to self-direction, 115, 167; ignorance, general, 87, 89, 210; ignorance of developmental psychology, 77, 139; ignorance of ethics, 75–76, 77, 81, 101; ignorance of secular society, 139; ignorance of sex, 77, 139, 204, ignorance of theology, 51–52, 81, 87, 99, 139; imposition of monasticism on young laywomen, 83, 90; ineffective communication, 50, 78; injustice, 57, 79, 82, 88, 166; insularity, 89–90, 92, 93, 218; intellectuality, 92; preference for males, 166, 185; supportiveness, 74, 146, 152, 153, 155; threats of damnation, 77, 81; triviality of, 57, 83, 90, 175, 210; uniformity demand, 57, 74–75. *See also* Carroll; Farrell; Schoffen; Wolff; Wong; *names of individual orders*

Obedience: and marriage, 125, 137–38; and nuns, 57, 82–83, 137–38; to parents 77, 81–82, 89; problems of, 41–42, 64–69, 74, 80–85, 99–103, 137–38, 143–44, 147, 168–69, 188–90, 200–203; to trivial rules, 57, 75, 77, 82, 84; unwarranted punishments, 75–77, 80–83, 88, 99–100

Official Revised Baltimore Catechism Number One, ix, x, 51, 64–65, 67–68, 70, 76, 96, 136, 190

Olney, James, 26

Ordination, 123

Oversocialization, 42

Paganism, 211, 221

Parents, ecclesiastical role of: autobiographers' critique of, 200–202; as delegates of popes, 129–30, 133, 137, 138, 139–44; religion teachers, 86, 87, 89–90, 124, 125–26; as representatives of God, 65–67, 68–69

Pascal, Roy, 7

Pemán, José María, 123, 137

Persuasive orientation of narrative structures: causes, 84, 87–88; circumstances, 210; closure, 28; contrast, 62, 104–5, 222–26; definition, 192; distinction, 175, 203; examples, 55, 201, 204; harmful results, 50, 75–76, 81–82, 83–84, 108–9, 169, 199; hypertext, 182–83, 218; plots, 197–98, 220–21; process, 168–69, 171, 192, 208, 209; reclassification, 54, 62, 87–88, 200, 201, 204; repetition, 205–7; shift of emphasis, 175–76. *See also* Strategies of autobiographers

Physical abuse, 76, 79–83, 97, 99, 117, 188; and canon law, 127; incest, 99–101, 166; in marriage, 101, 105–6

Pillay, Linda Marie, xiii, xiv, 93; allies, 177; artistic talent, 174; and authority figures, 143, 166; bisexuality of, 101; and Catholic reform school, 93–94, 166, 185; and dependence, 94; father's abuse of, 79, 99–100, 143; femininity training of, 94, 166, 184; friendship, 100, 171; and fully human life, 32–33; goodness of, 100–101, 171; harm done to, 100–101; justice of, 171; strategies as autobiographer, 73; strategies as girl, 166, 169, 170, 174, 177, 185

Pius IX, 131

Pius X, 128, 129

Pius XI, 128, 132–33

Pius XII, 128, 133

Popes, 14, 128–33. *See also names of individual popes*

Postmodernists, 31

Priests: abusive, 101, 185; anger aroused by, 49, 52–53, 186; betrayal by, 78–79, 88, 110; charity of, 227; contempt for females, 87, 101, 104, 115–41, 143–44; discouragement of learning, 88, 89; encouragement of females, 147, 148, 150–51, 152, 227; extension of father's authority to, 66; as flawed representatives of God, 40, 79, 185; helpfulness of, 45; inconsistency, 87; inflated rank, 66, 181; loyalty to papal teachings on women, 108, 117, 127, 134, 136; opposition to, 146, 202, 216; as representatives of Church, 162; sexual offenses of, 83, 183–84; support of abusive husbands, 105–6; theological orientation, 75

Princess of Eboli, 214

Protestantism: Catholic reactions to, 44, 141–42, 199, 218; effects on women, 21–22; gender views, 16, 21–22, 67, 138; reactions to Catholics, 64, 199

Public life, 129, 132–33, 153–54, 198

Pueyo y Abadía, Luis, 150–51

Purgatory and women, 52

"Purity," 76, 95, 97, 102, 138, 205–7

Rationality in Catholic women: and Aquinas's teaching, 14, 122–25, 137; and creativity, 16, 212, 213–26; desire to prove, 4–5, 16, 196, 208–10, 227–28; and education, 73, 125; failures of, 188–90; and internal censorship, 124; natural, to women, 15, 146–50, 161, 163, 190–91, 212; and surrealism, 213; and writing, 124, 212–13

Realism, 47–48, 54, 59–60, 220–21

Reflection of literary movements: cubist fragmentation, 60; realism, 54, 59–60; romanticism, 222; surrealism, 60, 204, 213–14; symbolism, 54, 59–60

Religious of the Sacred Heart. *See* Madams of the Sacred Heart

Repplier, Agnes, xiii, xiv, 56; artistry, 34, 56, 58, 212; authority, styles of, 57, 74, 75, 152; autobiographical pact, 56; defeats, 58, 188; and femininity training, 57, 75, 86, 132, 135, 137; and friendship, 167, 175, 201; humor of, 185, 203; literary prestige, 10; narrative form, 34; rationality, demonstration of, 212; and sacrifice, 58, 175, 203; self as process, 58; strategies as autobiographer, 32–33, 34, 56–59, 54, 203, 212; strategies as girl, 65, 167, 175, 185; truth in autobiography, 71, 75, 137, 152

Robinson, Richard, 11, 117, 118

Roessler, Augustine, 130–32, 134, 147, 189

Rose, Wendy, xiii, xiv, 98; artistry, 25, 98–99, 167, 217; cold maternal figures, 98–99; and justice, 32, 99; literary experience, 9; strategies as autobiographer, 25, 32, 73, 98–99, 193; strategies as girl, 167

Rouget, Marie Melanie. *See* Noël, Marie

Ruether, Rosemary Radford, 11, 14–15, 16, 22, 150, 172

Saari, Jon, 20

Sacrifice of women, 108–9, 136, 175

Sanford, Linda Tschirhart, 21–22

Sartre, Jean-Paul, 165, 168, 206–7, 220

Saturnal (Chacel), 103

Schoffen, Elizabeth, xiii, xiv, 88–89; and bogus nuns, 88–89; and cultural enclosure of girls, 198–99; desire to learn, frustrated, 85–86, 89; desire to live a just life, 32, 89; girlhood strategies, frustrated, 164, 166, 170; girlhood strategies, successful, 183, 187, 188; opponents of, 89, 118, 163; strategy as autobiographer, 73, 198–99

Schools, Catholic, intellectual discipline, 73, 171–72. *See also* Nuns as teachers

Schools, secular: broadening effect, 33; feared by Catholic authority figures, 88, 139; not necessarily offensive to God, 156, 198; social pressure in, 169; superiority, 87–88, 89

Scrupulosity, 8–9

The Second Sex (Beauvoir), 6, 23, 25, 74

Secrecy as strategy, 16, 167–70, 184; and camouflaged writing, 53–56; and deceit, 169–70; and truthfulness, 71

Self: autobiographical split of, 35, 193; and autobiography, 22–24; completeness of, 6, 147; continuous/discontinuous, 34; defense of, 184; development of, 115, 143, 147–50, 191; narrative definitions of, 191, 192; opposition to, 85, 100; as process, 31; psychological history of, 6; real vs. social, 22; remembered, 35, 193, 199; theoretical definitions of, 22, 24, 26, 27, 31; wounds to, 107–8

Self-Analysis (Horney), 22

Self-defense. *See* Strategies

Self-development caused by struggle: theory, 4; reactions to repression, 55, 56, 58, 90, 110, 161–91

Self-sacrifice: autobiographers' revision of, 147, 203; demand for, 116, 134, 136, 175; girls' revision of, 175–78

Self-strengthening as strategy, 164, 171–78, 181

Sewing, 92–93, 131, 141, 168, 192

Sexuality, Church's war against: "animality," 119–21, 205; and "Catholic Woman," 4; enforcement, 138, 204–5; inhibition resulting from, 116, 206; misinformation about, 138, 204, 205; loss of physicality, 206; "purity," 205; "sinfulness," 5, 95–96, 97–98, 116, 135; suppression, 94–97, 205, 207. *See also* Erotic history

Sexuality, defended: opposition to compulsory heterosexuality, 207–8; opposition to compulsory monogamy, 207; criticism of, 204–8; rebellion against, 172–73; sexual love, 54–55, 93, 94, 151–52, 204; sexuality and wholeness, 4, 24, 87, 206. *See also* Erotic history

Shapiro, Stephen A., 28

Showalter, Elaine, 22

Similarity across differences in scale, 219–20

Sin: as autobiographical topic, 29–30; faulty sinfulness training, 8–9, 75–76,

143–44, 197; gender and, 68; mortal, 95; and reproduction, 121–22; types of, 51, 68, 95; virtues as, 68, 200. *See also* Sexuality, Church's war against

Sister Formation Program, 89

Sisters: companions, 90, 201; comrades-in-arms, 186, 187; helpfulness, 35; importance, 35, 201, 222, 223–24, 226; shared suffering, 47, 84, 91, 105, 205; sorrow concerning, 147, 166

Sisters (Fishel), 201

Sisters of Charity, 40

Sisters of Mercy, 40

Sisters of Providence, 89

Social criticism and autobiography, 39, 55, 71, 194–95

Spain, Catholic Church in, 120–21, 123, 137, 150–51. *See also* Asquerino; Chacel; Franco; Janés; León; Matute; Varo

Spelman, Elizabeth V., 3–4, 191

St. Thérèse of Lisieux (Delarue-Mardrus), 222–25

Stanley, Liz, 8, 12, 22

Stanton, Domna C., 23

Starobinski, Jean, 35, 196

Stations of the Cross, and self-respect, 148, 172

Strategies of autobiographers: autobiographical integrity, 195; camouflage, 54, 56; "Catholic Woman" characters, 62, 209–10; characters opposed to Catholic feminity, 61, 146, 153; comedy, 51–52, 57, 84, 86, 203–4, 209–10; concerning the prohibition of criticism, 71; concerning the prohibition of self-interest, 29–33; description of alternative paths in general, 196; description of alternative paths for girls, 55, 198, 200–202; description of alternative paths for women, 62, 178–79, 204, 207; eulogy, 41, 44; modeling a more complete life, 29–33, 71, 210, 212; open criticism, 46–47, 50–53, 73, 86–93, 195–96, 197–211; paratextual comment, 216–19; restraint, 197; textual secularization, 62, 171–72; tone, 90. *See also* Persuasive orientation of narrative structures

Strategies of girls: adaptability, 186–87; alliance, 164–67; all-out fighting, 187–88; applicability of *The Art of War*, 11, 157, 162–63, 164, 183; attacks on girls, 183; and autobiography, 191; counterattack, 184–85; defeats, 188–89; espionage, 181–83; ethics of, 161, 184, 190; evasive action, 187; geographical moves, 170–71; redirection of opponent's resources, 171–81; restraint, 183–84, 187; secrecy, 167–70; secularization, 62, 63, 171–81, 196, 216; self-defense as religious duty, 161, 190; successes, 190–91; theory of, 162–64; thwarting, 186; versatility, 185–86

Study: devotion to, 87–92, 155–56, 174, 176; discouragement of, 91–92, 118, 131, 143, 166

Subordination: Christian theology of, 14, 15, 16, 54; Catholic theology of, 122–23, 125, 130, 134

Suffering, 21, 136–37, 177. *See also* Sacrifice of women

Suitors: 40, 44, 47, 96, 101, 206–7

Summa Theologica (Aquinas), 122

Sun-tzu. *See Art of War*

Surrealism, 204, 213–14

Symbolism 214, 216; divine pelican, 147; Mother of God, 147; in names, 212; Snow Queen, 107; spiral, 221, 223; world tree, 211

Synthesis, 178–81, 219

Teresa of Avila, 26, 29, 196

Tertullian, 118, 134, 137, 150

Textuality: architextuality (genericity), 213, 221–22; hypertextuality, 54, 213, 218, 222–26; interpretation, 8, 9, 10–12, 193–94; paratextuality, 213, 216–19; textual secularization, 62–63. *See also* Autobiographies by twentieth-century Catholic women; Autobiography, theory of; Language

Theology of equivalence. *See* Woman, minority theology of

Theology of subordination. *See* Woman, official theology of

Thérèse of Lisieux, 9, 30, 213, 222–26

Truthfulness and autobiography 48–49, 71

Twentieth century, impact on Catholic women, 33

Uniformity, 57, 134–35, 142–43, 147, 198; and convent, 210; and convent schools, 57, 74–75, 85

United States, Catholic Church in: censorship, 86; contrast with non-Catholic education, 67, 86, 92; misogyny taught, 119, 120, 137; relations with Protestants, 64, 67, 199. *See also* Benoist; Brave Bird; Carroll; Farrell; Fontenot; McCarthy; Mellish; Mullen; Norris; *Official Revised Baltimore Catechism Number One*; Pillay; Repplier; Rose; Schoffen; Wolff; Wong

Universities, 33, 91, 139, 210

Variations among twentieth-century Catholic women autobiographers: in attitude toward remembered self, 194; in censorship evasion, 53, 70–72; in courage and integrity, 188–91; in criticism/defense of Church, 70–72, 73, 194, 227; in criticism of Catholic gender training, 53, 74, 109; in erotic history, 135; in issues addressed, 195; in questions raised, 110; in writing skill, 225–26

Varo, Remedios, xiii, xiv, 17; artistry of, 74, 93, 168, 187, 213; autobiographical reference of triptych, 187; and Catholic education, 93; and close surveillance, 83; comparability to verbal narrative, 17; and cultural enclosure, 93; and femininity training, 83, 93; and hypertext, 168; and sexuality, 93; strategies as autobiographer, 13, 17, 74–75, 83, 93, 187; strategies as girl, 168, 187; surrealism of, 93, 168, 187, 213; and uniformity, 74–75

Vatican II, 8, 57, 85, 133

Verbal abuse: as causing sin, 118; as identified with immoral persons, 88, 137; as less than feminine, 91, 140; as sinful, 75,

76, 77, 79, 138; as subhuman, 101, 102, 140–41

Virginity, 138. *See also* Celibacy

Wiggins, David, 27

With Jesus: Prayers and Instructions for Youthful Catholics, 68

Wittgenstein, Ludwig, 3–4, 11, 135, 195–96

Wolff, M. Madaleva, xiii, xiv, 44; attitude toward self, 46, 121, 189, 193, 227; defects as autobiographer, 44, 45–46, 53, 132, 227; defense of Church, 44, 45, 194, 227; devotion to parents, 44–45; ecclesiastical approval of, 44, 118, 121, 132; and educational reform, 45, 89; egoism, 199–200; harm done to, 45–46, 132, 189, 193; literary prestige, 10; rationality in women, demonstration of, 10, 44, 118, 227; and secular schools, 44, 45, 189; strategies as autobiographer, 31, 45, 53, 199–200, 227; strategies as girl, 189

Woman/women: defined, 3–6, 19–22. *See also* Family resemblances among twentieth-century Catholic women autobiographers; Variations among twentieth-century Catholic women autobiographers

Woman, minority theology of: 8, 11, 15; created in God's image, 150; Eve, equal to man, 150; equal in charity and friendship, 150; morally improvable, 129; not guiltier than Adam, 150; not more sexual than man, 151; sexuality as love is sacred, 151

Woman, official theology of: x, 11, 14, 15; created in God's image, 123; equal to man, but not in this life, 129, 130; equal to man if celibate, 121; as Eve, evil by nature, 118, 119, 135; familial and subservient, 119, 122, 123, 125, 129, 131, 133; not created in God's image, 136; subordinate by nature, 119, 122, 123, 129, 130, 132, 134; subrational by nature, 118, 122, 123, 131, 135

The Woman Question (Roessler), 130

Women and Self-Esteem (Sanford and Donovan), 217

Women's language, 22

Wong, Mary Gilligan, xiii, xiv, 108; as ex-nun, 108, 121; strategy as autobiographer, 73, 108–9, 136; strategy as girl, 187; and suffering of Catholic mothers, 108–9, 136

Writing: derivation of literary forms from life patterns, 220–21; as evidence of rationality, 16, 124, 211–18; imaginative aspects, 213–16; intention in, 194, 213; literary prizes, 9–10; similarities across differences in scale, 219–20. *See also* Autobiographies by twentieth-century Catholic women; Reflection of literary movements; Strategies of autobiographers